The Latin American
Story Finder

ALSO BY SHARON BARCAN ELSWIT

The East Asian Story Finder:
A Guide to 468 Tales from China, Japan and Korea,
Listing Subjects and Sources (McFarland, 2014 [2009])

The Jewish Story Finder:
A Guide to 668 Tales Listing Subjects and
Sources, 2d ed. (McFarland, 2012)

The Latin American Story Finder

A Guide to 470 Tales from Mexico, Central America and South America, Listing Subjects and Sources

Sharon Barcan Elswit

McFarland & Company, Inc., Publishers

Jefferson, North Carolina

ISBN 978-0-7864-7895-8 (softcover : acid free paper) ∞
ISBN 978-1-4766-2229-3 (ebook)

LIBRARY OF CONGRESS CATALOGUING DATA ARE AVAILABLE

BRITISH LIBRARY CATALOGUING DATA ARE AVAILABLE

Front cover image © Juliia76/iStock/Thinkstock

Printed in the United States of America

*McFarland & Company, Inc., Publishers
Box 611, Jefferson, North Carolina 28640
www.mcfarlandpub.com*

In memory of my mother,
who got me started on a lifetime of sharing
stories with children by reading aloud each day

Acknowledgments

Much appreciation goes to the New York Public Library and the MidHudson Library System for their wonderful collections of books.

I am grateful to Constance Vidor for suggesting that this one come next and to Susan Bromberg Skolnick for sharing the stories as I discovered them.

Thank you, John Bierhorst, for the graceful scholarship of your own work and your kindness in answering questions.

I owe special thanks to my daughter Kate, keeper of gates for the Community chapter, and to Michael, who accompanied me everywhere on this journey.

I was going to bring you a plateful of the wedding food, canapes, and all, but there at the street corner a dog snatched it out of my hands.
    —Teodora Paliza in "The She-Calf," story #335

Table of Contents

Preface

Everything is possible when you step into the magically real world of Latin American folklore—a buzzard can change places with a wife's lazy husband; a hunter may hurl lightning bolts and thunder down on the tribesmen who cheated him of his share of the meat; a shapeshifting pink dolphin from the Amazon may seduce a young woman to his underwater city; and the lizard a padre scoops off a dusty road may become an emerald when he hands it to a poor peasant who needs to buy medicine for his wife. Here, a lone man after a cataclysmic flood sees his black dog slip out of its skin and become a young woman who cooks tortillas and will become his companion in the new world. The folktales deal with timeless key human questions, and there are human truths in the magic they contain.

Which 470 Stories Are Here?

This *Latin American Story Finder* is a guide to selected tales told in 21 countries, where stories from people in over 75 indigenous tribes melded with the culture of Spanish and Portuguese colonials who arrived in the 16th century. Tales collected and told by Catholic missionaries and Sephardic Jews fleeing the Inquisition from Europe also were adopted and changed by native Quechua, Maya, and Amazonian cultures. And then, added to the mix are the myths from the ancient Inca and Maya civilizations, Anansi stories which came over with African slaves, and tales told by indentured servants from India.

This mix makes the stories richly captivating and unique, and yet they have been greatly underrepresented in both folklore collections and individual books in English. I hope this book can change that. My job is to pick interesting stories for people to use. This guide points the way to tales of transformation, with supernatural beings and many magical objects; tales of love and devotion; tricksters; journeys up to the sky, underwater, and under the earth; reversals of fortune, and stories which explore the workings of nature and the relationship between gods and humans. These stories were told to make sense of the world people could not control, to reinforce traditions, and to pass along wisdoms. They cry out to be shared.

What Is in the Tales?

Especially present in the Latin American tales are stories of how things came to be and why they are what they are. A buzzard carefully rebuilds a jaguar queen's eyesight with resin after she loses her own eyes which she has sent flying out over the lake on a lark. This resin accounts for the gleam found in all big cats' eyes. Even the tales that do not center on a particular plant or animal or celestial body will end "and that's why...." We learn where corn and parrots came from, why the moon didn't marry the sun, how curious humans climbed down a rope from a hole in sky to reach earth, and how laughter originated when bat-people tickled a Cayapo man.

There is both earthiness and fantasy in many of the tales. A dog which the Quechua courier hits with a stone next appears as a beguiling young woman whose hip is sore. A Warao man resists being herded with the others from his tribe who are docilely being transformed into peccaries day by day, complete with bristles and multiple teats. A Maya husband ends up with two heads for a while, when he salts the neck of his witch-wife's headless body so her head cannot reattach.

The folktales share an interest in teaching values and taboos, the religious and social mores of their cultures. A Miskito husband discovers that the living belong with the living, when he accompanies his beloved wife who has just died to Mother Scorpion country. Punishment is meted out for shirking work; for being disrespectful to a parent; for cutting down too many trees or hunting more animals than are needed for food; for not being generous; and for being boastful, vain, or greedy. A toad who disparages the smell of the buzzard who is kindly giving him a ride through the air gets dumped off in one Maya tale. A magic canoe which thunks on feet in a story by the Kamaiurá people of Brazil swallows the fisherman who does not give it his first catch of fish. The outsider Asin in a tale by the Pilaga people of Bolivia sets a deep freeze over the land where people have ridiculed him for being different.

"The Ancestors Are All Around Us" reads the title of one story from the Ona people, who even now blow a kiss to the spirits when they leave the house or go on a journey. Humans who do not show gratitude and respect to the gods or spirits in nature suffer. It took five tries for the Aztec gods to create humans who did not neglect them.

The folktales also teach resilience in the face of economic, political, and social hardship. They bring solace through humor. Indigenous people may struggle to earn a living compared with the Spanish colonials, but little Rabbit in the trickster tales will outsmart the larger and more powerful Coyote who is after him every time. Mischievous exploits where Pedro de Urdemalas makes fools of gullible owners and fancy horsemen are celebrated in Chile, Argentina, Mexico, Brazil, and Guatemala.

New realities transformed old stories on both sides when Christian belief in a single God met indigenous belief in many gods, who may be the duenos, or owners, of hills, lakes, and other places in the natural world, which also are home to souls and spirits. The beloved Mexican Virgin of Guadalupe is described as having beautiful dark skin and long black hair. The Brazilian one-eyed monster Mapinguari tears apart the hunter who insists on hunting even on a Sunday. The Virgin Mary replaces the fairy godmother in a Mexican Cinderella tale, where young Maria goes looking for the fish which made off with entrails her mean stepmother sent her to wash and ends up calming a crying baby Jesus. A cat and dog in an African American slave tale from Guadalupe go to ask God whether life goes on after death. As Juan Carlos Galeano writes, "Amazonian realities are still a present and active part of the lives of the non-indigenous, who now represent the majority of the population in most cities throughout the region."

Chapters and Challenges

Despite the large numbers of diverse cultures represented here, different tribes and people in Latin America share some of the same customs and values. In addition to the usual trickster and family life tales common to all folklore, certain unifying themes, such as concerns for social justice and a decent living, clamored to become whole chapters for this guide, different from those chosen for my previous two Story Finders. New chapter headings developed specifically for *The Latin American Story Finder* are: When Cultures, Classes or Species Collide; Winning and Losing with the Gods; Making Bargains, Good and Bad; Seeking Justice; Punishments and Rewards; Defenders of the Earth; and Supernatural Seducers.

I did wrestle with applying *supernatural* to a realm where shapeshifting and the supernatural are natural. It is considered education in regional tales of the Amazon, for instance, for a man whose spear has stuck in a dolphin to be arrested by two policemen in a speedboat and taken underwater to treat the dolphin's wounds. However, supernatural is the descriptive term we understand in our North American culture.

The stories began as oral tales, many recorded by people outside of Latin American culture and over many years, which presents some language challenges. *Pumas* are often referred to as *tigers*, even when they have spots. The words for *anaconda* and *boa* are applied interchangeably in Spanish-speaking Amazonia. I left most spellings and terms as I found them, including use of Spanish and Portuguese diacritical marks, so that users would get a feel for the language used within a particular tale.

Many of the books I read are the only sources for particular tales. The majority of stories were published before 1970 when it was acceptable to use the word "Indian" rather than "indigenous people" to describe people of Native American descent. "Indian" shows up even in stories collected by anthropologists directly from indigenous tribes. If a story was compelling and well-told and did not insult the dignity of the protagonist, then I could not push it away because the protagonist is called "Indian." The term "Indian" in summaries is used only to refer to people from South Asia who were brought over by the British as indentured servants to work on the sugar plantations of Guyana.

Changing sensitivities in our modern world did mean that I had to reject other tales, though, since I am promoting stories to be shared with diverse groups. A humorous story from sixty years ago which disparages women just isn't funny now. It is the same with stories which depict native people stereotypically. I also did not feel comfortable including the one version of how night was released where black slaves are the disobedient servants who have been turned into monkeys. Luckily, there were other less emotionally-charged variations of the Brazilian night story to choose from. The only Mexican do-it-manana tale which I included concerns the legendary fools of Lagos. The core of the story is how the fools fill one hole in the road by creating another and then another. It does not need the men dragging their heels at making the repairs to be funny. However, it was published in 1960 and continues to be the only version of the story around in English.

Again, some stories transcribed directly from native sources may be of interest anthropologically, but are just too raw in content or writing to be enjoyed by a general audience. However, buried in a collection of tales directly from the Yupa people, most of which I could not use, was the surprising "Women Who Want to Be Men," where the tribe totally accepts the affection and commitment between two women. Teachers, librarians, and storytellers count on my guides to find the right story for the right time to use with others. The tales selected in this *Finder* speak coherently, forge bridges, and capture the imagination.

Featured Stories and Variants

As a subject guide to stories, *The Latin American Story Finder* describes stories with enough detail to give their flavor and send readers to the tales themselves. Many of the stories from Latin America are one of a kind even though they are part of the oral tradition in their countries. When available and worthy, though, all variants of a story have been listed, so that someone who might not have one particular version may find a similar tale in a different collection closer at hand. Major differences are described.

It was often hard to choose which version to highlight. All of the retellings are worthy narratives, or they would not have been included here. I could summarize only one. Two criteria influenced my choice of featured story: the story appears in a publication readily available to a contemporary reader, and the way it is told calls to me personally. The stories listed below each featured story are of two types: *reappearances*, i.e., the very same story reprinted in a new collection, and *retellings*, i.e., the basic plot retold in a new version. Stories listed under "Where Else This Story Appears" are reappearances, including audio and video recordings. Stories under "How Else This Story Is Told" are retellings—usually by different authors, though sometimes one author will offer one version for children and another for adults. Story titles from collections are given in standard roman type; a story title in italics indicates that the story is published as an individual picture book.

Sometimes these versions closely match each other and the featured story. Other times, they may end differently, or one story may wrap around the featured story or be contained within it, a story within its story. Characters may have different names and variant stories may contain their own unique elements, but if the narrative or thematic thrust of the story is close—if the reason a person would choose this story is the same— then it has been included as a variant.

To insure that readers do not miss a particular character or setting, the special characteristics of variant tales are accessible through the Subject Index. So, for example, when a featured Mexican story involves Little Conejo getting stuck to the wax doll while raiding the farmer's garden, but Monkey and Guinea Pig are the protagonists in variants from Brazil and Peru, you will find all three animals and all three countries listed in the subject index. Neither will you miss the fascinating Maya tale about the origin of the moon, which is not in the Beginnings chapter. "Lord Sun's Bride" shows up in the chapter of love stories, but it has been marked for the index with Origin tales, as well as with Kekchi Maya People. All stories, featured and variant, appear in the Story Title Index.

Using the Connections

A list of story *connections* follows the main entry for each tale. These define the main subjects covered by a particular story. They are identical to terms referenced in the subject index. Placed together here the connections serve as guideposts to help a reader quickly recognize whether this story will suit their needs. They reveal the essence of a summarized story—the emotions and nuances and the premises it evokes—so that the user may efficiently select an appropriate tale from many offerings.

As "The Story of the Vitória Régia" shows, a single story may have many applications. This is as much a tale about the origin of water lilies, as what happens when an indigenous woman falls in love with someone outside her tribe. The story itself is located in the chapter with collisions of culture, but you will also find its connections with Origin tales and Love listed in the Subject Index.

Using the Subject Index

Each featured story has been given a number. References in both the subject index and the title index are to that story number. That number includes subjects for all variants listed below the featured story, too. For example, if the subject index cites a particular entry number for a fox, the fox may not appear in the featured story of that number, but he will appear in one of the variants listed below. A descriptive note with the variant will let you know in which tale you will find him.

For ebook readers, all subject index terms have been linked directly to the story numbers. Since the diacritical markings for Spanish and Portuguese words which appear in the index are necessary for successful searching, users will want to click on a term right from the index. Copying and pasting a term into the search box will also work.

The index also references indigenous tribes and country sources as they appear in the *Finder*. I took them from the sources I consulted, but spelling for tribal names which originated in a non–English-speaking world appeared with myriad spellings—and sometimes even with a totally different name—from one book to the other. I have used the Library of Congress as an authority control and created Appendix A to list all 75 indigenous tribes which have stories here with their alternate names and spellings. The Subject Index will list only the one authoritative name and country found with the story number itself.

Appendix A is a must if you are looking for stories from a particular people which you do not see in the index. Countries, when identified, are listed, but as indigenous peoples' groups cross country borders, Appendix A will also let you know where the story may have originated if the country does not appear with the tribal name beside a story. Some tales were identified only as Maya, for example, but that could mean any of fourteen separate Maya groups in any one of four countries. A story just identified as originating in Amazonia might have come from any one of nine countries. A story from the Andes Mountains might be told in one or more of seven lands. In almost every case here, the place where a story originated is the place where the story is set. People were talking about the world around them.

Which Collections Are Included

The purpose of *The Latin American Story Finder* is to make it easy for people to use and share these stories. References are made to the latest or most available edition of books in English at the time of writing this guide. In case the reader has access to earlier editions of books, citations in the bibliography include reissues and alternate titles. I have also included some outstanding video and audio presentations.

The collections and picture books included in this guide are also chosen for readability. I wanted readers to be able to turn to any listed anthology or collection and feel confident in sharing the proffered story from there just as it is. Many of those books in turn, through their notes on the origins, history, significance, and folkloric archetypes of a particular story, will lead readers who desire to know more to primary source and scholarly material in reference books.

Over the past ten years, I have been gratified by the feedback from librarians, teachers, and storytellers on how my *Finders* have been useful to them and the people they serve. The majority of these tales have had little exposure in the English-speaking world. And yet, as the anthropologist Claude Lévi-Strauss has said, "South American mythology belongs to the spiritual inheritance of mankind on a par with the great masterpieces of Greek and Roman antiquity and the Near East." The stories themselves are relevant within and outside of Latin America because they contain universal truths which help people think about their lives. They also invite readers to find commonality with people from cultures which may be very different from their own.

Four hundred and seventy stories from Latin American cultures are listed and described in this *Finder*, with many published variants. Look up a specific topic or country in the subject index, or peruse chapters where stories have been gathered into broader themes. Check the subject index for particular characters and themes, or the story title index for a story you know by name. My work has been to get resonant stories out there and then to help people find what they need. From the charming Venezuelan "Light Keeper's Box" I learned that the sun which first sped too quickly from east to west across the sky now moves at just the right speed in order to walk with a slower, newfound turtle friend. You'll find many other surprises here.

I

Beginnings and Balance

Earth, Sun, Moon, Night, People, Floods, Fire, Sky, Food, Music

1. THE HUNGRY GODDESS

Mary-Jo Gerson, *Fiesta Femenina*
Aztec People. Mexico

All that exists below the gods in the heavens in the beginning is water. One goddess, *La Diosa Hambrienta*, is always hungry. The eyes and mouths everywhere on her body loudly and constantly cry out for food. The other gods beg powerful Quetzalcóatl and Tezcatlipoca for help to stop the noise. With Quetzalcóatl's giant wings and Tezcatlipoca's rattlesnakes to hold her securely, they bring *La Diosa Hambrienta* down to the water world below to soothe her. She floats quietly for a while, but then starts crying "¡Tengo hambre!" again. Quetzalcóatl dives, but there is nothing alive under the water to bring for *La Diosa Hambrienta* to eat. He and Tezcatlipoca decide to stretch her body long, so she will feel less hungry. Oceans churn as the goddess fights them, and then, she suddenly pulls apart. Quetzalcóatl and Tezcatlipoca are appalled at what they have accidentally done. They carry the two halves of *La Diosa Hambrienta* back to the heavens. A god suggests they cover the world with the bottom half of her body, which creates the sky. The different parts of her top half form the diverse geographical landscape of earth and supply all that is required to support human life.

CONNECTIONS

Creation. Earth. Geography. Gods and goddesses. Hunger. Hungry Woman. Origin tales. Quetzalcoatl. Sky. Sky worlds. Tezcatlipoca. Water.

HOW ELSE THIS STORY IS TOLD

The Hungry Goddess / La diosa hambrienta—Olga Loya, *Momentos Mágicos / Magic Moments*
The Hungry Woman—John Bierhorst, *The Hungry Woman: Myths and Legends of the Aztecs*
Quetzalcoatl and Tezcatlipoca Create the World—David West, *Mesoamerican Myths* (Graphic nonfiction)

2. MOSNI'S SEARCH

Judy Goldman, *Whiskers, Tails & Wings*
Seri People. Mexico

After Hant Caai, god of creation, sings the sky and waters into being, he decides to bring sand up from the bottom of the ocean to make an earth. The ocean is deeper than Hant Caai can reach, and he asks the sea creatures for help. Mosni the sea turtle is mocked by the others as being too clumsy when she volunteers to make the long, dangerous journey. However, after other animals hide in fear or get distracted and do not return, Hant Caai asks for Mosni's help. It is not easy for Mosni to maneuver past those who would prey on her, and it takes her so long that the other creatures are sure she will not return. When Mosni does surface, she is unhappy, for she did reach the sand at the bottom at last, but most of it slid from her flippers as she rose back up through the water. She only has a few grains to give to the god, but Hant Caai thanks her sincerely. With those few grains of sand, he is able to sing beaches and deserts and mountains into existence. Mosni is honored by being first to walk on the land.

CONNECTIONS

Animal helpers. Courage. Creation. Earth. Gods and animals. Hant Caai. Heroes and heroines. Journeys. Origin tales. Tasks. Tortoises and turtles. Water worlds. Unselfishness. Water.

3. WHEN THE WORLD WAS DARK / CUANDO EL MUNDO ESTABA EN TINIEBLAS

Olga Loya, *Momentos Mágicos / Magic Moments*
Aztec People. Mexico

Four times before, the gods have tried to bring a sun to light and warm the world, but none have succeeded. Finally they decide that two gods must throw themselves in a fire. Humble Nanahuatzin and powerful Tecuzistecatl volunteer. The gods tell them not to be afraid, that they will soar through the air and up to the sky. Tecuzistecatl goes first. He walks the line-up of gods to the fire and throws his jewelry in and silver in. Then he walks back and runs toward the fire, but halts three times, afraid to throw himself in. Nanahuatzin walks down the line and throws his serape into the fire. Then he runs down between the gods and leaps in joyfully. Flame arcs up and shoots a ball of fire into the sky. Ashamed, Tecuzistecatl jumps in. Now there are two suns in the sky. They begin to wobble. The gods send Falcon to see what they want. Nanahuatzin says the other gods must jump into the fire, too. The gods call Morning Star to shoot the suns, but his arrows cannot touch the power of the suns. The gods agree to sacrifice themselves, but before they do, one god throws a rabbit at Tecuzistecatl. He says the coward should not shine as brightly as brave Nanhuatzin. The rabbit smashes into the second sun, knocking away some of his light. Nanahuatzin becomes the only sun, then, and Tecuzistecatl, the moon. You can still see the sihouette of the rabbit on full moon nights.

Connections

Courage. Gods and goddesses. Heroes and heroines. Journeys to other realms. Moon. Morning
Star. Nanahuatl. Origin tales. Sacrifice. Sky worlds. Spirits. Sun. Tecciztecatl. Underground
worlds.

How Else This Story Is Told

The Fifth Sun—John Bierhorst, *The Hungry Woman*. Nahuatl Aztec People. This story focuses
on Nanahuatl, who is told to purify himself before leaping into the fire, because he is covered
with sores. Once he jumps, Nanahuatl travels underground to the earth's eastern edge. The
sun's brilliant light appears fiercely on the horizon and then starts to shake. Nanahuatl's
demand that the spirits, too, jump into the fire explains the Aztec need to wage war in order
to keep a supply of human hearts to nourish the sun.
The Fifth and Final Sun—Juliet Piggott, *Mexican Folk Tales*
The New Sun—Douglas Gifford, *Warriors, Gods & Spirits from Central & South American
Mythology*
The Sun God—E. Adams Davis, *Of the Night Wind's Telling*. Toltec People

---

4. The Light Keeper's Box
Carolyn McVickar Edwards, *The Return of the Light*
Warao People. Venezuela

At the beginning of the world there is no day. A chief by the Orinoco River sends
his older daughter to bring some light back from a man who is said to keep it. When
she does not return from the house of the Deer, he sends his younger daughter, blowing
first on her face to keep her safe from evil spirits. He plays his flute, which she can hear
as she chooses the path which takes her to the light keeper. The light keeper says he
has been waiting for her. He opens a box of woven *itiriti* leaves, and light pours out.
Once each day, he opens it so they can play. Then she remembers that she needs to
bring the light back to her father. The light keeper gives her the box as a present. Her
father hangs it from a stilt, and light rays drift out. Many people travel by canoe to see
it. They pack the river and marvel at the light and the dreams that come while they
sleep. So many people want the light, the chief throws the box into the sky. Its light
becomes the sun, and the box itself becomes the moon. Day and night both last for too
short a time, though. At her father's request, the younger daughter brings a small grey
turtle, which the chief blows on and offers it to the sun as a present when it is directly
overhead. This turtle slowly journeys to the sun on the notes of his flute. The sun slows
its walk so they can move along the sky together. The moon also shifts pace, out of
respect for their friendship.

Connections

Animal helpers. Caciques and chieftains. Friendship. Gifts. Heroes and heroines. Journeys. Light.
Magic turtles. Moon. Origin tales. Parents and children. Problem solving. Sun. Tortoises
and turtles.

5. *THE LIZARD AND THE SUN / LA LAGARTIJA Y EL SOL*
Alma Flor Ada
Mexico

People and animals are distressed that the sun has disappeared for days, turning everything dark and cold. They search unsuccessfully, until the lizard discovers a rock that seems to glow and runs to tell the emperor. The rock is too heavy for her to move alone, so the emperor accompanies her with a woodpecker, whom he commands to break the rock open with his beak. Inside, the sun is curled up, asleep. They try to convince the sun that he is needed on earth, but all the sun wants to do is go on sleeping. The emperor has an idea to ask musicians and dancers to play and dance for him, and the sun agrees to wake up if they keep playing. To the sound of the musicians' loud, joyful sounds, the sun climbs back into the sky.

CONNECTIONS
Animal helpers. Bird helpers. Emperors, kings & queens. Lizards. Music. Origin tales. Problem solving. Sleep. Sun. Woodpeckers.

6. BADGER NAMES THE SUN (WHY THE BADGER LIVES UNDERGROUND)
Angel Vigil, *The Eagle on the Cactus*
Yaqui People. Mexico

The creatures on earth do not know what to call the Sun, since they are not sure whether it is male or female. Badger notices one morning that the Sun rises from a hole in the ground, just like he does. He tells the other animals that the Sun must a man, like him. The other animals cheer to have this settled and continue to name other things around them. Badger thinks the loud noise means they are angry with him. He hides in his hole ever since.

CONNECTIONS
Badgers. Gender. Misunderstandings. Names. Origin tales. Sun.

7. *HOW NIGHT CAME: A FOLK TALE FROM THE AMAZON*
Joanna Troughton
Tupi People. Amazonia, Brazil

In the old days, there is no night, for the Great Snake has imprisoned it beneath the water, along with the creatures of the dark. His daughter Great Snake marries a man from the land, but she becomes ill, unable to sleep in the constant daylight. Her husband sends three trusted servants to ask her father to release the night for her. The Great Snake will help. He seals the night in a palm nut, which he warns the men only his daughter may open. As the men paddle home, strange noises emanating from the nut arouse their curiosity. They break the seal, and night emerges over everything. Sticks in the forest turn into animals, like the jaguar; leaves become birds; weeds and stones from the river become frogs, snakes, and fish. The three servants, now fearful, are transformed into monkeys for disobeying. All is dark, and the Great Snake's daughter sleeps. When she wakes, she turns two balls of string into birds, one to sing to signal the beginning of day and one to signal night. Since then, night sleeps beneath the ocean during the daytime.

CONNECTIONS

Captivity. Curiosity. Disobedience. Gods and humans. Journeys. Night. Origin tales. Parents and children. Punishments. Snakes. Supernatural beings. Supernatural husbands and wives. Transformations.

HOW ELSE THIS STORY IS TOLD

The Creation of Night—Mercedes Dorson and Jeanne Wilmot, *Tales from the Rain Forest.* Once night is released from the *tucumâ* tree fruit, the Great Water Serpent's daughter pulls out a strand of her hair to separate Day from Night.
How Night Came—Douglas Gifford, *Warriors, Gods & Spirits from Central & South American Mythology*
How the Night Came to Be—Livia de Almeida and Ana Portella, *Brazilian Folktales*
How Night Came from the Sea—Mary-Joan Gerson. Here the sea serpent is female, a goddess of the sea, named for the African *lemanjá.*
The Sea Serpent's Daughter—Margaret H. Lippert

---

8. THE LAKE OF THE MOON

Pleasant DeSpain, *The Emerald Lizard*
Inca People. Andes Mountains. Peru

One clear night, the moon beams a calm lake down to the Andes Mountains in which to cast a perfect reflection of herself. However, the next day when the lake vanishes because it has been absorbed into the meadow ground, she angrily blames the animals for drinking it. The moon sends down new water with a magic spell which will put any animal who now drinks it to sleep forever. Three stars tell the sun about this lake and how llamas, jaguars, and chinchillas have disappeared from the mountains. The sun decides that the moon is jealous of his light. He sends shrimp to stir up the lake so it becomes muddy. The moon begs the wind to stop blowing the water so she can see herself, but the wind says it is not to blame. The moon breaks up the lake and its spell, and the animals return. Sometimes, the mountains shake, though, when the moon thinks angrily about losing her perfect lake.

CONNECTIONS

Accusations. Anger. Earthquakes. Gods and goddesses. Jealousy. Mirrors. Moon. Origin tales. Shrimp. Spells. Sun. Vanity. Water.

9. How the Gods Created the Finger People: A Mayan Fable
Elizabeth Moore and Alice Couvillon
Maya People. Honduras

The gods have created plants and animals, but they now want something to love them. They form a man out of clay, which dissolves when the God of Water tests his sturdiness. The figure they next make out of wood does float in water, but it burns when the God of Fire tests him. The God of Gold makes a man from gold which does not burn or dissolve, but this golden statue coldly does not interact with the animals on earth. The Good-Hearted God proposes that they make a human from part of themselves, who can relate with feeling to others the way the gods do. He slices off the fingers of his left hand, which become people when they fall to earth. The people run everywhere with delight, too fast for the gods to test them in fire and water. While the gods are napping, the finger people discover the cold gold statue in the garden. At first, the gold man does not react at all when they bring him home and treat him kindly, but after a long while, he does thank them. The God of Gold says the finger people will not be punished for running away because of their kindness to the gold man, but they will have to work for him and remain poor. The Good-Hearted God knows that the finger people have feelings and deserve better than this. He proclaims that the rich people must pay the finger people who work for them fairly. And when they die, a rich gold man will have to take the hand of a poor finger person so that they enter heaven together.

Connections
Clay. Creation. Fingers. Fire. Gods and humans. Gold. Humans. Justice. Kindness. Origin tales. Poverty. Punishments. Sky worlds. Status. Tests. Water. Wealth. Wood. Work. Worship.

How Else This Story Is Told
The Golden Man and the Finger Men—Juliet Piggott, *Mexican Folk Tales*. Maya People. Mexico
The Man of Gold—Douglas Gifford, *Warriors, Gods & Spirits from Central & South American Mythology*. Maya People

10. How We Came to the Fifth World / Cómo vinimos al quinto mundo
Harriet Rohmer and Mary Anchondo
Aztec People. Mexico

People keep neglecting the gods in the first world, and the gods are dissatisfied. The water god is chosen to tell a poor man and woman to make a boat from the ahuehuete tree and ride it with some fire and one ear of corn to plant in the new world after he floods the first world. Drowning people who ask are transformed into fish. In the second world, there is peace until the children of the man and woman fight over land and food. Quetzalcoatl, god of the air, is chosen to destroy the world with wind this time. He finds one worthy woman and man who remember the gods to hide in a mountain cave with a small fire and an ear of corn. Storm-battered people who ask are transformed into animals. The god of fire is chosen to destroy the third world with earthquakes and volcanoes after telling one unselfish man and woman to shelter in a cave. Some people beg to become birds to fly above the flames. The fourth world works for a while, until people neglect the gods again. The earth goddess tells the other gods to rest. She kills the crops and only sends food down at night to the good people. Hungry people ask to be eaten by jaguars. In the fifth world, after five creations and four destructions, people do not forget the gods, and peace and happiness reign.

CONNECTIONS

Animals. Conflict. Creation. Destruction. Earth. Floods. Gods and humans. Gratitude. Humans. Origin tales. Peace. Punishments. Quetzalcoatl. Selfishness. Transformations. Worship.

HOW ELSE THIS STORY IS TOLD

The Four Destructions of the World—E. Adams Davis, *Of the Night Wind's Telling*

---

11. FEATHERED SNAKE AND HURACAN

Margaret Mayo, *When the World Was Young: Creation and Pourquoi Tales*
Quiché Maya People. Guatemala

After Huracan, god of sky, and Feathered Snake have spoken the earth and animals into existence, they want to create creatures who will thank them. The first people they make from mud wash away in the rain. Stick people have no thoughts or speech. The gods destroy them with tarry rain, and some escape to become monkeys in the trees. Next they pound and shape yellow and white corn kernels into four men. These men are strong and smart. They even praise the gods before the Huracan and Feathered Snake ask them to. But now, the gods think these people may be too good, too much like gods. Huracan blows a mist so that the men do not understand everything, and the world will still hold mystery and wonder for them. Satisfied, Huracan and Feathered Snake make four women to lay beside the men while they are sleeping so they will not be lonely. This story comes from the first part of the Popol Vuh, the narrative of creation and history of the Quiché Maya.

CONNECTIONS

Corn. Creation. Gods and humans. Gratitude. Gucumatz. Humans. Huracan. Knowledge. Mud. Origin tales. Monkeys. Popol Vuh. Praise. Pride. Punishments. Wood. Worship.

HOW ELSE THIS STORY IS TOLD

The Creation of Man—Dorothy Sharp Carter, *The Enchanted Orchard*.
The Creation of People According to the Popol Vuh—Michael A. Schuman, *Mayan and Aztec Mythology*. It's the mountain cat, coyote, crow and parrot who bring the Creators to the Broken Place to get the corn they then use to make men.
The First Monkeys—Shirley Climo, *Monkey Business*

The First People—Douglas Gifford, *Warriors, Gods & Spirits from Central & South American Mythology*

How People Came to Be—Yolanda Nava, *It's All in the Frijoles.* After the mud people melt and the stick people are flooded, the creators, Tepeu and Gucumatz, shape four men—Balam-Quitze, Balam-Acab, Mahucutah, and Iqui-Balam—from corn dough.

How People Came to Be / De cómo se creó la gente—Olga Loya, *Momentos Mágicos / Magic Moments*

Legend of the Perfect People—Grant Lyons, *Tales the People Tell in Mexico.* After the Shaper wipes out the first people who give glib answers, he creates races of different colors and languages and keeps them in darkness, with only one fire, which they can take if they give thanks to the God of Storms.

Making Humans—Robert Hull, *Central and South American Stories*

People of Corn: A Mayan Story—Mary-Joan Gerson

---

12. *WHY THERE IS NO ARGUING IN HEAVEN: A MAYAN MYTH*
Deborah Nourse Lattimore
Yucatec Maya Speakers. Mexico

Lizard House and Moon Goddess are arguing which of the gods is the greatest next to Hunab Ku, the first Creator God. Hunab Ku chastises them, saying a great god is one who creates instead of arguing. He pours a jar of water with his spit into the darkness to begin the earth. However, when the animals and birds there cannot thank the gods, Hunab Ku offers a challenge. The god second to him will be the one who makes a creature which can praise the gods with intelligence and gratitude. He spits life into a man of earth from Lizard House and then a man of catzim tree roots from Moon Goddess, but these men cannot speak. The Maize God saves some mud and one stick from them before Hunab Ku has the Rain Gods, the Chacs, drown them. Hunab Ku is thinking to destroy the earth altogether, when the Maize God asks to plant some seeds with better spirit. The spirits of the Maize God's two men survive the tests of fire water which Moon Goddess and Lizard House put them through. When, jealous and angry, Lizard House and Moon Goddess throw the spirits into the river, Hunab Ku punishes them. He gives permission for Maize God to plant his seeds and spits life into the spirits which flow with the river to become bronze people who express gratitude to the gods for creating them. And so it is Maize God who sits beside Hunab Ku.

CONNECTIONS

Chac. Competition. Conflict. Corn. Creation. Gods and goddesses. Gods and Humans. Gratitude. Hunab Ku. Humans. Lizards. Mud. Origin tales. Status. Worship.

---

13. THREE BIRDS AND A LITTLE BLACK DOG
Idella Purnell, *The Merry Frogs*
Huichol People. Mexico

A farmer becomes frustrated when all the trees and vines he has cleared from the field grow back by morning several days in a row. He hides and sees an old woman emerge from the ground. Trees grow back in all the four directions she points her staff. He yells for her to stop, and she tells him she is Great-grandmother Nakawé who makes things grow and wants to tell him to prepare for the great flood which will be coming. He is to build a box from the fig tree, paint it colorfully, and put in five each of corn grains and beans of different colors plus a small fire with pumpkin stems to feed it. He will also take a small black dog, a woodpecker, a sandpiper, and a parrot into the box. Then Great-grandmother Nakawé secures the cover for the box and rides on top with a macaw as the rain pours down. After fifteen days, the floodwaters go down, and the box comes to rest on a mountain near Santa Catarina. The macaw and parrot shape valleys, which curves their beaks. The birds separate waters into seas. When the sandpiper does not sink in the mud, the man comes out onto solid ground at last. Plants begin to grow again. Great-grandmother Nakawé becomes the wind. One day the man comes back to his cave to find tortillas already cooked. He hides and sees the black dog take off her skin and transform into a woman with shining black hair. The man throws her skin into the fire. He comforts the woman and washes her in corn water, and they live happily together.

Connections

Bird helpers. Boats. Dogs. Earth. Farmers. Floods. Gods and humans. Nakawe. Origin tales. Rescues. Supernatural beings. Transformations. Warnings.

How Else This Story Is Told

The Flood—*The Emerald Lizard*, Pleasant DeSpain. The black dog here has been sent as a gift from the Earth Goddess.

The Rain of Five Years (The Story of the Creation of the World)—Angel Vigil, *The Eagle on the Cactus*

The Story of a Flood—Juliet Piggott, *Mexican Folk Tales*

The Tree That Rains: The Flood Myth of the Huichol Indians of Mexico—Emery Bernhard

---

14. When Animals Were People / Cuando los animals eran personas

Bonnie Larson

Huichol People. Mexico

After the flood, Takutsi Nakawe, Grandmother of All Growing Things, brings new life back to plants and animals with her magic walking stick, but creatures have not fully settled into their true natures. A singing stranger finds Turtle Person cooking meat and goes off to get some toasted corn to eat with it. Squirrel Person warns Turtle Person that the singing stranger is a wolf, who will return with his wolf friends to eat not only all the meat, but both of them as well. They go up into a tree. The wolf does return with other wolves who try to knock the tree over. Hanging onto Squirrel Person's tail as the squirrel leaps to another tree. Turtle Person falls into a puddle. The wolves eat him, splashing all the water out of the puddle. However, now the wolves are thirsty. Grandfather Vulture sends them in different directions five different times. Finally, he tells the wolves that there will be no water until they revive Turtle Person. The wolves work to fit all the pieces together. At last Turtle Person is alive again, and the wolves get to quench their thirst. Since that time, squirrels live safely up in trees, wolves are smart hunters of their own meat, and turtle shells look patchworked from the fall.

CONNECTIONS

Birds. Buzzards. Friendship. Gods and animals. Interspecies conflict. Justice. Nakawe. Origin tales. Restoring life. Righting a wrong. Squirrels. Tortoises and turtles. Unkindness. Wolves.

HOW ELSE THIS STORY IS TOLD

Bigú—Marcos Kurtycz and Ana García Kobeh, *Tigers and Opossums: Animal Legends.* The buzzard is one of the animals God sends to check out if it is time to resettle the planet. He eats dead animals and does not obey God's order to return. A turtle pushes to meet God, so the buzzard finally gives in to ride him up on his back. But the turtle criticizes the buzzard's smell, and the buzzard tips him off. The creature's shell breaks into a hundred pieces, which God collects and puts back together. God calls the turtle Bigú, which means fragments.

Note: See also *Jabuti the Tortoise* (140) and A Party in Heaven (140), where turtles and tortoises crack their shells, getting dropped by other animals.

---

15. THE BIRD WHO CLEANS THE WORLD

Victor Montejo, *The Bird Who Cleans the World and Other Mayan Fables*
Jakaltek Maya People. Guatemala

When the floodwaters start receding in ancient times, the trumpet bird goes out first to see whether the earth is livable. The water is still too high. The buzzard goes next. He finds a hill that sticks up above the water. On that hill are decaying animals, and buzzard forgets that he is supposed to be scouting and begins to eat the meat. When he returns to the house where all the other animals are waiting, he smells terrible and they will not let him in. *Usmiq*'s punishment becomes his work once all of the water is gone. He can eat only dead animals, but this keeps the world free from stench and rottenness for others.

CONNECTIONS

Angels. Bird helpers. Buzzards. Floods. God. Gods and animals. Identity. Meat. Origin tales. Punishments. Rabbits. Tasks. Tortoises and turtles. Vultures.

HOW ELSE THIS STORY IS TOLD

Mexican variations:

The Rabbit Flood—Margaret Read MacDonald, *Five Minute Tales.* Otomi People. It is a rabbit who tells the man to build a box to float out the flood in and rides on top. When the floodwaters recede, the man and his family cook meat from a cow which had drowned. God sends some angels down to see what is burning, but warns them not to eat any of it. The meat smells so good that they taste a little piece. They wash well, but God turns them into vultures, who eat only meat from then on.

The World—Manuel Vidal Valderrama. In Américo Paredes, *Folktales of Mexico*. The rabbit can see from a hole in the roof that the box they are riding out the floodwaters in has now reached the sky. When the waters recede, the humans cook some of the dead cattle. The Lord sends angels down to check on the smoke. When the angels eat some of the meat, against God's command, they become the vultures in the new world.

16. *THE GREAT CANOE: A KARINA LEGEND*
Maria Elena Maggi
Carib People

When Kaputano the Sky Dweller arrives to tell the Kariña people that the world will be covered by water, most people do not believe him. Kaputano tells the four couples who fear the coming flood to help build a canoe to save some of his people. The eight people ride out the flood in this giant canoe with two of each kind of animal and seed from each kind of plant. When the waters recede, Kaputano asks the survivors if they want the earth to stay bare, but they desire palm trees for leaves to weave and mountains where crops may be grown and rivers with fish and trees for shelter. And Kaputano gives it all to them, his children.

CONNECTIONS
Boats. Floods. Gods and humans. Kaputano. Origin tales. Rescues. Warnings.

17. *THE GOOD LLAMA: A PICTURE STORY FROM PERU*
Anne Rockwell
Peru

A llama has stopped eating and tells the man concerned about him that it is because there will be a catastrophic flood when the earth tries to drown the sun with tears for making her too hot. The llama leads the man and his family up to Villacoto Mountain. As they climb, the llama convinces other birds, insects, and animals to come along. The foxes refuse to believe there will be a flood until the waters begin to rise. At the top, the llama reassures each creature in its own language. It suddenly becomes dark and terrifying, when the sun topples into the water. The sun swims desperately to reach the sky again. He begs the earth for help, and at last the earth agrees never make such a flood again if the sun promises to bathe in the western sea each evening and let the moon bring cool light for the night. The sun reluctantly agrees, and the floodwaters recede. Since that time, llamas only speak their own tongue, and the tips of foxes' tails are black where they dipped into the earth's tears.

CONNECTIONS

Accusations. Animal helpers. Conflict. Earth. Floods. Foxes. Gods and humans. Gratitude. Heat. Herders. Heroes and heroines. Language. Llamas. Mama Cocha. Moon. Origin tales. Promises. Rescues. Sun. Temperature. Warnings.

HOW ELSE THIS STORY IS TOLD

The Llama's Secret: A Peruvian Legend—Argentina Palacios. The llama warns that the goddess of the sea and fish, Mamachocha, will be flooding the earth. At the end, people gratefully decorate their llamas with bells and entertain them with flutes.

---

18. THE DISOBEDIENT GIANT

Genevieve Barlow, *Latin American Tales from the Pampas to Mexico City*
Cuna People. Panama

People are suffering with hunger when winter storms flood the plains of Panama. Together they pray to the god Oba, and the oldest wise man tells them that Oba is sending his son, the giant Ologuitur, to help. Ologuitur is not doing anything in the heavens, but it still takes him several days to appear. By then the land is so wet, he sinks in up to his waist. Ologuitur sees some boulders which could be rolled to block with ocean. When he tries to return to the heavens before actually doing the work, Oba pushes him back to Earth so hard that Ologuitur falls into the center of the earth. It is frighteningly dark down there, and the weight of the earth pushes heavily down as the giant stands and crawls underground. He never does find his way out. Though Ologuitur's movement below can cause earthquakes and his voice calling through can make volcanoes, the Cuna people thank him for the beauty of the mountains which now block the ocean from flooding their land.

CONNECTIONS

Disobedience. Farmers. Floods. Giants. Gods and humans. Gratitude. Hunger. Journeys to other realms. Laziness. Mountains. Origin tales. Parents and children. Punishments. Supernatural beings. Topography. Underground worlds.

---

19. HOW THE BAT SAVED THE WORLD

Idella Purnell, *The Merry Frogs*
Cora People. Mexico

The earth is so flat in the beginning that standing water makes the corn mildew. The head man decides to consult the Vulture first about how to get rid of the water. The Vulture, however, does not really care, for if people die, he will be able to eat them. The Owl, too, thinks only about himself. It seems unlikely that an old man with a cane will be able to help, but the old man is a Bat and offers to see what he can do in the night, since he is blind during the day. At night, the Bat swoops down with his sharp-pointed wings and cuts paths to lead the water away from the fields. The head man thanks him, but complains that the canyons and valleys are too deep for people to travel. Bat asks if they want everything to go back the way it was, but the head man just requests gentler slopes with some flat areas for corn. Bat darts again to change some of the land, and people are most grateful for the reshaped sections, where they can plant and the water drains.

CONNECTIONS
Animal helpers. Bats. Birds. Buzzards. Earth. Farmers. Gratitude. Origin tales. Selfishness. Topography. Valleys. Water.

---

20. THE MERRY FROGS
Idella Purnell, *The Merry Frogs*
Cora People. Mexico

In a time of severe drought, five chief men ask the hummingbirds to call the rain clouds in the east. The clouds, however, kill the messengers for their brightly colored robes and run back to their caves. The hummingbirds are able to come back to life and report what happened, but no one else wants to go for the rain clouds. Frog volunteers. He leaves one son on each mountain along the way. At the last mountain, he calls out to the clouds and starts running away as the clouds give chase. Frog hides under a stone, and the clouds chase the fifth son they think is frog. Then he hides, and they chase the fourth son. This goes on until the rain clouds come to the western sea. Rain falls, and they return grumbling to their caves, while the frogs laugh.

CONNECTIONS
Bird helpers. Conflict. Drought. Frog helpers. Frogs and toads. Hummingbirds. Origin tales. Restoring life. Tricksters.

---

21. TLACUACHE'S TAIL
Judy Goldman, *Whiskers, Tails & Wings*
Huichol People. Mexico

Back in a time when people pray to the gods for a way to keep warm because they have no fire, a light flashing from sky to earth causes some dry branches to become bright and hot. One Old Woman runs away with a branch of the Bright Thing to her hut, saying it is a gift from the gods. The Old Woman will not share the Bright Thing. Opossum Tlacuache, who has been watching her, notices that she does not leave the Bright Thing even to gather food or to sleep. He tells the Headman that he thinks he can help if people promise not to hunt him or be mean to him anymore. When the Headman finally agrees, Tlacuache tells them to have branches ready. He carries ripe *tunas*, cactus fruit, to the Old Woman's hut. Right away, she suspects he has come to steal fire. Tlacuache convinces her that he has brought her fruit in exchange for being able to sleep near the warmth. He pretends to sleep. As the Old Woman's eyes close,

Tlacuache goes closer to the Bright Thing. The Old Woman awakens and yells. Startled, Tlacuache turns, and the Bright Thing leaps onto his bushy tail. He runs to the village with his burning tail and jumps onto the branches which have been prepared. The Bright Thing feeds on them. Water helps cool Tlacuache's tail at last. Grateful to have fire, people do treat Tlacuache more kindly. He also starts feeling better about having no hair on his tail when he realizes it's useful for hanging from trees.

CONNECTIONS

Animal helpers. Bargains. Courage. Fire. Generosity. Gods and animals. Gods and humans. Heroes and heroines. Iguanas. Opossums. Origin tales. Selfishness. Tails. Theft. Unkindness.

HOW ELSE THIS STORY IS TOLD

How the Opossum Stole Fire—Fernanco Benitez. In *Jade and Iron* Cora People. Mexico. Brave Yaushu, the opossum, makes a long journey with a gift of corn flour so the Lord of the Fire will let down his guard. When he sneaks some embers, the Lord of the Fire accuses Yaushu of stealing from his own grandfather and throws him down the mountain, but the opossum succeeds.

Opossum and the Great Firemaker: A Mexican Legend—Jan M. Mike. Opossum bravely climbs up to the sky where Iguana is hoarding fire he stole.

Opossum Steals Fire—Pablo Guerrero. In John Bierhorst, *The Mythology of Mexico and Central America*. Mazatec People. Mexico

The Possum's Tail (How Fire Came to the World)—Angel Vigil, *The Eagle on the Cactus*. Mazatec People. Mexico

See also Fire and the Jaguar (250).

---

22. THE GODS OF LIGHT
Alicia Morel in *Jade and Iron*
Mapuche People. Chile

One night, in a time before the Mapuche people have learned to make fire, Caleu sees a shooting star. Though he worries that it may portend trouble, Caleu does not say anything, except to warn his family to return before dark when the women and children climb the mountain to gather nuts. Caleu's wife, Mallén, leads the others to a cave as night begins to fall, and from there they see a shooting star with a golden tail. Is this a message from the ancestors? Just then, an earthquake sends stones crashing down around them. Sparks fly as stone hits stone. Grandmother Collalla calls these little lights a gift from their ancestors. The sparks set fire to a tall *coihue* tree. The men arrive, looking for their families. They pick up burning branches to lead the way down the mountain. After that, people collect those stones to make fires by striking them together.

CONNECTIONS

Discoveries. Earthquakes. Fire. Flint. Gods and humans. Grandparents. Origin tales. Parents and children. Stones.

23. FIRE-TAKING
Josepha Sherman, *Trickster Tales*
Makiritare People (now Yacuana). Venezuela

Kawao, the toad woman, and her jaguar husband, Manuwa, have killed and eaten the Water Mother, Huiio the fish woman, and are raising her twin sons. They intend to eat them also when they have grown. Iureke and his brother Shikiemona do not know any of this. They also do not know that Kawao holds fire secretly within her. One day Iureke gets so angry when Kawao does not tell them the truth about how she is able to cook that he jumps into the forbidden river and his brother follows. There they meet other fish for the first time. The spirit of Huiio, tells them who they are and about Kawao's plot. The twins return to avenge their mother's murder. When Kawao sends the twins out to play, Iureke hides in the roof and puts one of his eyes on the back of his neck to learn how Kawao cooks. The eye shows that Kawao breathes fire from her mouth. Kawao has decided to kill the boys, but the twins pin her to the floor until she coughs out the fire and dies. Iureke throws the fire in a pot along with Kawao, and both boys run. Manuwa comes roaring after them, pulling a fresh jaguar from his body each time they hurt him. Then Manuwa finds the twins swinging on a vine. They say it gives them magic power. Manuwa says he will stop chasing them if they let him swing on it. The twins push him so high, the vine snaps. Manuwa falls and is killed. Iureke puts half of the fire he stole in one tree and half in another. He thinks clever people will figure out how to coax the fire out of hiding by rubbing sticks from one tree against sticks from the other.

CONNECTIONS
Fire. Fish. Frogs and toads. Jaguars. Magic. Murder. Origin tales. Parents and children. Revenge. Secrets. Spirits. Sticks. Supernatural beings. Twins.

24. *HOW IWARIWA THE CAYMAN LEARNED TO SHARE: A YANOMAMI MYTH*
George Crespo
Yanomami People. Amazonia, Venezuela

In a time when animals in the Amazon rain forest have no fire and eat their food raw, one bird tells the others that, flying over the caymans' roof, she saw Iwariwa's wife pull sweet potatoes with a stick from something orange and crackling. The potatoes smelled wonderful. She then saw Iwariwa collect the fire into a little basket afterwards and hide it in his mouth. The others do not think it is fair that the caymans keep this wonderful thing all to themselves, and the jaguar Dihi is sure they can find a way to grab the basket. He invites the caymans to a feast. Everyone is eating at the feast except for Iwariwa, who keeps his mouth closed. Everyone is laughing at the entertainment, except for Iwariwa, until the anteater pretends to fall. Then Iwariwa lets out a large belly laugh and the basket with fire shoots up into the air. The bird snatches it and passes it to the tortoise who swims across the river and passes it to the armadillo who ducks into his burrow where Iwariwa gets stuck, until he agrees to share the fire.

CONNECTIONS

Bargains. Birds. Caimans. Fire. Jaguars. Origin tales. Rescues. Secrets. Selfishness. Teamwork.

---

25. ALETÍN AND THE FALLING SKY
Melinda Lilly
Mocoví People. Argentina

The Earth is still very much in transition when it is new. One evening, after days of sunshine, Aletín throws his stick hard at the western horizon to remind the Sun where to go to rest. The stick tears a hole where air meets land. The Sun does slip down, but now the sky rips more, and a star falls into Aletín's hammock. Aletín climbs a palm tree to stitch the star back up in the sky, but when he wakes in the morning, the whole blue Sky has come down and covers him heavily like a blanket. Aletín works with his frightened people to prop the Sky up with branches. With all their strength, they manage to toss the Sky on top of the Sun. That works until the Sun can no longer hold Sky's weight and rolls down to Earth starting fires. People who run to the river turn into water animals; those in the forest become land creatures. Aletín rises up as a toucan. With his new beak, he stabs the Sun and sticks it back up into the Sky.

CONNECTIONS

Animals. Birds. Fear. Gods and humans. Leadership. Origin tales. Problem solving. Sky. Stars. Sun. Tasks. Teamwork. Toucans. Transformations.

---

26. ÑUCU THE WORM
Jürgen Riester in *Jade and Iron*
Chimane People. Amazonia, Bolivia

In the old times, when the sky is so close to earth that it sometimes crushes people, a poor woman notices a shiny thing in the yucca plants one day. She does not investigate until a dream tells her the thing is alive. She then finds a white worm, which she brings home and tenderly cares for. Ñucu quickly outgrows each jar she places him in and is always hungry, which is difficult, since she struggles to find her own food. Then one day, Ñucu lies across the river, and his giant body creates a dam. Fish jump out, and the woman now has plenty to eat. She is catching so many fish, though, that none are left for the villagers. Ñucu tells his mother to invite them to fish with her. He reassures her once she has helped them, the villagers will make sure she, too, has enough to eat. Ñucu, grows even larger and arcs across the earth to hold up the sky. The old woman misses him, but she can see him shining as the Milky Way at night.

CONNECTIONS

Dreams. Fish. Food. Generosity. Heroes and heroines. Hunger. Kindness. Magic worms. Milky Way. Sky. Stars. Supernatural beings. Tasks. Transformations. Worms.

HOW ELSE THIS STORY IS TOLD

Ñucu, the Worm / Ñucu, el gusano—Paula Martin, *Pachamama Tales*

27. HOW THE RAINBOW WAS BORN
Lulu Delacre, *Golden Tales*
Zapotec People. Mexico

Cosijogui, god of lightning, dazzles people on earth when he orders the lizard Cloud Guardian to open one of his secret pots and send clouds and lightning into the dark sky. When people are thirsty, he has the Water Guardian open a second secret pot, but the deluge of rain and lightning frighten them. However, messengers who arrive from earth to ask Cosijogui to stop are curious to see what is in the other two pots. Cosijogui commands his lizard-guard to release hard hail from the third pot. While the lightning god and his guards are enjoying the stormy chaos down below, people and creatures on earth pray to Gabicha, the sun, for help. Cosijogui knows his own power over the skies is diminishing as Gabicha sends rays of light through the clouds. Gabicha tells the last lizard-guardian to open the pot of wind to blow the storm away. Now recognizing Gabicha's dominion and kindness, Cosijogui lays down a multicolored bridge between the sky and the earth to help Gabicha bring the message of peace.

CONNECTIONS

Gods and humans. Hail. Lightning. Origin tales. Peace. Power. Rainbows. Rescues. Status. Storms. Sun. Water. Wind.

28. THE BOY HORTICULTURIST
Frances Toor, *A Treasury of Mexican Folkways*
Tepoztlán. Mexico

A mamma cannot find food which will stop her baby boy from crying. He rejects her milk as well as white and corn flour gruel, even with sweeteners. The child just keeps crying. The mamma sends her servant to bring the curandera, the medicine woman. The curandera sees that the baby has a maguey plant painted on his stomach, and he calms as soon as she feeds him some pulque. The curandera advises the mother to feed him pulque until he is seven years old. She smokes herbs over him, sucks the blood from above his stomach, and rubs out the paint. When the boy is seven, the curandera smokes him with herbs again and discovers pictures of many fruits on his back, along with an ear of corn in one hand and a calabash plant. She says he is to eat only fruit now. She sucks his hand and his back, and then washes his back with specially prepared tea. All the fruit painted on his back disappears. He becomes the one responsible for planting all the fruit trees, and people call him "el niño horticultor."

CONNECTIONS
Food. Fruit. Healers. Hunger. Magic. Origin tales. Parents and children. Plants. Pulque. Trees.

---

29. THE LEGEND OF MANIOC
Joel Ruffino Dos Santos in *Jade and Iron*
Brazil

Zatiamaré is so angry when Atioló gives birth to a daughter instead of a son that he will not give the baby a name or even speak to her. Her mother calls her Mani. When Atioló gives birth to a boy next, however, Zatiamaré cherishes this son. Mani asks her mother to bury her alive in hopes that she may be worth something someday. Atioló weeps, but at last, consents and buries Mani in a shallow grave. That night Atioló dreams that Mani is too hot, so she digs her up. Mani tells her she needs to be moved by the river. When Atioló bathes nearby, however, she hears Mani say it is too cold on the riverbank, so she takes her into the forest. Mani tells her mother only to come visit next when she can no longer remember her face. Time passes, and Atioló is thinking about Mani, missing her daughter. She walks to her grave, where she finds a tall green plant. Just as Atioló says that the plant cannot be her daughter, one part separates and becomes a root, which she takes home to cook. Manioc becomes a mainstay food for people of the Amazon.

CONNECTIONS
Death. Despair. Dreams. Favoritism. Food. Gender. Manioc. Origin tales. Parents and children. Plants. Self-esteem. Transformations.

HOW ELSE THIS STORY IS TOLD
The Gift of Manioc—Frances Carpenter, *South American Wonder Tales*. When an old woman tells the chief that his daughter has married a stranger with milk-white skin and will give birth to a child who will bring blessings to the land, he feels only rage. His daughter insists that she was with no man, and in a dream a young man tells him that his daughter speaks the truth—he is the son of the gods who made all things on earth, who married her. The child Mani is born, but she dies when she is very young. Mani is buried inside a hut, where a special plant grows with white roots which nourish people when specially prepared.
The Origin of Yuca / El origen de la yucca—Paula Martin, *Pachamama Tales*
The Story of Mani—Livia de Almeida and Ana Portella, *Brazilian Folktales*. Tupi People. Amazonia. When a daughter becomes pregnant, a warrior comes to her father in a dream and tells him to believe that his daughter lay with no man and that she will bear a gift to all. She gives birth of a girl, Mani, who dies when she is one year old. The plant which grows where she is buried gives people strength.

30. The Quest for Corn

John Bierhorst, *The Mythology of Mexico and Central America*
Mopan Maya People. Belize and Guatemala

Before the time when people grow crops, they live on the plants and fruits they find. Only the leaf-cutter ants know that corn is hidden under a large rock, with cracks so small they are the only ones who can get at it. The animals want to know what fox has been eating that makes his wind smell so sweet and follow him to where the ants have dropped a few grains. The ants agree to bring up some corn for the others, but there are just too many animals. People ask the *mam* for help. Three thunder lords try to break the rock, but they need Yaluk, the fourth and greatest thunder lord. Yaluk says he is too old, but sends a woodpecker to tap on the rock to find the spot where it is thinnest. He directs his thunderbolt there. When the rock breaks open, some of the white corn turns red and yellow from fire and smoke. Old Yaluk, who has fainted from the effort, is left with only red and yellow corn, but the corn he plants comes up sooner than the white corn which the other mam took. The woodpecker ends up with a red crest because he forgets to hide, and a rock hit him on the top of his head.

Connections

Ants. Bird helpers. Birds. Corn. Discoveries. Fireflies. Food. Foxes. Gods and animals. Gods and humans. Gratitude. Insect helpers. Leaf-cutter ants. Lightning. Origin tales. Punishments. Quetzalcoatl. Rocks. Secrets. Tasks. Teamwork. Thunderbolts. Woodpeckers.

How Else This Story Is Told

Maya variations:
(Variants of this tale are also told by the Cakchiquel, Mam, Pokomchi, Yucatec, and Tzeltal Maya)

The Corn in the Rock—John Bierhorst, *The Monkey's Haircut and Other Stories Told by the Maya*. Kekchi Maya People. When the fox refuses to tell the other animals what he has been eating that fills his belly, the firefly successfully follows him.
The Spirit of the Maize—Douglas Gifford, *Warriors, Gods & Spirits from Central & South American Mythology*. Maya People. The gods decide people have grown too comfortable and hide the maize, so people will turn to them in hunger and appreciate them more. However, animals also miss the maize. An ant talks a bird out of eating him and finds a way into the rock.

Mexican Aztec variations:
The Legend of Food Mountain / La montaña del alimento—Harriet Rohmer. The humans which Quetzalcoatl creates from bones have nothing to eat, until he sees a red ant emerging from a mountain with a piece of corn. Once the mountain is open, rain dwarfs steal the food, which is why people call for rain to bring the food back.
The New People and Their Food—Juliet Piggott, *Mexican Folk Tales*. Quetzelcoatl turns himself into a black ant to join their procession into a mountain and bring corn to people from where it is hidden. Gods tell people to plant the corn and offer thanks to them. They punish the ant for poking around by fastening him to his anthill.

31. THE FEATHERED SNAKE: HOW MUSIC CAME TO THE WORLD

Margaret Mayo, *Mythical Birds and Beasts from Many Lands*
Aztec People. Mexico

In the beginning, the only music on earth is in the House of the Sun, who will not share. The creator god Smoking Mirror convinces the reluctant feathered snake Quetzalcoatl, Lord of the Winds, to bring some music back from the sun to earth. Quetzalcoatl journeys to the sun, where he hears the wonderful sounds of musicians dressed in the colors of the different kinds of music they play: white, blue, red, golden. The Sun has warned the musicians that Quetalcoatl will try to steal them, and they are silent and afraid as Quetzalcoatl tries to persuade them of the joy their music would bring to a silent earth. Finally, Quetzalcoatl grows angry and causes a terrifying storm that covers the Sun's light with dark clouds. The musicians run to him, and Quetzalcoatl gently wraps his body around them and brings them to earth. They teach humans and animals all the melodies of nature and people now heard.

CONNECTIONS

Captivity. Conflict. Generosity. Gods and goddesses. Journeys. Moon. Music. Musicians. Origin tales. Quetzalcoatl. Rescues. Seflishness. Storms. Sun. Tasks. Tezcatlipoca.

HOW ELSE THIS STORY IS TOLD

All of You Was Singing—Richard Lewis

The Coming of Music—Robert Hull, *Central and South American Stories*. Quetzalcoatl reaches the sun on a bridge made of the intertwined bodies of Tezcatlipoca the sky god's three servants: Cane and Conch, Water Woman, and Water Monster.

How Music Was Fetched Out of Heaven—Geraldine McCaughrean, *The Golden Hoard: Myths and Legends of the World*

Musicians of the Sun—Gerald McDermott. Alligator Woman, Turtle Woman, and Fish Woman carry the Wind across the sea to the place where he can then leap up to the Sun, where the musicians are being held captive.

---

32. THE MURMUR OF THE RIVER (HOW MUSIC CAME TO THE WORLD) / EL MURMULLO DEL RÍO (CÓMO LA MÚSICA LLEGÓ AL MUNDO)

Angel Vigil, *The Eagle on the Cactus*
Maya People. Mexico

The Earth feels incomplete to the gods without something to lift the spirits of people in hard times. The Earth itself contains sounds, and Ah Kin Xooc asks each god to contribute a sound: river murmurs, rain taps, wind whispers, corn leaf rustles, wave crashes, ice cracks, tree creaks, bird chirps, fire crackles. He swallows these sounds of nature and brings them to the center of the Earth. When he opens his mouth, all of the sounds escape and rise. Ah Kin Xooc teaches people the whole range to match the emotions in their hearts. People imitate the sounds of nature and add more sounds and instruments to create music which speaks to them.

CONNECTIONS
Gods and humans. Music. Origin tales. Respect for nature. Teamwork.

---

33. THE ORIGIN OF MUSIC
John Bierhorst, *The Hungry Woman: Myths and Legends of the Aztecs*
Zapotec Aztec People. Mexico

In a time long ago, people in each of the three parts of the Zapotec land excel in different skills, which contribute to the whole. The women of the north weave cloth; artists of the south make pots, drums, and flutes from clay and wood; men in the center trade goods made by the others and women run the markets. The gods do not know that none of the people feel appreciated for their work. When they send the goddess Tangu Yuh down to earth on the New Year to celebrate the Zapotec's cooperation, instead, her magnificent presence causes grief, as each group vies for her attention. Tangu Yuh returns to heaven. Now, all of the Zapotec people are sad. They would like her to return. They try to recall Tangu Yuh's face. Then the people of the south compose a song imagining her eyes; the potters create a clay figure of her; the people of the north dress that figure as they remember, like themselves. Over time, their sadness fades, and they gather together in a joyful fiesta each year on New Year's Day, singing the song of Tangu Yuh and making dolls of her with arms reaching out. The Zapotecs hope that Tangu Yuh will visit again when the potters can capture her likeness more precisely.

CONNECTIONS
Art. Competition. Despair. Dolls. Gods and humans. Music. New Year. Origin tales. Skills. Tangu Yuh. Teamwork. Weaving.

HOW ELSE THIS STORY IS TOLD
The Legend of Tangu Yuh—Mary-Jo Gerson, *Fiesta Femenina*
The Zapotec Legend of Tangu Yuh—Frances Toor, *Treasury of Mexican Folkways*

II

Journeys to Other Realms

---

34. WHAT HAPPENED WHEN ARMADILLO DUG A HOLE IN THE SKY
Natalia M. Belting, *Moon Was Tired of Walking on Air*
Cayapo People. Brazil

Long ago, people live in the sky where they have to keep cutting down trees, which grow like weeds. A hunter catches up with a giant armadillo, which disappears into a hole. The man digs after him and four days later makes a grab for the armadillo's tail. The bottom of the burrow breaks through, and the armadillo falls to earth. The earth the man sees through the hole looks beautiful with grasslands and water full of fish. The headmen say they will go down to see if this is a better place to live. Eventually, the rope they make from everyone's belts, bracelets, and anklets is long enough to touch the earth. The first headman to climb down secures the rope to a tree trunk. Many villagers follow. A boy shouts up to the villagers who hesitate to come and cuts the rope. They become stars in the sky. The first people who remain on earth are the Ancestors.

CONNECTIONS
Ancestors. Armadillos. Discoveries. Earth. Humans. Journeys to other realms. Origin tales. Ropes. Sky worlds. Stars. Transformations.

HOW ELSE THIS STORY IS TOLD
The Hole in the Sky—Anton Lukesch. In Johannes Wilbert, *Folk Literature of the Gê Indians, Vol. 1.* Gê People. Brazil and Paraguay

---

35. LEGENDS OF THE WARAUS. THE DISCOVERY OF THE EARTH
W. H. Brett, *Guyana Legends*
Warao People. Guyana

In the land above the sky where the Warau live, there are no animals, except birds. Okonorote tracks one beautiful bird for many days, and when his arrow strikes true and it falls, he discovers a pit in the ground of the sky. Peering over the edge, Okonorote can see forests and rivers and strange creatures way down below. He brings the other young men to the edge and then all of them convince the old men that another world is there. Okonorote suggests that he travel down alone on a cotton rope, just in case there is danger. At last, the rope is long enough, and Okonorote descends. He roasts a deer and brings some of the meat back up to the sky. The Warau people yearn to eat more of this, and they all climb down the rope, all but one woman who becomes wedged in the opening. She is still there, which is why people cannot see through the sky.

CONNECTIONS

Carib people. Curiosity. Death (Character). Discoveries. Earth. Humans. Journeys to other realms. Okonorote. Origin tales. Ropes. Sky worlds.

HOW ELSE THIS STORY IS TOLD

A Home Beneath the Clouds—Roy Heath. In Andrew Salkey, *Caribbean Folk Tales and Legends.* People travel down on rope of lianas. When a pregnant woman gets caught in the hole, Death kills her, blocking their path back up.

Legend of Okonoróté—William Henry Brett, *Legends and Myths of the Aboriginal Indians of British Guiana.* In rhyming verse.

The Sky People—Douglas Gifford, *Warriors, Gods & Spirits from Central & South American Mythology.* This story continues on beyond Okonorote's descent to earth to the beginning of the warrior Carib people.

---

36. THE BOY WHO ROSE TO THE SKY

John Bierhorst, *Black Rainbow: Legends of the Incas and Myths of Ancient Peru*

Peru

On the third night that a young man is sent to guard the family garden, glowing princesses descend from the sky and begin digging up potatoes. They are stars, and as he grabs one, the others rise back up. He asks this princess to be his wife, though she wants to return to the sky. He lies about having his own house and brings her to his parents, who care for her, but keep her shut indoors. When she becomes pregnant, the child dies. She escapes and returns home. A condor offers to fly the heartbroken young man up to the sky for the price of two llamas, one to eat right away and the other for food along the way. It takes one year to reach the sky, and when the llama meat runs out, the young man feeds the condor pieces from his own leg. The condor lands at a lake which makes them younger and heals the man's leg. On the other side, at the temple of the Sun and the Moon, are many identical maidens. One tells him she is going to come back to him. She gives him a little quinoa to cook. When he adds too much, and it overflows, she tells him he must leave. The condor carries the sad young man back to earth. His star wife is the only woman he will ever love.

CONNECTIONS

Captivity. Condors. Deceit. Interspecies conflict. Journeys to other realms. Love. Magic. Magic
waters. Mourning. Quinoa. Sky worlds. Stars. Supernatural husbands and wives.

HOW ELSE THIS STORY IS TOLD

The Girl from the Sky—Douglas Gifford, *Warriors, Gods & Spirits from Central & South American
Mythology*

---

37. JUAN IN HEAVEN
M.A. Jagendorf and R.S. Boggs, *The King of the Mountains*
Costa Rica

Sometimes Juan feels bad that he always misunderstands things. He only feels free
from ridicule when he is alone at night. Staring at the sky one night, he finds himself
outside of heaven. Juan requests entrance, telling St. Peter that he never harmed anyone,
and it would be a sanctuary from all the teasing, but St. Peter tells him that he is not
ready to enter. St. Peter brings Juan to a room where lights of different brightness indi-
cate the length of a person's life. Juan sees that his own lamp is not so bright. He is
trying to add oil, when St. Peter stops him and takes him back to the waiting room.
One day, when angels escort the soul of a Pope into heaven Juan follows them in. God
notices that Juan has no wings, so an angel brings him some. It is wonderful there in
heaven, a dream that makes Juan very happy.

CONNECTIONS

Deceit. Dreams. God. Gods and humans. Heaven. Journeys to other realms. Juan Bobo. Justice.
Life span. Reputation. Peter, Saint. Self-esteem.

---

38. THE ENCHANTED CITY
Juan Carlos Galeano, *Folktales of the Amazon*
Peru

Sitting on the riverbank one afternoon, a young logger falls in love with a beautiful
girl who appears there. She describes her home as enticingly free of overwork and abun-
dant with food and riches and invites him to meet her family. With magic words, she
opens a stone door beside a chacruna shrub and leads him down a tunnel through
another door guarded by two ranaco trees with boas to an ancient-looking city made
of stone. There the logger sees people bathe in fountains which help them to live longer.
When he tells the young woman he needs to return to send word to his parents in Iquitos, she leads him back to the logging camp. His friends, who thought he had drowned,
try to convince him not to return to her, but he gives them a letter and leather bag filled
with gold and precious stones to take to his parents. No one ever sees him again.

CONNECTIONS

Enchanted cities. Journeys to other realms. Love. Magic doors. Mysteries. Seduction. Supernatural beings. Treasure.

---

39. THE BOY WHO WAS LOST

M.A. Jagendorf and R.S. Boggs, *The King of the Mountains*
Brazil

Led deep into the forest by a *bacurau* bird he is trying to hunt, a boy becomes miserably lost for a few days. He wishes aloud that a woodpecker could fly him across the stream, and the woodpecker grows huge and takes him on a frightening ride, which ends with the boy screaming and the woodpecker putting him back down in the same place. Now an alligator takes the boy on his back, but mid-stream taunts the boy to call him a bad name. The boy doesn't say the bad name until he reaches the other side. The alligator comes after him, but a heron hides the boy in his crop. On the other side, the boy is still lost. He comes to the house of the Wild Pig people, who resemble humans with pig heads. Not knowing what else to do, he accepts their invitation to stay and puts on a Wild Pig skin, until one day he recognizes a certain garden and hides until the pigs all leave. He is very happy to be home, but he always feels part Wild Pig and will never let anyone come close.

CONNECTIONS

Alligators. Bird helpers. Herons. Journeys to other realms. Lost. Nighthawks. Pigs. Reunions. Supernatural beings. Woodpeckers.

---

40. JUAN FETCHES THE DEVIL

Anthony John Campos, *Mexican Folk Tales*
Mexico

When his parents can no longer afford to feed Juan's enormous appetite, they tell him to go bring the devil back. Juan sadly leaves to find him. An old man tells him that the devil lives across the ocean in a fiery cave. An eagle with a large appetite will fly him there, if Juan has seven cows to feed him during the trip. Juan steals the cows and finds an eagle, and they set off. After a while of flying, though, Juan gets hungry, too. He and the eagle argue, and the eagle dumps him off into the ocean. Luckily, Juan is close enough swim to shore. He starts walking to the desert. Hungry, Juan runs after a coyote, who pleads that he will take Juan to the cave with fire if Juan doesn't eat him. The coyote takes Juan to a bear he can eat the first day and then to a wolf to eat the next. On the third day, however, when Juan is hungry enough to eat the coyote, the coyote tells him to grab the nose of whoever is in a certain cave. It turns out to be the devil. Holding the devil's nose with pliers, Juan forces the devil to fly him home. Frightened, Juan's parents ask him to forgive them. The devil tells Juan to pull a hair from the coyote's tail every time he gets hungry, and the hair will become a cow to feed them all.

CONNECTIONS

Bargains. Changes in attitude. Coyotes. Devil. Eagles. Forgiveness. Hunger. Journeys to other
  realms. Magic. Magic hairs. Parents and children. Quests.

---

41. THE STORY OF THE GODDESS OF THE LAKE

Don Bonifacio Soto Bizarro and Benjamin Bizarro Temó in James D. Sexton, *Heart of Heaven, Heart of Earth*
Maya People

When a sudden whirlwind in the lake causes their parents to drown, the older children push the youngest boy out. In two nights of dreams, his parents tell him not to
grieve, that they peacefully serve the dueña down in the lake and will always care for
him. They warn him to stop crying so he can remain in the world above. The next day,
searching the beach at Santa Cruz where he saw them, the boy meets a senorita with
a transparent blue face, green eyes, and long white hair, who wears jade necklaces and
gold rings. The dueña of the lake demands to know why he has come. He describes his
loneliness. The dueña insists he come to see his parents. He knows they are dead and
fears to go, but she sings a haunting song as they travel. They reach a place that looks
like a regular community with people cooking together. His parents are there, but when
he tries to take their hands, they are just air. They invite him to stay with them, but the
boy answers that now that he has seen that they are happy, he will go. The houses and
people vanish, and the lady of the lake is walking with him underwater. He can feel the
farewell kiss she gives him, but when he tries to kiss her, she, too, is only air. He returns
to his village, but soon afterward, mysteriously disappears.

CONNECTIONS

Death. Despair. Dreams. Gods and humans. Journeys to other realms. Loneliness. Orphans. Parents and children. Shipwrecks. Spirits. Supernatural beings. Water worlds.

---

42. JUAN BOA: THE MAN WHO TURNED
INTO A RIVER SERPENT

Juan Carlos Galeano, *Folktales of the Amazon*
Amazonia, Colombia

Juan and his sister disappear when traveling by canoe one day. In a dream, his
mother learns that Juan has turned into a water boa, living in the Amazon River between
upper Ucayali River and Santarem. He would like to escape the dangers of dealing with
giant leeches and giant pirarucú fish and asks her for help. His family goes to a shaman,
whose charms do not work. One day Juan is even attacked by his own boa sister, who
has been put up to it by a power-hungry male boa. He kills them both and keeps wandering, disheartened. When he reaches a garrison of soldiers, Juan calls out that he is
a man and can become one again if the soldier shoots him right in the star on his fore-

head. The soldier agrees to help, but accidentally hits Juan in the eye as Juan swims toward him. Still, Juan's snakeskin peels off. He emerges from the water grateful to be human again, even with one eye, and grateful to now know some of the wonders of that other world.

Connections

Amazon River. Boas. Brothers and sisters. Journeys to other realms. Rescues. Rivers. Parents and children. Snakes. Soldiers. Transformations. Water worlds.

---

43. The Prince of the Sword

Yolando Pino-Saavedra, *Folktales of Chile*
Chile

When an enchanted prince rides off with a young man's sister whom he has fallen in love with, the brother follows their trail to the sea. He flings himself into the water and walks the street down there to the prince's castle. His sister is there and tells him that her husband returns from war every afternoon. She hides her brother, but it turns out that the prince does not mind that that the young man has come. The prince does warn him, though, never to touch the gold which flows from the spring. Exploring the castle grounds the next day, the brother touches the golden spring. When he sees that his finger has turned to gold, he figures he might as well get into trouble for more than that and dips his whole body and a sword in. The golden brother then gallops off to help the prince on the battlefield, where he fights with bravado, unrecognized. Finally, he reveals himself to the prince and says it the gold which gave him such power. The sea disenchants, and the castle disappears, leaving a great city, where they all live happily.

Connections

Brothers and sisters. Conflict. Gold. Journeys to other realms. Magic. Magic springs. Princes and princesses. Transformations. Water worlds.

---

44. The Fisherman and the King

Ignacio Bizarro Ujpan in James D. Sexton, *Heart of Heaven, Heart of Earth*
Maya People

A clever but lonely muchacho, called Ton Tun, uses the magic ring his father has left him to hunt and to fish underwater without air. The people of Sansiriwux complain to the king that Ton Tun isn't leaving any game for them. This is not true, but it angers the king, who orders the muchacho to bring him a dead jaguar, though the forest doesn't have any. The ring plays a drum and a *chirimía* to summon the jaguar from an enchanted place. When the boy drags in the dead jaguar, the king demands that he bring it back to life. Ton Tun blows on the eye where the arrow went in, and the jaguar revives. Now the king is frightened, so the muchacho gently leads the jaguar back to the forest and thanks him. However, townspeople get soldiers to capture Ton Tun once more. The boy again tells the king that he has done nothing wrong, but the king commands that he find two engraved axes and an engraved gold ring dropped into the sea. The ring's music brings a dueno of the sea, who calls upon sea creatures who find everything. After Ton Tun passes one more test, the king beheads the townspeople who told lies about him.

CONNECTIONS

Deceit. Emperors, kings, & queens. Gods and goddesses. Jaguars. Journeys to other realms. Justice. Magic. Magic rings. Resentment. Restoring life. Spirits. Supernatural beings. Tests. Water worlds.

45. THE ORIGIN OF TUBERS

Johannes Wilbert, *Yupa Folktales*
Yupa People. Sierra de Perijá, Venezuela

A Yupa man, inadvertently left behind during a communal boar hunt, trips into a net of the tiger people and becomes trapped. At dawn, Tiger-Son compassionately lets the shivering Yupa escape before his father can eat him. As the Yupa runs toward the sun, he finds the son of the Moon, calling up to tell his uncle, the Sun, that his father sent him to pick up a bird. The Sun lies that he has no bird to share and grabs the Yupa. The son of the Moon runs home to get his father to save him. The Moon arrives and drinks the rest of the tobacco juice which the Sun has been using to drug the Yupa. The Moon takes the man with him. For two months, the Moon hides the Yupa in a cave where young girls go when they first menstruate, a place forbidden for the Sun to enter. The man only goes out at night when the Sun sleeps. The Moon is so impressed with everything the Yupa tells him about human life that he offers one of his daughters in marriage. Though everything is fine there, the Yupa wants to return to his village after a while. The Moon understands and gives the man some yucca roots and batata for planting on earth. With the Moon's warning not to drink hot chichi, for he has been in their cold land for a long time, the Yupa makes the long journey home. He shows villagers how to plant and harvest the tubers. However, he is always cold, and one day, the Yupa drinks a calabash of warm chichi and dies.

CONNECTIONS

Captivity. Curiosity. Deceit. Drink. Gifts. Gods and humans. Journeys to other realms. Kindness. Lost. Moon. Origin tales. Parents and children. Rescues. Sky worlds. Sun. Tigers. Tubers. Warnings.

46. THE ENCHANTED PALACE

Genevieve Barlow, *Latin American Tales from the Pampas to Mexico City*
Tehuelche People. Patagonia, Argentina

An old Tehuelche shepherd walks alone to the Andes Mountains, which he has always longed to see. Taycho does not believe his wife's warning that invisible ones there bewitch visitors until singing awakens him in a cave. The voices reassure him that they are friendly. They invite him to their palace, which mysteriously appears out of a mist. The door shuts behind him, but voices continue to reassure him that they will let him go soon. They want to know everything about his home. They are kind, but after a few days, he misses his wife. Reluctantly, they agree to let him return to her, but warn him not to tell anyone about them. They gift him with a golden vase filled with jewels. He thanks them, and the palace vanishes as soon as he steps outside the door. His wife rejoices when he returns, for he has been gone for a year. She promises to keep the true story of his journey secret and does, but two visitors see the jewels. The chieftain demands to know and goes to see the palace for himself. Voices in the cave refuse to let him enter, saying they admit a human only once every thousand years. The jewels and the vase itself all disappear from Taycho's house.

Connections

Ancestors. Andes Mountains. Caciques and chieftains. Curiosity. Enchanted cities. Gods and humans. Husbands and wives. Journeys to other realms. Magic. Mysteries. Palaces. Promises. Punishments. Secrets. Shepherds. Spirits. Storytelling. Supernatural beings. Supernatural voices.

How Else This Story Is Told

Variation from the Chibcha People of Colombia and Panama:

The Lost City of Gold—Alex Whitney, *Voices in the Wind.* A Chibcha boy enters a cave he's never seen before, with a tunnel that leads through the mountain to a great golden city with a columned palace below. He is sure this is his ancestors' ancient home, which had disappeared for centuries, but when he tries to reenter, mist hides the cave entrance from being found.

---

47. Seeking Wisdom

Adriana and Tosca Balter in Nadia Grosser Nagarajan, *Pomegranate Seeds*
Jewish People. Chile

When a brother and sister ask more questions than their uneducated parents can answer about right and wrong and what lies beyond the volcano they can see, a wandering Mapuche suggests they ask the wise man who lives on the mountain peak far away. With their favorite llama, their parents' permission, and blankets and food, the children set off to find him. It seems like a good sign when they find a rare pink flower in bloom before they begin the icy cold climb up rocky hills to the lip of a volcano crater. The small old man, Emmanuel, who lives in a hut above hot lava, invites them in. When they are warm and fed, he says he will answer one question. The sister Araceli asks about truth. He gives them a practical answer and food for the trip home. When Araceli turns to wave goodbye, however, the hut and the man have vanished.

Connections

Brothers and sisters. Curiosity. Journeys to other realms. Knowledge. Mysteries. Questions. Quests. Truth. Volcanoes. Wise men and wise women.

48. THE STRANGE ADVENTURES OF ALCAVILU
Genevieve Barlow, *Latin American Tales from the Pampas to Mexico City*
Araucanian People. Chile

With his father's blessing, the chieftan's son, Alcavilu, rides off to see what lies beyond the mountains. He helps a shivering old man. Grateful, the old man predicts that Alcavilu will not return home alone. He gives Alcavilu a magic leaf to chew so he can understand the language of birds and animals. The next morning a lion gives Alcavilu a hair with which he can transform into any animal or bird and travel wherever he wishes. Alcavilu soars to the edge of a volcano where he sees a frightened girl. He flies off as a bird before the god of the volcano can throw him in. Alcavilu rests beside a cottage. When he wakes, he is placed gently in a cage. The kind daughter, Kallfuray, slips seeds in for him to eat, but Alcavilu is really hungry and crawls out as an ant. The family discovers that he is human and tells him that the captive girl at the volcano is their daughter. Alcavilu rescues her. When the grateful father asks what he can give him, Alcavilu requests to marry Kallfuray, who loved him as a bird, too. The old man returns Alcavilu's horse with saddlebags full of gold and gems, and Alcavilu's father heartily welcomes his son and his new bride home.

CONNECTIONS
Captivity. Curiosity. Heroes and heroines. Journeys to other realms. Kindness. Knowledge. Love. Magic. Magic leaves. Magic hairs. Prophecies. Rescues. Rewards. Sorcerers. Transformations. Wise men and wise women.

---

49. THE MAGIC GROCERY STORE
Anita Brenner, *The Boy Who Could Do Anything*
Mexico

With nothing to eat on New Year's Eve, Manuel leaves his wife's scolding and goes out to his cornfield, where even the dry leaves call him poor. A young man steps out of a whirlwind right in front of him and invites him into the colorful swirl. Manuel guesses the young man is Tepozton. They travel to the foot of a mountain with an open door, a magic grocery store. Tepozton gives Manuel a little money to buy whatever he wants, but warns that he must leave at midnight when the door will close for a whole year. Manuel joins his sleeping wife when he returns home with food. The next morning, they discover the grocery bag is full of gold.

CONNECTIONS
Gods and humans. Hunger. Husbands and wives. Journeys to other realms. Magic. Magic stores. Mysteries. New Year. Poverty. Tepozton.

50. THE GREEN SERGEANT

Elsie Spicer Eells, *The Brazilian Fairy Book*
Brazil

Jealous of his daughter's popularity in the palace and angered by her dreams of surpassing him, a King orders his soldiers to kill her and bring him her little finger as proof. The soldiers bring the King her finger, but leave the princess alive in the forest. She wanders into a hole in the ground and through a cave to a hall where she finds a man's green suit and a horse who says he will serve her. When her clothes wear out, she puts on the man's clothes, cuts her hair, and exits into a different kingdom, where she becomes a King's guard. The Princess Lucinda there falls in love with her and becomes angry when the Green Sergeant does not return her love. Princess Lucinda makes up stories of what the Green Sergeant boasts he can do, and the King sets up impossible tests, which the horse helps the Green Sergeant accomplish. Meanwhile, the Green Sergeant princess continues to dream that her father is kissing her hand. After the Green Sergeant presents the King with a jewel she has seized from a sea-serpent, the magic horse becomes a handsome prince, his enchantment broken. Their stories are told. The King wants to marry the Green Sergeant, and Princess Lucinda now loves the horse prince. When the Princess's father comes to the wedding, he is truly glad to find his daughter alive.

CONNECTIONS

Animal helpers. Changes in attitude. Deceit. Disguises. Dreams. Emperors, kings & queens. Gender. Jealousy. Journeys to other realms. Love. Magic horses. Parents and children. Princes and princesses. Sea serpents. Status. Storytelling. Supernatural beings. Tests. Transformations. Underground worlds.

---

51. *CUNA SONG / CANCION DE LOS CUNAS*

Harriet Rohmer
Cuna People. Panama

When Inatopiler's little sailboat is overturned by the wind, he enters a new world underwater. Uncle Shark brings the boy to his house where a girl Olowilsasop, with ringing coral and glass beads, offers Inatopiler a maize drink and a hammock to sleep in. The next day, the whole family sails off to the great chicho feast at the castle of Uncle Nia. Fish swim in and out of Olowilsasop's hair as they bathe in the river. Everyone is friendly, but Inatopiler misses his mother throughout the festive drinking and dancing. He can even see her in the world above. When Uncle Shark tells Inatopiler to be happy for there is no returning to that world, Inatopiler hits him. A fight with all the water people ensues. Inatopiler stops fighting, but he cannot stop thinking about how to reach his mother's house. That night Olowilsasop finds Inatopiler's hammock empty and goes looking for him. She climbs the golden ladder to Morning Star's house. Morning Star sends her on the back of the great eagle to find Inatopiler at the mountain lake. She wakes Inatopiler, who smiles at Olowilsasop's bravery and tells her that he now accepts that his human life is over.

Note: Written in verse and sung over three nights, this journey is told as part of a longer story where village men go looking for Inatopiler. When he is not found, the neles, or wise ones of the village, visit the underwater in their dreams to see what has befallen him.

CONNECTIONS

Changes in attitude. Courage. Death. Discontent. Friendship. Interspecies conflict. Journeys to other realms. Morning Star. Mourning. Sky worlds. Water worlds.

---

52. THE FLIGHT OF QUETZALCOATL
Jerome Rothenberg, *Shaking the Pumpkin*
Aztec People

When the god Quetzalcoatl sees himself in the bark of a tree and discovers that he has become old, he sets off on a journey to the sea. Voices come to him from the past, and he weeps, leaving indentations in a rock where he sits at Temacpalco. He digs up a stone to make a bridge which leads to a lake of serpents, who tell him to turn around. When Quetzalcoatl counters that it is too late for that, they tell him to leave all of the precious Toltec crafts he inspired humans to create behind there, in what later becomes known as The Lake of Jewels. In the City of Sleepers, a shaman hands him pulque to drink, and Quetzalcoatl falls to the road and dreams. The town is empty when he wakes, and his hair is shaved off. He continues on, singing and weeping, with snow falling, and the weight of remembering companions who froze. Serpents on the beach form into a boat and sail him into Red Daylight, where he becomes handsome once again. He throws himself into a fire on the beach, and his ashes rise as birds circle. There are seven days of darkness when he journeys to Death's Kingdom, and then his body transforms to light, burning forever as the morning star in the sky. This telling is in free verse.

CONNECTIONS

Death. Despair. Drink. Gods and goddesses. Journeys to other realms. Morning Star. Old age. Origin tales. Quetzalcoatl. Sea serpents. Shamans. Sky worlds. Stars. Supernatural beings. Transformations.

WHERE ELSE THIS STORY APPEARS

The Flight of Quetzalcoatl—Jerome Rothenberg. At *Spoken Web: Concordia University*—*Jerome Rothenberg* 1969 (Online audio).

HOW ELSE THIS STORY IS TOLD

The Flight of Quetzalcoatl—John Bierhorst, *The Red Swan: Myths and Tales of the American Indians*
The Story of Quetzalcoatl—Douglas Gifford, *Warriors, Gods & Spirits from Central & South American Mythology*. This telling of Queztalcoatl's journey to the spirit world includes the beginnings of his life and his daughter's marriage to the green chili seller, who hypnotizes the Toltecs, which is when Quetzalcoatl knows it is time to leave.

III

Winning and Losing with the Gods

---

53. LEGENDS OF THE CARIBS. THE FIRST PEOPLE
W.H. Brett, *Guyana Legends*
Carib People. Guyana

Curious Carib people in the land of the moon descend to earth and become faint with hunger when the clouds which brought them down disappear. They call on Tamosi Kabo-tano, the Ancient One, but receive no answer. Only Maipuri the tapir has found the great food tree Tamosi Kabo-tano created on earth. Each branch of this tree holds different fruit. Plantains, maize, cassava, yams, and potatoes grow underneath at its base. The Caribs can see that Maipuri has become fat, but the tapir will not tell them where the food comes from. They send the woodpecker to spy on him, but the woodpecker taps each tree along the way and loses the tapir. Rat succeeds in tracking the tapir, but then sneaks food only for himself. Telltale scraps on rat's face give him away, though, and the people make him take them to the food source. They arrive at the enormous tree, and a voice from above tells them to cut it down. It takes many months of chopping before the great tree crashes to the ground. Each person takes cuttings from the branches, trunk, and roots to grow so they can have food close to where they live.

CONNECTIONS
Agoutis. Bridges. Clouds. Curiosity. Despair. Earth. Farming. Floods. Food. Generosity. Gods and humans. Hunger. Journeys to other realms. Magic trees. Makunaima. Moon. Origin tales. Rats. Selfishness. Tamusi. Tapirs. Trees.

HOW ELSE THIS STORY IS TOLD
The First People—*Legends of Guyana's Amerindians: Legends of the Caribs* (Online).
The First People—William Henry Brett, *Legends and Myths of the Aboriginal Indians of British Guiana*. In rhyming verse.
The Moon People—Melinda Lily. Two sisters convince other villagers to come with them to visit the Earth they can see from the moon.
Tamosi and the Tree of Life—Richard and Judy Dockery Young, *1492: New World Tales*. Kalinago Carib People. It's the agouti who grows sleek and fat here, eating secretly from the tree.
The Tree of Life—Douglas Gifford, *Warriors, Gods & Spirits from Central & South American Mythology*. Acawai People. Orinoco River Delta. The great spirit Makunaima creates the

39

world and this tree which the agouti finds. Once the tree is cut, Makunaima's son Sigu brings fish from the hollow trunk to streams, lakes, and rivers, but water bubbling up from an underground spring threatens to flood the land. He covers the stump with a tightly woven basket which troublesome Iwarrika the monkey pushes up. It takes a while for things to settle down.

54. THE ANCESTORS ARE ALL AROUND US

Natalia M. Belting, *Moon Was Tired of Walking on Air*
Ona People

The earth is empty when Kenos arrives from the sky with his three friends. He shapes the land, arranges the Ancestors into tribes, and gives them language. The gods are exhausted and old now, but have a hard time resting. Kenos suggests that another place may give them stronger sleep. In a village far away, Kenos instructs the people there to wrap them in mantles of guanaco fur and lay them on the ground, as if for burial. The villagers mourn these four as friends. The gods do not stir or breathe for many nights, but then they wake and wash and become invigorated and young again. After this, older Ancestors also wrap and sleep as if dead and wake to become young, watched by their families. When they tire of the cycle, Kenos transforms the elders into animals and birds. Some Ancestors return with Kenos to the sky and become clouds and stars. People are connected to them everywhere.

CONNECTIONS

Ancestors. Community. Earth. Gods and humans. Journeys to other realms. Kenos. Life span. Old age. Origin tales. Sky. Sleep. Transformations.

55. HEART OF HEAVEN, HEART OF EARTH: A TZUTUHIL TALE

Valerio Teodoro Tzapalíc in James D. Sexton, *Heart of Heaven, Heart of Earth*
Tzutuhil Maya People. Guatemala

When the Spanish start killing indigenous people, tribal leaders meet on the lakeshore at Chuitinamit to decide what to do. The old men themselves know how to make offerings in the hills and volcanoes and how to call upon the Heart of Heaven and the Heart of Earth to prevent wars. They can become invisibly part of nature, but they do not want to see the rest of their people destroyed. A shaman and Tzutuhil prince proposes that those who can become invisible do, but that no one else fight. By remembering those who have disappeared, people on earth will never be alone. It becomes traditional for people to offer a kiss with their hand when they leave, requesting that the fathers, mothers, grandmothers, and grandfathers go with them through whatever day will bring. Bad things befall people who do not make a connection to the Heart of Heaven and their invisible forefathers.

CONNECTIONS

Allegories and parables. Ancestors. Cautionary tales. Cultural conflict. Generations. Honoring parents. Invisibility. Prayer. Princes and princesses. Punishments. Remembrance. Shamans. Spanish Colonial People. Supernatural beings. Traditions. Worship.

---

56. OUCH!

Judy Goldman, *Whiskers, Tails & Wings*
Trique People. Mexico

Man and Woman are very comfortable on the new earth the God of Creation has given them, perhaps too comfortable. Fruit just falls into their hands; they lie around with no work to do. The God of Creation does not want to destroy Man and Woman and begin again, so he comes up with a plan. He forms little balls of dirt and water, adds vines and other pieces, and names them as they dry. Then he shapes a very tiny ball from the leftover mix, so small it has no name. He breathes the balls to life. As they flutter, scuttle, and buzz, the God of Creation tells them what their various jobs are. Mosco (mosquito), Piojo (louse), Araña (spider) Abeja (bee), Mariposa butterfly), Avispa (wasp), Hormiga (ant) are all sent to annoy Man and Woman so they will move, but Man and Woman swat them away and go back to sleep. Only when the tiniest creature Pulga (flea) jumps on them do Man and Woman get up and stay up to build their home and plant crops and raise a family.

CONNECTIONS

Cautionary tales. Fleas. Gods and humans. Humorous tales. Insects. Laziness. Lice. Mosquitoes. Origin tales. Punishments. Wasps. Work.

---

57. THE FIGHT OVER LIFE

Roger D. Abrahams, *African American Folktales*
African American People. Guadalupe

Cat and Dog are arguing about whether or not Man can come back to life after he dies. Cat says no, and Dog argues that he can. Cat suggests they consult with God. Dog wants to get to God first. He puts butter here and there along the road to distract Cat. Cat does the same thing with bones for Dog. Cat ignores the butter, knowing it is a trick, but Dog cannot resist stopping to gnaw on bones. Cat reaches God first and humbly asks their question. God listens to what Cat thinks, that people just stay dead when they die, and responds that it sounds right. When Dog arrives and poses the same question, God scolds him for getting distracted and coming late. "It shall be as Cat has said it then: 'People when they die will not come back to life again.'"

CONNECTIONS

Arguments. Cats. Death. Dogs. God. Gods and animals. Humorous tales. Questions. Restoring life. Tricksters.

58. DOG ASKS FOR A NEW NAME

Harold Courlander, *A Treasury of Afro-American Folklore*
African American People. Suriname

Tired of being called "thieving Dog" all the time, Dog asks the Master to change his name. So God kills a fat cow and starts the barbecue. Then God sets Dog to guard the cooking meat so none will go missing. This watching and waiting is too much for Dog, who finally gives in and eats a piece of the meat. The next day God tells Dog he did a good job, but his new name will be "Just-the-same-as-ever."

CONNECTIONS

Discontent. Dogs. God. Gods and animals. Humorous tales. Names. Reputation. Responsibility. Temptation. Tests. Theft.

59. MONTEZUMA'S WOUND

John Bierhorst, *Latin American Folktales*
Mexico

An eagle swoops down and lifts a poor farmer right out of his garden near Coatepec one day. The eagle flies him to a cave on a mountain peak, calling out to an unseen "lord of all power" when they arrive. King Montezuma lies unconscious in the cave. A mysterious voice tells the farmer to hold a hot smoking tube against the king's thigh, and he will see that the king notices nothing outside of himself. He does, and the king does not respond. The voice then commands the farmer to tell Montezuma back on earth the story of what has happened up in the cave. The burn on the king's thigh will prove that what the farmer says is true. The farmer is also to tell Montezuma that the Lord of Creation finds him too proud to continue to rule much longer. When the farmer reaches the palace and tells Montezuma the story, the king remembers the dream where a poor man burned him. Now the burn is hurting him, and Montezuma has the farmer imprisoned.

CONNECTIONS

Allegories and parables. Arrogance. Aztec people. Class conflict. Dreams. Eagles. Emperors, kings & queens. Farmers. Gods and humans. Illness. Journeys to other realms. Leadership. Messengers. Montezuma. Perspective. Prophecies. Pride. Punishments. Supernatural voices. Tests. Warnings. Wounds.

WHERE ELSE THIS STORY APPEARS

In John Bierhorst, *The Hungry Woman*

60. THE TALKING STONE

John Bierhorst, *Latin American Folktales*
Aztec People. Mexico

Montezuma is determined to be the emperor to have made the grandest altar for prisoner sacrifices ever built to Huitzilopochtili. At last, stonecutters locate the perfect round boulder at Acolco. It is so large men from six cities need to wrestle it from the hillside to a place for carving. Once the stone has been carved and anointed as Montezuma commands, the stone itself announces that it will not move for the great procession to the capital. Montezuma does not believe the runners who tell him that the stone has spoken. Men manage to slide it to Tlapitzahuayan, where the stone talks again, proclaiming that Montezuma has become too arrogant to think himself grander than the creator and that his reign will end. This message frightens Montezuma, but he orders the men to carry on. In stops and starts, the stone is finally slid onto the causeway to Mexico. There it breaks through and sinks into the water. Montezuma sends divers down who tell the emperor that they found only a path through the water. The stone is found back on its hillside in Acolco.

CONNECTIONS

Allegories and parables. Arrogance. Emperors, kings & queens. Gods and humans. Huitzilopochtili. Language. Magic stones. Montezuma. Pride. Stone. Stonecutters. Supernatural beings. Supernatural voices. Tasks.

WHERE ELSE THIS STORY APPEARS

In John Bierhorst, *The Hungry Woman*

HOW ELSE THIS STORY IS TOLD

The Magic Stone—Amelia Martinez del Rio, *The Sun, the Moon and a Rabbit*

---

61. THE GODDESS OF THE EARTHQUAKES
Margaret Campbell, *South American Folklore Tales*
El Salvador

The water level in Lake Ilopango rises before an earthquake. To prevent the Goddess of the Blue Cape from punishing all of Cuscatlán, the priests have been commanding that beautiful maidens be thrown into the lake to carry a message to the goddess. The princess Solisál and her friends Atlóx woi and Atonál question that the goddess can be so bloodthirsty. Solisál is determined to end the practice when she becomes queen. However, young Solisál has now been selected for sacrifice this time. As the priests swing her to throw her in, her friends grab her and run to the forest. People in the kingdom blame all three for the terrible earthquake which follows. Soldiers search the forest to no avail. Now the Chief Priest himself walks around the lake. When he senses motion in the top of a tree he calls out that beautiful Solisál become water, strong Atlóx woi a tree, and gentle Atonál a breeze. Ever since then, the lake is calm.

CONNECTIONS

Conflict. Earthquakes. Friendship. Gods and humans. Heroes and heroines. Lakes. Priests and priestesses. Princes and princesses. Punishments. Resistance. Sacrifice. Transformations.

62. THE RABBIT'S EARS / LAS OREJAS DEL CONEJO

Genevieve Barlow and William N. Stivers, *Stories from Mexico /
    Historias de México*
Maya People. Mexico

Rabbit does not mind having small ears, but he would definitely like his body to
be greater. At owl's suggestion, rabbit hops up the hill to the god of animals to ask if
the god can make him big enough to possibly become king of the animals one day. The
god tells rabbit he must return with the skins of a crocodile, monkey, and snake first.
Rabbit asks the animals to lend him their skins for a party, which they graciously do.
Seeing how clever this rabbit is, the god worries now that rabbit may hurt other animals,
even inadvertently, if he is any bigger. The god makes only rabbit's ears tall, so he will
hear enemies approach. It happens so quickly, Rabbit does not have time to be upset.
He thanks the god, returns the skins to his friends, and happily accepts owl's compliments on his new ears.

CONNECTIONS

Alligators. Appearance. Cleverness. Coexistence. Crocodiles. Discontent. Ears. Friendship.
    Gods and animals. Origin tales. Rabbits. Size. Snakes. Status. Tasks. Tests. Tigers. Trick-
    sters.

HOW ELSE THIS STORY IS TOLD

Nicaraguan variation:
Ha! Tío Rabbit Is Bigger—M.A. Jagendorf and R.S. Boggs, *The King of the Mountains.* Papa Dios
    gives rabbit the task of bringing back monkey tiger, and alligator skins in order to change
    his size.

Warao variation:
Rabbit Gets a Jaguar's Paw and an Alligator's Tooth—Johannes Wilbert, *Folk Literature of the
    Warao Indians.* Warao People. Venezuela and Guyana. God still will not make rabbit's body
    bigger, only his ears, even when rabbit tricks alligator into telling his weakest spot and pre-
    tends to be tying vines around himself to protect from a hurricane in order to bring God a
    paw from jaguar.
See also The Affair of the Horns (106), The King of the Animals (132) and Why Rabbits Have
    Long Ears (263) for other explanations of rabbits' ears.

---

63. HOW THE PORCUPINE OUTWITTED THE FOX

Genevieve Barlow, *Latin American Tales from the Pampas to Mexico City*
Maya People. Honduras

The god Noh Ku created porcupines with fur to live in the evergreen forest. One
evening, no longer hungry, Mrs. Porcupine tells her husband that they should go home.
Mr. Porcupine wants to go eat some clover and dismisses her worry about his safety
with foxes in the tall grass. He suggests she return alone. Mr. Porcupine is eating clover

deeper and deeper into the meadow when he hears a fox. With no possible escape and terrified, he calls to Noh Ku for help. A chill ripples through his body. The fox springs at him, but then yelps and flees. Mr. Porcupine does not know why he has been spared until he returns home, and Mrs. Porcupine shows him that his back is now armed with sharp-tipped quills. Mrs. Porcupine's relief at her husband's safety turns to dismay that her husband no longer looks like part of the family. Mr. Porcupine is regretting his greed which is now making her unhappy, when Noh Ku gifts Mrs. Porcupine with a coat of armor, too.

CONNECTIONS
Appearance. Escapes. Foxes. Gods and animals. Husbands and wives. Interspecies conflict. Origin tales. Porcupines. Transformations.

---

64. CHARITY
Manuel de Jesús Aráoz in John Bierhorst, *Latin American Folktales*
Argentina

It is the practice of a king who cares about helping people in his town to personally distribute food to the needy each week. One day a man shows up the king has never seen before. They talk. The king wants to give more to this man, who struggles to provide for his own family and his parents, without offending others. The king hides a gold coin inside one of the two meat pies he hands the man, without telling him. When the man shows up again the next week, the king thinks he may have squandered the doubloon. It turns out the poor man unknowingly gave the meat pie with the gold to another poor man on his way home. The king then wants to give him a treasure from his storeroom. The Lord's voice interrupts, then, saying that the king must help this man the same as he helps others; it is only up to God to give him more.

CONNECTIONS
Allegories and parables. Charity. Emperors, kings & queens. Generosity. God. Gods and humans. Hunger.

---

65. A FARMER LEARNS A LESSON
Anthony John Campos, *Mexican Folk Tales*
Mexico

As three brothers work together on their father's farm, the two younger men grow closer, but the older son feels left out. When their father does not leave all the land to him, the older brother becomes even more bitter. As they work the dry land, the younger two brothers accept God's will; the older brother becomes angry with God. One day, a bearded man on a burro stops and asks for water. He asks the younger brother who brings him a drink what he is planting. The brother says barley, and the man tells him that's what he will reap. He tells the second brother who is planting wheat, that he will reap wheat. He tells the oldest brother who replies that he is planting rocks that he will reap rocks, which is just what happens. The oldest brother becomes less resentful as he realizes "that what you sow in life, so shall you reap."

CONNECTIONS

Allegories and parables. Changes in attitude. Brothers and sisters. Cautionary tales. Farmers. Gods and humans. Perspective. Punishments. Resentment. Work.

66. THE FIRST PEOPLE

Mercedes Dorson and Jeanne Wilmot, *Tales from the Rain Forest*
Tupi People and Guarani People. Brazil

When the sorcerer Aroteh, who lives on the earth with his sorcerer twin Tovapod, notices that their harvest is disappearing, the brothers take turns guarding at night. One dawn, a lovely woman rises from behind a calabash. She gathers food, but swiftly vanishes into a small hole in the earth when she hears Tovapod. He goes over and sees many arms reaching up out of the ground. Tovapod is trying to enlarge the hole, when a boulder shifts and blocks the whole thing. With the Wind's help, the brothers tip up the boulder. Hundreds of hungry humans try to rush through the narrow opening from the darkness below. They have webbed fingers, heads with horns, and sharp teeth and chins. Some have tails, and they are jostling to get out. The beautiful woman returns below, not understanding when Tovapod tries to tell her that they cannot hold the heavy boulder any more. Aroteh brings mats and benches to make the people comfortable. Tovapod reshapes their sharp teeth, fingers, toes, horns, and tails so they will not hurt each other and be able to move more easily. Aroteh pushes the sun to keep it from setting before their work is done. Tovapod teaches the people to sing and talk. Some stay, some roam. From these people the different tribes and different languages are born.

CONNECTIONS

Earth. Gods and humans. Humans. Hunger. Journeys to other realms. Rescues. Origin tales. Sorcerers. Theft. Tribes. Underground worlds.

67. *THE BOY WHO WOULDN'T OBEY: A MAYAN LEGEND*

Anne Rockwell
Maya People. Mexico

Monkey is telling stories about the great lord, Chac, who makes the good rain, but can also cause trouble with thunder, lightning, and wild winds, when Chac himself grabs the boy Monkey's talking to and takes him to be his servant in the clouds. This boy tends to do whatever he wishes; he doesn't follow instructions. He digs a hole in the sky with the jade shovel Chac told him not to use. The boy's family is calling for him, so the boy ties a rope to a tree to get down to earth, but it is not long enough. Chac sees him dangling and lets loose the winds until the boy begs for them to stop. Eventually the boy gets better at listening. However, the boy unknowingly chases off some frogs that arrive dripping water when he has been told to prepare for guests. Chac is angry, for those frogs were the guests he wanted to honor for singing to him. Now, the boy is angry, and steals Chac's tools and causes a storm not in his control. He falls into the sea. Chac blows the boy back home, tired of having him as a servant.

CONNECTIONS

Angels. Captivity. Chac. Changes in attitude. Disobedience. Gods and humans. Impulsivity. Journeys to other realms. Punishments. Rain. Servants. Sky worlds. Tasks.

HOW ELSE THIS STORY IS TOLD

The Boy Who Wouldn't Listen to His Parents—Yolanda Nava, *It's All in the Frijoles*. The disobedient boy who runs away becomes caught up in a scary storm, and the god who controls the skies, rescues him and makes him promise to behave.

Chac—John Bierhorst, *The Monkey's Haircut and Other Stories Told by the Maya.* Yucatec Maya. Guatemala

The Disobedient Child—Victor Montejo, *The Bird Who Cleans the World and Other Mayan Fables.* Jakaltek Maya. Guatemala. The disobedient boy runs away from home and finds old man in the woods and unleashes a great storm. The man is Qich Mam, first father of all people and founder of "*Xaqla,*" who makes him promise not to disobey his parents.

The Disobedient Child / El niño desobediente—Susan Conklin Thompson, Keith Steven Thompson, and Lidia López de López, *Mayan Folktales*.

No Help at All— Betty Baker. When the boy returns home, his parents are grateful for the wind he loosed, which inadvertently clears their field.

The Lord of the Clouds—John Bierhorst, *The Monkey's Haircut and Other Stories Told by the Maya*. Mam Maya People. Guatemala. A man carried off by the lord of the clouds sees angels up there, causing storms with their capes and swords. Later, he takes their capes, but the rain he causes will not stop. When they leave him to make supper, he adds too many beans. So, the angels send him back to earth.

Thunder's Apprentice—John Bierhorst, *The Mythology of Mexico and Central America*. Mam Maya People. Guatemala. A man is the disobedient helper here.

68. *THE RAINMAKER: A TZUTIJIL MAYA STORY FROM GUATEMALA*

Michael Richards
Tzutuhil Maya People. Guatemala

The youngest brother, Chep, is troubled that his eldest brother, Nawbey, acts lazy and buys expensive fruit, when the rest of them work hard in the garden after their father has died in a flood. He secretly follows his brother to a giant cavern where colorfully robed people in long capes kiss the hand of a powerful-looking man on a ledge. Discovered there, Chep is taken by guards deeper into the cave past stalagmites covered with robes, which seem to be alive and represent different kinds of rain. A black robe covers him and says it is Tempest. Chep cannot push it away, and so he puts it on and floats upward, feeling powerfully electric. The Lord of the Rain angrily orders him captured. Chep tells the Lord about Nawbey's behavior. The Lord of the Rain decides that Nawbey misused his power, and Chep will replace him and learn to drop right rains.

Connections

Arrogance. Brothers and sisters. Caves. Gods and humans. Journeys to other realms. Laziness. Power. Punishments. Rain. Responsibility. Reversals of fortune. Work.

---

69. The Origin of the Nopal Cactus / El origen del nopal

Genevieve Barlow, *Stories from Latin America / Historias de Latinoamérica*
Aztec People. Mexico

When after a long and difficult journey, the Aztec people come to a large island, they wage war against peaceful tribes around the lake in order to collect human hearts to offer in daily sacrifice to their god of war, Huitzilopochtli. The god's sister and her husband abhor the suffering Huitzilopochtli's cruel demands are causing. Their son Copil takes one thousand warriors to stop him in a surprise attack. Huitzilopochtli's spies, however, tell him Copil is there. The god sends priests who cut out Copil's heart and bury it in one of Lake Texcoco's islands. The next morning, a green cactus with red flowers grows from Copil's heart, the nopal, strong and beautiful. Now appeased, Huitzilopochtli proclaims that he will return to the sky to guide his people. Soon after, the Aztecs recognize the sign that Huitzilopochtli wants them to build on this island when they see an eagle with a serpent in its beak on a branch of the nopal cactus.

Connections

Conflict. Gods and goddesses. Gods and humans. Heroes and heroines. Huitzilopochtli. Magic plants. Murder. Nopál. Origin tales. Plants. Resistance. Sacrifice. Tenochtitlan. Transformations. Uncles and nephews.

How Else This Story Is Told

The Tale of the Nopál—Margaret Campbell, *South American Folklore Tales*

---

70. The Pot That Spoke in the Hard Times / La olla que habló en los malos tiempos

Pedro Cholotío Temó and Alberto Barreno, *The Dog Who Spoke / El perro que habló*
Tzutuhil Maya People. Santiago Atitlán, Guatemala

Though they are poor, a widow teaches her twelve children to live with respect, love, generosity, honesty, and without envy. Because no villagers help them, she prays to both the Heart of heaven and the *dueño* of the sacred world for food for her family. When God brings a drought which causes famine, the widow has a dream where the Heart of heaven and the *dueño* tell her to fill her clay pot with small stones and place it on the fire as if she were cooking food. She does this, and the pot fills with *tamalitos*. Her faith is rewarded, for when some people steal the pot, she is able to feed her family by placing mud on the griddle which turns into corn tortillas. The stolen pot turns hard as stone. Before it disappears, the pot scolds the villagers who kick it saying that it never hurt anyone like they mistreated the poor widow and her children.

CONNECTIONS

Allegories and parables. Charity. Faith. Gods and humans. Greed. Kindness. Magic. Magic pots. Parents and children. Punishments. Rewards. Spirits. Theft.

71. THE LAME MAN OF OLANCHO / EL COJO DE OLANCHO
Genevieve Barlow, *Stories from Latin America / Historias de Latinoamérica*
Honduras

Out of compassion, the poor farmer Isidro is the only one who visits Juan, a miserly, rich, lame man, who never thanks him for the company. Then, for the first time, when his wife is sick, Isidro asks to borrow money for medicine, promising to repay Juan with interest when his crops come in. The miser insists that he needs all his money and tells Isidro to ask the Lord. He says it is not his problem if the Lord does not respond. In despair, Isidro prays to the Lord again on his way home. When he reaches home, his wife is well, and together, they give thanks. The next day, Isidro returns to suggest that Juan pray to cure his lameness. The miser thinks he will offer the Lord a gold chain with his prayer and then begins to balk about actually giving it. Isidro assures him it is worth the price. When Isidro returns, Juan tells him he prayed and is no longer lame. And Isidro says he prayed for Juan, too. As soon as Juan bitterly complains that it did not cost Isidro anything to pray like it did him, Juan falls to the ground lame again, with the gold chain returned.

CONNECTIONS

Disabilities. Faith. God. Gods and humans. Healing. Illness. Kindness. Miracles. Misers. Prayer. Punishments. Unkindness.

72. THE OLD MAN AND THE BEANSTALK
Brenda Hughes, *Folk-tales from Chile*
Chile

A poor old man and his wife plant their very last beans, which grow plants astoundingly vigorous and tall. The stalks are so tall, the woman complains that they cannot even see beans to harvest. Her husband climbs the biggest plant to seek God's advice. God tells Saint Peter to give the old man a magic ring which will grant sensible wishes. Outside his home, the old man wishes for better clothes. He looks so different, his wife does not recognize him at first, but then they both wish for useful things to make their lives better. In gratitude, the man begins to attend church regularly. Worried that his wife may make a foolish wish, he takes the ring along and leaves it with a wise woman nearby. She substitutes that magic ring for another, with no magic at all. The woman feigns ignorance of any other ring, so the old man climbs up the beanstalk to Saint Peter again. He requests a tablecloth which produces food when unfolded. Once again, the wise woman tricks him by substituting another cloth. The old man returns to Saint Peter who warns this will be his last gift. The man chooses some magic sticks and tells the wise woman not to tell them to come out, but, of course, she does. The sharp points of the little sticks prick her over and over until she returns the old man's ring and tablecloth.

CONNECTIONS

Deceit. Gifts. God. Gratitude. Greed. Heaven. Journeys to other realms. Justice. Magic. Magic beans. Magic rings. Magic sticks. Magic tablecloths. Peter, Saint. Punishments. Reversals of fortune. Theft. Tricksters.

---

73. *THE THUNDER GOD'S SON: A PERUVIAN FOLKTALE*
Ariane Dewey
Peru

The thunder god, Parícaca, sends his son Acurí down to earth to learn about mankind when he turns thirteen. Overhearing two foxes, Acurí arrives at the house of a rich miser who has become very ill. He tells the rude, sick man that he can cure him by getting rid of the two-headed toad under his grindstone, if the man promises to share his wealth. The man is agreeing, when his wife shows up, unhappy at this beggar in her house. Acurí pulls out gold rings she has stolen and says two serpents are on their way to swallow her. She promises to stop stealing, and Parícaca flies down to help Acurí tie knots in the serpents. Their vain son Rupay proposes several competitions to humiliate Acurí, so his father will throw him out. With his father's magic, Acurí outdresses, outdrinks, and outdances Rupay. Animals help him build a great house overnight (which the rich man claims that he now owns since it is on his land). In a bola stone throwing challenge, Rupay's stone hits a thunderbolt which Parícaca put there. Rain and hail cause a giant wave which washes the rich man's house away. Parícaca transforms the fleeing family into deer. Before he returns to the sky, Acurí gives their llamas as a gift for the villagers to share.

CONNECTIONS

Animal helpers. Competition. Earth. Gods and goddesses. Gods and humans. Greed. Journeys to other realms. Magic. Misers. Parents and children. Punishments. Rudeness. Theft. Thunderbolts. Vanity.

---

74. ZIPACNA
Margaret Campbell, *South American Folklore Tales*
Quiché Maya People. Guatemala and Mexico

The buzzard Xic reports to the Lord of the Heavens, that The Great Parrot, Gukúp-Cakix, has bragged to his sons that he is the one responsible for making the world they see below. The Lord decides to teach Gukúp-Cakix some humility. He sends twin orphans to kill Gukúp-Cakix with poisoned darts. After his father dies, Zipacna sets off on a journey. When he sees four hundred human boys struggling to carry the trunk of a ceiba tree, he shows off and takes the whole trunk on his shoulder. Frightened by Zipacna's superhuman strength, the boys form a plan to kill him. They decide to dig a pit near the tree trunk, ask Zipacna for help, and then let the tree trunk fall and crush him. But Zipacna has overheard. He digs a cave in the side of the pit which protects him when the tree falls. The boys keep watching for the ants to carry out pieces of Zipacna so they will know he is dead. Finally, on the third day, the ants emerge with bits of hair and nails, but they do not know Zipacna gave these to them. The boys are celebrating Zipacna's demise when he sneaks out and makes their hut crash down upon them. Saddened by the loss of these children, the Lord of the Heavens breathes new life into the bodies of the boys as Las Agrupadas, The Pleiades stars in the sky.

Connections

Arrogance. Braggarts. Cautionary tales. Gods and goddesses. Gods and humans. Journeys to other realms. Murder. Origin tales. Pleiades. Power. Punishments. Revenge. Stars. Transformations. Vanity.

75. The Gift of the Moon Goddess / El regalo de ladiosa luna

Genevieve Barlow, *Stories from Latin America / Historias de Latinoamérica*
Guarani People. Argentina and Paraguay

The Moon Goddess loves to descend from the sky to pick flowers on earth during the day with her friend the Cloud Goddess, both dressed as Guarani maidens. One spring, though, she and Cloud Goddess stay late and are cornered by a tiger in the forest. As the tiger leaps, a Guarani hunter hits him with an arrow and tells them to run, but they are too paralyzed by fear to move. The Guarani shoots at the tiger when he leaps again, and this time, the goddesses transform and rise into the sky. Only by seeing the dead tiger and their flowers can the hunter tell that maidens really have been there. The goddesses come to his dreams that night to thank him. Moon Goddess tells him she will place a special tree with nourishing leaves at the spot where he saved them. The hunter visits this tree and brings some of its leaves back for the villagers to roast. The Yerba mate tea gives them energy and quells hunger, and they offer thanks to the Moon Goddess in return.

Connections

Dreams. Gods and goddesses. Gods and humans. Gratitude. Hunters. Journeys to other realms. Magic plants. Origin tales. Rescues. Rewards. Tea. Tigers. Transformations. Trees. Yerba maté.

How Else This Story Is Told

The Gift of the Moon Goddess—Genevieve Barlow, *Latin American Tales from the Pampas to Mexico City*

---

76. *VOLADORES*
Patricia Petersen
Totonac People. Mexico

Tigre longs for the day when he will be able to put on colorful wings and fly round on the tall pole, like the village voladores chosen to honor the Sun and ask for a good harvest. He is impatient when his Uncle Quiche shows him how to make and play a flute, instead. Then there is trouble for the voladores. A volcano, jealous of the Sun, erupts and singes their wings. The rain god sends down so much water, his Uncle Teo's wings get too heavy, and he falls and becomes ill. The sky stays dark for so long, people think the Sun god has forgotten them. Tigre says he will ask the wind to move the clouds away to bring back the Sun. The elders laugh, but Tigre has been studying how his brother, the eagle, flies. He climbs the pole and flies beside the eagle. When Tigre tires, the eagle carries him to the house of the wind god, who snaps that he cannot help for the Sun's powers are stronger than his. Then, the wind god relents. He wants to know what the boy will give him if he does help, and Tigre offers his Uncle Quiche's flute. Tigre plays the flute hauntingly for a long time. At last, the wind agrees to grant his wish.

Connections

Bargains. Bird helpers. Courage. Discontent. Eagles. Flutes. Gods and humans. Heroes and heroines. Journeys to other realms. Impatience. Jealousy. Music. Power. Prayer. Rain. Sky worlds. Status. Sun. Uncles and nephews. Voladores. Volcanoes. Wind.

---

77. Why Corn Is Golden
Carlos Navarrete in Vivien Blackmore, adapter, *Why Corn Is Golden: Stories About Plants*
Mexico

Though his wife worries that the god may punish him for impertinence, a man who wants to know every detail of the Sun's life turns himself into a sparrow and then an eagle to go to where the Sun rises. He sees how the Sun spills gold into the water and how the sea swallows it up. The man desires that gold, but he thinks he will need dwarves to help lift it. The dwarves invite him to their cave that leads to the center of the earth. They are actually rays of the sun that warm the roots of plants. The man offers the dwarves some of the gold if they will help carry it. Then, the man tricks them into carrying it all. Afterwards, he thinks the sack of gold he takes away is getting heavier, but really he is getting smaller, until he turns into a buzzard. Ashamed, he flies away. The dwarves give half of the gold to the man's wife. The other half they tuck carefully into some of the roots, which become corn.

CONNECTIONS

Corn. Curiosity. Deceit. Dwarves. Gods and humans. Greed. Journeys to other realms. Origin tales. Sun. Supernatural beings. Transformations. Underground worlds.

78. THE MOLE CATCHER

John Bierhorst, *The Monkey's Haircut*
Lacandon Maya People. Mexico

Nuxi gets lost while looking for moles and climbs a tree. When he throws a golden spoon seed down at a beautiful woman walking by, she stops and takes off her scalp. He is sure she must be the daughter of Death Maker and throws another seed. It hurts her bare skull. Then he follows her into the earth to the house of Sukunkyum, elder brother of Our Lord. There, Sukunkyum's wife hides him from the Death Maker under a kettle disguised with chili peppers. The chilis make Death Maker sneeze, and he is suspicious, but goes away. Sukunkyum arrives home carrying the sun, whom he feeds and places at the bottom of the sky. He gives Nuxi old clothes and instructs him to specially wash them so Nuxi will not smell human. When the daughter of Death Maker arrives, Sukunkyum says that she now belongs to Nuxi because she brought him here. Sukunkyum transforms Nuxi into a hummingbird and sends them to Death Maker's house. Death Maker's daughter hides Nuxi when her father shoots him. Nuxi transforms from hummingbird to man at night. She decides to tell her parents about Nuxi. They vomit, but Death Maker wants to see this son-in-law. Finding him dressed all in blue, Death Maker accepts Nuxi, though Nuxi goes to cut wood for Sukunkyum, who has better food. Since Death Maker's daughter is Nuxi's wife, she must eat tortillas over at Sukunkyum's house, too.

CONNECTIONS

Birds. Death (Character). Fathers-in-law and mothers-in-law. Gods and goddesses. Gods and humans. Hummingbirds. Interspecies conflict. Interspecies marriage. Journeys to other realms. Mole catchers. Parents and children. Sukunkyum. Sun. Supernatural beings. Supernatural husbands and wives. Transformations. Underground worlds.

79. THE DEATH OF ARI

Daniel Munduruku, *Amazonia*
Bororo People. Amazonia, Brazil

Pranksters Meri the Sun and Ari the Moon pee on the fire where Bororo fishermen have set their fish to roast. Toad hops over and saves one ember from the fire inside his mouth. Seeing toad there, though, the fishermen think he's the one who put out the fire. To save his own life, toad tells on Meri and Ari. The fishermen send big birds running with embers in their head feathers to set fire to the dry grassland where Meri and Ari are. Meri gets away by climbing a strong angelim tree, but Ari's weaker tecoma tree falls into the flames. Afterwards, Meri places Ari's charred bones on a hill. The bones disappear. The wolf denies saying that it has eaten the burnt moon, so Meri declares a race to determine the truth. Wearing Meri's own belt tied so tightly his stomach swells, the wolf dies. Meri constructs a skeleton of his brother on the ground with sticks and fragments of Ari's bone from inside the wolf. He covers it with cooked herbs and leaves. The next day, Meri brings the figure to life. Then he motivates his brother to move by telling him that scary animal spirits are coming.

CONNECTIONS

Accusations. Birds. Bones. Brothers and sisters. Competition. Death. Fire. Fishermen. Gods and animals. Humorous tales. Justice. Magic bones. Moon. Pranksters. Restoring life. Revenge. Sun. Frogs and toads. Truth. Wolves.

80. 'MANO COYOTE

Camilla Campbell, *Star Mountain and Other Legends of Mexico*
Mexico

There are problems at the watering hole. The tough goats which belong to El Diablo, the Devil, are herded by coyotes and won't let the sheep, which are owned by Señor Dios and herded by dogs, get any water. Señor Dios offers to put men on earth to herd both the goats and the sheep, but El Diablo won't sell. Instead, El Diablo proposes that both flocks race to the water hole. Whoever's animals get there first will own both flocks. Señor Dios covers the valley with fog so the sheep arrive first. The coyotes say they will not obey Señor Dios, even though he tries to tell them that humans could take care of them, like they will the dogs, sheep, and goats. So, the coyotes who used to belong to El Diablo now steal sheep and chickens and become the enemies of men. One night 'Mano Coyote eats too many chickens and becomes stuck trying to squeeze out of the henhouse hole. He plays dead, and the farmer throws him over the wall. When he sees that he is safe, 'Mano Coyote runs off laughing. He gets his comeuppance, though, when 'Mano Tejón, a raccoon, almost gets him drowned by egging him on to jump into the water to get the cheese.

CONNECTIONS

Competition. Interspecies conflict. Coyotes. Devil. Dogs. Farmers. Goats. God. Gods and animals. Herders. Raccoons. Sheep. Tricksters.

81. *THE MAGIC BEAN TREE: A LEGEND FROM ARGENTINA*

Nancy Van Laan
Quechua People. Argentina

Hot relentless sun and a terrible drought has made it seem as if the gods of the Great Sky World—Pachamama the Life Giver, Pamero the South Wind who brings rain, and Mother of Storms—are no longer listening to the prayers of the llama herders or their animals. Little Topec is sure the rain has become lost and courageously sets off to bring it back. North Wind blows him to the pampas, where Topec wakes in the first Carob Tree, whose roots still hold water from the first rainfall on earth. The Carob Tree tells Topec that the wings of the immortal Great Bird of the Underworld are keeping the voices of those on earth from reaching the gods. Topec cannot kill the bird; he will need to make it move. The Carob Tree tells Topec that the bird comes there to rest each night. Topec returns with herders from his village, who make tremendously loud noise with instruments and voices until the Great Bird flies off. At last there is a rain that brings back plant life. The Carob Tree gifts Topec with its beans, which feed llamas and people and grow more carob trees.

CONNECTIONS

Birds. Carob tree. Courage. Drought. Gods and humans. Herders. Heroes and heroines. Journeys to other realms. Magic trees. Noise. Pachamama. Perseverance. Prayer. Rain. Rescues. Trees. Supernatural beings.

HOW ELSE THIS STORY IS TOLD

The Great Bird in the Carob Tree—Frances Carpenter, *South American Wonder Tale*s

---

82. THE FIRST INCAS

Alex Whitney, *Voices in the Wind*
Inca People. Peru, Educador, Bolivia and Chile

Because Atlantis is a corrupt place, filled with deceit, it is going to be sunk. The god Te-hooti tells the Oracle priest of Atlantis to warn people to leave, but few do. Two brothers, Ayar Oco and Manco Capac, are about to cut pines to build a raft to sail to Peru, the Land of Power, when a heavy rain raises the sea and their town of Ah-den begins to burn. They struggle to avoid falling timbers in the tidal wave, as Atlantis drowns. They emerge from the water in a new place, where they can see a green valley and beyond, a snow-capped mountain. A tall, bearded man leads a pure white llama and tells them he is Viracocha, Lord of Peru. Manco says his own will gave him the strength to fight the storm and reach this place. Ayar says he let the sea of turmoil carry him. Viracocha welcomes them to serve as rulers of the Inca Empire. Ayar governs people along the shores of Lake Titicaca in the highlands, who become known as Ayar Inca, People of the Reeds. Viracocha sends Manco to rule the fertile mountain valley, where he establishes the city of Cuzco, with Manco Inca, People of the Sun.

CONNECTIONS

Adaptation. Atlantis. Brothers and sisters. Gods and humans. Journeys to other realms. Leadership. Origin tales. Perseverance. Perspective. Peru. Punishments. Rain. Viracocha. Water worlds.

HOW ELSE THIS STORY IS TOLD

The First Incas—Douglas Gifford, *Warriors, Gods & Spirits from Central & South American Mythology*

83. WHY THE OLD NEVER GROW YOUNG
Martin Elbl and J.T. Winik, *Tales from the Amazon*
Amazonia

Troubled that he cannot cure death or old age, a knowledgeable witch doctor seeks guidance from the gods. The spirit of his dead father tells Veji that he must travel to Onoengrodi, the creator of men, who lives far away where the sky meets the earth. The ghost gives him three warnings: not to eat any of Onoengrodi's food or he will turn into a deer; not to smoke any tobacco there or he will become a field; and not to look at Onoengrodi's daughter or he will never be able to leave. Veji reaches Onoengrodi's house, and Onoengrodi says he will answer the healer's wish, even though it is not a wise one. He gives the healer a comb of youth to make a person young and strong. Veji has followed all of his father's warnings and is starting for home when he hears a woman say he has left his tobacco behind. He turns slightly and sees Onoengrodi's daughter, but in that instant, he falls in love with her and forgets all else.

CONNECTIONS
Death. Ghosts. Gods and humans. Healing. Journeys to other realms. Life span. Love. Magic. Old
age. Questions. Quests. Shamans. Temptation. Warnings.

---

84. THE KING OF THE MOUNTAINS
M.A. Jagendorf and R.S. Boggs, *The King of the Mountains*
Bolivia

There is much contention among the birds in Bolivia over which should become king. One wise old bird suggests that they either let Pachacámac, the god of the earth, decide or let the leader be the one who can come closest to Pachacámac's golden palace in the sun. Pachacámac approves of a competition to find the bravest bird. Many birds start, but after a while, only three are still circling closer to the sun—the eagle, the hawk, and the condor. Ferocious heat forces first the hawk and then the eagle down. Though the sun's fire scorches his head and neck, the condor pushes through to Pachacámac's throne. The god rewards the condor's courage, saying that the condor will live in a glittering ice palace in mountains that rise nearest to the sun and that he himself will assume the condor's majestic form whenever he visits earth.

CONNECTIONS
Birds. Competition. Condors. Courage. Eagles. Gods and animals. Hawks. Journeys to other realms.
Leadership. Origin tales. Pacha Kamaq. Rewards. Sky worlds. Sun.

---

85. THE TATEMA
Diane Wolkstein, *Lazy Stories*
Mexico

"If God wishes to give, he will give, even if He has to push it through the window." This is what lazy Mario tells his wife, when he sleeps late and refuses to help his storekeeper friend carry rocks for his house. However, when a runaway horse appears, Mario springs into action to stop it. The rescued white-bearded rider is most grateful and tells Mario to look under a certain rock for a tatema, which he says is a gift given to one person by God. Mario finds six wooden chests there, which each contain silver coins. He puts some coins in his pocket and covers the chests with leaves. Mario's friend offers his mules to carry the chests, if Mario will give him three. Mario agrees, but the friend who has been giving Mario food for free now believes he should have all the chests. He sneaks there that night without Mario, but the chests only contain mud, which he has his servants dump in front of Mario's house. However, Mario's faith is validated the next morning. When his wife opens the window, silver coins shower inside.

CONNECTIONS

Deceit. Excuses. Faith. God. Gods and humans. Gratitude. Humorous tales. Laziness. Miracles. Money. Perspective. Rescues. Reversals of fortune. Rewards.

HOW ELSE THIS STORY IS TOLD

To Whom God Wishes to Give He Will Give—Wilson M. Hudson, *The Healer of Los Olmos and Other Mexican Lore*

IV

Making Bargains, Good and Bad

86. La Madrina Muerte / Godmother Death

Olga Loya, *Momentos Mágicos / Magic Moments*
Mexico

When Death asks to become his son's godmother, Joaquín is torn. He does not want to anger her, but he also worries that she may hurt his child. At last he decides Death does treat everyone equally and brings her to his house. One day Godmother Death shows her godson José a pulsing red flower in the forest. She tells him he can heal people with a few petals from this flower, but he must defer to her if he sees her when he is treating a patient and let her take that person away. José agrees, and he does become a famous healer. José always leaves a bedside when Godmother Death appears, until the time he is treating the king, whose daughter he loves. He ignores La Madrina Muerta at the foot of the bed. She looks angry, but does not protest. He ignores her again when the princess, who is now his wife, becomes ill. Then La Madrina Muerta brings José to a cave where she shows him how little is left of the candle which is his soul. When José protests, she tells him that he disobeyed her twice. José dies as the flame flickers out. La Madrina Muerta never takes another godson.

Connections

Bargains. Candles. Death (Character). Emperors, kings & queens. Godparents and godchildren. Healers. Husbands and wives. Life span. Magic flowers. Princes and princesses. Punishments. Supernatural beings.

How Else This Story Is Told

La Madrina Muerte—Riley Aiken. In J. Frank Dobie, *Puro Mexicano*.

87. The Empty Boat / El barco vacío

Genevieve Barlow, *Stories from Latin America /
    Historias de Latinoamérica*
Venezuela

Alejandro, the young head of a wealthy but selfish family in Argentina, realizes that they are on the verge of bankruptcy. When he wishes aloud for someone to help him out of debt, an elegant stranger in black enters the library. He tells Alejandro to stick a pin anywhere into the world map on the wall, and Alejandro's family will receive the estate when a man who lives in that place dies. Frightened, Alejandro protests that he cannot kill anyone. When the gentleman pushes that the person who dies will be a stranger, Alejandro places the pin in the island of Margarita in Venezuela. Instantly, a rich prince proposes to marry his older sister and clear the family's debts. That same night, the boat of the fisherman Luis, who has been depressed, returns to Margarita empty after a storm. Only his wife Rosa still believes Luis himself may show up. Feeling miserable with guilt, Alejandro comes to Margarita. He connects Rosa's loss to his pin and works as a humble fisherman to help her family. One night, to Rosa's joy, Luis does return. He says he was rescued by a boat going to Europe. He became ill and battled nightmares where the devil was trying to take him, but is very happy to be back here with Rosa and his friends. Alejandro is also greatly relieved. He remains there and marries a woman from the island a few years later.

CONNECTIONS

Bargains. Debts. Devil. Fishermen. Guilt. Murder. Repentance. Reversals of fortune. Righting a wrong.

---

88. *THE BLACKSMITH AND THE DEVILS*
María Cristina Brusca and Tona Wilson
Argentina

Though Juan Pobreza, the blacksmith, is poor, he never turns anyone away from his hut on the pampas. After he makes a new horseshoe for a limping mule, the old gaucho tells him he is San Pedro and grants Juan Pobreza three wishes. Juan Pobreza does not believe that this old man really guards the gates of heaven. He playfully wishes to fix people in three places—in his chair, in his tobacco pouch, and up in his fig tree—until he gives permission for them to move. Juan Pobreza is thinking maybe he should have sold his soul to the devil for gold, when an elegant gentleman appears and offers Juan Pobreza just that. Now Juan Pobreza has twenty years to enjoy life with a bag of gold. After twenty years, when the devil comes with a helper to collect his soul, Juan Pobreza invites them to try some of his figs, and they get stuck in the tree. When they leave, Lucifer himself comes with all the devils. Juan Pobreza baits them by saying he bets they cannot all fit into his tobacco pouch. They get stuck inside, and he pounds them with his hammer. He lets them out after a while. Now Juan Pobreza has done everything and dies. Neither heaven nor hell wants him, so he roams the pampas, haunting people who are down on food or money.

CONNECTIONS

Bargains. Blacksmiths. Devil. Heaven. Humorous tales. Peter, Saint. Tricksters.

How Else This Story Is Told

Argentinian and Chilean variation:

Misery, the Blacksmith / El herrero miseria—Paula Martin, *Pachamama Tales*

Chilean variation:

Pedro the Blacksmith—Yolando Pino-Saavedra, *Folktales of Chile.* Pedro makes a deal with the Devil to be the best blacksmith. He is so good that God sends Saint Peter there to repair the keys to heaven. In payment, Pedro asks for those three wishes which hold someone captive in place until he gives permission. In the end, after the Devil is tricked, he does not want Pedro in hell. So Pedro goes to Saint Peter and asks to peek into heaven, and then slips into a chair there and cannot be moved, for God had granted him that wish to stay wherever he sits.

---

89. The Priest Goes Down to Hell

Anthony John Campos, *Mexican Folk Tales*
Mexico

Certain that he and his wife will never have a child, a poor husband signs a contract with the devil, promising his son's soul in exchange for money. A son is born to them, however, who studies to be a priest. When the son is to be ordained, his father in great sadness tells his son about the bargain. The son walks into the desert to try to find the devil. One hermit sends him to another, who directs him to the mean bandit Abrilio, who has become the devil's compadre. The devil shows up and takes the son to hell. When Lucifer hears that the man is looking for a contract made with one devil long ago, he tortures various devils and finds lame *el diable cojo*. When he threatens to throw lame *el diable cojo* in Abrilio's bed, this devil produces the contract, which Lucifer presents to the son. Abrilio drops dead when he hears that even a devil didn't want to share his bed. However, a starving hermit is sent to Abrilio's bed after he boasts to an angel that the celebration for his soul will be even greater than the one for Abrilio's.

Connections

Bargains. Devil. Hell. Hermits. Journeys to other realms. Parents and children. Priests and priestesses. Punishments. Quests. Souls.

---

90. The Castle of Master Falco

Margaret Campbell, *South American Folklore Tales*
Colombia

The boat builder Master Falco has come from Spain to the New World to become rich. He transports goods along the Colombian coast, until a storm washes him up onto a deserted island. When a ship shows up there, Master Falco begins a trade in coconuts and turtle meat and decides to stay on the island. He is doing okay, but one day he wonders what would happen if the Devil showed up. Suddenly an elegant stranger appears with glowing eyes. They start talking about the sea, which the Devil doesn't particularly care for. Master Falco extolls the joys of sailing in a good wind, and the Devil finally asks what he would charge for a ride. Master Falco says the Devil will have to answer three questions or grant his wish, and the Devil agrees. Master Falco asks his first question out on the water. The Devil is growing seasick and doesn't know how to answer. Back at shore, Master Falco poses the last two questions, which the Devil cannot answer, including who his grandfather is. Master Falco has won. He asks the Devil for a castle, and it appears. The rest of Master Falco's story is unknown, but the castle that people see when they sail near Isla Ceicén disappears when they land.

CONNECTIONS

Bargains. Boat builders. Castles. Devil. Humorous tales. Islands. Journeys. Questions. Mysteries. Seasickness.

---

91. THE SPIRITS OF THE STONES: EVIL SPIRITS
Juan Carlos Galeano, *Folktales of the Amazon*
Amazonia, Bolivia

Although his Christian parents are not happy when a young peasant tells them he would rather learn sorcery than work the land, his father gives his blessing for his son to find a teacher in the town of Cobija. From this master the young man learns how to use stones that contain spirits with healing power. Finally, he is ready to work on his own. The spirits in the stones are demanding. They warn him to protect them from the sun in bags of black fabric or be killed. With these stones he is able to help people. Other stones appear, though, which offer him power over life and death if he obeys them. He accepts, and his reputation spreads along the Madre de Dios River. The young sorcerer's father worries that his son may be tangling with evil. In fact, the stones have begun threatening him to kill people or else. He stabs clay models in the heart, and people die. When the stones demand more victims, he refuses, and is run down by a motorcycle. Townspeople begin to suspect evil sorcery. The son confesses to his father, who contacts someone who tells them to place the stones among roots of an almond tree so they can rest peacefully. And when the tree burns one day, as if struck by lightning, the son is free.

CONNECTIONS

Bargains. Evil. Healing. Magic. Magic stones. Murder. Parents and children. Rescues. Sorcerers. Spirits. Supernatural beings. Work.

---

92. THE STONECUTTER AND THE TREE OF FORTUNE /
EL CANTER Y EL ÁRBOL DE LA FORTUNA
Pedro Cholotío Temó and Alberto Barreno, *The Dog Who Spoke /*
El perro que habló
Maya People. Santiago Atitlán, Guatemala

Chepe's rock carving is respected, but he regrets not having gotten an education in order to earn a better living. One day, resting under a big fig tree, he dreams that a young man steps out of the trunk and tells him that treasure is buried under the tree, which he will give him when Chepe visits him four times at midnight. Chepe dismisses the dream, but it keeps recurring, so he visits the tree four times. Then, just as he dreamed, he picks up a silver coin and then a little gold coin. Chepe uses the coins to find different work, but he does not pay attention to what the dueno has also said in the dream about helping others. He uses all the money on himself. He even callously turns away the dueno from the enchanted tree who comes begging for money, disguised as a blind man. And so, the dueno takes Chepe's fortune away.

CONNECTIONS

Bargains. Cautionary tales. Discontent. Dreams. Duenos. Gods and humans. Magic. Magic trees. Money. Punishments. Reversals of fortune. Rewards. Selfishness. Spirits. Stonecutters. Tests. Treasure.

---

93. BLANCAFLOR

Mary-Jo Gerson, *Fiesta Femenina*
Mexico

The gambler Pedro bargains with the Devil for money in his pocket and five years of good luck. After that, Pedro must find him at the *Hacienda of Qui-quiri-quí* on the Plains of Berlin, where the Devil will give him three tasks. Pedro's five good years are up all too soon. He finds his way to the Plains when the hermit who can summon fish sends him to his brother who can summon animals, who calls a lion to take him to the third hermit in the desert. An eagle flies Pedro there and tells him only to speak to the third dove, Blancaflor, who is the devil's most special daughter. They sing together, and Blancaflor says she will help Pedro. With the help of Blancaflor's magic, Pedro accomplishes the Devil's first two impossible tasks. The third is to mount a horse that has never been ridden. Blancaflor says that the horse will be *el Diablo* himself and tells Pedro how to do this, too. Now Blancaflor wants to go to escape her parents' anger. She leaves spit in her room which answers in her voice, but her parents soon realize that the two have fled and come after them. Blancaflor throws down her hairbrush and then her mirror which become a thicket and a lake to slow *el Diablo* and *la Diablesa*. But, they keep coming. Her parents give up when they reach the little old man Blancaflor enchanted to answer their questions with lists of vegetables. Pedro promises to come back for Blancaflor after he tells his family about her, but she warns him not to kiss anyone or he will not remember. He does embrace his grandmother and forgets Blancaflor. At the fiesta to celebrate his return, one guest carries two doves on a silver tray. She tells the doves to tell the story of Blancaflor and the forgotten promise. Pedro does not think this story is about him until Blancaflor softly sings to herself, and then it all comes back. So they are married and live the rest happily together.

CONNECTIONS

Animal helpers. Bargains. Bird helpers. Devil. Doves. Eagles. Escapes. Gamblers. Giants. Illness.
  Journeys. Love. Magic. Magic birds. Magic breaths. Magic clubs. Magic combs. Magic dolls.
  Magic hairbrushes. Magic horses. Magic mirrors. Magic pins. Magic shawls. Magic spittle.
  Memory loss. Outsiders. Parents and children. Princes and princesses. Reversals of fortune.
  Tasks. Transformations. Warnings.

HOW ELSE THIS STORY IS TOLD

Blanca Flor—Riley Aiken. In J. Frank Dobie, *Puro Mexicano*

Blanca Flor, White Flower—A Fairy Tale from Mexico / Blanca Flor, Cuento de hadas de México—Olga Loya, *Momentos Mágicos / Magic Moments*. Here, when Juan goes home and forgets Blanca Flor, it is their dancing together that helps him remember.

Blancaflor—Alma Flor Ada and F. Isabel Campoy, *Tales Our Abuelitas Told*. A fearful voice asks
  Prince Alfonso what he will give for his father's health, and the prince promises to bring
  himself to the Three Silver Towers in the Land of No Return in three years. When he escapes
  from there, Blancaflor detains her parents by leaving some of her breath to answer for her.
  To slow them down when they give chase, she throws down a magic comb, magic pin, and
  magic shawl. Blancaflor and Prince Alfonso make it to the castle together.

Blancaflor—Américo Paredes, *Folktales of Mexico*

Rosalie—John Bierhorst, *The Monkey's Haircut*. Yucatec Maya. Mexico. A young man falls in love
  with the giant's youngest daughter and needs to accomplish four tasks in order to live there.
  With her help, he does, but she urges him to leave. She, too, leaves spittle on the floor which
  speaks for her to cover their escape. The giant turns back when they turn themselves into
  an orange tree and an old man, but when they transform into a sardine and a shark, his wife
  tells them they must remain in the water for seven years. They do, but Rosalie has not been
  baptized and cannot enter his grandparents' town. The young man goes to get some holy
  water and forgets Rosalie when kissed by his grandmother, until he feels pain when she
  whips a doll.

---

94. FISHERMAN'S DAUGHTER

John Bierhorst, *Latin American Folktales*
Colombia

A voice promises a poor fisherman plentiful fishing in the future if he brings the
one who will greet him first to the river. Certain that this will be his dog, the man at
last agrees. But it is his little daughter who runs out. Sadly, the man brings his daughter
to a house in the middle of the river and says goodbye. Though no one is there, the
house is furnished and supper appears. Sometimes in the dark, the voice asks her to
find the louse on his head. Sometimes a horse takes her back to her parents with money,
but the voice orders her not to let them touch her and to bring nothing back. However,
when she is checking his head for lice one night, her hand brushes his body and she
feels fish scales. The daughter disobeys orders the next time she visits her parents. The
matches and a candle she brings back show her that the man is a fish from the waist
down. Angry, he sends her in men's clothing to the palace to work. The young king tells
her to bring him a strand of hair from the mother of all the animals. She does not know

where to go, until she shares her food with an old woman and a boy. They direct her to a meadow and warn her only to approach the mother of all animals if grass covers the ground. She pulls one very long strand of hair from the mother of all animals, and the king pays her thousands of pesos and tells her she is free to go. The old woman gives her a wand which shows her the way home, with the grace of God.

CONNECTIONS

Bargains. Disobedience. Emperors, kings & queens. Fishermen. Generosity. Kindness. Magic. Magic hairs. Magic wands. Mermaids and mermen. Mother of all animals. Parents and children. Punishments. Reversals of fortune. Supernatural beings. Supernatural voices. Tasks.

---

95. THE MAGIC ARROWS

Douglas Gifford, *Warriors, Gods & Spirits from Central & South American Mythology*
Caraja People

On their way to catch two huge howler monkeys who have been frightening people in the forest, two brothers laugh at a toad woman who says she will help them if one agrees to marry her. Then the howler monkeys are racing through the trees and come at them with heavy sticks. The brothers flee and disappear. At this same time, their younger brother, whose body is covered with sores, searches for an arrow he has lost. A snake shows him where it is. They get to talking, and the snake offers the young man some ointment for his skin. He stays with the snake for several days, using the ointment, which heals his sores. The snake tells him that the howler monkeys are really demons, that he should agree to marry the toad woman, and that he should aim at both monkeys with his one arrow and they will vanish. The young man follows all these instructions and the toad woman helps him to aim. The monkeys leave their skins behind, which he brings back to the snake, who gives him magic arrows in return. The younger brother returns to his village, worried about what his grandmother may say about the toad wife. As she enters the hut, however, the toad changes into a beautiful young woman. His life, too, is transformed and happy from then on.

CONNECTIONS

Animal helpers. Appearance. Bargains. Brothers and sisters. Demons. Disrespect. Frogs and toads. Healing. Kindness. Magic. Magic arrows. Monkeys. Reversals of fortune. Snakes. Supernatural beings. Supernatural husbands and wives. Toad woman. Transformations. Unkindness.

---

96. THE MOUSE KING

Amalia de Ordóñez in John Bierhorst, *Latin American Folktales*
Bolivia

When a peasant's daughter picks up a white mouse in the forest, it offers to grant her wishes in exchange for being able to run free. Right then, she wishes that her family's hut become a farmhouse. It does. However, the daughter spurns her lover now as being beneath her. She requests more and more from the mouse at the oak tree, dissatisfied with all she gets, including marriage to a prince. The mouse warns her not to be too greedy and rejects her wish that she rule the kingdom. When the daughter returns home, there is her family's poor hut again.

CONNECTIONS

Allegories and parables. Animal helpers. Bargains. Cautionary tales. Discontent. Greed. Magic. Magic mice. Punishments. Warnings. Wishes.

97. *THE WITCH'S FACE: A MEXICAN TALE*
Eric A. Kimmel
Mazahua People. Mexico

En route to Mexico City, the gentleman Don Aurelio Martinez stops at a large black house, hoping to spend the night. Three women come to the door. Each seems to have the face of the same person at a different age. The youngest daughter, Emilia, is most beautiful, and she whispers that everything is not as it appears. Don Aurelio discovers that they are witches, when they pull off their faces and fly into the night. He wakes one morning shut in an iron cage. Emilia sadly tells him she will officially become a witch, too, when she has killed him. Don Aurelio argues that she should help him escape, so he can help her. Emilia gives him her beautiful face and makes him promise to burn it when he flies home on magic wings. She will come when he makes a new face for her and says her name. The face Don Aurelio fashions from a piece of leather seems so crude to him. He cannot bring himself to destroy the beautiful face he fell in love with. He whispers Emilia's name. The young witch arrives and smoothes on the leather mask he made. Though Emilia says that it does not matter what she looks like, Don Aurelio loves only the beautiful woman she was before. One night he smoothes her old face on her while she is sleeping, and Emilia flies out the window in horror. He tries to follow with the second pair of wings and falls, the magic gone. Don Aurelio never walks nor sees Emilia again, and he realizes love is what makes a face beautiful.

CONNECTIONS

Appearance. Beauty. Changes in attitude. Deceit. Disguises. Cautionary tales. Escapes. Faces. Love. Masks. Promises. Punishments. Warlocks and witches.

98. THE NOBLEST DEED
Grant Lyons, *Tales the People Tell in Mexico*
Mexico

As he lies dying, a father in Guadalajara tells his three sons that the one who does the most noble deed in the next week will inherit a diamond, the only wealth he has to give. The sons return and tell him their stories. The eldest has given half of what he owns to the poor. The middle son jumped into a river and saved a child from drowning. The youngest has quietly rolled with a man, who has previously threatened to kill him, away from the edge of a cliff. That man awakened, truly grateful to have been saved and no longer an enemy. The father compliments all three for their charity and compassion. He gives the diamond to the youngest son who had the courage to transform hatred into friendship with his kindness.

CONNECTIONS

Allegories and parables. Bargains. Changes in attitude. Charity. Competition. Courage. Enmity. Generosity. Heroes and heroines. Jewels. Kindness. Parents and children. Rescues. Rewards. Tests.

HOW ELSE THIS STORY IS TOLD

The Most Noble Story—Naomi Baltuck, *Apples from Heaven.* The diamond owner is a widow in this version, who tells the youngest son he has made the world a better place.
A True Hero—Anita Stern, *World Folktales*

99. THE LITTLE BOY WHO TALKED WITH BIRDS
Victor Montejo, *The Bird Who Cleans the World*
Jakaltek Maya People. Guatemala

A father wants to know why his son laughs whenever a bird sings as they take a break from working in the cornfields. The boy resists telling him, but when his father gets angry, he says that the bird predicts that his father will salute him one day. Thinking that his son does not respect him, the father sends the boy away. The boy wanders until he hears that the chief is offering his daughter in marriage and his kingdom to the person who can interpret the crows raising a racket outside his window. The boy tells the king that the male crow and female crow blame each other for not doing some of the work and are arguing about which one has claim to the babies who have hatched. The king asks the boy's advice, and the boy tells the crows that each should take one child. They fly off happily, and the king keeps his promise. The boy's father is among those who come to honor the new chief, and his son reassures him of his respect.

CONNECTIONS

Anger. Arguments. Bargains. Bird helpers. Crows. Disrespect. Emperors, kings & queens. Honoring parents. Language. Magic birds. Misunderstandings. Parents and children. Problem solving. Prophecies. Reconciliations. Respect. Reversals of fortune. Status. Tests.

WHERE ELSE THIS STORY APPEARS

At *Learning to Give* (Online).

HOW ELSE THIS STORY IS TOLD

The Little Boy Who Talked with Birds / El niño que hablaba con los pájaros—Susan Conklin Thompson, Keith Steven Thompson, and Lidia López de López, *Mayan Folktales*

100. Monkey Gets the Last Laugh

Martha Hamilton and Mitch Weiss, *Through the Grapevine*
Brazil

The other animals have had it with monkey's tricks and roll a large stone onto his tail while he is sleeping. Monkey breaks his tail off, trying to pull it free. Cat makes off with the tail. She says she will give it back when Monkey brings her milk from Cow. Cow says she'll give milk if Monkey brings her grass from the farmer. The farmer wants Monkey to get the cloud to give some rain. The cloud wants water from the river. When River tells Monkey to go ahead and take some water, Monkey says thank you and brings everyone all the things they want in exchange for what he needs. Cat gives the tail back, and Monkey feels whole again.

Connections
Bargains. Cause and effect. Cats. Clouds. Cows. Farmers. Monkeys. Punishments. Retaliation. Rivers. Tails. Tasks.

How Else This Story Is Told
Why the Monkey Still Has a Tail—Elsie Spicer Eells, *Folk Tales from Brazil*

101. Paisano Saves Baby Rabbit from Señor Rattlesnake

Dan Storm, *Pictures Tales from Mexico*
Mexico

Of all his paisanos, Rattlesnake fears the fast Roadrunner bird the most. One day Roadrunner catches Rattlesnake asleep in the desert and quietly surrounds him with thorny prickly pear leaves. Rattlesnake wakes to find himself held captive in a circle of cactus. He begs Roadrunner for mercy, and Roadrunner agrees to let him go if he promises not to harm any animal babies. Rattlesnake agrees. A few days later, though, Rattlesnake corners a terrified baby rabbit. He has just opened his mouth to eat the little rabbit, when the Roadrunner props his mouth wide with a long thorn.

Connections
Bargains. Birds. Deceit. Fear. Interspecies conflict. Justice. Promises. Rabbits. Rattlesnakes. Rescues. Roadrunners. Snakes.

102. The Ram in the Chile Patch

Judy Sierra, *Nursery Tales Around the World*
Mexico

A little boy yells at the little ram who has gotten into his patch of chile peppers. The ram not only yells back at him, but knocks him down. Then the ram kicks out a cow, a dog, and a burro who try to help and keeps eating the chile peppers. The boy sadly offers a little ant some corn to get the ram out. The ant wants to know how much corn. The ant turns down every large amount of corn the boy names as a reward, but does accept his offer of a modest handful. The ant climbs up and bites the ram's behind. At last, the little ram leaves.

CONNECTIONS

Ants. Bargains. Bullies. Chili peppers. Goats. Humility. Insect helpers. Punishments. Rewards. Size.

HOW ELSE THIS STORY IS TOLD

The Goat from the Hills and Mountains—Alma Flor Ada and F. Isabel Campoy, *Tales Our Abuelitas Told.* A large, bullying goat, threatens to eat everyone, until a little ant offers help for a two grains of wheat.

The Ram in the Chile Patch—Maria del Refulgio Gonzalez in Américo Paredes, *Folktales of Mexico*

---

103. TUP AND THE ANTS

John Bierhorst, *The Monkey's Haircut and Other Stories Told by the Maya* Yucatec Maya. Mexico

Tup is the laziest of the three brothers who marry three sisters. When his old father-in-law sends the young men out to cut trees to make a cornfield, the eldest two work for three days, while Tup goes off and sleeps. When he sees a leaf-cutter ant carrying off the end of his food, he threatens to kill it, unless the ant brings him to the lord of its nest. Tup demands that the ants either return the food they stole or finish his work. The ant lord brings the ants to work, and they clear the field for him. Meanwhile, Tup's brothers have hollowed all the tree trunks, which is what they thought their father-in-law meant by cutting trees. Still, without coming to look, the old man calls Tup an idler and won't let his wife give him as much food when he sends the sons out to the field to burn brush. For the next few tasks—burning, sowing, building earth ovens to roast ears of young corn—Tup takes food straight to the ants' nest in exchange for their help with the work. The father-in-law keeps scolding Tup, not knowing that his brothers continually misinterpret his instructions. Finally, the old man, his wife, his daughters, and the brothers set out with mules to harvest the fields and eat the roasted corn. The old man sees that only Tup's fields are thriving; his mother-in-law even gets lost among the plants. Tup is honored with a good dinner that night, and his brothers are sent packing.

CONNECTIONS

Animal helpers. Ants. Armadillos. Bargains. Brothers and sisters. Changes in attitude. Cleverness. Farmers. Fathers-in-law and mothers-in-law. Humorous tales. Iguanas. Insect helpers. Laziness. Leaf-cutter ants. Magic. Misunderstandings. Origin tales. Parents and children. Reversals of fortune. Sorcerers. Status. Work.

WHERE ELSE THIS STORY APPEARS

In John Bierhorst, *Latin American Folktales.*

How Else This Story Is Told

Variation from Honduras:

A Tale of Three Tails—Charles J. Finger, *Tales from Silver Lands.* A father believes the wizard
who tells him that his sons are lazy, when the wizard keeps undoing the boys woodcutting
so they will not discover his forest home. With magical help from an iguana, the boys are
able to stop the wizard, who flies off so fast his skin bakes hard, and he becomes an armadillo.

---

104. *The Harvest Birds / Los pájaros de la cosecha*
Blanca López de Mariscal
Mexico

No one expects much from Juan Zanate, who always has one or two zanate birds
on his shoulder or hat. After his father dies, Juan struggles when the land is divided
between his elder brothers. The richest man in town laughs at him when Juan asks for
a piece of his own land to farm. One of the zanates, Grajo, would like to see Juan succeed.
Juan then asks old Grandpa Chon for a piece of land to prove that he can make things
grow. Grandpa Chon gives Juan a chance, but, if Juan fails, he will have to work for the
old man for as many days as he tried to farm. Nobody believes Juan will be able to grow
anything, but Juan is determined. He sweeps the shopkeeper's floor to earn some seeds
for planting and to feed the zanates. Grajo advises Juan to plant weeds along the borders
of his land. Other farmers continue to laugh at Juan, but he brings in a fine harvest of
corn, squashes, and beans. The old man gives Juan the land he promised, and Juan tells
him the seceret the zanates shared, that plants are like brothers and sisters and grow
better together than alone.

Connections

Bargains. Bird helpers. Dreams. Farmers. Magic birds. Opportunity. Perseverance. Respect for
nature. Reversals of fortune. Rewards. Ridicule. Tests. Wise men and wise women.

Where Else This Story Appears

At *Learning to Give* (Online).

---

105. The Aztec Letter
Richard and Judy Dockrey Young, *1492: New World Tales*
Otomí People. Mexico

An Otomí trader stops by a village hut and offers to pay for a midday meal. The
woman there says she will cook tortillas and rabbit stew for him, if he will read her the
bark paper with pictograms which her husband has sent from Tenochtitlán. He agrees.
They eat and then she gives him the bark, which he turns different directions, telling
her it is such sad news. Very worried about her husband, she questions the trader, who
now explains that the unhappy thing is that neither of them can read.

CONNECTIONS

Bargains. Humorous tales. Letters. Illiteracy.

---

106. THE AFFAIR OF THE HORNS

Victor Montejo, *The Bird Who Cleans the World and Other Mayan Fables*
Jakaltek Maya People. Guatemala

Deer covets rabbit's antlers and leaps over rabbit's head one day, saying he is just admiring them. Deer asks to borrow the antlers. Rabbit answers that they were specially made by the Creator and Shaper for him when rabbits were made from decayed trees. Deer promises to be right back with the antlers, but runs off once they are on his head and never returns. Rabbit goes to the Creator and Shaper, who says rabbit was careless to lend them off like that. Instead, he draws rabbit's ears out long. And rabbit goes off a lot more cautious.

CONNECTIONS

Appearance. Cautionary tales. Deceit. Deer. Discontent. Ears. Gods and animals. Identity. Interspecies conflict. Origin tales. Promises. Rabbits. Tricksters. Trust.

HOW ELSE THIS STORY IS TOLD

Kanjobal Maya variation from Guatemala:
The Rabbit and His Cap—Don Pedro Miguel Say in Fernando Peñalosa, *Tales and Legends of the
Q'Anjob'al Maya* and as Rabbit and the Cap of Antlers at *Maya Culture—Traditional Storyteller's Tales* (Online). After Uncle Rabbit loses his antler cap, he goes to the king he calls
father who says he will make him taller if he brings back fifteen loads of skins. Rabbit tricks
many animals to get those skins, but the father accuses him of murdering his own brothers
and merely stretches his ears.

Mexican variations:
The Deer's Sandals—Idella Purnell, *The Merry Frogs*. Cora People. Deer has claws, which do not
allow him to run, and he wishes he had wings, or at least hooves like Rabbit. Deer begs to borrow
Rabbit's sandals and, though Rabbit is reluctant to trust him, he lets Deer put them on. Deer
dances in Rabbit's hooves and then runs off with them after his fifth circle over the mountain.
See also The Rabbit's Ears / Las orejas del conejo (62), The King of the Animals (132), and Why
Rabbits Have Long Ears (263) for other explanations of rabbits' ears.

---

107. MAICHAK

The Ekaré Writers Group in *Jade and Iron*
Pémon People. Venezuela

Maichak's brothers-in-law laugh at him because he cannot hunt or fish. One day a little man comes out of the river on Mount Auyan-tepuy and offers Maichak a magic *tapara* gourd for gathering fish. When Maichak puts a little river water in the gourd, the river dries up, so he can gather many fish. The little man warns him only to fill the gourd halfway and not to tell anyone. This works until Maichak's brothers-in-law sneak into his shoulder bag and take the gourd. They overfill it, causing a flood, and the gourd is swallowed by a fish. Unhappy about losing the gourd, Maichak seizes the rattle an armadillo is shaking to bring wild peccary pigs out of their burrow. The armadillo warns him not to lose this rattle like he did the gourd and not to shake it more than three times in a row. One of Maichak's brothers-in-law steals this maraca, too. He shakes it too many times, and a herd of peccaries take it away. Maichak then asks a howler monkey for his comb, which brings many birds close. The monkey gives it to him, warning that he shouldn't comb more than three times straight. When his brothers-in-law steal this too, Maichak leaves home. He travels far, has wonderful adventures, and learns many skills, which he teaches to his family when he returns many moons later.

CONNECTIONS

Animal helpers. Armadillos. Brothers-in-law and sisters-in-law. Fish. Hunters. Journeys. Magic. Magic combs. Magic gourds. Magic maracas. Monkeys. Music. Peccaries. Punishments. Reconciliations. Reversals of fortune. Ridicule. Secrets. Theft. Warnings.

108. THE BOW, THE DEER, & THE TALKING BIRD

Anita Brenner, *The Boy Who Could Do Anything*
Aztec People. Mexico

When he is dying, an Aztec merchant offers his sons their choice among three magic things which will make their fortune. The youngest son chooses the bird which speaks about what it sees. Over time, he becomes Prime Minister. His elder brothers are jealous and plot to steal the bird. The bird has overheard them, but the younger brother does not believe that his brothers are evil and lets them stay in the palace. When the bird informs him that a neighboring land is planning a surprise attack, he even tells the king that if he makes all three brothers nobles, they will save the country. With the magic door and magic arrow from their father, the brothers do help him send the enemy soldiers fleeing. The brothers realize what they can accomplish together. And ever since that time, when someone knows a secret they may say, "Oh, a little bird told me."

CONNECTIONS

Bargains. Bird helpers. Birds. Brothers and sisters. Changes in attitude. Emperors, kings & queens. Jealousy. Magic. Magic arrows. Magic birds. Magic doors. Rewards. Secrets. Teamwork.

109. SOMERSAULT STREET

Yolanda Nava, ed., *It's All in the Frijoles*
Mexico

Don Mendo Quiroga y Suárez, Marguis of Valle Salado, has always helped the poor. It distresses him that his nephew's daughter, now an orphan from Spain whom he has invited to stay in his house, can be elegantly charming to some people, but treats others with superciliousness. She ignores his advice about her manners, saying that she does not need the friendship of ignorant Mexicans. Don Mendo does not find a way to show his niece the error of her ways until he dies. Upon Don Mendo's death, his niece eagerly anticipates receiving enough money to return to Spain. His will states, however, that in order to inherit his property, his niece must turn three somersaults dressed up in finery in front of her uncle's friends in the public plaza. She desires the money enough to do it and thinks that none of them matter, anyway. No one laughs at her, though, and after the third somersault, people cheer her bravery. She cries as they extend friendship to her. The niece remains in the capital to help nuns in the orphanage and gives most of her inheritance to the Orders of Saint Francis and Mercedes. The street where she lives is immediately renamed Calle de La Machincuepa.

CONNECTIONS

Bargains. Cautionary tales. Changes in attitude. Charity. Friendship. Kindness. Manners. Orphans. Punishments. Selfishness. Somersaults. Uncles and nieces.

HOW ELSE THIS STORY IS TOLD

The Calle de La Machincuepa—Thomas Allibone Janvier, *Legends of the City of Mexico*
Somersault Street / La calle de la Machincuepa—Genevieve Barlow, *Stories from Latin America / Historias de Latinoamérica*

110. THE WITRANALWE WHO GUARDED SHEEP

Richard M. Dorson, *Folktales Told Around the World*
Mapuche People. Chile

Two poor nephews have no food to feed their wealthy uncle when he gets hungry on a visit to them one time. They slip out to his corral near Pitrugquén, telling themselves that he will not miss two sheep. At the corral, though, a large frightening horseman in black with long, sharp teeth and silver spurs, a *witranalwe*, stands guard. One nephew runs, but the other stays, boldly holding a lamb. He asks the horseman who he is. When the horseman rumbles that he is partner with the sheep's owner, the nephew exclaims that they are related, since the owner is his uncle who will be at the fiesta. The *witranalwe* agrees to let the nephew take the lamb, if he saves him a bowl of its blood. The *witranalwe* even helps carry the sheep. He gallops back later to down the bowl of blood pudding and wine, which the nephew has left outside and never tells his master about the lamb.

CONNECTIONS

Bargains. Cleverness. Ghouls. Humorous tales. Secrets. Sheep. Supernatural beings. Theft. Uncles and nephews. Witranalwes.

111. *JAMES THE VINE PULLER*

Martha Bennett Stiles
Brazil

An elephant yells at James, the turtle, for eating a coconut. The elephant says he is king of the jungle and every tree in it belongs to him. Intimidated, James goes to eat seaweed from the ocean, but a whale accuses him of stealing from his garden and says he is king there. James has to eat and comes up with a plan. The next day he challenges both the elephant and the whale separately to vine-pulling contests. The strongest will become king of the jungle or ocean and have to leave. They accept. He ties one end of the vine to the whale's tale and carries the other end on his leg to tie onto the elephant's trunk. Assuming their opponent is James, the elephant and whale pull against each other back and forth until they are exhausted. James goes to each and says that since neither has won, they all get to live and eat as they did before.

CONNECTIONS

Anansi. Bargains. Bullies. Competition. Elephants. Humorous tales. Interspecies conflict. Jaguars. Monkeys. Problem solving. Spiders. Status. Tapirs. Tricksters. Tortoises and turtles. Whales.

HOW ELSE THIS STORY IS TOLD

Brazilian variations:

Jabuty, the Strong—Frances Carpenter, *South American Wonder Tales*. Here the tortoise tricks a tapir into pulling against a whale.

The Fisherman and the Monkey—Elsie Spicer Eells, *The Brazilian Fairy Book*. A long adventure begins when angry Jaguar wants to get back at monkey for all the tricks he has played. Afraid, monkey borrows rope from a fisherman he promises to make rich. He connects the sleeping jaguar's tail to a sleeping whale. Later, the monkey helps the fisherman succeed in tricking giants for the king, and eventually the fisherman receives the riches and reward monkey promised him.

African American variation from Suriname:

Tug of War—Melville J. Herskovits and Frances Herskovits, *Suriname Folk-Lore*. Anansi the spider tricks the elephant and whale into tugging against each other here.

---

112. THE PULQUE VENDOR TRICKS THE DEVIL

Anthony John Campos, *Mexican Folk Tales*
Mexico

A pulque vendor who walks everywhere to sell his drink rues the fact that he will never be able to save enough money to build a bridge across the river near Guadalajara. Just then, a tall stranger in a black cloak asks what the vendor will give if he builds the bridge for him. The vendor offers whatever money he has plus some of his pulque. Instead, the devil wants the vendor's soul if he finishes construction before daybreak. The vendor will not promise that until the devil promises that the vendor will be free if the devil does not finish before the cock crows. The pulque vendor naps and wakes to see the whole bridge finished, except for one last tower. He suggests they drink to the devil's victory. The devil gulps down a glass of "the one which stays" and passes out before he can finish a second. Just then the cock crows dawn, and the devil bursts into flame and vanishes. Something always happens to keep anyone from finishing the bridge.

CONNECTIONS

Bargains. Bridges. Churches. Construction. Dawn. Demons. Devil. Drink. Fences. Humorous tales. Mayors. Mysteries. Pulque. Ranchers. Roosters. Tricksters. Vendors.

HOW ELSE THIS STORY IS TOLD

Mexican variations:

The Devil and the Railroad—Anita Brenner, *The Boy Who Could Do Anything*. A seven-foot man who says he is Satan, knocks down the first railroad bridge over a canyon because he doesn't want dirt and noise near his summer home. The superintendent offers one hundred fifty souls if the Devil will build the bridge himself by midnight.

The Rich Ranchero's Maguey Fence—Anthony John Campos, *Mexican Folk Tales*. The devil takes a ranchero up on his offer to give "anything I own to have the moat dug and maguey's planted" to encircle his vast land. When the devil fails, the ranchero keeps his soul, but he can never seem to finish the fence.

Variation from Honduras:

How the Devil Constructed a Church—Dorothy Sharp Carter in Joanna Cole, *Best-Loved Folktales of the World*. With the governor pressing him to get the construction done, the mayor of Curarén signs a contract in blood to give Enemigo MaloDevil unbaptized babies if he will build a church before cock crows. The Devil and his demon workers are outsmarted while it's still dark by an old woman with a candle in one hand and a rooster in the other.

---

113. THE TAILOR WHO SOLD HIS SOUL TO THE DEVIL

Neil Philip, *Horse Hooves and Chicken Feet*
Mexico

When a poor tailor says he would even accept money from the Devil to feed his family, the Devil himself appears. The Devil offers to help in exchange for the tailor's soul. The tailor says he will agree to the bargain if the Devil can turn a pile of cloth into a shirt faster than he can. Devil produces a sack of gold, and they start. The Devil has trouble threading his needle, so the tailor threads it for him with a thread so long that it keeps getting tangled as the Devil sews. The tailor threads his own needle with a very short thread that zips in and out, and he wins. After that, people try to avoid putting long, long thread in needles: "the Devil's thread."

CONNECTIONS

Bargains. Cautionary tales. Clothing. Competition. Devil. Humorous tales. Poverty. Reversals of fortune. Sewing. Tailors. Tricksters.

HOW ELSE THIS STORY IS TOLD

The Tailor Who Sold His Soul to the Devil—Petra Guzmán Barrón. In Américo Paredes, *Folktales of Mexico*

114. THE MAN WHO DEFEATED THE DEVIL / EL HOMBRE QUE VENCIÓAL DIABLO

Pedro Cholotío Temó and Alberto Barreno, *The Dog Who Spoke /
El perro que habló*
Tzutuhil Maya People. San Pedro La Laguna, Guatemala

The son of a rich miser squanders all of his inheritance and becomes a beggar. He keeps drinking. When the devil shows up for him, the son answers that the devil can only take his body and soul once he has died, for he wants to keep drinking and partying now. The devil agrees, only if he gets to drink the man's blood on the last day of his life. When the devil comes to check how the man is doing, the man says he needs more time to learn to become a thief. The devil helps him steal from townspeople. When the devil next shows up he tells the man he has had enough time. The thief bets that the devil cannot accomplish four things. All the bets, like filling a net with water or catching the thief's fart, are impossible for the devil to do. The thief wins, and the devil goes away.

CONNECTIONS

Bargains. Devil. Drink. Humorous tales. Life span. Thieves. Tricksters.

---

115. HOW THE BLACKSMITH FOOLED DEATH

Livia de Almeida and Ana Portella, *Brazilian Folktales*
Brazil

Life gets better for a struggling young man when he shares some food with an old lady who rewards him with three wishes. He wishes for iron and coal for his blacksmith work, a magic table covered with food when he and his wife need it, and a magic guitar that makes people keep dancing without being able to stop when he plays it. Then one day, Death arrives at the door and terrifies his wife. The man tells Death he will go with her, but asks to play his guitar one more time. Death allows this, but once the blacksmith starts playing, Death cannot stop dancing. The blacksmith is able to wrangle out two more years. Luckily, he is not home when Death next visits, and Death tells his wife she'll return in a week. When the man comes home, he puts on a disguise. His wife tells Death her husband had to leave. Death says they had a deal and finds the man, whom the wife claims is her uncle. In a hurry, Death says, she will take the uncle instead.

CONNECTIONS

Bargains. Blacksmiths. Dancing. Death (Character). Disguises. Husbands and wives. Kindness. Life span. Magic. Magic guitars. Magic tables. Music. Reversals of fortune. Tricksters. Wishes.

---

116. THE BANANA BET

Pleasant DeSpain, *Eleven Turtle Tales*
Panama

Mama Tortoise wants to find a way to reach the ripe bananas hanging high in the tree for her children's party. She tells monkey that she has been practicing climbing trees and suggests they race up the banana tree. She sets the bet at two bunches of bananas. Mr. Monkey is sure he'll win. He races to the top, while Mama Tortoise slowly climbs. She agrees that Mr. Monkey has won and then bets four bunches of bananas that she will reach the ground first. Monkey scoffs, but finally agrees. Mama Tortoise wins by pulling her body all into her shell and falling straight down into the sand. Mr. Monkey brings down four bunches of bananas, and now she has two to give him for the first race and two to bring home for her children's party.

Connections
Bananas. Bargains. Competition. Humorous tales. Monkeys. Tortoises and turtles. Tricksters.

How Else This Story Is Told
The Wagers—Dorothy Sharp Carter, *The Enchanted Orchard*

---

117. The Tricky Turtle
Bill Gordh, *Stories in Action*
Mexico

A father traps a turtle in a cage and brings it home so the family can have turtle soup for dinner. While he goes to gather firewood, their papa tells the children to make sure the turtle doesn't leave the cage. But when this turtle tells the children that it could play the flute for them if it had more room, they just have to open the cage a little. His flute playing is so wonderful, they beg the turtle to play more. He tells them he would also dance for them if they let him out of the cage and dance along. As the children dance, the turtle dances too, disappearing into the forest. The music stops. The children look for the turtle, and when they cannot find him, they put a big rock in the cage instead. They do not tell their father, but when he sees the rock, dinner is bread that night for everyone. The children apologize and tell him how wonderfully the turtle played and danced. Their father says the turtle's music will fill them more than turtle soup.

Connections
Captivity. Dancing. Disobedience. Escapes. Flutes. Forgiveness. Humorous tales. Music. Parents and children. Tricksters. Tortoises and turtles. Understanding.

How Else This Story Is Told
Mexican variation:
Clever Little Turtle—M.A. Jagendorf and R.S. Boggs, *The King of the Mountains*

Amazonian variations:
The Dancing Turtle—Pleasant DeSpain, *Eleven Turtle Tales*. Amazonia
Mira and the Stone Tortoise—Melinda Lilly. Kulina People. Brazil and Peru

118. TURTLE AND FOX

John Bierhorst, *The Red Swan*
Anambé People. Brazil

Fox asks to borrow Turtle's flute and says he will give it back, which Turtle doesn't trust Fox enough to do. But Turtle changes his mind after Fox compliments his playing. Fox takes the flute and runs away. Turtle daubs honey on his anus and hides under leaves on the path. Fox comes by and puts his hand in the hole to get some honey and then his tongue. Turtle squeezes his anus tight, trapping Fox until Fox admits he has the flute and will return it.

CONNECTIONS

Bargains. Deceit. Flattery. Flutes. Foxes. Honey. Humorous tales. Music. Tricksters. Trust. Tortoises and turtles.

119. THE FOX WHO WANTED TO WHISTLE

Genevieve Barlow, *Latin American Tales from the Pampas to Mexico City*
Argentina

Fox has been practicing whistling so he will sound like a partridge, but he doesn't. The puma suggests he ask the partridge herself to teach him how. The partridge warily agrees to give the fox lessons if the fox promises he will never hurt her or her family. The partridge sews the fox's long mouth closed on the sides in order for the whistle to sound. Fox is so delighted with the whistle that emerges with his breath now, that he says he can whistle as well as partridge without more help from her. Partridge bristles at that and starts to fly off, and the over-confident fox tries to open wide to snap at her and painfully rips all the stitches and his mouth.

CONNECTIONS

Arrogance. Bargains. Birds. Braggarts. Cautionary tales. Deceit. Discontent. Foxes. Huaychaos. Ingratitude. Music. Origin tales. Partridges. Punishments. Talents. Teachers. Trust.

HOW ELSE THIS STORY IS TOLD

Peruvian variation:

Why the Fox Has a Huge Mouth—John Bierhorst, *Black Rainbow: Legends of the Incas and Myths of Ancient Peru*. The fox asks to borrow a huaychao's flute-like bill, which requires getting stitches around his mouth to hold it securely. Fox has no intention of returning the bill, but when skunks start dancing to his music, he laughs and tears the stitches wide open, and the huaychao takes off with his beak.

120. DON'T MAKE A BARGAIN WITH A FOX

M.A. Jagendorf and R.S. Boggs, *The King of the Mountains*
Argentina

Two *viscachas* who live together in the pampas find two ragged red scraps in the brush. They take them to use as a blanket, but each piece is really too small. The *viscachas* are wondering where to find a needle and thread to sew the scraps together when along comes Señor Fox. He says he will give them a needle and thread, if they let him share the blanket. They agree. The blanket is sewn. When Señor Fox returns that night, he announces that he owns the middle where the stitching is, which happened all because of him. The *viscachas* get hardly any covers at all on each side of the large fox.

CONNECTIONS

Bargains. Blankets. Foxes. Humorous tales. Selfishness. Sharing. Tricksters. Viscachas.

---

121. THE LAZY FOX

Genevieve Barlow, *Latin American Tales from the Pampas to Mexico City*
Argentina

A lazy fox decides to trick an armadillo into planting his fields for him by promising a small share of the crops from his rich land. The fox tells him he can plant any crop he likes. Armadillo knows the fox is up to something, but when the fox tells the armadillo he can take the part that grows above the ground and he will only take what grows beneath, the armadillo and his family get busy planting wheat. They bring in a fine harvest of grain, and all the fox gets are roots. Now, the fox tells the armadillo to plant again, and this time he will take what is above the ground. The armadillo plants potatoes. Once again, the fox is left with nothing worthwhile. The hungry fox says he will take what grows below the ground and above the ground next time, and the armadillo can have what's left in the middle. The armadillo plants corn. The fox decides that he will plant his own fields next season and keep it all.

CONNECTIONS

Bargains. Carrots. Changes in attitude. Competition. Corn. Crabs. Devil. Farming. Foxes. Laziness. Pedro de Urdemalas. Potatoes. Rabbits. Sharing. Teamwork. Tricksters. Wheat. Work.

HOW ELSE THIS STORY IS TOLD

Chilean and Argentinean variation:

Pedro and the Devil—Maria Cristina Brusca and Tona Wilson, *Pedro Fools the Gringo*. Pedro outwits the Devil in four contests, the last of which is farming and who will gets to keep the tops and bottoms of different plantings.

Guatemalan variation:

The Rabbit and the Crab—Fernando Peñalosa, *Tales and Legends of the Q'Anjob'al Maya* and as Crab Tricks Rabbit (at last!) by Don Pedro Miguel Say. Also in Fernando Peñalosa, *Maya Culture—Traditional Storyteller's Tales (Online)*. Kanjobal Maya People. When arguments start over who's going to keep the tops and who the bottoms of carrots once they're harvested, the rabbit says he and crab should race, winner take all. The crab graciously offers the rabbit the handicap of going first and sneaks onto rabbit's tail, jumping onto the pile of carrots when rabbit turns to see how far behind he is.

122. WHEN THE FOX WAS TEACHER

Elsie Spicer Eells, *The Brazilian Fairy Book*
Brazil

A dog admires the way a fox is jumping on rocks. The fox agrees to give him lessons for a price. They meet for jumping lessons every day, until the dog has gotten quite good. The dog suggests they compete at jumping distances and heights. Sometimes one wins, sometimes the other. Then the dog suggests that they see which one can leap onto the hen with one jump. The fox jumps onto the hen, and dog leaps onto the fox, who instantly jumps sideways and escapes. When the dog complains that the fox has not taught him this sideways jump, the fox laughs that smart teachers do not share all they know.

CONNECTIONS

Bargains. Competition. Dogs. Foxes. Humorous tales. Knowledge. Teachers. Tricksters. Trust.

123. THE MONKEY BUYS CORN

Enid D'Oyley, *Animal Fables and Other Tales Retold: African Tales in the New World*
African American People. Brazil

With no money for dinner, the monkey asks his friend the cock if he can take corn now and pay for it tomorrow. He gives the cock a time to come collect the money. Monkey then borrows more food from the fox, the dog, and the tiger and gives each one a different time to arrive the next day, one-half hour after the other. The monkey is in bed, feigning pain, when the cock arrives, but just as he has invited the cock to get comfortable, the fox arrives, and the cock hides under the bed. Monkey points each one to hide under the bed. The fox eats the cock and gets eaten by the dog who gets eaten by the tiger. Monkey leaps into a tree to escape from the tiger, himself. The tiger's relatives are watching to catch the monkey by the stream, but the monkey rolls there in disguise. Then the monkey throws stones at the tiger, whom he spies hiding in a hole.

CONNECTIONS

Anansi. Bargains. Cockroaches. Coyotes. Dogs. Foxes. Hens. Humorous tales. Hunters. Interspecies conflict. Jaguars. Loans. Monkeys. Parrots. Roosters. Spiders. Tigers. Tricksters.

HOW ELSE THIS STORY IS TOLD

Brazilian variations:
How the Monkey Got His Food—At *Vida de Latinos: Folk Tales from Brazil* (Online)
Monkey and the Corn Cake—Livia de Almeida and Ana Portella, *Brazilian Folktales*. Monkey is the trickster who borrows from Rooster, Fox, Dog, and Jaguar.

African American variation from Belize:

Anansi Borrows Money—Ervin Beck. At *American Folklore Net* (Online). Bra Anansi and Mrs. Anansi have just gotten married, and Anansi borrows from his friends in order to pay the midwife.

Costa Rican variation:

Brer Rabbit, Businessman—Carmen Lyra. In Harriet De Onís, *The Golden Land* and in Joanna Cole, *Best-Loved Folktales of the World*. Brer Rabbit tricks a roach, a hen, a fox, a coyote, and a hunter.

Guatemalan variations:

Sometimes Right Is Repaid with Wrong—Victor Montejo, *The Bird Who Cleans the World and Other Mayan Fables*. Jakaltek Maya People. Rabbit has borrowed more money than he can repay. The animals he tells to hide under his bed are a cockroach, a hen, a coyote, and a jaguar. Each eats the one before, and the hunter shoots the jaguar.

Sometimes Right Is Repaid with Wrong / A veces el bion con mal se paga—Susan Conklin Thompson, Keith Steven Thompson, and Lidia López de López, *Mayan Folktales*

Mexican variation:

The Rabbit Who Wanted to Be a Man—Anita Brenner, *The Boy Who Could Do Anything*. Rabbit borrows money to pay the workers on his farm.

African American variations from Suriname:

Outwitting Creditors: Chain of Victims 1—Melville J. Herskovits and Frances Herskovits, *Suriname Folk-Lore*. Anansi the spider borrows fifty guilders from Hunter, Tiger, Cock, Cockroach (in reverse size order from the monkey variants above).

Outwitting Creditors: Chain of Victims 3—Melville J. Herskovits and Frances Herskovits, *Suriname Folk-Lore*. Anansi borrows guilders to buy a black coat for his wedding from a Cock, Wild-Dog, Tiger, and Hunter, offering to pay them back double.

Venezuelan variation:

The Very Clever Rabbit—Mary Hoffman, *A Twist in the Tail: Animal Stories from Around the World*. Rabbit and Parrot sell Rabbit's farm separately to a hen, a fox, a dog, a jaguar, and a man, who each think it will be theirs after the harvest.

V

The Community

Teamwork

124. THE STORY OF THE DOLPHINS
Johannes Wilbert, *Folk Literature of the Selknam Indians*
Ona People. Tierra del Fuego, Argentina

A woman brings her parents to the beach, worried about the dull rumbling she hears in the earth. Now, they all fear the powerful Xóše, the snowstorm which is coming. They decide to seek shelter in the sea. But the woman's husband, Kermánta, cannot swim. He tells them to go ahead, and he will stay on a rock and look for them afterwards. His wife will not leave him alone and continues to try to coax him into the water. Now it is urgent that they leave. Kermánta panics each time he tries to run into the water. Finally, his brothers-in-law push him into the sea and lift him up above the surface of the water the minute he begins to sink. Over and over, others lift Kermánta each time he sinks. The family stays together. At last, Kermánta can swim a little on his own. Everyone happily swims farther out into the ocean, which becomes their new home forever. They are the dolphins, who still stick together.

CONNECTIONS
Adaptation. Brothers-in-law and sisters-in-law. Devotion. Dolphins. Escapes. Fear. Husbands and wives. Journeys to other realms. Origin tales. Snow. Swimming. Teamwork. Transformations. Water worlds.

---

125. THE CUCKOO'S REWARD
Genevieve Barlow, *Latin American Tales from the Pampas to Mexico City*
Maya People. El Salvador

Chaac, God of the Fields and Crops, asks all of the birds to collect their favorite seeds and kernels of corn from the fields so they can plant them after the fire god burns off old plants at midday the next day. When the pretty cuckoo, distressed, asks what they are to do again, the owl accuses her of not helping last time. The parrot says cuckoo hides because she is afraid of fire. Chaac calmly says each will do his part. But way before expected, Owl hears fire crackling and alerts the others. They reach the field, and there is cuckoo bravely flying though fire and smoke to save their seeds. Cuckoo's brightly colored feathers have turned gray and her eyes, red. In thanks, other birds take over caring for her children.

CONNECTIONS

Birds. Chac. Courage. Cuckoos. Fire. Gods and animals. Gratitude. Heroes and heroines. Origin tales. Rewards. Righting a wrong. Tasks. Teamwork.

HOW ELSE THIS STORY IS TOLD

Mexican variation:
Cuckoo: A Mexican Folktale / Cucú: in cuento folklórico mexicano—Lois Ehlert. Maya People

---

126. *THE LITTLE RED ANT AND THE GREAT BIG CRUMB*
Shirley Climo
Mexico

Because she is so small, little red ant struggles to bring pieces of food back to the anthill for winter as easily as her cousins. She finds a heavy crumb of yellow torta and covers it with a leaf before hurrying off to find someone strong to help. The first five animals she meets—El Largo the lizard, La Araña the spider, El Gallo, the rooster, and El Coyote—seem strong, but defer to the next one as being stronger than they are. She thinks howling El Coyote may be the one, but then he runs, afraid of the Hombre. The Hombre is a tall farmer who doesn't notice little red ant at all until she runs up his leg and inside his shirt to yell in his ear. Then he begins to jump around and runs off. Little red ant realizes that she must be the strongest of all if she scared Hombre who scares El Coyote. She returns to the piece of cake and carries it home carefully on top of her head.

CONNECTIONS

Ants. Coyotes. Fear. Humans. Insects. Lizards. Perseverance. Roosters. Self-esteem. Size. Spiders. Status. Strength. Tasks.

---

127. *THE FROG AND HIS FRIENDS SAVE HUMANITY / LA RANA Y SUS AMIGOS SALVAN A LA HUMANIDAD*
Victor Villaseñor
Oaxaca, Mexico

In the Spring of Creation, a puzzling two-legged creature appears in the world. It is so different from them that the animals do not know how it will survive, skinless and weak. Lion and some of the other bigger animals think he may be food for them. Turtle warns that the creature may be poisonous. Frog thinks the creature may change over time, like she did from skinny pollywog to strong bullfrog. Armadillo bristles that it may be too late to add new creatures to earth. Frog rubs its soft belly, and the creature farts. Everyone laughs. Frog rubs its tummy and sings to the baby like his mother sang to him. Is the creature a mistake? Lion still wants to eat it. The baby farts and laughs, and the animals are laughing along. They decide that Mother Nature does not make mistakes and offer to protect it and take turns helping it to grow, like others helped them. That will make them feel good, and maybe the creature will become something beautiful and useful.

CONNECTIONS

Allegories and parables. Animals. Babies. Character. Coexistence. Frogs and toads. Humans. Humorous tales. Mysteries. Origin tales. Outsiders. Perspective. Respect for nature. Teamwork.

---

128. THE ROOSTER, THE GOAT AND THE DOG

Harold Courlander, *A Treasury of Afro-American Folklore*
African American People. Venezuela

Dog, rooster, and goat are frightened by what looks like a large tiger watching them from bushes across the river. Dog discovers it is the head of a tiger which has been cut and swims the others across, so he can eat tiger meat and the other two can eat the seeds and grass they like. Then dog pulls goat onto a branch and rooster flies into the tree where they will sleep. In the night, a pride of tigers finds the head beneath the tree. They are mourning the lost tiger when goat trembles so with fear he begins to fall. Seeing this, rooster claps his wings loudly, and the dog shouts "take the biggest." As goat crashes down on them, the tigers flee, sure that hunters are after them.

CONNECTIONS

Dogs. Fear. Friendship. Goats. Roosters. Teamwork. Tigers.

---

129. THE OLD ONES' FRIENDSHIP: THE DOG, THE JAGUAR, AND THE COYOTE

Victor Montejo, *The Bird Who Cleans the World and Other Mayan Fables*
Jakaltek Maya. Guatemala

A jaguar, a dog, and a coyote who have all been pushed out of their communities because they are too old to be useful decide to team up with each other. They agree to share food and protect each other. When the coyote finds a small piece of bread which won't feed them all, they decide that the oldest should get it. Senor dog says he has been alive since ancient times when a wise man was to come. Jaguar counters that he was there the first time the sun shone. While they debate, the coyote quietly eats the bread. When they realize the bread is gone, they send him away because he does not know how to behave among friends. Meanwhile, the jaguar and the dog decide they must have ridden in the Ark together and are the oldest animals on earth.

CONNECTIONS

Coexistence. Competition. Friendship. Humorous tales. Hunger. Old age. Punishments. Selfishness. Status. Teamwork.

---

130. OLD DOG AND YOUNG COYOTE

Richard and Judy Dockrey Young, *1492: New World Tales*
Otomi People. Mexico

A young coyote greets an old dog, who is sad because the humans he lives with think he is too old to be of much use. Young Coyote whispers a plan to Old Dog. The next day Woman brings Baby outside to the cactus den and leaves for a moment to get something from inside. Young Coyote runs up and tugs Baby gently by the foot. Woman screams; Man rushes out with his knife; and Old Dog races over barking at Young Coyote. Young Coyote lets go of Baby and runs off as if in fear. Woman tells Man they must keep Old Dog to guard the cactus den. That night Young Coyote sneaks back, and old Dog gladly shares his bone with rabbit meat still on it, a gift from the grateful family.

CONNECTIONS

Babies. Cleverness. Coexistence. Coyotes. Dogs. Old age. Problem solving. Teamwork.

---

131. THE ARRIVAL OF THE DOG INTO THE WORLD / LA LLEGADA DEL PERRO AL MUNDO

Pedro Cholotío Temó and Alberto Barreno, *The Dog Who Spoke /
El perro que habló*
Tzutuhil Maya People. Santiago Atitlán, Guatemala

The god of animals tells the dog what he is and that he must search for the owner who will be his friend and to whom he will be loyal in return. The god tells him this owner is the strongest being in the world. The lonely dog searches for a long time. The deer is swift, but eats only vegetation, and fears the jaguar and the mountain lion. The raccoon eats raw fish and also wants guarding from those big animals. The mountain lion and the jaguar need the dog to guard them against man. Now the dog knows that man is the strongest being in the world and finds him eating lunch. The man welcomes him. The dog will guard his house while the man works in the field and hunts for their food. The dog is grateful and tells the man where the animals who disappointed him live. Man and dog become friends, just as the god said.

CONNECTIONS

Bargains. Dogs. Friendship. Gods and animals. Identity. Journeys. Loyalty. Origin tales. Quests. Status. Strength. Teamwork.

Leadership

132. THE KING OF THE ANIMALS

Victor Montejo, *The Bird Who Cleans the World and Other Mayan Fables*
Jakaltek Maya People. Guatemala

Jaguar and mountain lion are competing to see which is worthy of top status. Rabbit tricks jaguar, who has come looking for him, by riding on his back and shaming him, because it looks like rabbit is in control. The decision is that jaguar's claws and impulsivity make him less trustworthy. The others just never know whether he is going to kill all the animals to satisfy his hunger. The mountain lion is calmer, and so he is chosen as king.

CONNECTIONS

Anansi. Character. Competition. Emperors, kings & queens. Jaguars. Leadership. Pumas. Rabbits. Spiders. Status. Tigers. Tricksters.

HOW ELSE THIS STORY IS TOLD

African American variation from Suriname:
Anansi Rides Tiger—Melville J. Herskovits and Frances Herskovits, *Suriname Folk-Lore.* Anansi the Spider tricks Tiger by seeming to ride and control him.
Note: See also Why Rabbits Have Long Ears (263) for a love story twist on this story.

---

133. THE ELECTION OF THE PAWI AS A LEADER

Dorothy St. Aubyn, *Caribbean Fables: Animal Stories from Guyana and the Antilles*
Guyana

The birds and animals around Roraima Mountain quarrel so much that a council forms to choose a leader who can solve their disputes. However, someone has an objection to everyone suggested to be that leader. Owl notices that a pawi is not part of the argumentative group and says he should lead. Pawi protests that neither his voice nor his whistle are loud, but Owl says that this quiet gives him wisdom. The others agree. Pawi is fine with keeping his own name, for he wants his family to recognize him, but he would like to have something to show that he is their leader. Owl suggests a crest for his head.

CONNECTIONS

Animals. Appearance. Arguments. Birds. Character. Coexistence. Interspecies conflict. Leadership. Origin tales. Owls. Pawis. Quiet. Status. Wisdom.

---

134. THE SACRED AMULET

Genevieve Barlow, *Latin American Tales from the Pampas to Mexico City*
Quiché Maya People. Guatemala

The Quiché soothsayer predicts that the chief's son Quetzal will be skillful and brave and have an uncommon future. At the ceremony to name Quetzal as chieftan, the soothsayer hangs an amulet, a tiny hummingbird wing, around Quetzal's neck and predicts that he will never die, protected by the gods. Queztal is beloved, and everyone in the tribe celebrates this honor except for Quetzal's uncle, Chiruma, who had hopes that he might become chieftain one day. Chiruma notices that arrows seem to deflect from Quetzal during battle and thinks the amulet may be what protects him. Chiruma steals that amulet one night. Noticing that it is gone, Quetzal is on his way to the soothsayer for help, when Chiruma shoots him with an arrow. The gods transform Quetzal into a breathtaking bird, with a green body and red breast and a blue-green tail three to six feet long, which is protected and sacred to Guatemalans.

Connections

Amulets. Aspirations. Birds. Caciques and chieftains. Deceit. Enmity. Jealousy. Magic. Magic amulets. Murder. Origin tales. Prophecies. Quetzals. Soothsayers. Theft. Transformations. Uncles and nephews.

How Else This Story Is Told

The Hummingbird King: A Guatemalan Legend—Argentina Palacios
The Lucky Charm—Anita Stern, *World Folktales*
Quetzal Will Never Die / Quetzal no muere nunca—Genevieve Barlow, *Stories from Latin America / Historias de Latinoamérica*

---

135. The Dwarf of Uxmal / El enano de uxmal

Genevieve Barlow and William N. Stivers, *Stories from Mexico / Historias de México*
Maya People. Mexico

When the witch in the woods asks for a son, the oldest wise man gives her an egg and tells her to keep it warm. A little boy is born from that egg, walking and talking right away. He stops growing when he is three, but is smart and knows the animals of the woods. When the boy rings the little bell with the rod he discovers under the witch's fireplace, a sound like thunder shakes all of Uxmal, and the king is afraid because prophecies say that the one who does this will be the next king. King's servants appear to lead the boy to the king, who challenges him to three tests of strength and intelligence. The boy bests the king in the first two tests, but the king really does not want to turn Uxmal over to a dwarf. The next morning, however, the king wakes to find that the dwarf has built a palace right next to his overnight. The last test is for the two of them to make statues of themselves to place in the fire. The one whose statue does not burn will be king. The dwarf's statues of clay survive where the king's wooden ones do not. So the dwarf of Uxmal rules, with the witch alongside.

CONNECTIONS

Animal helpers. Appearance. Competition. Drought. Dwarves. Emperors, kings & queens. Leadership. Magic bells. Prophecies. Rain. Size. Sorcerers. Strength. Temples. Tortoises and turtles. Uxmal. Warlocks and witches.

HOW ELSE THIS STORY IS TOLD

The Dwarf of Uxmal—Richard and Judy Dockery Young, *1492: New World Tales.* Yucatec Maya. Chichén Itzá, Mexico

The Dwarf Who Became King / El Enaño Rey—Idella Purnell. In Maite Suarez-Rivas, *An Illustrated Treasury of Latino Read-Aloud Stories.* In this version, the dwarf is not a good person, and people rise against him.

The Dwarf-Wizard of Uxmal—Susan Hand Shetterly. In this telling, when a drought comes, the old woman sends the boy dwarf back to order the governor to call for rain. No rains fall until the dwarf follows the old woman's snake friend into a hole in the jungle floor where forty tortoises sleep in a white cave. He tells them of the hardship the drought has brought to Uxmal and the animals. The tortoises walk out of the cave and growl, and thunder begins. The Rain God sends down rain, and the people of Uxmal believe Tol has magical powers.

---

136. THE WALL OF PALPAN

Alex Whitney, *Voices in the Wind*

Aztec People. Mexico

Harmony among the clans and in nature dies with the end of Quetzalcoatl's reign. Frost followed by drought causes a shortage of food, and marauding tribesmen who used to be farmers attack towns, taking goods, destroying buildings, and killing people. Some people flee to Palpan on a mountain plateau, where they are safe until the Warrior Chieftan Tok reports to Princess Mitla that he has seen smoke nearby. They are outnumbered, but Princess Mitla has a plan. She tells Tok to keep his warriors circling boulders, so it looks like the fighting force is huge. The ruse works, and the tribesmen retreat. Rain ends the drought, and a new emperor restores order. The Princess's brother rebuilds his own city and wants to know what kind of wall Mitla's people built that kept Palpan safe. She answers that every man was a brick.

CONNECTIONS

Conflict. Heroes and heroines. Illusions. Leadership. Princes and princesses. Problem solving. Rescues. Teamwork. Walls. Warriors.

The Residents

137. THE CURIOUS MICE

Victor Montejo, *The Bird Who Cleans the World and Other Mayan Fables*

Jakaltek Maya People. Guatemala

Some country mice are all very interested to know if the new human baby that arrives will be a boy or girl. The future ease or difficulty they will have surviving and finding food depends on this. One mouse says women cover pots, but men are more careless. Another says men lay out traps, whereas women are afraid. As they debate, a hungry cat sends them fleeing. It turns out, twins are born—a boy and a girl.

CONNECTIONS

Babies. Coexistence. Curiosity. Gender. Humorous tales. Identity. Mice. Perspective. Twins.

---

138. THE STORY OF THE TOAD AND THE DEER / EL CUENTO DEL SAPO Y EL VENADO

Pedro Cholotío Temó and Alberto Barreno, *The Dog Who Spoke / El perro que habló*
Maya People. Guatemala

Drought on earth is causing suffering because of the sins of humans. The animals want to send a delegation to ask the god for forgiveness and implore him to send rain to fill the rivers and streams. The rabbit says the mountain lion and jaguar will not be admitted to heaven because they are too evil and ugly, even though they are swift. The animals elect turtle, who takes many days gathering everything she will need. Their pleas are heard, and the god sends rain. Everyone rejoices, except for toad, who does not know how to be happy. When toad proposes a race, the other animals laugh because he can only hop. At last the deer agrees to race him, certain he will win. Toad says he is smarter. He arranges toads all along the path and places himself close to the finish line. The next toad answers that he is going ahead and jumps each time deer calls to see where he is. And so toad wins, without running at all.

CONNECTIONS

Arrogance. Basilisk. Braggarts. Character. Competition. Deer. Drought. Foxes. Frogs and toads. Gods and animals. Horseflies. Insects. Jaguars. Messengers. Origin tales. Rabbits. Rain. Speed. Tortoises and turtles. Tricksters.

HOW ELSE THIS STORY IS TOLD

Brazilian variation:

The Deer and the Turtle—Carlos Estevâo de Oliveira. In Johannes Wilbert, *Folk Literature of the Gê Indians, Vol. 1.* Apinaye People. Turtle challenges Deer to a race when deer complains that he has eaten Deer's fruit. Turtle plants many other turtles along the route and wins.

Chilean variation:

The Fox Who Was Not So Smart—M.A. Jagendorf and R.S. Boggs, *The King of the Mountains.* When the Fox challenges Horsefly to a race, Horsefly hides quietly in Fox's tail. When the Fox refuses to pay up, Horsefly gathers his family to bite Fox to death.

Variation from Guyana:

The Jabuty and the Jaguar—Frances Carpenter, *South American Wonder Tales*. Many tortoises placed along the race route fool the jaguar.

Maya variations from Guatemala:

The Rabbit and the Crab—Fernando Peñalosa, *Tales and Legends of the Q'Anjob'al Maya* and as Crab Tricks Rabbit (at last!)—Don Pedro Miguel Say. Also in Fernando Peñalosa, *Maya Culture—Traditional Storyteller's Tales* (Online). Kanjobal Maya. Rabbit and Crab team up to grow carrots, but then they argue about who should get the tops and who the bottoms of the harvest. They run a race to decide, and though Rabbit is overconfident, Crab wins by hiding on Rabbit's tail.

The Rabbit and the Crab / El conejo y el cangrejo—Susan Conklin Thompson, Keith Steven Thompson, and Lidia López de López, *Mayan Folktales*

The Race of Toad and Deer—Pat Mora. The race is proposed when the deer scolds the toad and his friends for singing.

Mexican variations:

How the Basilisk Obtained His Crest—Alfredo Barrera Vazquez. In Frances Toor, *A Treasury of Mexican Folkways*. Maya. Quintana Roo, Mexico. Everyone thinks Big Deer is sure to outrun everyone, but young Basilisk tells everyone to shut their eyes and wins by jumping on the tail of Big Deer. The prize is a big sombrero from the Lord of the Woods.

Rabbit's Last Race—Pleasant DeSpain, *Thirty-Three Multicultural Tales to Tell*. The braggart Rabbit is so confident about his own swiftness, that he lets Frog choose the course. Frog lines up four hundred frogs all the same size as himself through the tall swamp grass and wins.

The Race Between the Rabbit and the Frog—Dan Storm, *Pictures Tales from Mexico*. Frog is fed up with Rabbit's bragging about his speed with Frog and tricks him in the race.

---

139. WHO'S STRONG?

M.A. Jagendorf and R.S. Boggs, *The King of the Mountains*
Guyana

Jaguar is hungry and growling. When he pounces on Lightning, who seems to shrug him off, Jaguar gets mad. Jaguar starts showing off how strong he is. Lightning doesn't say anything, until Jaguar sits down, tired. Then Lightning swings his club, and thunder and rain roar. Frightened, Jaguar climbs a tree, but Lightning smashes all the trees around, and Jaguar falls out. Jaguar runs to hide in a cave, but Lightning smashes the rocks. Wherever Jaguar goes, Lightning follows. Shivering with cold and fright and very wet, Jaguar stops running. Lightning stops, too, and tells him others are also strong, and he should quit boasting.

CONNECTIONS

Allegories and parables. Braggarts. Cautionary tales. Character. Competition. Fear. Gods and animals. Hunger. Jaguars. Lightning. Origin tales. Punishments.

140. THE TOAD'S SPOTS / LAS MANCHAS DEL SAPO

Genevieve Barlow, *Stories from Latin America / Historias de Latinoamérica*
Argentina

Toad sneaks into Crow's guitar case, when Crow refuses to take him to the party in the sky, which he says is only for beautiful birds. Once there, Toad is having a great time singing and dancing, though he does worry about how he is going to return to earth. Mr. Crow is surprised to see him and suspects a trick, but he does not see when Toad sneaks back into the guitar while he making a thank-you speech. The guitar turns over on the way home, and though toad begs stones to move out of the way as he is falling, they do not. He is bruised with spots and never wants to fly again. Toad never deceives a crow again, either, but his trip to the clouds does let him know ever after whenever it is going to rain.

CONNECTIONS

Angels. Birds. Buzzards. Cause and effect. Crows. Deceit. Ducks. Eagles. Flight. Frogs and toads. Hawks. Heaven. Jealousy. Journeys to other realms. Origin tales. Rabbits. Revenge. Sky worlds. Tortoises and turtles. Tricksters.

HOW ELSE THIS STORY IS TOLD

Argentinan variation:
Las manchas del sapo / How the Toad Got His Spots—Marjorie E. Hermann. Here, toad's carrier
    is an eagle.
Toad's Spots / Las manchas del sapo—Paula Martin, *Pachamama Tales*

Brazilian variations:
How the Toad Got His Bumps and Bruises—At *Vida de Latinos: Folk Tales from Brazil* (Online).
    Buzzard is flattered, when Toad asks him to take him up to the party in the sky, but sneaks
    into his violin case and gets inadvertently dropped by Falcon on the way home.
Icarus the Frog—Nurit Baker. In Nadia Grosser Nagarajan, *Pomegranate Seeds*. Jewish People.
    When Rana the frog gets left behind up at the heavenly party, a kindly angel brings her a
    pair of wax wings. However, the sun is up when she flies, and the wings melt. Rana falls
    hard, but you can tell from her croaks how happy she is to have survived.
Jabuti the Tortoise: A Trickster Tale from the Amazon—Gerald McDermott. Tupi People and
    Guarani People. Amazonia. Vulture is jealous of the way Jabuti plays the flute and offers to
    give him a ride up to the festival in heaven and then turns upside down in midair on purpose.
    After the tortoise's shell breaks, the King of Heaven commands the birds to gather up the
    pieces of shell and patch him back together. He gifts the birds who helped patch Jabuti with
    bright new colors.
A Party in Heaven—Livia de Almeida and Ana Portella, *Brazilian Folktales*. Turtle gets Vulture
    to take him up to the party and then hides in Vulture's guitar case.

Maya variation from Guatemala:
Toad and Hawk—John Bierhorst, *The Monkey's Haircut*. Chorti Maya. Guatemala. Toad wants
    to come along when Hawk goes to Our Father up in the sky. Even though Hawk has agreed
    to take him the toad hides himself inside Hawk's bag and will not tell Hawk how he got
    there. Toad tries to float back down by himself, but crashes, which explains his fat belly.

Variations from Nicaragua:

Mister Frog's Dream—Genevieve Barlow, *Latin American Tales from the Pampas to Mexico City.* Nicarao People. Mister Frog is a show-off who dreams of flying. He gets dropped by some ducks who are also showing off, when he opens his mouth to tell them he is getting dizzy.

Uncle Rabbit Flies to Heaven—M.A. Jagendorf and R.S. Boggs, *The King of the Mountains.* Buzzard wants to get even with Tío Conejo for playing tricks, so when Rabbit wants to go up to the clouds for the feast, Buzzard tells him to brings his guitar and then flies wildly around, until Rabbit whacks him on the head with the guitar and they both fall.

Note: *See also* Señor Rattlesnake Learns to Fly (223), where the rider gets punished for being ungrateful and insulting to others.

---

141. THE FLY WHO DREAMED THAT HE WAS AN EAGLE

Augusto Monterroso in Marcos Kurtycz and Ana García Kobeh,
    Tigers and Opossums: Animal Legends
Mexico

A fly dreams that he is an eagle and can soar over the mountains. But then his dream turns. His big, heavy body will not let him do the little things a fly can do. He bumps into walls and cannot land on a cowpat. Still, the fly wakes disgruntled that he is still a fly.

CONNECTIONS

Allegories and parables. Aspirations. Discontent. Dreams. Flight. Identity. Perspective.

---

142. *MOON ROPE: A PERUVIAN FOLKTALE /* *UN LAZO A LA LUNA: UNA LEYENDA PERUANA*

Lois Ehlert
Peru

Fox has always dreamed of going to the moon. Now he plans to hook a grass rope to the tip of the moon when it is crescent and climb up. He invites his friend Mole to come along to eat the worms he likes up there. They braid the rope together. But how to get it up there? The rope keeps falling back when Fox tries throwing it high. Mole suggests that they convince birds to attach one end to the moon. The birds do, and the two start climbing. Fox makes it up, but Mole nervously slips. A bird flies him home, where other animals tease Mole about having let go on purpose. Mole runs and hides underground; he never sees Fox looking down when the moon is full.

CONNECTIONS

Aspirations. Bird helpers. Condors. Discontent. Fear. Foxes. Friendship. Jealousy. Moles. Origin tales. Parrots. Ridicule. Teamwork. Unkindness.

How Else This Story Is Told

The Fox and the Mole—Genevieve Barlow, *Latin American Tales from the Pampas to Mexico City*. Condor flies the rope up for them, but the mole is nervous about climbing. The parrot laughs that mole will never make it, and mole accuses the parrot of being jealous that he's not going. Fox makes it up safely, but the parrot pecks at the rope so it breaks. Condor catches mole.

---

143. The Coyote and Juan's Maguey

Dan Storm, *Pictures Tales from Mexico*
Mexico

Juan's only crop is a giant maguey, which he cares for tenderly. He takes honey water from a hole in the center of the plant with a gourd and sells it in jars. His giant maguey gives him enough agua miel to sell and make pulque from. One day, however, Juan's gourd comes out dry. Tracks tell him a coyote thief has come in the night. Juan makes a corral around the maguey with a little door just big enough for a coyote and leaves a little agua miel and pulque as bait. When he hears the coyote, he yells. The startled coyote starts zooming around inside the corral so fast, he cannot see the way out. Juan is laughing so hard, he doesn't club the coyote when it finally runs away.

Connections

Coyotes. Farmers. Fences. Humorous tales. Maguey. Plants. Thieves. Traps.

How Else This Story Is Told

Juan's Maguey Plant—Pleasant DeSpain, *Thirty-Three Multicultural Tales to Tell*

---

144. Why Armadillos Are Funny

Barbara McBride Smith in David Holt and Bill Mooney,
　　More Ready-to-Tell Tales
Guyana

Long ago, when armadillos were awake during the day, friendly Apollo makes others laugh by making his eyes bulge and wiggling his tongue. One day, he leaps straight up out of a ditch just as roadrunner is racing by and makes that face. Roadrunner falls backwards, frightened, and then laughs when he sees Apollo's silly face. Apollo does this over and over to many creatures. Meanwhile lightning resents the armadillo's ability to halt creatures suddenly. She thinks that is her specialty. Lightning sneaks up on Apollo as he hides and strikes him on the head. He goes through contortions and then curls into a ball and faints. When Apollo revives, he rolls into a tree, which cracks his shell. Acorns fall. As onlookers gather, he pretends he planned all this. The crowd laughs, including lightning, until she realizes he is stealing her show. The new bolt she aims at him misses. Animals keep laughing, which is good protection for armadillo.

CONNECTIONS
Armadillos. Character. Conflict. Jealousy. Laughter. Lightning. Origin tales. Practical jokes.
    Resentment. Status.

---

145. THE CARVERS
Alex Whitney, *Voices in the Wind*
Maya People. Yucatan, Mexico

Though they argue a lot, Apu and Coh are woodcutters and friends. They work as a team, with Apu chopping down trees and Coh making blowgun darts from the wood for hunters. Both villagers hope to achieve something that will be of service to their ruler Hunac. When Apu sees some fine-grained wood, he decides to use half to make an ornament for Hunac's pyramid. Coh will make an ornament, too, from the other half. Coh says Apu's axe is too clumsy, and Apu says Coh's knife is too small. They work secretly on their ornaments and carry them to the king, wrapped in bark, wondering all the way whether the other's criticism about their work is valid. Hunac waits at the top of his palace pyramid in a long cloak and headdress made of colored feathers and asks if they have brought something for him. They uncover their carvings, and each looks only at what his friend has made. Hunac admires both, which look very similar and invites both to stay with him as master craftsmen.

CONNECTIONS
Art. Competition. Doubt. Emperors, kings & queens. Friendship. Hunac Ceel. Rewards. Sculpture.
    Self-esteem. Talents. Teamwork. Tests. Woodcutters.

---

146. THE PADRE WHO NEVER WORRIED
Elsie Spicer Eells, *The Brazilian Fairy Book*
Brazil

A Padre has posted a sign saying that he never worries, and the King wants to know if this is true. He tells the Padre to return in three days to answer three questions or be put to death. The Padre's servant offers to take his place. The servant answers the first two questions in a way that the king cannot contest. To the King's third question—"What am I thinking?"—the servant cleverly tells the King that he thinks he is talking to the Padre who never worries.

CONNECTIONS
Character. Cleverness. Emperors, kings & queens. Humorous tales. Identity. Kings and queens.
    Perspective. Priests and priestesses. Questions. Servants. Tests. Worry.

147. Señor Coyote and the Old Lion

Dan Storm, *Pictures Tales from Mexico*
Mexico

Mountain Lion is hungry in his old age. No longer fast enough to run after prey, he tries to entice smaller animals to come into his cave. When Señor Coyote shows up, Mountain Lion points out all the different tracks of animals who have come to look inside the cave. But Señor Coyote notices that the tracks only lead one direction—in. Mountain Lion tries to convince him that those who enter, like it so well that they stay. Señor Coyote comes closer, wondering if those animals do stay and exit through a back door. At that moment, Mountain Lion snaps at him, but Señor Coyote gets away.

Connections
Coyotes. Escapes. Interspecies conflict. Lions. Old age. Tricksters.

148. So Say the Little Monkeys

M.A. Jagendorf and R.S. Boggs, *The King of the Mountains*
Brazil

Little monkeys with black mouths live in the tall palms along the Rio Negro. At night, they get pricked by thorns when they try to sleep and get drenched by rains and shiver in the wind. Every night the father monkeys say that tomorrow they will build a house to protect them. But every morning, the monkeys are so happy to swing among the trees. They chatter to each other, and even when the mothers remind the fathers about building a house, everyone is too busy playing and eating fruit; they say they will do it tomorrow. So the day goes, and they never build houses, always putting it off, saying *amambâ*.

Connections
Character. Monkeys. Procrastination. Tasks.

How Else This Story Is Told
Monkeys in the Rain—Margaret Read MacDonald, *Five Minute Tales* and in *Teaching with Story*
So Say the Little Monkeys—Nancy Van Laan
The Tomorrow Monkeys—Bill Gordh, *Stories in Action*

149. The Ant Who Learned to Play the Flute

Angel Vigil, *The Eagle on the Cactus*
Mexico

A hardworking ant imagines something greater than this work digging tunnels in the anthill and hauling back pieces of food. He teaches himself to play melodies on an abandoned flute he finds, and one day leaves, hoping to find work with his music. He arrives at a much larger anthill and plays for the queen, who invites him to stay on as the royal musician. When a messenger announces that fierce army ants are almost upon the anthill, the musician tells the queen his plan. He will play from a hidden spot in hopes of distracting the enemy so the queen's soldiers can surprise them. His plan saves the anthill. Not only is the ant able to continue his dream of making music to live, but he also wins the heart of the queen.

CONNECTIONS
Allegories and parables. Ants. Aspirations. Discontent. Heroes and heroines. Identity. Insects. Music. Problem solving. Rescues. Talents. Work.

---

150. TOO CLEVER
Pleasant DeSpain, *The Emerald Lizard*
Uruguay

Señor Fox wakes Señor Rooster, who is up in a tree. He urges the rooster to come down to hear some news, but Señor Rooster does not trust the hungry fox. At last, Señor Fox calls up that a new law says no animal can hurt another in the forest now. Again, he asks Señor Rooster to come down so he can explain it to him, and Señor Rooster can spread the word in the morning when he crows. Señor Rooster is thinking this may be real, when he sees some wild dogs heading their way. He tells Señor Fox that these new friends are heading over to join them. Señor Fox desperately wants to know which direction the dogs are coming from. He runs in what he thinks is the opposite direction, not knowing that Señor Rooster has sent him right straight to the pack.

CONNECTIONS
Allegories and parables. Chickens and hens. Cleverness. Coexistence. Coyotes. Deceit. Dogs. Foxes. Interspecies conflict. Peace. Roosters. Tricksters. Trust.

HOW ELSE THIS STORY IS TOLD
Kanjobal Maya variation from Guatemala:
The Coyote and the Hen—Fernando Peñalosa, *Tales and Legends of the Q'Anjob'al Maya*
Coyote Doesn't Fool Old Hen At All (The Coyote and the Hen)—Don Pedro Miguel Say. In Fernando Peñalosa, *Maya Culture—Traditional Storyteller's Tales* (Online).

Variation from Uruguay:
Oversmart Is Bad Luck—M.A. Jagendorf and R.S. Boggs, *The King of the Mountains* and in Lila Green, *Folktales of Spain and Latin America*

---

151. SEÑOR COYOTE AND THE DOVE
Dan Storm, *Pictures Tales from Mexico*
Mexico

Mother Paloma, the dove, is not worried at first when Señor Coyote finds her singing to her babies in a tree. She feels like she is far enough away. Señor Coyote asks politely at first for her to give him the ugliest *palomito* and then snarls that he will knock down the tree and eat all three babies if she doesn't give him one. Now Mother Dove is starting to feel afraid. Still, she tells the arrogant coyote that he cannot sing the way she can. Señor Coyote tries, and Mother Dove tells him to make his yodels louder and louder. She knows there are two dogs that live nearby and wants them to hear. Señor Coyote thinks she is just trying to distract him and zooms in circles around the tree to make the dove dizzy enough to fall. The dogs do not come. Then Mother Paloma remembers that the ranchero calls them by imitating her own whistle. So, she sends her song out as strongly as she can. The dogs arrive.

CONNECTIONS

Birds. Cleverness. Coyotes. Dogs. Doves. Fear. Flattery. Interspecies conflict. Music. Rescues. Tricksters. Trust.

---

152. The Coyote and the Two Dogs

Dan Storm, *Pictures Tales from Mexico*
Mexico

Chased from different directions by two pairs of dogs, Señor Coyote takes refuge in a small cave up on the mountainside, just as all four close in on him. The dogs cannot get in and whine, and then all is quiet. Señor Coyote congratulates himself on cleverly escaping. He cockily asks different parts of his body what they did to help. His feet, ears, and eyes all have good explanations, and Coyote praises them. He looks disparagingly at his tail, which doesn't answer. Coyote scolds the tail for slowing him down with weight. Its feelings hurt, the tail says it had originally waved the dogs over to start the chase. Señor Coyote accuses the tail of being on the side of the dogs and tells the tail to go. When it doesn't, he starts backing his tail out of the cave. The dogs, who have never left, pounce.

CONNECTIONS

Accusations. Arrogance. Coyotes. Dogs. Foxes. Humorous tales. Interspecies conflict. Resentment. Tails.

Where Else This Story Appears

Señor Coyote and the Dogs—Dan Storm in Joanna Cole, *Best-Loved Folktales of the World* and in Harold Courlander, *Ride with the Sun*

How Else This Story Is Told

Coyote's Tail—Bill Gordh, *Stories in Action*
Fox and His Tail—Martha Hamilton and Mitch Weiss, *Tales Kids Can Tell*. Mexico and Nicaragua

153. *THE FARMYARD JAMBOREE*
Margaret Read MacDonald (Book with CD)
Chile

Clucking red hen, quacking white duck, purring yellow cat, barking black dog, bleating white sheep, oinking pink pig, mooing brown cow, and neighing grey horse—a little boy loves the growing farmyard pet collection his relatives keep adding to, in a cumulative counting song.

CONNECTIONS
Counting tales. Farms. Pets. Songs.

WHERE ELSE THIS STORY APPEARS
On *YouTube*, sung by Bob King (Online)

154. THE DANCING FOX
John Bierhorst, *Black Rainbow: Legends of the Incas and Myths of Ancient Peru*
Peru

A fox who flatters the women hides his tail inside pants when he goes dancing. All the young women want to dance with him. One woman is annoyed that she doesn't get more of his attention. She eggs the others on to make him stay longer. The fox stays, but when he tries to leave and they hold him, the fox growls and bites as foxes do. His bushy tail flies out as he flees. Humiliated by their laughter, the fox never returns.

CONNECTIONS
Character. Dances. Disguises. Flattery. Foxes. Humiliation. Identity. Jealousy.

155. TASI AND THE ORANGES
Shirley Climo, *Monkey Business*
Amazonia, Brazil

From high in the brazilwood tree in the forest, a young howler monkey is enticed by the oranges she sees in the farmer's grove. Her family warns that her father never returned from that orchard, but she thinks she can sneak into the grove before the farmer arrives. She tries two more times and gets chased off. Then she sees the farmer put a funny little man in the tree. She calls up to that man, and when he doesn't answer, she climbs up the tree and strikes him and becomes firmly stuck. She shakes the branch hard until the limb falls down into a fire ant's nest. She is still stuck to the little man and gets badly bitten. Then, the little man starts melting, for he is just made of beeswax and seeds. She is able to pull herself free bit by bit and run home. But when the little howler monkey thinks of those oranges, she remembers what happened and howls.

CONNECTIONS

Curiosity. Dolls. Escapes. Farmers. Howler monkeys. Interspecies conflict. Monkeys. Origin tales. Oranges. Perseverance. Punishments. Theft. Traps. Warnings.

Note: For other stories where the farmer has made a wax figure to catch a thief see many variants under The Wax Doll, the Coyote, and Rabbit (385).

156. BETTER ALONE THAN IN BAD COMPANY

Marcos Kurtycz and Ana García Kobeh, *Tigers and Opossums: Animal Legends*
Mexico

A stranger fox invites a dog to accompany him to the next village, but keeps changing which side he would like the dog to walk on. The fox says it is because people will be critical since he is a stranger. The dog acquiesces and keeps switching, right, left, right again once they are past the village. However, when hunters fire at them, the fox runs to the other side. The dog is hit in the paw, and the fox runs off. The hunters tell the dog he is better off without that fox.

CONNECTIONS

Character. Deceit. Dogs. Foxes. Friendship. Hunters. Interspecies conflict. Outsiders. Selfishness.

157. THE GENTLE PEOPLE

Susan Milord, *Tales Alive! Ten Multicultural Folktales with Activities*
Patagonia, Argentina

There is a time when gentle people, ruled by a kindly prince, live in peace with each other and the natural world. Each month the prince grants them one wish, but they hardly need anything they do not already have. He only forbids them to travel north beyond the stars of the Southern Cross. One day a man follows a colorful bird into the forbidden forest. He walks into a clearing where men with pointed teeth are eating animals raw and fighting with each other. They attack him, and he flees. The prince tells him those greedy, selfish people will invade now that they know others are here. The people ask to be transformed so they can hide. They follow the prince to a river and turn into guanacos. Legend says that when a guanaco dies, a gold-tipped blue flower will bend toward earth and return a gentle person to the land.

CONNECTIONS

Allegories and parables. Coexistence. Cultural conflict. Ecology. Escapes. Guanacos. Greed. Kindness. Magic. Magic flowers. Origin tales. Peace. Princes and princesses. Selfishness. Supernatural beings. Transformations.

158. *Uncle Nacho's Hat: A Folktale from Nicaragua / El sombrero del Tío Nacho: Un Cuento de Nicaragua*

Harriet Rohmer
Nicaragua

When Uncle Nacho's niece Ambrosia presents him with a new hat one morning, he thanks her, but now he does not know what to do with his beloved old hat. Even though the old hat has so many holes it is no longer good for keeping the sun off or fanning kitchen flames, it has becomes so much a part of him. Uncle Nacho places it on top of the garbage, thinking someone who needs it will take it, but Ambrosia's mother recognizes it and brings it back to him. Uncle Nacho hangs the hat on a tree at the edge of town, thinking someone may appreciate it. A gentleman takes it, but then two boys who recognize the hat as Uncle Nacho's think he stole it. They return it to Uncle Nacho. Uncle Nacho takes the new hat off. Ambrosia suggests he introduce the new hat around. So he does and even comes to like it, too.

Connections

Appearance. Discomfort. Gifts. Hats. Humorous tales. Identity. Recycling. Uncles and nieces.

159. The Old Man and the Robbers

Elsie Spicer Eells, *The Brazilian Fairy Book*
Brazil

The royal treasury has been robbed, and none of the royal magicians have a clue who did it. A huge reward is offered. As one last try, the King has a poor old man brought to the palace, whom some think may be a magician, and gives him three days to find the thief. The old man pushes back from a full meal and says he has seen one. The royal servant quakes, sure he has been found out as one of the robbers. His companion serves the next meal, and the old man says now he has seen two. Certain now that they have been identified, both servants confess to the robbery.

Connections

Emperors, kings & queens. Humorous tales. Misunderstandings. Theft. Words.

160. Half a Blanket

Bill Gordh, *Stories in Action*
Mexico

After Juanita's grandmother dies, her grandfather comes to live with them. Juanita loves listening to his stories, but her parents feel like the house is just too small. They move Grandpa to the shed. Juanita finds him shivering one day in the cold. She searches for a blanket for him. When her father finds one, she asks him to cut it in half, so she can save part for when he gets old. Her father realizes then that Grandpa belongs inside the house with them.

CONNECTIONS

Allegories and parables. Blankets. Changes in attitude. Generations. Grandparents and grand-children. Honoring parents. Kindness. Old age. Parents and children. Respect. Righting a wrong.

161. THE CUPÊNDIA AMAZONS

Carlos Estevâo de Oliveira in Johannes Wilbert,
   Folk Literature of the Gê Indians, Vol. 1
Apinagé People. Brazil

Two Apinaye warriors decide to visit a settlement of women who have formed their own tribe near Sâo Vicente. Friendly Cupêndia hunters direct them to their village. The warriors tell the Cupêndia chief they have come to visit and are allowed to stay as guests. The women are not only good hunters, they work hard and grow many crops, too. There are only women there; even the children are all female. The Apinaye think they would each like to marry someone from the village, but Cupêndia law dictates that first they will have to win the woman in a race. The Apinaye run many races to try, but no matter how swift they are, the women run faster. Perhaps it is because the women consume only one meal at midday, all liquid. After four months, the men return alone to their own village, carrying gifts from the Cupêndia women.

CONNECTIONS

Aspirations. Competition. Gender. Independence. Marriage. Outsiders. Tests. Warriors.

162. TALE OF THE TEACHER

Ignacio Bizarro Ujpán, *Heart of Heaven, Heart of Earth*
Maya People

After lecturing the country *naturales* about the importance of education when they do not understand the Castilian he speaks, a city schoolteacher manages to arrange for a boatman to row him across a large river. He lectures the boatman that without knowing how to read and write, he has only half a life. The boat overturns midway across the river. The teacher cannot swim and starts to drown. The boatman says that without knowing how to swim the teacher could lose his whole life. Then he relents and saves the teacher, who gratefully acknowledges the usefulness of many kinds of knowledge.

CONNECTIONS

Allegories and parables. Arrogance. Boatmen. Changes in attitude. Cultural conflict. Humorous tales. Knowledge. Teachers.

163. WHO IS WISE? / ¿QUIÉN ES SABIO?

Genevieve Barlow and William N. Stivers, *Stories from Mexico /
Historias de México*
Mexico

It is the 19th century, and two meteorologists from the University of Mexico are traveling north of Mexico City to study the weather over their vacation. They arrive in a small town with all of their books and equipment and ask an old woman if they may sleep in her courtyard. She welcomes them, but says they would be better off inside because it is going to rain. The professors insist that is impossible, according to their equipment and knowledge. She simply repeats that she knows it is going to rain. The meteorologists think that she is ignorant and go to sleep in the courtyard. That night a heavy rain falls. In the morning, they apologize and ask the woman how she knew. She tells them her donkey, like all the donkeys in this town, is clever. Whenever it is going to rain, the donkey gives her a sign by heading for the stable and braying three times.

CONNECTIONS

Burros. Changes in attitude. Fools. Humorous tales. Knowledge. Rain. Teachers.

---

164. WOMEN WHO WANT TO BE MEN

Johannes Wilbert, *Yupa Folktales*
Yupa People. Sierra de Perijá, Venezuela

A Yupa girl, Uretane, wants no husband. She insists she is a man and looks like a man. When bathing, she discreetly goes to a different spot in the river from the other women. One woman comes to bathe with her. They fall in love and marry, and no one in the community objects. Uretane does the same work the men do, and the settlement accepts the pair. It only seems strange to visitors when one woman orders another around.

CONNECTIONS

Appearance. Coexistence. Gender. Homosexuality. Identity. Love. Perspective.

---

165. A MASTER AND HIS PUPIL

John Bierhorst, *Latin American Folktales*
Guatemala

Don Gumersindo Drydregs decides his son needs to learn a trade. The son keeps giving him reasons why this trade or that won't work out. Exasperated, his father sends him to apprentice to Juan Idler, so he can learn how to beg and thieve and live by his wits. Juan tells the son he will climb up and drop down figs for them to eat. The boy lies down on the ground and opens his mouth wide and waits for figs to fall right in. Juan says this boy does not need to learn how to loaf.

CONNECTIONS

Apprentices. Excuses. Humorous tales. Laziness. Parents and children. Teachers. Work.

VI

Reaching Out with Kindness

---

166. THE EMERALD LIZARD
Pleasant DeSpain, *The Emerald Lizard*
Guatemala

Well-known for his good deeds in Santiago de Guatemala in the late 1600s, Brother Pedro San Joseph de Bethancourt meets an indigenous man who is walking to town and looks down-hearted. When Brother Pedro asks, Juan tells him that he has no money to buy medicine for his sick wife and doesn't know what else to do. Brother Pedro swiftly bends down and catches a small green lizard. He holds the lizard to his heart and hands it to Juan. The lizard is now an emerald in Juan's hands. He thanks Brother Pedro. With that emerald, Juan is able to purchase medicine, as well as food and cows for the future. His wife recovers, and Juan earns a better living. Years later, he buys back the emerald lizard to return it to Brother Pedro. Juan finds the monk in the countryside and thanks him for his help long ago. Brother Pedro holds the emerald to his heart. It becomes alive once again and skitters away.

CONNECTIONS
Animal helpers. Bethencourt, Pedro de San Jose (Saint). Gratitude. Illness. Jewels. Kindness. Lizards. Magic. Magic lizards. Magic scorpions. Miracles. Monks. Poverty. Restoring Life. Reversals Of Fortune. Scorpions. Transformations. Vendors.

HOW ELSE THIS STORY IS TOLD
Guatemalan variations:
Emerald Lizard—Harold Courlander, *Ride with the Sun*
Golden Goodness—M.A. Jagendorf, *The King of the Mountains*

Mexican variation:
The Friar and the Scorpion / El fraile y el alacrán—Genevieve Barlow and William N. Stivers, *Stories from Mexico / Historias de México*. Down on his luck when three of his ships sink one after another with all of their cargo, the wealthy merchant don Lorenzo walks to the monastery of Friar Anselmo, where the friar catches a scorpion crawling up the wall and tells him to bring it to the pawnbroker.

167. THE MARRIAGE OF THE LITTLE HUMMINGBIRD

Marcos Kurtycz and Ana García Kobeh, *Tigers and Opossums: Animal Legends*
Mexico

Hummingbird needs to find more little dry branches for her nest, or she will not be able to marry. Her husband is also poor and cannot provide other items for their wedding. Saying that women are smart and two birds should be able to solve this problem, the sweet singer Xkokolché calls their friends with a tender, riveting song about a little bird who wants to get married and needs help. Deer, spider, Bacalché tree, iguana, spring, Xomzanil bird, and bee each offer a special gift, and others finish building the nest. Ever since then, hummingbirds have been happily adorned, and Xkokolché's song is the lullaby Mexican mothers sing to their children.

CONNECTIONS

Appearance. Birds. Friendship. Hummingbirds. Kindness. Music. Marriage. Origin tales. Poverty. Teamwork. Transformations.

168. HOW THE HUMMINGBIRD GOT ITS COLORS

Bill Gordh, *Stories in Action*
Mexico

Puma doesn't know she crushed Mouse's babies when walking through the grass, but in retaliation, Mouse glues Puma's eyes shut with pitch, dirt, and leaves while she is sleeping. Hummingbird hears the roar when Puma wakes and patiently cleans the sticky layers from Puma's eyes. Grateful, Puma opens her eyes and offers to dress up Hummingbird's gray feathers with color. She gathers green, black, red, blue, and silver colors from nature and orders Hummingbird to close his eyes. The colors fly up into the air and color Hummingbird's feathers splendidly as they drift down onto him.

CONNECTIONS

Accidents. Anger. Appearance. Birds. Colors. Eyes. Gratitude. Healing. Hummingbirds. Kindness. Mice. Pumas. Revenge. Transformations.

169. KING SOLOMON AND THE BEE / EL REY SALOMÓN Y LA ABEJA

Pedro Cholotío Temó and Alberto Barreno, *The Dog Who Spoke / El perro que habló*
Maya People. Panajachel, Guatemala

One day King Solomon helps a bee escape by opening a window in his house. Not too long afterward, the king's wisdom is going to be tested. He will be expected to choose the one real flower amid many artificial blooms. The bee returns to assure the restless king that he has come to return the favor, "Agrado quiere agrado," and will help Solomon recognize the real flower by alighting on it. This happens, and the next day people rejoice that they are governed by a king so wise and intelligent.

CONNECTIONS

Bees. Emperors, kings & queens. Gratitude. Insect helpers. Kindness. Reputation. Rescues. Solomon. Tests. Wisdom.

170. THE LITTLE FROG OF THE STREAM
Genevieve Barlow, *Latin American Tales from the Pampas to Mexico City*
Peru

A sad shepherdess who was stolen away from her llamas to serve King Condor up the mountain convinces the condor to let her go down to the stream to wash clothes. She reassures the condor that he will hear her beating clothes on the rocks and know she has not run away. There at the stream the weeping shepherdess meets a little frog who offers to help her escape. The frog says that she will magically transform to look like Collyur and beat the clothes, so Collyur can flee. Before she leaves, Collyur kisses the little frog on the forehead in thanks. After a while, King Condor flies down to see what is taking the shepherdess so long. He sees her step into the water and disappear. Underwater, the little frog becomes a frog again. The frog always considered herself ugly, but when she returns home, her family sees a star-shaped jewel on the spot where Collyur kissed her.

CONNECTIONS

Animal helpers. Appearance. Captivity. Condors. Escapes. Frogs and toads. Gifts. Gratitude. Herders. Heroes and heroines. Kindness. Magic. Rescues. Self-esteem. Stars. Transformations.

171. CRAB WITH THE FLYING EYES
Livia de Almeida and Ana Portella, *Brazilian Folktales*
Tualipang Pemón People. Amazonia, Brazil

Crab can sail his eyes out over Lake Palaná and summon them back into place again. Onça sees him and wants to do this, too, but Crab warns the jaguar queen that it is too dangerous, for the sharp-toothed *traíra* fish may try to eat those eyes. Still, Onça insists, so Crab sends jaguar's eyes out over the lake. When he calls for them to return, though, they do not come back. Onça is now blind and furious with Crab. She asks Buzzard for help. He flies away and brings back two bowls of crystal clear resin from the *jatoba* tree, which he heats. Telling her to be brave, Buzzard pours the milk into Onça's sockets and washes her eyes with water. Now the jaguar has eyes that shine like glass in the dark forest. Grateful, Onça asks what she can do in return, and Buzzard requests a tapir to eat now and for her to leave him part of every animal she kills.

CONNECTIONS

Blindness. Buzzards. Crabs. Eyes. Gratitude. Healing. Jaguars. Kindness. Magic eyes. Origin tales. Water.

HOW ELSE THIS STORY IS TOLD

Tualipang variation from Brazil and Guyana:

Little Crab with the Magic Eyes—Margaret Read MacDonald, Jennifer MacDonald Whitman, and Nathaniel Forrest Whitman, *Teaching with Story*

Pemón variation from Venezuela:

Tossing Eyes—Pleasant DeSpain, *The Emerald Lizard.* Little Crab warns Jaguar that the Oonka-Loonka Fish might swallow his eyes, and when he does, Vulture replaces them with two blue berries.

---

172. THE MESSENGER OF THE LORD AND THE POOR MAN WITH SEVEN CHILDREN / EL ENVIADO DEL SEÑOR Y EL POBRE HOMBRE ON SIETE HIJOS

Pedro Cholotío Temó and Alberto Barreno, *The Dog Who Spoke / El perro que habló*

Tzutuhil Maya People. Panajachel, Guatemala

A poor man's wife has always told him to be patient, that it is preferable to go from poverty to riches than the other way around. One day a *viejito*, a little old man with a long beard wearing an old hat and priest's cassock, asks if he can spend the night with them. Apologizing that they have no bed or food, the señor still welcomes the viejito to shelter with them. In the morning, the viejito tells the señor he will make him rich soon for his gracious hospitality, and the señor responds that he will continue to be patient. The viejito says, "He who listens to the advice of the old lives to be old." Now their house transforms for the better. When the viejito returns, the señor thanks him for his advice and the gift of their new house. He asks how he can return the favor. The viejito responds that he owns the riches of heaven and earth and leaves them money, which he says will never run out as long as they reach out and help poor people.

CONNECTIONS

Allegories and parables. Advice. Charity. Gods and humans. Generosity. Gratitude. Hospitality. Kindness. Patience. Poverty. Rewards. Wise men and wise women.

---

173. THE OLD MAN OF TEUTLI

Dan Keding, *Elder Tales: Stories of Wisdom and Courage from Around the World*

Mexico

Running thirstily over parched land, a little rabbit meets an old man, whom he recognizes as the Old Man of Teutli from his flat hat, long white hair and beard, and crutch. The little rabbit kisses the ground and worries aloud that the frail old man is out in this unforgiving landscape when he is needed by others. The rabbit offers him his own blood to drink, but the old man refuses. He says he will be able to find liquid in a cactus, and that the young rabbit must go to the spring at Mexcalco, where he will find what he needs to stay alive. After the rabbit runs off, the old man throws away his crutch. He says that he was testing the rabbit's love, and the rabbit's unselfishness will enrich the rabbit's own life.

CONNECTIONS
Animal helpers. Gods and animals. Kindness. Love. Old age. Rabbits. Self-sacrifice. Tests. Unselfishness.

HOW ELSE THIS STORY IS TOLD
The Old Man of Teutli—Idella Purnell, *The Merry Frogs.* Aztec People Milpa Alta, Mexico

---

174. THE GOOD MAN AND THE KIND MOUSE
M.A. Jagendorf and R.S. Boggs, *The King of the Mountains*
Chile

Little Mouse wants to repay Juan Hollinao's kindness in sharing food with her and suggests he marry the king's daughter. Juan is sure the king will not let his daughter marry a poor man, but Little Mouse has a plan. Transformed into a page boy, she asks the king to borrow a bushel basket so her master can measure his gold. The king thinks Juan Hollinao is rich and agrees, only if Juan Hollinao will return the basket himself. Little Mouse has a plan so Juan can arrive dressed well. The king's daughter falls in love with Juan, and the king agrees to their marriage. Little Mouse runs interference every time Juan tries to tell the king the truth about his poverty. She reassures Juan Hollinao that if God wills, "it rains when there is need of rain." Sure enough, Juan Hollinao returns with the princess to find his home is now a palace. Everything goes well, but Juan forgets Little Mouse until one day he finds her on the garbage pile, dead. Juan Hollinao is filled with remorse. Even though Juan apologizes and asks Little Mouse to stay with them, she says she must leave. Little Mouse becomes an angel and always looks out for Juan Hollinao's family.

CONNECTIONS
Angels. Animal helpers. Emperors, kings & queens. Faith. Friendship. Gratitude. Ingratitude. Kindness. Magic. Magic mice. Mice. Princes and princesses. Remorse. Reversals of fortune. Rewards. Transformations.

---

175. THE GIRL WHO TURNED TO STONE
Brenda Hughes, *Folk-tales from Chile*
Chile

A cacique whose wife has died returns to his village with a new wife who resents his daughter's beauty. The stepmother smears thick cream from a sorceress on the sleeping daughter's face the night before her wedding. It turns the daughter's face to stone. The cacique notices that one of the stepmother's fingers is also stone and confronts her. The stepmother confesses and is put to death. However, neither the village shaman nor the sorceress can undo the enchantment. The sorceress says that to reverse the spell, the daughter will have to gather all of the dead man's bones which went into the cream from where they have been scattered. The wedding is called off, and the daughter tells her unhappy father that she must live alone in the wild. There, she saves an ant's life, and it tells her to dig. The daughter digs and finds some white bones to put in her bag. A toad and a deer lead her to more bones when she rescues them. Now the daughter is missing only the skeleton's head. In the mountains she pulls a thorn from a puma's paw, and the skull is in its cave. When a thorn prick causes a drop of her blood to fall on the bones, the skeleton springs up, a live young man, now released from his enchantment. He kisses her, and her face becomes beautiful once again. They live together in the mountains, guarded by the puma.

CONNECTIONS

Animal helpers. Ants. Appearance. Bones. Caciques and chieftains. Deer. Enchantment. Frogs and toads. Heroes and heroines. Jealousy. Kindness. Love. Magic bones. Magic ointment. Pumas. Quests. Rescues. Shamans. Skeletons. Sorcerers. Stepmothers and stepdaughters. Stone. Transformations.

---

176. THE GOLDEN JARS

Livia de Almeida and Ana Portella, *Brazilian Folktales*
Brazil

An old lady, a stranger at the door, asks the kind stepdaughter for fire for her pipe and steals a golden jar from the table while the girl is in the kitchen. Frightened that her stepmother will punish her, the stepdaughter goes to find the old lady. She binds a golden bird's broken leg, and the bird sends her to a white rabbit who requests aid and sends her to the cow who requests water and then directs her to the old lady's hut. The cow tells the girl to enter the house and do what her heart tells her to do. The old lady is out, but she cleans up the messy house and falls asleep. When the old lady returns, she orders the girl to peel all the string beans and then with her fingers comb tangles from her hair, which is full of little creatures. The girl does all this, uncomplaining. The old woman then hands her a string of dried beans, which she says will make her wishes come true. Frightened of her stepmother, the stepdaughter decides to see what the beans can do. She pulls one bean off and wishes, and a palace appears. The stepdaughter stays there. When her stepmother finds her, the princess tells her the whole story. The stepmother wants her daughter to do everything that the stepdaughter did. The stepsister, however, is mean to all the animals and then yells at the old lady. When she wishes on the dried bean, her wish lands her in a cave forever surrounded by toads, snakes, and scorpions. The kind daughter marries a kind prince.

CONNECTIONS

Cautionary tales. Character. Kindness. Magic. Magic beans. Punishments. Reversals of fortune. Rewards. Stepmothers and stepdaughters. String beans. Theft. Unkindness. Warlocks and witches.

HOW ELSE THIS STORY IS TOLD

Venezuelan variation:

Poor Little Girl, Rich Little Girl—M.A. Jagendorf and R.S. Boggs, *The King of the Mountains*. A poor, kind girl prays to end conflict between bulls and to fill a dry stream with water as she looks for work. At the castle, she does not complain when an old lady asks her to help scrub dishes and scratch her back, which is covered with glass shards. She is rewarded with a barrel of gold coins. The rich girl across the street wants gold coins, too, but her unpleasant behavior only punishes her with insects.

---

177. ANTUCO'S LUCK

Juana González in John Bierhorst, *Latin American Folktales*
Chile

After losing his job as a cowherd, Antuco heads for Santiago to join the army. That night he dreams that an old woman sharing the warmth of his little fire tells him that she is his luck. She says that to become rich he must do a favor for the first Christian who asks. When the man who gives him a ride on the back of his horse the next day requests that Antuco stand in to be the godfather for his new baby, Antuco agrees. After the baptism, Antuco shares his dream. Then the husband tells what he dreamed about a genie and an underground passage that leads to treasure, and Antuco realizes he knows the place. He borrows the compadres' horse and rides there. As the genie in the man's dream instructed, he digs up a ball of red yarn, which he tosses at a genie who startles him. The genie says he must now obey Antuco and leads him to the treasure chest. From his new palace in Santiago, Antuco sends the genie back to his compadres with their horse and some of the treasure. A while later, he sails to France. Antuco presents the royal family with treasures from his chest. The princess decides she would rather marry this prince from Chile, than the king of England's son. Though the king of England declares war, Antuco captures the entire English navy with the help of the genie and his ball of yarn. Antuco of Chile marries the French princess.

CONNECTIONS

Dreams. Fortune. Genies. Herders. Kindness. Magic. Magic yarn. Princes and princesses. Quests. Reversals of fortune. Supernatural beings. Treasure. Yarn.

---

178. PROTECTION OF THE DEVIL

Elsie Spicer Eells, *The Brazilian Fairy Book*
Brazil

When a fortune-teller informs the Queen that the Prince will die violently when he is eighteen, the Prince leaves, thinking it will cause his mother less pain if he dies away from home. In a faraway kingdom, he hires workmen to repair a chapel to Saint Miguel and scolds the workman who neglects to give new paint to the image of the Devil, too. The Prince then moves on to another city, where an old woman lies that he has robbed her. The Prince is arrested and taken away. Saint Miguel asks the Devil if he knows who is resposible for his spruced-up image in the chapel. When the Devil learns that it was prince, who is now unjustly condemned to death, he charges to the old woman's house and forces her to confess her lie. The Prince is freed and returns to Saint Miguel chapel. He does not know whom to thank for his release. A monk on a fiery horse rides up. The Devil removes his hood and informs the Prince that he is the one who secured the Prince's freedom in gratitude for having been restored like the other images. The Devil tells the Prince that he can now return home to live out his life well.

CONNECTIONS

Appearance. Art. Deceit. Devil. Gratitude. Kindness. Miguel, Saint. Paint. Parents and children. Princes and princesses. Rescues. Reversals of fortune.

WHERE ELSE THIS STORY APPEARS

In Frances Frost, *Legends of the United Nations*

HOW ELSE THIS STORY IS TOLD

Mexican variation:
The Devil Does a Good Deed—Anthony John Campos, *Mexican Folk Tales*. The old lady has grown accustomed to seeing the painting of the devil which a bandit compadre gave her husband. When she is dying and the devil himself shows up, she calls him "old friend," and he rushes off to bring a priest to administer her last rites.

---

179. CHIAPANECO

Carlos Navarrete in Vivien Blackmore, *Why Corn Is Golden: Stories About Plants*
Mexico

Chiapaneco may arrive as an old man, a tramp, or a beggar and ask for some food to eat and a place to sleep. He may be disabled. Still, he will help with chores if he can. When people help Chiapaneco, their crops thrive, but if they send him away, bad fortune comes to their fields and homes.

CONNECTIONS

Allegories and parables. Beggars. Charity. Hospitality. Kindness. Punishments. Reversals of fortune. Rewards.

VII

Seeking Justice

---

180. GOOD IS REPAID WITH EVIL
John Bierhorst, *Latin American Folktales*
Venezuela

A father cautions his son not to free a trapped snake because he may bite. The boy releases the snake anyway, and the snake goes immediately to bite the boy. When the father yells that his son just saved him, the snake replies that he is just behaving the same way everyone else does. A burro, a horse, and a dog all agree that humans have not been kind to them after they gave many years of good service. The father whispers to a fox that he will reward him with chickens from his ranch if he helps save his son. The fox talks the snake out of hurting the boy, but back at the ranch, the man's wife tricks the fox and puts a dog inside the sack instead of the chickens promised to the fox.

CONNECTIONS
Animal helpers. Alligators. Anansi. Bargains. Bulls. Burros. Cautionary tales. Cleverness. Coexistence. Coyotes. Deceit. Emperors, kings & queens. Foxes. Gratitude. Humans. Injustice. Justice. Rabbits. Rescues. Snakes. Spiders. Tigers.

HOW ELSE THIS STORY IS TOLD
Jakaltek Maya variation from Guatemala:
The Ungrateful Alligator—Victor Montejo, *The Bird Who Cleans the World and Other Mayan Fables*. Rabbit saves the boy by sending the alligator back to the streambed.

Mexican variations:
Repaying Good with Evil—Riley Aiken. In J. Frank Dobie, *Puro Mexicano*. 'Mano Coyote saves the day, but after a while the man releases his dog as a "reward," instead of the promised chicken.
Repaying Good with Evil—Dan Storm, *Pictures Tales from Mexico*. Alligator accuses the ranchero of starting the whole concept of repaying good with evil, but Brother Coyote still tricks Alligator back into the mud bank.
Señor Coyote Settles a Quarrel—Dan Storm, *Pictures Tales from Mexico*. Señor Conejo and Señor Coyote roll the stone back onto Señor Rattlesnake.

111

Nicaraguan variation:

Uncle Rabbit and Uncle Tiger—Yolanda Nava, *It's All in the Frijoles*. Uncle Rabbit is the one who rescues Tío Bull from Tío Tiger by pretending not to understand the situation.

African American variation from Suriname:

The Trouble With Helping Out—Abrahams, Roger, *African-American Folktales* and at *Learning to Give* (Online). After being rescued by Hunter and then wanting to eat him, Snake argues that everyone acts this way. Anansi the spider helps trick Snake back into being pinned, but Snake wriggles free eventually and makes his way to the palace where he decides to help Hunter by biting the king who has imprisoned Hunter for poaching and giving Hunter the antidote with which to save the king. This ends with Hunter marrying the princess.

Venezuelan variation:

The Man, the Snake, and the Fox—Harold Courlander, *A Treasury of Afro-American Folklore*

181. The Hero in the Village

M.A. Jagendorf and R.S. Boggs, *The King of the Mountains*
Aymara People. Bolivia

A burro who works very hard for his Aymara master and gets little to eat is freed by the foxes every night, so they can all eat from the garden. However, every morning, the master finds the burro untied and the crops eaten and beats the burro. The burro wants to get even. He stretches out as if dead. The foxes tie him to their tails to drag home to eat. The burro springs up and drags the foxes back to the garden. The foxes are now the ones who get beaten for stealing the crops, and the burro is treated with new respect.

Connections

Burros. Cleverness. Coexistence. Foxes. Justice. Respect. Reversals of fortune. Righting a wrong. Work.

182. When Señor Grillo Met Señor Puma

Judy Goldman, *Whiskers, Tails & Wings*
Tarahumara People. Mexico

When Señor Puma almost steps on Señor Grillo and then pushes him away, Señor Grillo accuses the big cat of cowardice. Señor Puma challenges the cricket to fight him in a war. For his army, Señor Puma gathers bears, more pumas, foxes, bobcats, skunks, and snakes. Señor Grillo gathers crickets and wasps for his. The next day Señor Puma does not see Señor Grillo on the battlefield, but when the puma's army charges into the meadow crickets jump out everywhere, confusing them, and wasps sting them all the way to the lake. The victory song Señor Grillo composes is one crickets now sing every night.

CONNECTIONS

Anger. Bullies. Cleverness. Coexistence. Crickets. Injustice. Interspecies conflict. Jaguars. Lions. Noise. Origin tales. Pumas. Retaliation. Righting a wrong. Size.

HOW ELSE THIS STORY IS TOLD

Jakaltek Maya variation from Guatemala:

The War of the Wasps—Victor Montejo, *The Bird Who Cleans the World and Other Mayan Fables*. When the jaguars are angry with the cricket for chirping all night, the cricket challenges them to fight.

Mexican variations:

Cricket and Jaguar Fight—Margaret Read MacDonald, *Five Minute Tales*. Maya People. Zinacantán, Chiapas, Mexico

The Lion and the Cricket / El león y el grillo—Genevieve Barlow and William N. Stivers, *Stories from Mexico / Historias de México*. Maya People. Mexico. There's no stinging here, just many friends who hide and help the cricket.

The Lion and the Cricket / El león y el grillo—Angel Vigil, *The Eagle on the Cactus*

War Between the Cricket and the Jaguar—Romin Teratol. In Robert M. Laughlin, *The People of the Bat: Mayan Tales and Dreams from Zinacantán*. Maya People. Mexico

The War Between the Lion and the Cricket- Dan Storm, *Pictures Tales from Mexico*. The Lion mocks the cricket as being too small and agrees to fight to teach the cricket some respect.

---

183. THE ORIGIN OF RAIN AND THUNDER

Mercedes Dorson and Jeanne Wilmot, *Tales from the Rain Forest*
Amazonia, Brazil

Bebgororoti and the other men from his village hunt and kill a large tapir together. Bebgororoti, alone, cuts up the animal. He takes the entrails to the river and lays them on a rock to dry, but when he returns the other hunters have left no share of meat for him. They laugh at the blood on his hands and tell him to keep the entrails. Angry, Bebgororoti returns to the village wanting revenge. He shaves a triangle of hair from the crown of his wife's head and their children's and asks her to do the same to him. Bebgororoti paints his family to look like wild animals in black and red from crushed fruit and seeds. Then, though she begs him to stay, Bebgororoti tells his wife he is leaving for the sky and that she and the children should stay inside the *maloca* if they see black clouds or hear rumbling. Bebgororoti makes a club-sword and shouts so angrily as he walks high up the mountain that the villagers think wild peccaries are there. Lightning flies at them from Bebgororoti's club. Still, they mock him. Their arrows fly, but cannot touch him. Bebgororoti kills them in a white flash. Bebgororoti's wife and children have run outside, but their painted bodies protect them from harm. They see Bebgororoti climb up to the sky, where he becomes rain and thunder.

CONNECTIONS

Anger. Appearance. Generosity. Hunters. Husbands and wives. Injustice. Journeys to other realms. Lightning. Rain. Revenge. Ridicule. Sky worlds. Thunderbolts.

HOW ELSE THIS STORY IS TOLD
The Man Who Turned into the Rain—Anton Lukesch. In Johannes Wilbert, *Folk Literature of the Gê Indians, Vol. 1*. Cayapo People

---

184. THE FEAST ON THE MOUNTAIN AND THE FEAST UNDER THE WATER
Roger D. Abrahams, *African American Folktales*
African American People. Suriname

Anansi has invited all the animals to his birthday party, but decides to shut Tortoise out by demanding that the animals wash their hands before they eat. He knows Tortoise walks on his hands and will get them dirty even after he washes. Tortoise wants revenge. He invites the animals to a feast underwater, knowing that Anansi the spider will be too light to stay down. Anansi, however, borrows a coat and fills the pockets with stones so he can sink down to the table. Tortoise announces that everyone must take off their coats before eating. Anansi tries to ignore him, but Tortoise insists Anansi remove his coat, and Anansi floats up.

CONNECTIONS
Anansi. Cleverness. Feasts. Foxes. Hospitality. Humorous tales. Interspecies conflict. Justice. Retaliation. Spiders. Tortoises and turtles. Toucans. Water worlds.

HOW ELSE THIS STORY IS TOLD
Brazilian variation:
The Fox and the Toucan—Elsie Spicer Eells, *The Brazilian Fairy Book*. A fox serves a toucan mandioca porridge on a flat rock, which the toucan's beak will not let him pick up. Hungry and angry, the toucan invites the fox to his house and serves the mandioca porridge in a narrow-necked jar, which fox cannot reach into.

African American variations from Suriname:
Feast on the Mountain and the Feast Under the Water—Harold Courlander, *A Treasury of Afro-American Folklore*
Grudging Hospitality: the Feast on the Mountain and the Feast under the Water—Melville J. Herskovits and Frances Herskovits, *Suriname Folk-Lore*

---

185. THE ARMADILLO AND THE MONKEY: A FOLKTALE OF BRAZIL
Luis Jardim
Brazil

Armadillo needs work, and so he agrees to build a fence for Dr. Monkey, who says he will pay him some money up front and the rest when the job is done. Armadillo builds a beautiful fence, but not only does Dr. Monkey not pay the rest of what he owes, the doctor nastily dismisses Armadillo every time he tries to collect. Getting Fox, Bull, Opossum, Snake, Alligator, Guinea Pig, and even Milleped to help him, Armadillo tears down the fence, so the bull gets into the cornfield and devours everything while Dr. Monkey is off trying to impress Dona Agouti. Dr. Monkey goes to bed, without knowing that he has no corn left or that Armadillo has been responsible. Armadillo digs underneath Monkey's house while he sleeps, and the house collapses in the morning breeze. Now, Dr. Monkey sees all the devastation and comes to Armadillo to help him rebuild, but Armadillo retorts that since he was not paid, the wrecking part is free.

CONNECTIONS
Armadillos. Deceit. Humorous tales. Justice. Monkeys. Revenge. Wages. Work.

---

186. THE HUNGRY PEASANT, GOD, AND DEATH
Frances Toor, *A Treasury of Mexican Folkways*
Mexico

A poor peasant near the city of Zacatecas saves most of the little food he grows for his wife and children. One day, he steals a chicken to eat all by himself. Up a steep mountain, he cleans and cooks the chicken. A man approaches just as he is about to eat. He hides the pot and says he doesn't have any food to share, but the stranger can see the fire and smell the chicken. The stranger insists that the peasant will not refuse to give food to him once he knows who he is. Finally the peasant asks, and the man reveals that he is God, the peasant's Lord. The peasant answers that his Lord gives unfairly, so some people get nothing, and therefore he will not share his chicken. Finally, God leaves. A pale man approaches and also asks for food. The peasant refuses to give him any, too, until the stranger says he is Death. Now the peasant changes his mind; he will share some chicken with Death, who takes from all the same.

CONNECTIONS
Allegories and parables. Death (Character). Generosity. God. Gods and humans. Hospitality. Humorous tales. Hunger. Justice. Peasants. Reputation. Theft.

HOW ELSE THIS STORY IS TOLD
Jakaltek Maya variation from Guatemala:
The Loudmouth and Death—Victor Montejo, *The Bird Who Cleans the World and Other Mayan Fables*. Loudmouth and Death are compadres. Loudmouth likes that color, race, clothing, age, or power mean nothing to Death, who never plays favorites. This is something Death has to remind Loudmouth, who loudly protests when Death comes to take him.

Mexican variation:
The Hungry Peasant, God, and Death—Kevin Crossley-Holland, *The Young Oxford Book of Folk Tales*

187. The Pongo's Dream
John Bierhorst, *Latin American Folktales*
Quechua People

A native servant has been publicly humiliated by his arrogant master many times. Now the servant tells the master that he has had a dream of both of them in heaven. He tells how they stood before Saint Francis, who is judging them. The saint tells an angel to anoint the master with honey and to anoint the servant with excrement. The master is thinking this is just how it should be, when the servant tells the next part of the dream—how Saint Francis commands that they lick each other's bodies forever.

Connections
Allegories and parables. Arrogance. Cautionary tales. Class conflict. Dreams. Excrement. Francis of Assisi (Saint). Heaven. Justice. Masters. Punishments. Ridicule. Self-esteem. Servants. Storytelling.

How Else This Story Is Told
The Pongo's Dream —John Bierhorst, *The Red Swan: Myths and Tales of the American Indians*

188. The Burro and the Fox
Angel Vigil, *The Eagle on the Cactus*
Mexico

A burro decides to run away from a master who beats him even when he gives good service. He is enjoying the freedom of being his own master, when a fox suggests the burro meet the lion he serves. It makes the burro very uncomfortable the way the lion keeps narrowing the circles he walks around him as they talk. When the lion actually nips him, the burro runs. The fox insists that the lion just wanted to greet him, but the burro, heading back home, answers that he would rather be beaten than eaten.

Connections
Burros. Cautionary tales. Class conflict. Foxes. Independence. Injustice. Lions. Masters. Respect. Work.

189. Juan Bobo and Old Tiger
M.A. Jagendorf and R.S. Boggs, *The King of the Mountains*
Venezuela

All Juan Bobo can find of his dear burro one day are his skin and bones and tiger footprints. Juan Bobo wants to get even. With a thick branch he goes looking for Old Tiger. Little Vine and then Little Onion ask to come along and help. Old Tiger's cave is empty when they get there, except for a meat stew cooking. Little Onion jumps into the pot to look out from there; Little Vine watches from the cave entrance; and Juan

Bobo hides behind the woodpile. Old Tiger returns growly with hunger. Little Onion starts singing that they have come to kill Old Tiger. The tiger gets more and more furious when Onion won't stop singing and knocks the pot down. Little Onion bounces into Old Tiger's eyes so he cannot see. Old Tiger runs out of the cave where, Little Vine trips him, and Juan Bobo beats him with the branch. And Old Tiger doesn't go after neighborhood animals any more.

CONNECTIONS

Anger. Justice. Murder. Plant helpers. Punishments. Revenge. Tigers.

190. NO JUSTICE ON EARTH

Roger D. Abrahams, *African American Folktales*
African American People. Suriname

The Devil complains that whenever he tries to do something good, people still don't think well of him. He requests that God place a big stone in the path so he can leave a bag of money on top. Still, a person walking along the path who stubs his toe on the rock cries, "What the Devil!" The next person walking down the path sees the money and praises God. How is the Devil to change his image?

CONNECTIONS

Changes in attitude. Devil. Discontent. God. Humans. Humorous tales. Injustice. Reputation. Tests.

HOW ELSE THIS STORY IS TOLD

The Devil Complains—Harold Courlander, *A Treasury of Afro-American Folklore*

191. THE LITTLE TENCA AND THE SNOWFLAKE

Brenda Hughes, *Folk-tales from Chile*
Chile

A little tenca bird scolds the biting winter snow when a snowflake burns her foot, while she is out trying to find food. The snowflake says it is the fault of the sun, which was causing it to melt. The sun tells her the cloud is at fault for covering it. The cloud blames the wind; the wind blames the wall; the wall blames the mouse who blames the cat who blames the dog who blames the stick who blames the fire who blames the water who blames the knife who blames the man responsible for making it. The man tells the little tenca to ask God who made him. Very tired now, the little tenca flies up to God and wants to know why God created man. Sympathetic to her grief, God tells the little tenca to fly back and take care of her hungry babies. She does and finds her foot healed.

CONNECTIONS

Accusations. Ants. Birds. Cause and effect. God. Gods and animals. Humans. Insects. Journeys to other realms. Justice. Knives. Miracles. Murder. Responsibility. Snow.

HOW ELSE THIS STORY IS TOLD

Chilean variation:

The Thrush—Yolando Pino-Saavedra, *Folktales of Chile*. A little thrush breaks her claw trying to look for food in the frost and demands justice from the sun, clouds, winds, wall, rat, cat, dog, stick, fire, water, ox, and knife, who each blame the next one, until the blacksmith finds the thrush annoying and kills her.

Jakaltek Maya variation from Guatemala:

Author's Preface—Victor Montejo, *The Bird Who Cleans the World and Other Mayan Fables*. A wild dove pleads for cotton cloth because her leg is broken and to protect her from the cold, that has been caused by a string of characters.

Mexican variation:

The Little Ant—Américo Paredes, *Folktales of Mexico*. An ant breaks her leg in the snow and asks the judge to sue the snow. The snow blames the sun who blames the cloud; the cloud blames the wind, and the list goes on up to God. The judge stops there because he cannot question God.

---

192. THE PROOF OF THE MICE

Victor Montejo, *The Bird Who Cleans the World and Other Mayan Fables*
Jakaltek Maya People. Guatemala

A kind man has opened his house to a poor husband and wife, but he begins to doubt their honesty when some valuable things of his go missing. To quiet his suspicions, he trusts them to guard two big mice in a basket without telling them what is inside. They lift the lid, and the mice run away. The man realizes their host was testing them, but he cannot find the mice to put them back. The ungrateful couple is sent away.

CONNECTIONS

Cautionary tales. Deceit. Generosity. Honesty. Husbands and wives. Ingratitude. Justice. Mice. Tests. Theft. Trust.

---

193. UNIAÍ'S SON AND THE GUARANÁ

Mercedes Dorson & Jeanne Wilmot, *Tales from the Rain Forest*
Amazonia, Brazil

Uniaí's two brothers count on her to provide everything they need from Noçoquém, the enchanted jungle, where they live. One day Snake sprinkles magic scent, stares into Uniaí's eyes, and wishes. Instantly they are married, and she is carrying a child. Uniaí's brothers angrily turn away from their sister. They had expected her to continue caring only for them. Saddened, Uniaí leaves her beloved home. As her son grows, she tells him such stories of the wonders of Noçoquém, with its majestic nut tree and his skillful uncles, that the boy begs to go there. It is dangerous, but Uniaí sneaks him in and roasts him special nuts right there. Later, armadillo and bird guards report the presence of ashes to the brothers, who suspect their sister and set a howler monkey to capture anyone at the nut tree. The boy cannot resist returning alone, and the monkey's sharp arrow shoots him down. Missing her son, Uniaí runs to Noçoquém and finds him lifeless. She sings to make an extraordinary healing plant from his body, one which can end illness and give strength in love and war. From his eyes, Uniaí wills the guaraná plant into being, with fruit which resembles human eyes. When she returns to see the plant, she wants to cry for the fruit reminds her of her son's eyes, but then Uniaí sees him behind the leaves, strong and happy. Uniaí's son begins the Maué tribe, responsible for discovering the powers of guaraná.

CONNECTIONS

Brothers and sisters. Eyes. Guarana. Healing. Injustice. Interspecies seduction. Jealousy. Magic. Magic plants. Maue People. Murder. Origin tales. Parents and children. Plants. Restoring life. Snakes. Transformations. Trees.

HOW ELSE THIS STORY IS TOLD

The Creation of Guaraná—Momentum Arts, *Reminiscence Site of Untold Stories Untold Stories* (Online)
The Story of Guaraná—Livia de Almeida and Ana Portella, *Brazilian Folktales*

---

194. THE TWO MARIAS
Neil Philip, *Horse Hooves and Chicken Feet*
Mexico

After her mother dies, Maria urges her father to marry the neighboring widow, who seems kind. Her father does not think the kindness will last, and he is right. After they marry, the widow and her daughter, also named Maria, are mean to his Maria when he is away with the sheep. They kill a lamb he has sent her. Sent to wash its entrails and not lose any, Maria knows she will be punished when a fish makes off with some. She follows the fish and enters a house where Baby Jesus is crying. Maria calms him and tidies up the house. When the Virgin Mary returns, she places a gold star on Maria's forehead in thanks for her kindness. Her stepmother sends her daughter to wash lamb entrails, so she will get a gold star, too, but she is harsh with Baby Jesus and the Virgin Mary. The stepsister comes home with horns on her head, which keep growing back. A prince sees the gold star on Maria's forehead while she is working and falls in love with her. Her stepmother says Maria can marry him if the wedding feast is prepared by the time she returns from her walk. A mysterious woman makes it happen. But the stepmother assigns two more impossible tasks. With the magic whistle a bird gives Maria, birds stuff twelve mattresses with bird feathers and fill ten bottles with birds' tears. Annoyed that all of her demands have been met, the stepmother locks Maria in the cellar and tells the prince she has run away. She tries to substitute her own Maria, but the cat sings out the truth, and the prince and the right Maria ride away.

CONNECTIONS

Animal helpers. Bird helpers. Cats. Dogs. Cinderella tales. Cows. Deceit. Fish helpers. God. Grass. Injustice. Insect helpers. Jesus. Kindness. Love. Magic. Magic cups. Magic plants. Magic sashes. Miracles. Murder. Music. Parents and children. Princes and princesses. Punishments. Ranchers. Rebozos. Reversals of fortune. Sheep. Stars. Stepmothers and stepdaughters. Tasks. Transformations. Truth. Virgin Mary. Wishes.

HOW ELSE THIS STORY IS TOLD

Variation from Argentina:

Rice from Ashes—Aída Agüero de Agüero. In John Bierhorst, *Latin American Folktales*. A magic dove and then a queen ant help the daughter with impossible tasks her mean stepmother has set. However, when the stepmother orders her to kill a beloved lamb which helped spin wool, the lamb tells the girl to keep the golden cup she will find inside. The kind daughter is the only one who gives God in disguise a drink of water. At the end, a bird sings out to expose the stepsisters' deception, so the prince can find her.

Brazilian variations:

The Fish Mother—Livia de Almeida and Ana Portella, *Brazilian Folktales*. A rich woman throws her poor friend in the river in order to be able to use her daughter as a servant. A giant silver fish comes to her aid, which the wicked stepmother roasts. When a rosebush grows where the fish scales are buried in the palace garden, a search ensues for the one girl who can pick its rose.

The Singing Grasses—Livia de Almeida and Ana Portella, *Brazilian Folktales*. There are no step-sisters in this version; the wicked stepmother kills the girl and buries her under a fig tree, but the grass that grows there sings truth to the gardener.

Waving Locks—Elsie Spicer Eells *The Brazilian Fairy Book*. A girl with long beautiful hair, whose mother has died, is buried alive by the wicked old woman who looks after her. Long-waving grass grows up under tree and sings her story in the breeze. Waving Locks comes back to life through miracle wrought by Our Lady.

Chilean variation:

Maria Cinderella—Yolando Pino-Saavedra, *Folktales of Chile*. Here, a dog gets the prince to turn back by barking a riddle about burro dung being the one up on the horse, instead of golden star. The prince finds Maria Cinderella with the gold star in the oven.

Mexican variations:

Adelita: A Mexican Cinderella Story—Tomie dePaola. The rancher's son falls in love with the girl, who was wearing an embroidered red *rebozo* at the fiesta. There is no magic helper in this story, but a kindly family servant is on her side when the stepsisters act mean.

Cinderella—Tonik Nibak in Robert M. Laughlin, *Of Cabbages and Kings* (Print) and at Smithsonian Institution Libraries (Online). Tzotzil Maya. Zinacantán. Cinderella has a magic sash which helps her.

---

195. THE WONDERFUL CHIRRIONERA / LA MARAVILLOSA CHIRRIONERA

Angel Vigil, *The Eagle on the Cactus*
Mexico

Three poor brothers whose mother has died make a game of stealing fruit from miserly Señor Mariano's orchard. Their father works hard in the fields all day. Though he gives Señor Mariano permission to whip them, whipping hurts the old fruit grower's arm more than the boys. They keep taking fruit. One day Señor Mariano sees two oxen pulling a wagon with a whip that seems to be working all by itself. He finds out that the whip is a *chirrionera*, a snake that can stand on its head and whip its tail in the air, hitting true. Señor Mariano wants one. He catches a *chirrionera* in the mountains and trains it and sings to it. He calls his *chirrionera* Angelito and sets him after the brothers. The boys see Señor Mariano feed the *chirrionera* cut up fruit and sneak hot *habanero* chili into each piece. When the *chirrionera* eats the fruit, it writhes with pain. Then the *chirrionera* whips Señor Mariano and rolls back to the mountains. The brothers apologize to Señor Mariano and even begin to help out in the orchard. Señor Mariano changes, too; he sets extra fruit out for people to take home to their families.

CONNECTIONS

Brothers and sisters. Cautionary tales. Changes in attitude. Chili peppers. Chirrionera. Coexistence. Fruit. Generosity. Justice. Misers. Orchards. Parents and children. Punishments. Snakes. Supernatural beings. Theft. Tricksters.

HOW ELSE THIS STORY IS TOLD

The Marvelous *Chirrionera*—Grant Lyons, *Tales the People Tell in Mexico*

---

196. AUNT MISERY'S PEAR TREE

Livia de Almeida and Ana Portella, *Brazilian Folktales*
Brazil

A poor old lady feels frustrated that the village children steal the pears from her tree, when she has so little to eat. When a hungry man asks for some food and shelter, she shares what she has with him. The next day he offers to grant a wish for her. Right away, Aunt Misery wishes that anyone who climbs up to steal her pears will get stuck up in the tree until she frees them to come down. The children now stop taking the pears. Then Death comes for her, a tall woman carrying a sickle. Now that she feels stronger, though, Misery wants to live. She asks Death to climb the tree and bring her four pears. Death gets stuck up there for many years, but people around the world who need release from life begin to suffer. Misery relents and lets Death come down, on the condition that she herself not die. This explains why there is despair in the world today.

CONNECTIONS

Allegories and parables. Bargains. Cleverness. Death (Character). Despair. Fruit. Hospitality. Immortality. Justice. Magic. Misery (Character). Old age. Poverty. Rewards. Theft. Wishes.

HOW ELSE THIS STORY IS TOLD

Brazilian variation:

Tia Miseria—Olga Loya, *Momentos Magicos / Magic Moments*

Kanjobal Maya variation from Guatemala:

The Poor Old Woman—Fernando Peñalosa, *Tales and Legends of the Q'Anjob'al Maya*

VIII

Punishments and Rewards
Teaching Good and Wise Behavior

197. SPREADING FINGERS FOR FRIENDSHIP
Roger D. Abrahams, *African American Folktales*
African American People. Suriname

The plantation overseer Ba Yau brings food to both of his wives and instructs them to spread their fingers when they eat. When he dies, the first wife sits alone, while people bring a cow, sugar, and coffee to the second wife. The first wife goes to ask the second wife about this difference. When the second wife asks what she did with the provisions Ba Yau brought, the first wife spreads her fingers in the air. The second wife tells her that only the air will bring her things now, whereas the second wife invited other people to share what she cooked. Those people she gave food to now bring her things in return.

CONNECTIONS
Allegories and parables. Cautionary tales. Friendship. Generosity. Husbands and wives. Misunderstandings. Punishments. Rewards. Selfishness.

HOW ELSE THIS STORY IS TOLD
Spreading the Fingers—Harold Courlander, *A Treasury of Afro-American Folklore*
Spreading the Fingers—Melville J. Herskovits and Frances Herskovits, *Suriname Folk-Lore*

---

198. THE RICH SEÑORA
Grant Lyons, *Tales the People Tell in Mexico*
Mexico

A woman, whose son is the Mayor of Motúl and has enough to share, never gives anything to beggars. She is downright rude to the poor old woman at the door, but when she returns to eat her food, snakes are crawling through her house. The next day when the beggar returns, she gives her a few old onion skins. The old woman thanks

123

her. That night, however, the mayor's mother wakes so hungry, she eats thirty tortillas, but never feels full enough. She grows thinner and thinner, while the beggar woman grows healthy. When the mayor's wife dies, two angels bring her the only thing she ever gave to anyone else—those onion skins—to hold onto as they fly her toward heaven. The skins break, and she tumbles down.

CONNECTIONS

Allegories and parables. Angels. Beggars. Cautionary tales. Charity. Heaven. Journeys to other realms. Justice. Misers. Punishments.

199. HOW FLINT-FACE LOST HIS NAME
Anita Brenner, *The Boy Who Could Do Anything*
Mexico

A greedy, rich man who overcharges on interest to poor people is called Flint-Face because of the mean expression which matches his deeds. One night at a party, he is afraid to go home and spends the night counting his money until he falls asleep. He dreams that he runs to a bakery and buys bread for a crowd of beggars who are pulling apart his house looking for food. The next day, Flint-Face goes to collect money people owe him, and that night he dreams he has died and arrived at heaven. The Lord says Flint-Face is evil for charging so much interest. When Flint-Face argues that it is not illegal, the Lord says it is still immoral and Flint-Face never did anything for anybody because he wanted to, including distributing the bread. The Gates of heaven slam shut. When Flint-Face wakes in the morning, all of his money is gone. He himself becomes a beggar, repentant of his selfish ways.

CONNECTIONS

Bankers. Beggars. Changes in attitude. Dreams. God. Gods and humans. Greed. Heartlessness. Heaven. Journeys to other realms. Punishments.

200. HOW THE SERPENT WAS BORN
Victor Montejo, *The Bird Who Cleans the World and Other Mayan Fables*
Jakaltek Maya People. Guatemala

A loving mother stops by the house of her grown son, anticipating the tortillas he will share with her. The son, however, directs his wife to hide the pot of chicken soup she's prepared for their own dinner. He brusquely tells his mother there is no food to give her. His hungry mother waits for a while, saddened by her son's unkindness and ingratitude, and then leaves. When the son and his wife lift the pot lid, however, they find a poisonous snake waiting inside. From such hard-heartedness as theirs, the serpent comes into being.

CONNECTIONS

Allegories and parables. Cautionary tales. Heartlessness. Honoring parents. Hospitality. Ingratitude. Magic. Origin tales. Parents and children. Punishments. Selfishness. Snakes. Unkindness.

HOW ELSE THIS STORY IS TOLD

How the Serpent Was Born / De cómo nació la víbora—Susan Conklin Thompson, Keith Steven Thompson, and Lidia López de López, *Mayan Folktales*

---

201. THE CREATURE OF FIRE

Livia de Almeida and Ana Portella, *Brazilian Folktales*
Brazil

Because he does not want to share, a man takes his family far away into the woods, so neighbors will not see him roast a lamb. He searches all day to find the perfect spot free from trees, insects, and people. Then he realizes they have nothing with which to light a fire, and no one to ask. The man sends his eldest son to request some embers from two small lights he sees in the dark. The boy heads out, frightened, when suddenly he is blinded by the fiery eyes of a giant creature with large hairy ears. He flees toward his family with the creature roaring that it will burn him if he does not give it what it wants. The man and his family run all night. A woodsman invites them to hide inside his hut. He shoots the creature with his shotgun when it tries to push past him into the house. The man comes out, and they hit the creature until it is dead. The woodsman advises the man to forget about finding places without fleas and flies, since monsters are more dangerous. After this experience, the man reaches out to share with his neighbors and travelers.

CONNECTIONS

Cautionary tales. Changes in attitude. Escapes. Fear. Monsters. Punishments. Scary tales. Selfishness. Supernatural beings.

---

202. THE LOST PRINCE

Yolando Pino-Saavedra, *Folktales of Chile*
Chile

Lost in the forest, the youngest prince finds a palace and is hired as gardener there on the condition that he bring the king a fresh bouquet of flowers every day. The princess is miffed to be left out and tells lies about the prince claiming to be brave. Believing her, the king sends the prince off to bring back his three-colored mare from the land of the pirates or else. With the help of a magic wand from an old crone, he does, but now the princess is even more jealous, and has the king send him to retrieve a man-eating snake. The crone tells the prince how to lure the snake, but when he brings it back, the snake loudly hisses for the princess to appear. The snake throws out its breath and pulls her in and eats her. The king realizes that the princess is the one who caused all the trouble. He asks the prince to bring the snake back to the woods and stay on as his friend.

CONNECTIONS

Cautionary tales. Deceit. Emperors, kings & queens. Humorous tales. Jealousy. Lost. Magic. Magic wands. Monsters. Parents and children. Princes and princesses. Punishments. Snakes. Supernatural beings. Tasks. Warlocks and witches.

203. THE WOMAN WHO DIED FOR THREE DAYS AND WENT TO GET ACQUAINTED WITH HELL

Elena de Dios in James D. Sexton, *Heart of Heaven, Heart of Earth*
Maya People

A wealthy, self-centered woman buries her worldly goods and papers rather than let them go to anyone else. When she dies, her poor neighbors take up a collection for her burial. On her third day in the coffin, the woman speaks, admitting that she has lived wrong and wants to change so she will not suffer like her parents. She gets out of the coffin to show her neighbors where to dig up her money and documents, which will allow them to sell her land and divvy up her livestock. Now, she is satisfied to let go.

CONNECTIONS

Cautionary tales. Discontent. Changes in attitude. Ghosts. Hell. Journeys to other realms. Punishments. Selfishness.

204. KÁKUY

Lulu Delacre, *Golden Tales*
Quechua People. Bolivia

A brother and sister are on their own in the jungle after their parents die. The brother continues to provide and protect their hut just as his father did. The sister, however, lives selfishly, and does not appreciate all that he does for them both. One day, when the brother returns tired, she calls him lazy and throws the dinner he cooked on the floor. He does not want to abandon her, but this behavior cannot continue. The brother asks his sister to help him get a beehive with a certain honey she likes down from a tall tree. Desiring that honey, she offers to climb up. He tells her to wrap her shawl around her face to protect herself from the bees' fierce stings. She is high up in the tree, waiting for instructions, and then realizes with fright that he is gone and all the branches below have been cut so she cannot get down. The bees begin to sting. She prays to her brother, but can only cry "Kákuy, turay" which means, "Stay, my brother." As she falls, she begs the gods to help her find her brother, and they transform her into a bird, which can only fly short distances and sing plaintively in the night.

CONNECTIONS

Abuse. Bees. Birds. Brothers and sisters. Cautionary tales. Fear. Gods and humans. Heartlessness. Ingratitude. Origin tales. Orphans. Punishments. Selfishness. Transformations. Unkindness.

HOW ELSE THIS STORY IS TOLD

Variations from Argentina:
Kakuí, Bird of the Night—Harold Courlander, *Ride with the Sun*
The Sad, Sorry Sister—Frances Carpenter, *South American Wonder Tales*

205. BAHMOO RIDES THE WRONG FROG

M.A. Jagendorf and R.S. Boggs, *The King of the Mountains*
Guyana

When the boaster Bahmoo shows up at a neighboring village, the people there decide to teach him a lesson. They invite Bahmoo to bring a club when they go to hunt frogs "as big as bush hogs" the next morning. Bahmoo brags that he will not need a weapon; he will just jump on the frogs' backs and wring their necks. He says this aloud as they enter the swamp, and the king of the frogs overhears. Unsettled by the very loud croaking of frogs all around, Bahmoo wants to show the others that he is not afraid. He jumps on the king frog's back, but the giant frog winds his legs firmly around Bahmoo's neck and threatens to take him away. Now terrified, Bahmoo flails and howls in the water, as the villagers laugh. Bahmoo is ashamed when the frog king tosses Bahmoo up onto land, chastising that humans do not show the same mercy to frogs.

CONNECTIONS

Braggarts. Changes in attitude. Frogs and toads. Humiliation. Interspecies conflict. Swamps.

206. HOW THE STARS CAME

Philip Ardagh, *South American Myths & Legends*
Bororo People. Brazil and Bolivia

With his grandmother's permission, a boy accompanies the women of the village to help them find corn. Once they pound the corn, however, he sneaks some of the flour into a bamboo shoot. The boy asks his grandmother to make cakes with this flour. He lies, telling her he did not steal it. His grandmother makes cakes for all of the children. However, she begins to doubt that her grandson has told the truth. When her macaw loudly repeats the word "thief," which she murmured, the boy cuts out the bird's tongue. One bad deed leads to another. Then, worried about punishment, the grandson convinces all of the children that they must climb to the sky where adults will not find them. A hummingbird fastens one end of a creeper vine to the sky and the children start climbing up. The mothers are frantic when they return and cannot find their children. They spy the legs of the very last child and try to follow, but the creeper vine collapses under their weight. Hitting the ground, the women are transformed into different animals. The children become stars up above, their eyes sparkling with tears.

CONNECTIONS

Bird helpers. Birds. Corn. Deceit. Grandparents and grandchildren. Guilt. Hummingbirds. Journeys to other realms. Macaws. Origin tales. Parents and children. Punishments. Sky worlds. Stars. Theft. Transformations. Truth.

HOW ELSE THIS STORY IS TOLD

How the Stars Came—Vic Parker, *Traditional Tales from South America*

How the Stars Came to Be—Mercedes Dorson & Jeanne Wilmot, *Tales from the Rain Forest*. Bororo People. Amazonia, Brazil. In this version, corn is something the women prepare only for themselves, as the men consider it poisonous to eat. The very last child to reach the sky cuts the rope, which causes the women to fall. They become different types of animals depending on where and how they fall.

Star Fate of the Bororo Boys—Livia de Almeida and Ana Portella, *Brazilian Folktales*. Bororo People. Amazonia, Brazil. Here, the Women prepare corn dishes that only men are allowed to eat. The falling women all become wildcats and howl at the sky.

207. THE BLACK SHIP

Pablo Antonia Cuadra in *Jade and Iron*
Zapatera Island, Nicaragua

When someone on Redonda Island signals their ship with a sheet as they cross Lake Nicaragua, the crew does land. The people there are in pain, sick from food poisoning. They have no money to pay them, and the captain will not wait for the time it will take for his sailors to cut firewood and gather bananas in exchange for transporting the families to Grenada. As they sail away, an old woman curses the crew for closing their hearts. The ship vanishes forever. Are the captain and crew sailing endlessly back and forth? People claim to have seen the ship and heard cries from sailors asking for direction, but it never lands.

CONNECTIONS

Boats. Cautionary tales. Curses. Ghosts. Heartlessness. Lakes. Nicaragua, Lake. Punishments. Ships. Unkindness.

208. THE GOLD AND SILVER FISH

Ignacio Bizarro Ujpan in James D. Sexton, *Heart of Heaven, Heart of Earth*
Maya People

A poor señor in San José works hard selling firewood and mushrooms, and his wife washes clothes for a living. One sunrise, after a rich comadre and compadre make them feel bad by claiming that they have more because they work harder, the senora prays to the goddess of the lake for help with their struggles. The goddess tells the woman that she will be rewarded, but that she and her husband must not forget others in need and disappears. A fish jumps into the senora's basket. She places that fish on her altar at home. The wooden image of Jésus turns gold; the Virgen María becomes silver; and the fish turns gold on one side and silver on the other. She and her husband give thanks to the goddess and to God. Three weeks later, the coffer the fish is in becomes full of coins. Now their fortune changes, and the senor and senora do not forget to help the poor. Envious, the rich compadre and compadre ask how this came about. The rich comadre goes to wash clothes hoping for a reward. The goddess of the lake asks why she is doing this when she already has enough. The turtle and crab the goddess sends the rich comadre fill her house with toads, tortoises, and poisonous snakes.

CONNECTIONS

Animal helpers. Cautionary tales. Comadres and compadres. Gods and humans. Jealousy. Justice. Magic. Magic fish. Miracles. Prayer. Punishments. Reversals of fortune. Rewards. Unkindness.

---

209. THE MAGIC CANOE
Margaret Read MacDonald, *Five Minute Tales*
Kamaiurá People. Brazil

A man leaves the canoe he has just made from the bark of a jatobé tree in the forest. Tomorrow, he will pull it to the river and go fishing. The next morning, however, his canoe is not there. Then it thumps into the clearing with a face and four strong legs. It waves a paddle for him to climb in. He does and tells the canoe to take him to the river. It does, and he commands it to catch fish. Fish jump in, filling the boat full. The canoe swallows them all. Surprised, the man commands the canoe to catch more fish. This time when it is full, the boat walks out of the river and back to the forest. The man is delighted to bring home so many fish. The next day, he takes a sack with him, thinking he will collect enough fish to sell. When the fish begin to fly into the boat, he stuffs them immediately into the bag, forgetting to let the canoe eat first. The canoe glares. He tries to take some fish out of the bag, but it is too late. The canoe swallows him up.

CONNECTIONS

Boats. Cautionary tales. Greed. Magic. Magic canoes. Punishments. Retaliation. Selfishness. Supernatural beings.

---

210. THE CHOCOLATE THAT TURNED TO STONE
Carlos Navarrete in Vivien Blackmore, *Why Corn Is Golden: Stories About Plants*
Mexico

Warrior bullies demand that the villagers give them more and more cocoa beans, until warriors are the only ones who can eat chocolate. Fed up, an old man brings the warrior chief a recipe for sweets which the chief orders him to prepare. The warriors love those sweets which he makes from the cocoa beans. One day they gobble down a new stash of sweets which the old man has left purposefully unattended. The next day their stomachs are stone hard. Villagers throw the chief in the river, where he sinks.

Connections

Bullies. Cautionary tales. Chocolate. Greed. Punishments. Selfishness. Warriors.

211. Greed in Heaven, Growth on Earth

M.A. Jagendorf and R.S. Boggs, *The King of the Mountains*
Bolivia

Since animals on the ground all have little mouths, there is too much competition for food. Señor Fox, called Tío Antonio, convinces Mallcu, the condor to lift him to a feast in the sky. The king of the birds makes him promise that the fox will use good manners and not throw bones under the table. Tío Antonio agrees, but when the birds finish and fly away, he begins to eat wildly. Angry, Mallcu also flies off, saying he will not bring Tío Antonio back to earth. Tío Antonio is frightened now, as he peers over the edge of a cloud. It is a long way down. His crying brings some small *papachiuchi* birds who sympathetically tie a long rope from the *cortadera* plant to a cloud for him to slide down. Tío Antonio is sliding, his paws sore, when he cannot resist taunting some parrots who fly by. Angry, the parrots threaten to cut his rope. Tío Antonio pretends that he is joking, then starts in again two more times, and the parrots hack away at the rope until he falls. When Tío Antonio breaks apart, everything he has been eating scatters over the earth and becomes the food people live on.

Connections

Bargains. Bird helpers. Birds. Cautionary tales. Condors. Earth. Flight. Food. Foxes. Greed. Journeys to other realms. Manners. Origin tales. Parrots. Promises. Punishments. Ridicule. Sky worlds. Unkindness. Vanity.

How Else This Story Is Told

Quechua variation from Peru:
The Vain Fox / La zorra vanidosa—Paula Martin, *Pachamama Tales*

212. The Parrot Who Sings Kra-Kra-Kra

Daniel Munduruku, *Amazonia*
Bororo People. Amazonia, Brazil

At a time when the parrot is a boy, one boy goes fishing with his father and brings back fish, which are shared in the village. However, the boy becomes dissatisfied with his portions and keeps taking larger shares, even hiding food away. One day he sneaks some mangabas his mother is roasting right out of the fire. The pasty mass sticks in his throat. He cannot spit it out. His neck swells and his head becomes smaller. His mouth becomes a pinched hard beak. Now he has tail feathers, and everywhere he scratches his itchy body, a green feather grows. He cries with a scratchy voice and flies up to live in the trees. There is some question whether he ever becomes a boy again.

Connections

Birds. Cautionary tales. Greed. Origin tales. Parrots. Punishments. Transformations.

---

213. Why You Must Not Strike Children

Douglas Gifford, *Warriors, Gods & Spirits from Central & South American Mythology*
Tapuyu Chaco People

A little girl slips out of the locked hut to see where her parents have gone to party. Just as the girl sees her mother tipsily losing her balance, the mother sees her looking in and angrily shouts at her daughter for disobeying. The mother hits the girl, shoves her back to the family hut, and returns to drink maize beer. The other children want to know why their sister has been beaten. She tells them, and the locked hut opens by itself. The children move outside in a line, chanting softly, and moving to a new beat. As they wend through the village, more and more children join their line. They dance out of the village and slowly up into the sky where they become stars. After the loss of those children, all parents try hard to be more understanding.

Connections

Allegories and parables. Abuse. Anger. Brothers and sisters. Cautionary tales. Changes in attitude. Drink. Heartlessness. Journeys to other realms. Parents and children. Punishments. Sky worlds. Stars. Transformations.

---

214. The Skull Takes Revenge

Livia de Almeida and Ana Portella, *Brazilian Folktales*
Brazil

Pedro can be funny, but when he drinks too much, his jokes belittling others are mean. One evening, as he cuts through a cemetery, he takes a skull which seems to be laughing down from a tree and invites it to come to his house the next night at midnight. Then he kicks the skull. Pedro wakes with a bad headache, but his neighbor is sure he is joking, because Pedro has this grotesque grin on his face. The tea he drinks dribbles out of his mouth. Then he sees that his mouth is open wide and grinning. He shrugs this off and starts preparing dinner for guests. At midnight a mysterious visitor arrives wrapped in a cloak. When the new guest lets his hood drop back, his friends shriek to see a grinning skull. The skull finds it very funny that Pedro faints and dies with a grin on his face.

Connections

Cautionary tales. Character. Drink. Practical jokes. Punishments. Ridicule. Skulls. Supernatural
beings. Transformations. Unkindness.

---

215. The Inheritance of the Old Man / La herencia del Viejo

Pedro Cholotío Temó and Alberto Barreno, *The Dog Who Spoke /
El perro que habló*
Tzutuhil Maya People. Santiago Atitlán, Guatemala

A poor compadre turns down his rich friend's first suggestion on how to become
wealthy because it would mean leaving his wife or children for the *dueño* up on an
enchanted hill. Together, though, they do bring the town drunk up there as an offering.
The drunkard disappears, and the poor compadre becomes rich. At the end of his life,
the compadre tells his sons about the enchanted hill. The sons squander their father's
wealth and go to the hill to perform *costumbres* and get rich. At midnight, however, their
father's voice tells them his body is being endlessly cut and fed to the *dueño's* wild animals.
They flee with their father's sandals and handkerchief, but the *dueño* keeps their spirits.

Connections

Cautionary tales. Comadres and compadres. Duenos. Gods and humans. Greed. Murder. Parents
and children. Punishments. Sacrifice. Selfishness. Supernatural voices.

---

216. The Girl and the Kibungo

Livia de Almeida and Ana Portella, *Brazilian Folktales*
Brazil

Long ago, children are not allowed to go out at night alone for fear they may be
seized and eaten by the kibungo. However, one daughter pooh poohs her mother's
warnings and continues to visit neighbors and relatives after dark. One night, however,
a kibungo sneaks up behind her and puts her inside his back where his stomach is. She
begins to cry and sings out. She calls to her mother who sings back that she warned
her. The girl keeps crying and singing out to various people as the kibungo passes their
houses. Everyone is afraid and answers like her mother, except for her grandmother,
who immediately starts to prepare. When the kibungo passes her window, the grandmother pours boiling water on his legs. In pain, the kibungo throws the girl out. Her
grandmother plunges a hot skewer into his neck, and the kibungo runs off. The girl,
however, no longer walks by herself at night.

Connections

Cautionary tales. Changes in attitude. Fear. Grandparents and grandchildren. Heroes and heroines. Kibungo. Monsters. Night. Parents and children. Punishments. Supernatural beings.
Warnings.

217. ¡El Cucuy! A Bogeyman Cuento in English and Spanish

Joe Hayes
Mexico

Two lazy, older sisters tease their younger sister and make things difficult for their father, who needs their help since their mother has died. They are sure their father is pretending when he threatens them with el Cucuy, the monster who carries away children who do not behave. Especially exasperated one day, their father calls for Cucuy to take them. Nothing happens until sunset, when el Cucuy comes and takes them to his hidden mountain cave. The sisters are so frightened. A goatherd hears the sisters crying and helps them escape. They meet their father and sister who have come to find them. After that, the girls pitch in to help, and their father never mentions el Cucuy again.

Connections

Brothers and sisters. Captivity. Cautionary tales. Changes in attitude. Cucuy. Fear. Heroes and heroines. Laziness. Manners. Monsters. Parents and children. Punishments. Rescues. Warnings. Work.

218. The Mother Who Never Wanted Her Son to Work / La madre que nunca quiso que su hijo trabajara

Pedro Cholotío Temó and Alberto Barreno, *The Dog Who Spoke / El perro que habló*
Tzutuhil Maya People. Panajachel, Guatemala

A mother never asks her son to pitch in and help with the work after her husband dies. As she gets older, however, she could use his assistance. She tells him it is now his turn, after all she has done for him. Her son asks if she thinks a certain crooked tree can be straightened. She answers that the time has passed for that. The muchacho answers that it is the same with him; it is too late now. The muchacho brings his mother's heart to his married sister to cook, telling her it is the heart of a bull. The heart screams out on the grill that it is her mother, and the sister goes to the police. The muchacho's mother needed to teach him the value of work when he was young.

Connections

Accusations. Allegories and parables. Brothers and sisters. Cautionary tales. Heartlessness. Ingratitude. Knowledge. Laziness. Murder. Parents and children. Punishments. Work.

219. Snake-in-the-Water

Idella Purnell, *The Merry Frogs*
Aztec People. Milpa Alta, Mexico

Little Pancho always wriggles out of helping with work. When the old woman asks him to fetch water from the well, he says there is a snake there. One day, though, he readily accompanies his friend to the spring for water, even though the boy's mother tells them there is a snake there. And there is a long snake, who comes right at them. Pancho flees, but the snake wraps around him. The donkey, the horse, and the ox say they will not help him, because people have always mistreated them. Pancho cries out to the eagle who asks why the snake wants him. Pancho says it is because he made up the story about there being a snake in the well whenever he was asked to go for water. The eagle lifts the snake off of Pancho then, so he can run home. He never makes up that snake story when asked to fetch water again.

Connections

Allegories and parables. Bird helpers. Cautionary tales. Changes in attitude. Deceit. Eagles. Laziness. Monsters. Punishments. Snakes. Storytelling. Work.

---

220. The Bad Compadre

Francisco Sanchez in John Bierhorst, *Latin American Folktales*
Cakchiquel Maya People. Guatemala

Juan would like to make money and has his wife ask their compadre, the wealthy merchant Mariano, if Juan can accompany him on his next selling trip. Mariano agrees. When Juan lags behind, the merchant casts spells which put threatening leaf-cutter ants, then snakes, coyotes, hawks, and jaguars in his path. Juan has to give away all the food he brought to sell just to get past them. When they reach the plantation, Mariano tells the owner privately that Juan is a terrific servant who can separate sugar from salt, clear and plant a cornfield by morning, and build a multi-story house all plastered and complete with the daughter of the patron suckling a baby. The animals Juan fed along the way help him accomplish these tasks. Mariano requests greater pay from the owner for all that "his servant" Juan has accomplished. In a dream, the animals tell Juan that as a punishment from God, they will end Mariano's life and bring Juan the money. It comes to pass.

Connections

Animal helpers. Bird helpers. Cautionary tales. Comadres and compadres. Coyotes. Deceit. Dreams. Gods and humans. Hawks. Insect helpers. Jaguars. Justice. Leaf-cutter ants. Magic. Murder. Patróns. Punishments. Reversals of fortune. Snakes. Tasks. Vendors.

Where Else This Story Appears

In John Bierhorst, *Latin American Folktales* and in John Bierhorst, *The Monkey's Haircut*, both also at *Open Library* (Online)

---

221. The Cheating Milkman

Rajini Persaud in *Caribbean Indian Folktales*
Indian People. Guyana

A milkman cheats his customers by mixing water with the milk he sells. One day, thirsty, when he stops by a pond, something heavy splashes into the water. Then something else splashes. He thinks someone is throwing bricks at him. When he returns to his milk cans on the road, though, he sees that what had gone flying into the pond was all of his watered-down milk-money. He begins again after that and sells only milk that is all milk.

CONNECTIONS

Allegories and parables. Cautionary tales. Deceit. Greed. Money. Milkmen. Punishments. Water.

---

222. THE TWO LITTLE ELVES

Hugh Lupton, *Tales of Mystery and Magic*
Chile

A poor woodcutter finds two elves, hopping from foot to foot in the forest and singing a song which counts three days of the week, Monday to Wednesday. He joins in and then adds Thursday to Saturday to make six days. They are delighted and all sing his new version together. Then the elves decide such a good song deserves a reward. They each hand him one of their feet for wishing on. He will be able to make all the wishes he can say in one breath, and then a foot will disappear. He brings the feet home to show his family. They wish for good food plus livestock and then clothes and a palace to live in. The feet disappear, and their wishes are granted. When the woodcutter's wealthier brother learns about the new riches, he dresses like a poor woodcutter and finds the elves. He adds Sunday to their song and demands two wishes. His wife scoffs at the idea that the feet can really grant wishes and impulsively asks for whiskers and a beard on their baby. When that happens, they need to use their second wish to remove all the hair.

CONNECTIONS

Appearance. Brothers and sisters. Calendar. Cautionary tales. Comadres and compadres. Dwarves. Elves. Greed. Humorous tales. Husbands and wives. Magic. Magic feet. Manners. Music. Punishments. Rewards. Supernatural beings. Wishes. Warlocks and witches. Woodcutters.

HOW ELSE THIS STORY IS TOLD

Argentinian variation:
Sunday Seven / Domingo siete—Paula Martin, *Pachamama Tales*

Chilean variation:
The Four Little Dwarfs—Yolando Pino-Saavedra, *Folktales of Chile*

Costa Rican variation:
And Sunday Makes Seven—Robert Baden. Twelve witches reward the poor man who adds days and rhyme to their song by removing the mole from his nose and sending him home with gold. They yell that his rich brother has ruined their song and send him home with two moles and no gold.
The Two Comrades—Lupe de Osma, *The Witches' Ride*

223. SEÑOR RATTLESNAKE LEARNS TO FLY
Pleasant DeSpain, *Thirty-Three Multicultural Tales to Tell*
Mexico

Two buzzards feel sorry for Señor Rattlesnake when he frets about always being earthbound. They take him up for a ride through the sky. Rattlesnake is holding onto a stick with his mouth as they fly, and he is loving it. But then Señor Eagle taunts him. Dove tells the snake not to be angry, that Eagle is provoking him so he will open his mouth and fall. The rattlesnake does forget the eagle, because now he is looking at the dove—at the dove whom he desires to eat! The snake opens his mouth wide to get the dove and falls.

CONNECTIONS
Anger. Birds. Buzzards. Cautionary tales. Discontent. Doves. Eagles. Flight. Friendship. Frogs and toads. Ingratitude. Interspecies conflict. Journeys. Kindness. Origin tales. Punishments. Rattlesnakes. Ridicule. Snakes.

HOW ELSE THIS STORY IS TOLD
Mexican variations:
Pokok Up High—Judy Goldman, *Whiskers, Tails & Wings*. Tzeltal Maya People. A little frog who is taken up into the air starts insulting Xulem the buzzard, who is treating him to this wonderful ride. Shaken off by the buzzard, the frog splats down on the ground, which explains his flattened shape.
Señor Rattlesnake Learns to Fly—Leslie Goldman, *Dora's Favorite Fairy Tales*. The rattlesnake, king of the land, falls when he opens his mouth to strike at the eagle, king of the sky, who is teasing him.
The Snake Who Wanted to Fly—Dan Storm, *Pictures Tales from Mexico*

Jakaltek Maya variation from Guatemala:
The Toad and the Buzzard—Victor Montejo, *The Bird Who Cleans the World and Other Mayan Fables*. Toad disparages buzzard's smell a couple of times, and the buzzard dumps him.
See also The Toad's Spots / Las manchas del sapo (140).

224. HOW THE BRAZILIAN BEETLES GOT THEIR COATS
Elsie Spicer Eells, *Brazilian Fairy Tales*
Brazil

When a large gray rat taunts a modest little brown beetle about how slowly she is crawling, the parrot overhead suggests a race. He offers a bright coat made by the tailor bird as the prize. As the beetle thinks about the coat she would like to have, the rat mocks the possibility of her ever winning. The parrot signals for the race to start and then flies to the royal palm tree where the race will end. The rat runs fast and gets tired, but pushes himself, even though he is sure the beetle will be far behind. When he reaches the royal palm tree, though, there is the beetle already sitting beside the parrot.

The rat wants to know how she did it, and she shows him her tiny wings. The rat had no idea she could fly, and the parrot scolds him for judging by looks alone. The beetle chooses a coat of green with golden lights from the splendid colors she sees in nature around her. The rat remains plain gray.

CONNECTIONS

Appearance. Beetles. Braggarts. Cautionary tales. Clothing. Colors. Competition. Insects. Knowledge. Origin tales. Perspective. Rats. Rewards. Ridicule.

HOW ELSE THIS STORY IS TOLD

The Beetle and the Paca—Frances Carpenter, *South American Wonder Tales*
How Brazilian Beetles Got Their Gorgeous Coats—Martha Hamilton and Mitch Weiss, *How & Why Stories*
Why Beetle Is Beautiful—Pleasant DeSpain, *The Emerald Lizard*. Parrot offers the brown Beetle a louder color if she will do something brave. He then proposes a race, annoyed with Paca the rat's boasting.

---

225. BIRD CU
Genevieve Barlow, *Latin American Tales from the Pampas to Mexico City*
Mexico

There is going to be a reunion of birds, and Bird Cu is complaining about how plain she looks. The eagle asks the owl what to do, and the owl suggests that birds all contribute some of their colorful feathers to dress her up. Once she is covered with pitch and new feathers, Bird Cu does nothing but admire herself. The owl says she needs work. He is certain that once she serves as their messenger, Bird Cu will have no time to be vain and will help those who helped her. Still, Bird Cu fails to deliver the eagle's message summoning all birds to an impending storm meeting. The birds resent both Bird Cu and the owl for promoting her. Tonotiuh tells the eagle that those two shall only come out after dark now to be safe from the anger of the other birds.

CONNECTIONS

Anger. Appearance. Arrogance. Bats. Beauty. Bird helpers. Birds. Cu (Bird). Discontent. Eagles. Feathers. Generosity. Gods and animals. Kindness. Music. Origin tales. Owls. Punishments. Selfishness. Trust. Vanity. Work.

HOW ELSE THIS STORY IS TOLD

The Biguidibela—Marcos Kurtycz and Ana García Kobeh, *Tigers and Opossums: Animal Legends*. Here, the plain animal is a bat, called *biguidibela*, which means naked bird. She goes to God, who says there are no feathers left, but to ask some of the birds to share their extras. They do, but *biguidibela* becomes so unbearably boastful, the other birds complain to God. As *biguidibela* spins to show off her feathers to God, they fly off until she is plain again and hides in the night.
The Owl and the Painted Bird / La lechuza y el pájaro pintado—Angel Vigil, *The Eagle on the Cactus*. An old owl takes on the responsibility for returning all the feathers lent to Pi-coo,

but she flies off with them. The birds' anger turns on owl, who now only comes out at night, still trying to find her, calling Pi-cooo.

El Pájaro-cú—Camilla Campbell, *Star Mountain and Other Legends of Mexico*
El Pájaro Cú—Riley Aiken. In J. Frank Dobie, *Puro Mexicano*

226. THE PEACOCK AND THE PUHUY

Genevieve Barlow, *Latin American Tales from the Pampas to Mexico City*
Maya People. El Salvador

When the god Chaac announces that King Eagle is retiring, the peacock—who was not beautiful back then, but could certainly sing—has a plan to become king. He asks the puhuy if he can borrow his splendid coat until after the election. The peacock not only reassures the shy puhuy that he will return it, but also promises to share the honors of being king with him. The puhuy lends the peacock his magnificent coat with colorful tail feathers, neck feathers, and a crest and hides his own bareness in the bushes. When the peacock struts out the next morning, with such beauty of looks and song, he is chosen to be king. Days later the peacock is still strutting around in the puhuy's coat. Chaac finds the puhuy and gives him a plain coat, telling the shy bird no one will take advantage of him in this. But the puhuy knows Chaac is punishing him for having foolishly trusted the peacock. Then Chaac punishes the peacock by taking away his kingship and his gift of song.

CONNECTIONS

Appearance. Bargains. Beauty. Birds. Cautionary tales. Chac. Colors. Deceit. Discontent. Feathers. Generosity. Gods and animals. Music. Origin tales. Peacocks. Promises. Puhuys. Punishments. Shyness. Trust. Vanity.

HOW ELSE THIS STORY IS TOLD

Mexican variations:

The Disappointed Peacock—Idella Purnell, *The Merry Frogs.* Zapotec People. Peacock is strutting with pride, when sparrow-hawk decides to punish his vanity and tells him that beautiful feathers are not everything. He cannot sing like the goldfinch or dove. Peacock decides to get another opinion. Hen tells him that beauty requires other qualities, like being useful and giving eggs. When the vulture agrees that the peacock isn't of any good to other birds or humans, the peacock insults his feet. The peacock then tries to imitate a goldfinch, but cannot sing, and realizes what the other birds say about the qualities required for beauty are true.

The Puhuy Bird (Story cards)

227. *MEDIOPOLLITO / HALF-CHICKEN*

Alma Flor Ada
Mexico

The thirteenth chick in the farmyard brood hatches with only one wing, one leg, and one eye. He becomes vain about his uniqueness and decides to hop to the court of the viceroy in Mexico City. Along the way, he helps to clear branches from a stream, build up a small fire, and untangle wind from branches. The viceroy's guards laugh at Mediopollito and send him to the kitchen, where the cook plunks him in a pot to heat on the stove. After Mediopollito calls on his friend the stream to put out the fire, the cook throws him out the window. His friend wind carries Mediopollito up to the top of the viceroy's palace where he becomes the first weathercock, pointing where the wind blows and watching all that goes on below.

CONNECTIONS

Appearance. Chickens and hens. Disabilities. Friendship. Journeys. Kindness. Origin tales. Punishments. Rescues. Ridicule. Selfishness. Transformations. Unkindness. Vanity. Weather vanes.

HOW ELSE THIS STORY IS TOLD

The Little Half-Chick—Lucía M. González, *Señor Cat's Romance.* This Medio-Pollito has no time to waste helping others, and so wind, water, and fire don't help him either. He repents once he serves to help people as a weathervane up on the roof. The story here takes place in Spain, but was shared with the author by a Latin American.

Medio Pollito (half-chick): A Mexican Folktale—Amanda StJohn. In this version Medio Pollito only helps the wind, which helps him escape from the cooking pot by blowing him up to the roof.

228. THE PROUD HORSEMAN
Pleasant DeSpain, *The Emerald Lizard*
Costa Rica

A peasant, carrying a bundle of food and water, stops to rest on his hot walk to Nicoya. When a wealthy horseman greets him, the peasant requests a ride, since they are both going to the festival of the Virgin of Guadalupe. The horseman brushes him off, saying the weight will be too much and rides away. However, a little further down the dusty road, the horseman becomes thirsty and hungry and returns. This time he offers the peasant a ride for provisions, but the peasant turns him down, saying he'll be fine since his bundle is now much lighter.

CONNECTIONS

Arrogance. Cautionary tales. Class conflict. Horsemen. Hunger. Justice. Peasants. Punishments. Unkindness.

HOW ELSE THIS STORY IS TOLD

The Peasant and the Horseman—Harold Courlander, *Ride with the Sun*

229. THE ETERNAL WANDERER OF THE PAMPAS
M.A. Jagendorf and R.S. Boggs, *The King of the Mountains*
Argentina

A gaucho who claims to be the best weaver in all of Argentina determines to weave the most wonderful poncho ever made. Concentrating on that poncho day and night, he stops caring for his family, his friends, and his cattle. Colors and designs are all that matter. When a friend tells him about a fiesta in three days, the gaucho brags that he will finish in time, even though there is a lot left to weave. He pushes so hard that his fingers and eyes are sore, and he does not realize that the designs themselves are sloppy and the shape irregular. The night of the fiesta, he forgets to bring his family and races off on his horse eager to show off the poncho. Frightened by a bird, his horse throws him and runs away. The gaucho finds himself on the ground, attacked by long claws of the brush and held down by the heavy poncho. Voices scream that because he neglected his wife and children for his own vanity over a poncho, he will ride endlessly across the pampas forever.

CONNECTIONS

Arrogance. Braggarts. Cautionary tales. Clothing. Gauchos. Magic plants. Ponchos. Punishments. Responsibility. Selfishness. Supernatural beings. Vanity. Supernatural voices. Weaving.

230. MARIA SAT ON THE FIRE

Anita Brenner, *The Boy Who Could Do Anything*
Mexico

For ten years, Maria has cooked for a rich family, wasteful the whole time. She keeps the fire burning even when she isn't cooking and throws out food. The year after she dies, Maria returns to the house and tells the lady of the house that God has sent her to work without pay as a punishment for being wasteful before. Maria serves and cleans diligently, without eating anything herself. When the lady sees Maria sitting on the stove fire, though, she goes to the priest who comes to speak with her. Maria tells the priest God has told her to do this because she wasted the fire when she was alive. The priest blesses Maria, and she disappears as the fire goes out.

CONNECTIONS

Cautionary tales. Ecology. Ghosts. God. Gods and humans. Priests and priestesses. Punishments. Repentance. Supernatural beings. Wastefulness.

231. BROKEN PLEDGE: ALL THINGS TALK

Harold Courlander, *A Treasury of Afro-American Folklore*
African American People. Suriname

A man plants some peanuts and announces he will dig them up on his birthday. They are ready a few days earlier. When he tries to dig them up, however, the peanuts accuse him of breaking his word. His walking stick and everything else in his house now back the peanuts. Fearful, he runs outside, where a man carrying wood on his head scoffs that he would never run because of something so ridiculous. His bundle of wood contradicts, saying he would run even faster. At that, the men decide it's always important to do what you say.

CONNECTIONS

Accusations. Cautionary tales. Fear. Language. Peanuts. Promises. Supernatural voices. Wood. Words.

HOW ELSE THIS STORY IS TOLD

Broken Pledge: All Things Talk 1—Melville J. Herskovits and Frances Herskovits, *Suriname Folk-Lore*

IX

When Cultures, Classes
or Species Collide

---

232. THE VIRGIN OF GUADALUPE
Mary-Jo Gerson, *Fiesta Femenina*
Mexico

On a December morning in 1531, Juan Diego, is walking to church. Christianity is new for him, since the Spanish have forced indigenous people to give up their Aztec religion. As Juan climbs the hill of Tepeyac, he hears music and reaches a dark skinned woman in a beautiful rebozo, surrounded by light. The Virgin Mary asks him to tell the Bishop to build her a church on this hill, promising to protect the people of Mexico if this is done. Juan is filled with trepidation. How will he, a poor Indian who speaks Nahuatl, be able to convince Bishop Fray Juan de Zumárraga? Still, Juan walks to Mexico City to deliver the Virgin's message. Juan is certain he has failed when the Bishop asks him to return. Back on the hill, the Virgin tells Juan to try again. The guards belittle him, but Juan insists on speaking with the Bishop, who tells Juan to bring proof that his story is true. The Virgin sends Juan to Tepeyac where the hill is filled with roses impossibly blooming in December. The Virgin blesses the flowers Juan gathers in his *tilma*, and he returns to Mexico City. The Bishop's guards threaten Juan, but when the Bishop sees an image of the Virgin herself on the unwrapped *tilma* full of roses, he promises to build a church on the hill of Tepeyac. For the rest of his life, Juan lives beside the chapel, guarding the image of the Virgin on his *tilma*. Pilgrims now visit the basilica there every December.

CONNECTIONS
Bishops. Churches. Cultural conflict. Diego, Juan (Saint). Faith. Heroes and heroines. Magic flowers. Magic tilma. Messengers. Miracles. Perseverance. Saints. Virgin Mary.

HOW ELSE THIS STORY IS TOLD
How the Queen of Heaven, Our Beloved Lady of Guadalupe, Appeared in the Place Known as Tepeyacac Near the City of Mexico—Luis Lasso de la Vega. In Harriet De Onís, *The Golden Land* and as The Virgin of Guadalupe. In John Bierhorst, *The Hungry Woman*.

Our Lady of Guadalupe—Camilla Campbell, *Star Mountain and Other Legends of Mexico*
The Lady of Guadalupe—Tomie DePaola
The Miracle of Our Lady of Guadalupe—Lulu Delacre, *Golden Tales*. Zapotec People
The Miracle of Our Lady of Guadalupe—M.A. Jagendorf and R.S. Boggs, *The King of the Mountains*
The Virgin of Guadalupe / La Virgen de Guadalupe—Genevieve Barlow and William N. Stivers, *Stories from Mexico / Historias de México*
The Virgin of Guadalupe—E. Adams Davis, *Of the Night Wind's Telling*
The Virgin of Guadalupe—Olga Loya, *Momentos Mágicos / Magic Moments*

233. THE VICEROY AND THE INDIAN
E. Adams Davis, *Of the Night Wind's Telling*
Mexico

This Viceroy, Juan Vicente de Guemes Pacheco y Padilla, the Conde de Revillagigedo, cares about being a good governor to all the people in New Spain. One morning, an indigenous man tells the Viceroy that he has been wrongly accused of theft. Two days before he had found a small bag of gold lying on the ground. As his family could use the money, he was considering keeping it, when a street crier called that a certain gentleman was offering a reward for its return. The poor man knew it was right to bring the bag to its owner, but when he did, the Don accused him of stealing two ounces from it and turned him out with no reward. The poor man tells the Viceroy he saw the Don slide two ounces into his waistcoat pocket as he was counting. The Viceroy listens to the Don accuse the indigenous man of stealing. He tells the Don that the man would not have returned the bag at all if he were a thief. Therefore, the Viceroy concludes that the indigenous man must be honest, and this bag with 26 ounces instead of 28 must not be the same bag which the Don lost. Since no one else has claimed a bag of gold with 26 ounces, the Viceroy says it is only right that the finder take it home.

CONNECTIONS
Class conflict. Cultural conflict. Deceit. Gold. Honesty. Justice. Theft. Truth. Viceroys.

234. MALINTZIN OF THE MOUNTAIN
Mary-Jo Gerson, *Fiesta Femenina*
Aztec People. Mexico

Born an Aztec princess, Malintzin becomes a slave when her father is defeated in battle. She learns to speak Nahuatl, Mixtec, and Mayan, serving the Tabascans, who trade all over Mexico. When Malintzin is sold to the conquistador Hernán Cortés, she also learns Spanish. Cortés appreciates her knowledge and begins to rely on Malintzin for guidance in conquering her own people. She acts as interpreter when Cortés meets Moctezuma. The Aztec king thinks Cortés, with his white face and beard, is the spirit of the god Quetzalcoatl who has returned as it was foretold. Moctezuma gives Cortés gold, jewels, and chocolate. Malintzin helps Cortés with the deception, perhaps for a chance to make a better life for herself or perhaps to exert a kinder influence over his decisions. After a time, though, Malintzin realizes that Cortés and his soldiers want more and more riches and are cruel to the natives. Malinztin weeps so hard she floats away from Cortés. The wind carries her to the mountain of Texocotepec, where she lives, now a larger-than-life woman, crying for all the terrible things that happened to her people when the Spanish arrived. She soothes the tempers of the Nahuaques there, who have the power to bring rain to make things grow and rallies them to blow bugles and bang drums to give Mexicans courage to fight for their rights.

Connections

Aztec people. Betrayal. Captivity. Changes in attitude. Conquerors. Cortés, Hernán. Cultural conflict. Deceit. Emperors, kings & queens. Gold. Greed. Interpreters. Justice. Malintzin. Misunderstandings. Montezuma. Remorse. Slavery. Supernatural beings. Texocotepec, mountain. Transformations.

How Else This Story Is Told

Malintzin—Anita Brenner, *The Boy Who Could Do Anything*
The Return of Quetzalcoatl—John Bierhorst, *The Hungry Woman*

---

235. The Bat-Boy and the First Laughter

Horace Banner in Johannes Wilbert, editor, *Folk Literature of the Gê Indians, Vol. 1*
Cayapo People. Amazonia, Brazil

A Cayapo man alone in a forest hears a strange murmur. There, hanging upside down from a branch, is a Kuben-niêpre. It has a man's body with the wings and feet of a bat. The friendly Kuben-niêpre comes down and begins to stroke the Cayapo firmly. Though the man doesn't really like this, the Kuben-niêpre's cold hands and long nails tickle him and make him laugh. No one in the world has ever laughed before. The Kuben-niêpre flies the Indian to the stone cave where his people hang from the ceiling. There the Cayapo receives so many tickling caresses, that he collapses from laughter. When he finally returns home, his people are angry at the indignity with which he was treated and set out to retaliate. They arrive by day when the Kuben-niêpre are sleeping and set fire to dry leaves inside their cave. All but one young Kuben-niêpre escape through an opening at the top. This bat-boy is brought back to their village, alive. Even though they make him a rack to sleep upside down from and teach him to walk, he does not survive for long. Ever since then, laughter and tickling are considered appropriate only for women and children, not for warriors.

Connections

Bats. Captivity. Cultural conflict. Humiliation. Interspecies conflict. Kuben-niêpre. Laughter. Origin tales. Outsiders. Revenge. Supernatural beings.

236. THE COFFIN CONTEST / ATAUDKUNA MAQANAKUY

Sara Vargas de Mayorga in Johnny Payne, *She-Calf*
Quechua People. Peru

Things are tense between the people in the very cold land up high who have less food than the people who live without hardship in the warm, lush valley below. The cold-land people fear they will be taken over. Once, a coffin from the cold place brags it must be the stronger one now, since it has had to haul so many corpses to the graveyard. The coffin from the warmer place insists it is stronger. They agree to fight it out on the Ch'aqo Bridge. A man who hears them ka-chunking there hides, afraid of demons. The coffins fight until the thinner warm valley coffin is in pieces. The bigger cold-land coffin says the hot-lands now belong to him. The other coffin agrees to fight again, reclaims all its splinters, and thunks downhill. Sick with terror, the hiding man runs all the way back to his house in the valley. He tells his wife about the coffins fighting, but she is certain he is just covering up some misbehavior of his own. A friend suggests they smash the cold-land coffins before they can take over. The coffins realize what they are planning and threaten to carry the man off. The man dies of fright right then.

CONNECTIONS

Allegories and parables. Coffins. Class conflict. Competition. Cultural conflict. Fear. Hunger. Husbands and wives. Geography. Status. Strength. Supernatural beings. Temperature.

---

237. THE MORNING STAR

Idella Purnell, *The Merry Frogs*
Cora People. Mexico

Annoyed with the Sun's hot rays, the Morning Star, Chuvlavete, shoots the Sun right out of the sky one day. The Sun falls to earth, where he is healed with a poultice from an old man. Chuvlavete regrets his impulsive deed, and he and the Sun agree it's best to avoid each other. Chuvlavete is poor, but some rich people invite him over to eat. When he shows up almost naked, they call him a "sneaking Indian." The next night, Chuvlavete disguises himself with a big beard and nearly white skin. He dresses in a fine three-piece Mexican suit and gallops up with a silver sword on a white horse with a richly inlaid saddle. This time the rich people welcome him to their bountiful dinner. Chuvlavete rubs the bread over his arms and legs. When they ask why he is doing this, he answers that they have only invited his clothes to dinner, not him, and continues to pour food all over himself. Chuvlavete chastises them for disliking him as a native man God put in the world and forever "little brother of the Indians," rides away.

CONNECTIONS

Allegories and parables. Clothing. Class conflict. Cultural conflict. Food. Impulsivity. Manners. Morning Star. Stars. Sun. Temperature. Values. Wealth.

238. THE TREES OF WHITE FLOWERS
Yolanda Nava, *It's All in the Frijoles*
Pre-Columbian Mexico

This is a time when the Zapotecs face constant threat from the Aztecs. Emissaries from King Ahuizolt warn that the Aztecs will conquer Zapotec and own all of King Cosijoeza's trees with white flowers if the Zapotec king does not send some willingly. King Cosijoeza refuses. His warriors successfully defend the city with poisoned arrows. King Ahuizolt, angry at being defeated, asks his daughter to seduce the Zapotec king. The beautiful Coyolicatzin appears at the edge of King Cosijoeza's forest. She tells him that she has been traveling, seeking happiness. He invites her to stay at his palace. Once King Cosijoeza has fallen in love with her, Coyolicatzin reveals only that she is the Aztec princess and needs to go home. King Cosijoeza lets her return, knowing nothing of her deception. He believes that their love can conquer the enmity between the lands. Soon after, he sends emissaries to ask King Ahuizolt for her hand. Delighted that the plan is working so well, the Aztec king consents. Coyolicatzin has agreed to pass along Zapotec defense secrets to her father. King Cosijoeza and Coyolicatzin marry, but Coyolicatzin comes to truly love the wise, brave King Cosijoeza and the Zapotecs. She can no longer betray them and confesses her father's plot to the king one morning. Grateful for her love and loyalty, King Cosijoeza sends trees with white flowers to the Aztec king in Tenochitlán.

CONNECTIONS
Aztec people. Changes in attitude. Coexistence. Cosijoeza, King. Cultural conflict. Deceit. Emperors, kings & queens. Love. Loyalty. Parents and children. Princes and princesses. Seduction. Trees. Zapotec People.

HOW ELSE THIS STORY IS TOLD
The Trees of White Flowers / Los árboles de flores blancas—Genevieve Barlow, *Stories from Latin America / Historias de Latinoamérica*

---

239. THE STORY OF THE VITÓRIA RÉGIA, THE AMAZON WATER LILY
Livia de Almeida and Ana Portella, *Brazilian Folktales*
Amazonia, Brazil

Caititi, New Moon, is the bravest of all the men and women warriors in her tribe by the Jamunda River. Out in her canoe, one day, Caititi sees a tall, white-skinned man. He seems god-like, but when he moves toward her, she shoots an arrow into his shoulder. She leaves, but that night, unable to forget him, she returns to tend his wounds. Though he cannot understand her language, she tells the white man that she is linked to him and rows to him every day. When he heals, they walk in the woods together, and she teaches him the ways of her people. However, a village warrior who loves Caititi, becomes suspicious. Torigo follows her and discovers that this stranger is using Caititi to gather information to share with people who plan to attack and enslave the tribe. The native warriors, men and women, attack the white men first. When the man Caititi loves is felled by a poison arrow, she brings his body to her canoe and cries out to the moon to change him into the most beautiful flower on the river. Caititi vanishes, but a while later, a white flower, the symbol of their love appears on the river.

CONNECTIONS

Accusations. Amazon River. Betrayal. Cultural conflict. Death. Deceit. Flowers. Jamunda River. Jealousy. Love. Magic flowers. Moon. Origin tales. Outsiders. Mourning. Stars. Transformations. Vitória Régia. Wounds.

HOW ELSE THIS STORY IS TOLD

Vitoria Regia—Mani Fagundes, *Myths of the Amazon River Video* (Online video)
The Legend of the Vitória Régia—Momentum Arts 2008, *Reminiscence Site of Untold Stories* (Online)

Colombian Amazon variations:

Vitória Régia: Giant Water Lily—Juan Carlos Galeano, *Folktales of the Amazon.* In this version, Caititi has fallen in love with the warrior her father has told her lives in the moon and throws herself into the water to be close to the moon reflected there. It is Caititi who becomes the flower.

---

240. OLLANTAY AND THE INCA

Douglas Gifford, *Warriors, Gods & Spirits from Central & South American Mythology*
Inca People

Cusi-Coyllur, daughter of the Inca emperor Pachacutec, and the courageous Inca general Ollantay fall in love. They marry in secret for Inca law forbids anyone to marry out of their social position. Pachacutec angrily sends Cusi-Coyllur away when Ollantay openly asks to marry his daughter. Cusi-Coyllur gives birth to a daughter, who is taken from her to be raised elsewhere by priestesses in the temple of the Sun. Ollantay believes the law is unjust and seizes the fortress, Ollantaytambo. The general Ruminawi pretends to be on Ollantay's side, but once admitted to the fortress, he lets the emperor's army in at night while the tired rebels are sleeping. Ollantay is now a prisoner, being led in chains to the capital, when a royal runner comes to tell Ruminawi that Pachacutec has died. Ollantay despairs over what will happen to Cusi-Coyllur and their child and what Pachacutec's son, the new Inca, will say the next day. Ollantay tells the Inca Tupac Yupanqui that he did not fight against his father, only against the law that says the person who is a god and the person who is human may not touch each other. The young Inca said it is laws that hold the empire together, but he agrees with Ollantay that Inca strength comes from faith and courage. The new Inca returns Ollantay's titles and sets him free to officially live with Cusi-Coyllur and their true daughter.

CONNECTIONS

Class conflict. Emperors, kings & queens. Forbidden love. Husbands and wives. Justice. Laws.
Love. Rebellion. Soldiers.

---

241. LA LLORONA: THE WEEPING WOMAN
Joe Hayes
Mexico

Beautiful María intends to marry someone grander than any of the young men
from her village. She is attracted to a handsome, wealthy ranchero, newly arrived, and
he is beguiled by her. They marry and have two children. Then the ranchero starts
spending months away, taming horses. He returns only to visit the children and speaks
of remarrying. When the ranchero's carriage rides in one day with a new, richly dressed
woman sitting by his side, María is consumed with rage. She throws her children into
the river. Then, frantically realizing what she has just done, she runs along the bank,
but they have vanished. She runs herself to death looking for them, and, even after she
is buried, villagers continue to hear her crying to them and wailing. Sometimes they
even see her ghost, by the river. They call her La Llorona and use her story to warn
children to come home before it gets dark so La Llorona will not get them, too.

CONNECTIONS

Anger. Betrayal. Cautionary tales. Class conflict. Cultural conflict. Despair. Husbands and wives.
Ghosts. Llorona. Love. Magic seeds. Murder. Parents and children. Ranchers. Selfishness.
Supernatural beings. Tiempo, Señor.

HOW ELSE THIS STORY IS TOLD

La Llorona: A Hispanic Legend—Joe Hayes. In *Teaching from a Hispanic Perspective, a Handbook
for Non-Hispanic Educators* (Online)

La Llorona: The Crying Woman (Bilingual) and as *Maya's Children: The Story of La Llorona*—
Anaya, Rudolfo. In a gentler telling, this immortal Mexican girl does not deliberately harm
her children. They are born from seeds she grows in clay bowls. She is tricked into throwing
the pots in the lake, thinking that will keep the children from being taken by Señor Tiempo,
Father Time.

La Llorona, The Wailing Woman—Olga Loya, *Momentos Mágicos / Magic Moments*. Pressured
by his parents to marry a more suitable wife, the Spanish lover comes to take the children
away from his Indian mistress. Distraught, Luisa throws the children into the river and
jumps in afterwards.

La Llorona told by Joe Hayes—Joe Hayes (Online video)

The Tale of La Llorona—Linda Lowery and Richard Keep. In this version, Maria is only concerned
with marrying a rich man to live a better life. The children drown when she is neglectful,
watching Don Ramón step out of the carriage with the rich woman he is going to marry.

The Wailing Woman, A Tale from Tenochtitlán—Richard and Judy Dockrey Young, *1492: New
World Tales*. Aztec People. A widow of low birth falls in love with a handsome prince of the
Aztec Emperor's family, who toys with her affection. He tells her that he cannot not marry
her because her children could never be considered princes, since he was not their father.

242. THE COMING OF ASIN

Kevin Crossley-Holland, *The Young Oxford Book of Folk Tales*
Pilaga People. Bolivia

Pilagá villagers mock the crooked, ugly stranger in the fox skin who does not say where he comes from, only that his name is Asin. They treat him as a beggar. Chief Nalaraté laughs when Asin asks to borrow a comb from his daughter for Asin has no hair, but Nalaraté's daughter lends him the comb. Curious, she follows Asin to the river, where he transforms into a handsome young warrior with long black hair, like the warriors of her tribe. The daughter determines to marry this man with special powers. When she tells him this, he says they should sit together on his skin publicly. Nalaraté is angry, but his daughter refuses to wed anyone else. That night Asin uses magic powers to protect them with mosquito netting and to provide food and a beautiful red skirtcloth for his wife. When Nalaraté prepares for an expedition against another tribe, he tells Asin he will only bring shame if he comes along. Asin follows behind on a donkey, anyway. Once the battle begins he transforms into mighty warrior, and, alone, drives all of the enemy horses back to his village. Afterwards, Asin leaves this place where he has been mistreated. He brings his wife, her mother who never ridiculed him, and the horses to a new place by a river. Many Pilagá warriors now join them. Asin hears that Nalaraté is planning to attack him. He claps his hands, and a cold wind blows the roofs away from those villages and makes people suffer for their meanness. When Asin stops the wind, he changes the old men of Nalaraté's village into yulo and mazmorras birds, the middle-aged people into hawks and vultures, and the children into ducks and herons. They all fly away, and Asin turns Nalaraté into an alligator.

CONNECTIONS

Appearance. Birds. Caciques and chieftains. Cultural conflict. Heroes and heroines. Justice. Love.
  Magic. Outsiders. Revenge. Ridicule. Supernatural husbands and wives. Transformations.
  Warriors.

HOW ELSE THIS STORY IS TOLD

Bolivian variation:
The Coming of Asin—Harold Courlander, *Ride with the Sun*
Toba variation from Argentina:
Asin—Josepha Sherman, *Merlin's Kin*

243. ATZIMBA, THE PRINCESS / ATZIMBA, LA PRINCESA

Genevieve Barlow and William N. Stivers, *Stories from Mexico /*
  Historias de México
Mexico

None of the tribal doctors or wise men her grandfather Aguanga summons can cure the beautiful, kind princess, Atzimba. Resting on the beach, Atzimba falls instantly in love with a Spanish soldier who gallops by. Already so weak, she faints and will not wake. At that time, uneasy peace prevails between the indigenous people and Cortez's soldiers. No one is around when Captain Villadiego, the soldier who caused Atzimba to faint, rides by two days later. He sees Atzimba sleeping and kisses her. Atzimba opens her eyes then, and he also falls in love with her. Together they tell Aguanga they wish to marry. Though Aguanga loves his granddaughter, he cannot permit this, for the captain is Spanish and not a prince, which goes against the laws of their tribe. Atzimba begs her grandfather, saying Captain Villadiego saved her life. When Aguanga sees that they will not be deterred, he sends them far away with an escort of men from the tribe. The tribal men close the lovers in a cave with rocks. Years later, Spanish soldiers discover two skeletons there in an embrace.

CONNECTIONS

Caciques and chieftains. Cultural conflict. Forbidden love. Grandparents and grandchildren. Illness. Laws. Love. Princes and princesses. Punishments.

---

244. THE GRANDFATHER AND THE FAULTFINDERS
Ignacio Bizarro Ujpan in James D. Sexton, *Heart of Heaven, Heart of Earth*
Maya People

An indigenous grandfather and his grandson Chito carry big loads of charcoal, which they sell for their living. One after another, people in town find fault with how they are carrying it. Some accuse the grandfather of giving the boy too much to carry, and when the grandfather carries everything, people tell the grandson he has no respect. When Chito carries it all, some young men say the grandfather should because he is much stronger. A señora comments that they really need *caites* for their bare feet. They can only afford one pair, but that causes another round of criticism from onlookers and more switching around, which pleases no one. When the priest chastises Chito for wearing the sandals, they throw the *caites* away in frustration. Then at another senora's suggestion, they buy a burro to carry the charcoal, but everyone has an opinion about this, too. When they both ride the burro and a priest accuses them of making the animal suffer, they tell him that they are tired of being judged. They give their burro to the priest and walk away.

CONNECTIONS

Accusations. Class conflict. Cultural conflict. Faultfinders. Frustration. Grandparents and grandchildren. Justice. Perspective. Problem solving. Work.

---

245. THE THREE GRINGOS / LOS TRES GRINGOS
Pedro Cholotío Temó and Alberto Barreno, *The Dog Who Spoke /*
   El perro que habló
Tzutuhil Maya People. Panajachel, Guatemala

Some gringos who only speak English want to learn Spanish. They can say three phrases: "the three," which people said when pointing to them; "For one ear of corn that this man has stolen," when the police grab a thief; and "With much pleasure," which a vendor says to a señora who has asked for a quarter-pound of cheese. When a dead body is found in the market and the police question the gringos, these are the only phrases they know how to respond with. The police now think the three of them killed the man for an ear of corn. The third gringo answers, "With much pleasure," when the police take them to jail. The judge, however, realizes that they are innocent. He releases them, and the gringos decide to learn more Spanish.

Connections

Cultural conflict. Gringos. Humorous tales. Knowledge. Language. Misunderstandings. Outsiders.

How Else This Story Is Told

Chilean variation:

We Ourselves—Yolando Pino-Saavedra, *Folktales of Chile.* The three young men are naïve country bumpkins.

---

246. Seven Colors

Yolando Pino-Saavedra, *Folktales of Chile*
Chile

Confident of his experience with sheep, the son of a poor couple rides to the palace on a sheep, wearing pants with patches of many colors. To get rid of him, the king sends him to fetch one cow from a certain ranch, something no one else has been able to accomplish. The boy has just caught a cow when a giant challenges him to fight, so he rides his sheep under the belly of the giant's horse and stabs him. Then he takes the giant's diamond ring and brings back the cow. The king, who calls him Seven Colors, thinks he'll now have to put up with this strange young man. Seven Colors dines with the king's three daughters and gives the diamond ring to the oldest daughter when she compliments it. The king sends him back to that ranch again, and Seven Colors kills a second giant and returns with another cow and another diamond ring. The third giant is more ferocious, but Seven Colors slays him, too, and then investigates to see where they all might have come from. He finds a palace guarded by a fierce and gigantic frog who says that if he really killed the giants, he could also free her from enchantment. Seven Colors is afraid of this frog, but follows her instructions, and she transforms into a beautiful princess. The princess summons servants to bring fine clothes for him. The king apologizes to Seven Colors and stands as godfather when Seven Colors marries the frog princess he freed.

Connections

Appearance. Changes in attitude. Class conflict. Emperors, kings & queens. Frogs and toads. Giants. Herders. Magic. Outsiders. Perspective. Princes and princesses. Rescues. Supernatural beings. Tasks.

247. THE JAGUAR'S WIFE

Douglas Gifford, *Warriors, Gods & Spirits from Central &*
South American Mythology
Opaye People. Brazil

Just as a girl is wishing that she were a jaguar's daughter in order to have plenty of meat to eat, a jaguar is there and asks her to come with him. He promises not to hurt her. No one is around to give her advice, and she leaves with him. In a few months, the girl returns, healthy and happy, to tell her family that she is now married to the jaguar, who has offered to bring them meat. They request tapir. The jaguar gets tired of carrying meat to their roof and suggests they move into her village together. The jaguar's wife's family enjoys the meat and their daughter's skill in hunting, but they are still suspicious of the jaguar husband himself. Then the grandmother notices the girl is beginning to show black spots, claws, and sharp teeth. She prepares a spell, which kills the jaguar's wife. The family worries that the jaguar will harm them, but he calmly asks them to remember that he treated them fairly and leaves, saving his grief for when he is back in the forest.

CONNECTIONS

Betrayal. Grandparents and grandchildren. Interspecies conflict. Interspecies marriage. Jaguars. Love. Magic. Mourning. Murder. Outsiders. Supernatural husbands and wives. Transformations. Wishes.

---

248. TORORÕI, THE FROG

Galib Pororoca Gurib Ajuru in Betty Mindlin, *Barbecued Husbands*
Brazil

An indigenous man who is digging a hole to trap sauba ants for food invites the frog crying nearby to turn into a woman and become his wife. To his delight, the frog leaps away from his club and turns into a woman. She follows him home. Even though the frog-wife prepares *chicha* and *tacacá* for her husband, she herself eats only only toasted corn and sauba ants and prefers the queen ants which bite. The food she prepares seems to multiply by itself in the gourd, but her husband grows tired of being bitten by the ants they hunt every night. Irritated, he puts *tacacá* with hot pepper on his wife's tongue. It burns so much, she cries and then leaves for the river, where she turns back into a frog, still crying. Her husband regrets what he did and calls to her, but Tororõi is done with him.

CONNECTIONS

Abuse. Anger. Ants. Cultural conflict. Frogs and toads. Insects. Interspecies conflict. Interspecies marriage. Remorse. Supernatural husbands and wives. Transformations.

249. The Man Who Took a Water Mother for His Bride

Harold Courlander, *A Treasury of Afro-American Folklore*
African American People. Brazil

Farmer Domingos becomes aware that someone has been stealing corn from his meager garden for the past two nights. He hides with a knife to catch the thief. She turns out to be a beautiful water woman. He asks why he should not punish her. She answers that she has been very hungry and asks him to let her return to the river, for it will not help him to detain her. Domingos says he will not be alone if she marries him. She warns that another land man who married a water woman became abusive and ridiculed her. Domingos says this is not him, and so the water mother becomes his wife. His fortune and standing in the community change for the better. When Domingos drinks too much, however, he calls her a good-for-nothing Mãe d'agua. The water woman leaves silently, but Domingos's feet will not move when he tries to follow her. She walks into the river and disappears with their children and all of their livestock. Ears of corn, the house, and even the fence also fly through the air into the river. Domingos becomes poorer than he was at the beginning.

Connections

Abuse. Arrogance. Drink. Farmers. Husbands and wives. Interspecies conflict. Interspecies marriage. Magic. Punishments. Reversals of fortune. Ridicule. Supernatural husbands and wives. Theft. Water mothers.

---

250. Fire and the Jaguar

Philip Ardagh, *South American Myths & Legends*
Cayapo People. Amazonia Brazil

Botoque's brother-in-law does not believe Botoque when the boy calls down that the macaw's nest he's been sent to check on a high rock ledge contains only two stones and no eggs. His angry brother-in-law shakes the ladder. Botoque drops the stones to stop him. The stones hit his brother-in-law and knock over the ladder. The brother-in-law leaves him up there and tells the villagers that Botoque ran away. Botoque is stuck now on top of the ledge for days, hungry and scared. A jaguar notices him and climbs up to check out this curious human. Botoque tells him his story, and the jaguar invites him home, reassuring Botoque that it was a human who betrayed him, not a jaguar. Humans do not have fire yet, and Botoque is amazed to see a log burning in the middle of the jaguar's floor. Botoque enjoys eating cooked meat. Jaguar tells his wife that he has adopted Botoque. His wife objects that they will soon be having their own cub, but the jaguar treats Botoque like a son. He makes Botoque a bow and arrow, something else no human has seen before, and they go hunting together. The jaguar's wife resents Botoque. Once when she snarls and frightens him, he shoots an arrow into her paw and flees back to his village with some cooked meat. His family really enjoys the meat. They want to have fire and sneak to the jaguar's home, where a tapir steals a burning log for them. The jaguar, who was always kind to Botoque, feels betrayed. He becomes angry at humans, who cannot be loyal to animals or each other. He hunts now only with his teeth and claws and only eats meat raw.

CONNECTIONS

Anger. Animal helpers. Anteaters. Betrayal. Brothers-in-law and sisters-in-law. Fire. Husbands and wives. Ingratitude. Interspecies conflict. Jaguars. Life span. Magic trees. Meat. Ogres. Origin tales. Resentment. Theft. Transformations. Warnings. Weapons.

HOW ELSE THIS STORY IS TOLD

The Bird Nester and the Jaguar—John Bierhorst, *The Mythology of South America*. In this gritty version, the boy, frightened by the jaguar wife's wide-open mouth, shoves a stick into her throat, and she becomes an anteater.

Botoque, the Jaguar, and the Fire—Mercedes Dorson & Jeanne Wilmot, *Tales from the Rain Forest*

Fire and the Jaguar—Vic Parker, *Traditional Tales from South America*

The Fire of the Jaguar—Horace Banner. In Johannes Wilbert, *Folk Literature of the Gê Indians, Vol. 1*

How Fire Was Stolen—Curt Nimuendajú. In Johannes Wilbert, *Folk Literature of the Gê Indians, Vol. 1*. Crenye People

The Origin of Fire—Douglas Gifford, *Warriors, Gods & Spirits from Central & South American Mythology*. Caraja and Apinagé People. Once the jaguar has given the boy his own bow and arrow, he warns him not to answer any dead trees which may call out to him. The boy does, which condemns his people to a life span of fifty years. However, after escaping from an ogre on the way home, he brings his father back to meet the kindly jaguar, who gives him fire to take back, for love of this son.

See also Tlacuache's Tail (21).

---

251. LION AND MAN

M.A. Jagendorf and R.S. Boggs, *The King of the Mountains*
Chile

Sheltered Young Lion asks his father whether anyone or anything is braver or stronger than they are. Old Lion tells him that Man is trickier and can win without strength, which is why they live safely away in the Andes Mountains. Young Lion growls that he wants to see Man for himself and fight him. His father tries to convince him not to go, but Young Lion sets off down to the valley with his reluctant father's blessing. Along the way Young Lion asks Horse and Ox if they are Man, and each tells him how Man has hurt him. Dog, though, tells Young Lion that Man is a master he loves and obeys. Dog leads Young Lion to Man, after telling Man to bring a gun. Young Lion tells Man he wants to fight him. Man answers that they have no reason to fight, so Young Lion provokes him by accusing him of everything Horse and Ox told him. Man says he will use only one single word. He fires his gun at Young Lion's leg and shouts, "Bang." In pain, Young Lion flees back up into the mountains, thinking that his father was right.

Connections

Accusations. Andes Mountains. Betrayal. Burros. Changes in attitude. Competition. Courage. Coyotes. Curiosity. Dogs. Eagles. Horses. Humans. Identity. Interspecies conflict. Knowledge. Lions. Misunderstandings. Oxen. Parents and children. Quests. Snakes. Strength. Weapons. Words.

How Else This Story Is Told

Mexican variation:

The Lion Who Wanted to Fight Man—Dan Storm, *Pictures Tales from Mexico*. Here, lion meets Snake, Eagle, Ox, Burro, and Coyote. There is no gun, but the man lassos him. Lion thinks well of man for letting him then go free, and sometimes even helps man in the wilderness.

---

252. The Chontal Giant

Francisco Hinojosa, *The Old Lady Who Ate People: Frightening Stories*
Mexico

Chersjalm, strong and ferocious, the most frightening of the giants who live in the mountains, is bitten by a poisonous snake one day. He runs to the valley for the magic herb he knows can heal him, but collapses, too weak to stop the poison. Gayolicaltzin, queen of the Zapotecs, finds the giant in pain and brings him back from death with the magic herb. The king strongly objects when she has the giant moved to the palace. He wants to imprison Chersjalm, but the queen convinces him to let Chersjalm fight five warriors for his freedom when he recovers. Chersjalm easily throws those warriors in the air and says he will serve the queen and die defending her. The king still does not trust Chersjalm, but Chersjalm gets to prove his loyalty when Gayolicaltzin is kidnapped. He runs tirelessly to find her, tromps the evil warriors who hold her captive, and carries the queen gently back on a little throne on his back.

Connections

Captivity. Changes in attitude. Cultural conflict. Emperors, kings & queens. Giants. Gratitude. Healing. Heroes and heroines. Kindness. Loyalty. Outsiders. Poison. Rescues. Restoring life. Snakes. Supernatural beings. Trust. Zapotec People.

---

253. *The Treasure of Guatavita /
El Tesoro de Guatavita*

Harriet Rohmer and Jesús Guerrero Rea
Chibcha People. Colombia

Legend holds that long, long ago the goddess Bachue and her son arose from Lake Guatavita and wandered through the mountains, teaching the Chibcha people how to grow corn, build shelters, and find emeralds and gold. When the people grew old, they went to live in the cold water of the volcanic crater as serpents and watched over the nation. In gratitude, every spring, in a grand ceremony, the cacique would be rowed to the center of the lake and, dusted with gold paint. There he would offer his people's most beautiful creations to the water for the goddess and her son. He would then dive in afterwards, offering them even the gold from his body. When soldiers from the King of Spain conquered northern Colombia, they went looking for the chief they called El Dorado, the golden one. The cacique said nothing and was tortured. His son pointed south to the jungles. No one ever found the legendary treasures.

CONNECTIONS

Caciques and chieftains. Conquerors. Cultural conflict. El Dorado. Enchanted cities. Festivals. Gods and humans. Gold. Guatavita, Lake. Treasure.

HOW ELSE THIS STORY IS TOLD

The Legend of El Dorado—Nancy Van Laan. Each Chibcha king brings gold and ritually enters the lake so that the serpent down below will keep his kingdom safe.

---

254. THE MYSTERIOUS LAKE

M.A. Jagendorf and R.S. Boggs, *The King of the Mountains*
Colombia

Growing up high in the Andes, far from other people, Juan Martin has learned the languages of nature and respects the old stories, which his father shares. Now at the edge of an emerald green lake where native people used to worship, Juan overhears a zancudo say that the Golden Duck and Ducklings will emerge from the lake the next day. The legend says that the Golden Duck is a princess, and a person who catches all the ducks together within the circle of a rosary could become rich. Juan returns to see the ducks rise from the middle of the lake. He throws his rosary as the seven golden ducklings come close to shore. Suddenly, a beautiful bronze girl stands there with seven children. She sadly says she is a Chibcha princess and would like to return to the palace under the lake, where her father brought them to escape from the greed and cruelty of white men. Juan asks now how he can help them go back. The princess says he must come to live with them underwater. Juan wavers, but her need to return to the water is so great that he becomes an eighth duckling.

CONNECTIONS

Andes Mountains. Chibcha people. Cultural conflict. Ducks. Gold. Journeys to other realms. Lakes. Magic. Princes and princesses. Storytelling. Transformations. Supernatural beings. Water worlds.

---

255. THE COMET AND THE TIGER (WHY THE TIGER HAS BLACK SPOTS)

Angel Vigil, *The Eagle on the Cactus*
Mexico

One peaceful tiger in ancient times loves to watch the night sky. For several nights, though, he has resented the presence of a bright new comet, which he believes is trying to outshine the Moon he loves. The tiger cannot let his anger go. He demands to know why the comet is there, and, affronted, the comet answers that it is not for him to question what the gods find beautiful. The tiger responds that *Señora* Moon and her children the stars should be the only ones to light Earth at night. The comet says she must be respected, for her appearance foretells impending events such as the death of a king or famine or war. When the tiger does not accept this explanation, the angry comet burns him with arrows of fire from her tail. The tiger has been marked with those spots ever since.

Note: Pumas are often called tigers in Latin American tales.

CONNECTIONS

Anger. Coexistence. Comets. Interspecies conflict. Light. Moon. Origin tales. Outsiders. Pumas. Resentment. Tigers.

---

256. THE MONKEY'S HAIRCUT

John Bierhorst, *The Monkey's Haircut*
Yucatec Maya Speakers. Mexico

A monkey wishes to try to do everything his rich master does. When his master gets a haircut, the monkey thinks that would be a good idea for him, too. He eventually finds enough centavos and goes to the barber to request one. When the barber points out that the monkey has no hair on his head, the monkey asks to have his tail shaved, instead. Afterwards, the monkey leaves, but returns then for his hair clippings, for he remembers how the barber swept up the hair after his master's cut. By now, the monkey's hair is mixed in with everyone else's on the barbershop floor. Annoyed, the monkey swipes the barber's razor which he gives to the butcher when he hears him complain about the dullness of his knife. The razor breaks, though, so the monkey runs off with the butcher's guitar. The monkey is sitting on an old mud wall, singing and playing the guitar, when the butcher starts singing about the devil coming for the monkey. The wall collapses and the monkey is buried.

CONNECTIONS

Barbers. Discontent. Haircuts. Humans. Humorous tales. Imitation. Interspecies conflict. Magic. Misunderstandings. Monkeys. Swaps.

HOW ELSE THIS STORY IS TOLD

Brazilian variations:

The Monkey and His Tail—Enid D'Oyley, *Animal Fables*. African American People. Bored, Monkey sits in the middle of the road and stretches out his tail so that a man with a cart will run over it, and Monkey can demand his razor. This begins a whole set of trades, ending with Monkey happily going off with a loaf of bread.

The Spider Monkey's Close Shave— Shirley Climo, *Monkey Business*. A spider monkey gets upset to see his tail all bare after a shave and wants the barber to put the hair back on again. When the barber cannot, he grabs the razor and a series of swaps follows, where monkey gives things and then wants them back. After the girl monkey takes does not like swinging up in the trees, monkey decides to bring her back and be done with people things.

Mexican variation:
The Monkey's Whiskers—Anne Rockwell. When monkey is upset after his shave, the barber does magic, and monkey's whiskers come back redder and fuzzier.

---

257. The Magic Ibis

Douglas Gifford, *Warriors, Gods & Spirits from Central & South American Mythology*
Yahgan People. Islands south of Tierra del Fuego, Argentina

When an old man spies an ibis flying overhead and cries out that she is here and spring has finally arrived, the stately ibis is so affronted by the villagers' raucous celebration that she causes a deep freeze over the land. Many people die, unable to free their canoes from the ice to fish on frozen rivers. When the ibis allows the snow to melt, the land is changed. Rushing water carries soil away from the mountaintops, which stay bare. All year round, icebergs float between the islands, and ice too thick to melt clings to the mountain slopes. Since then, the people greet the arrival of spring quietly, pulling their children inside while the ibis flies by.

Connections

Birds. Coexistence. Disrespect. Ibis. Ice. Interspecies conflict. Noise. Origin tales. Punishments. Respect for nature. Spring. Traditions. Winter.

---

258. The Sparrow Shaman

Douglas Gifford, *Warriors, Gods & Spirits from Central & South American Mythology*
Yahgan People. Islands south of Tierra del Fuego, Argentina

Hespul the Sparrow, a mighty shaman, is angry when he shows up at a large feast where whale meat and blubber are being shared, and no one defers to him in any special way. He causes a frightening darkness to cover the land in the middle of the day and sends his voice out telling the people that he needs to be treated with respect. They plead with him to take the dark away and promise to honor him. The dark lasts for a long time, until one day Hespul paints his body and chants. As he slowly turns, dawn slowly rises in the east, and it still does to remind people of Hespul's power over day and night.

Connections

Anger. Birds. Day. Disrespect. Interspecies conflict. Night. Origin tales. Punishments. Respect for nature. Shamans. Sparrows. Status.

259. GODFATHER TO SKUNKS
Grant Lyons, *Tales the People Tell in Mexico*
Mexico

When Señora Skunk gives birth to a daughter, the proud papa rushes off to find a worthy godparent. Señor Fox, Señor Coyote, and Señor Mouse all laugh at the idea of being godparent to a skunk. Other creatures are insulted. Señor Lion accepts Señor Skunk's humble request, but he gets nervous at the christening fiesta. When Señora Skunk asks why, the lion tells her there is nothing to eat there for him, only skunk food: insects, eggs, and worms. The skunks are embarrassed. Señor Skunk accompanies Señor Lion to look for meat, but gets excited and sprays the ox, who would have trampled him, if Senor Lion hadn't been there to save him. Worried about her injured husband, Señora Skunk is angry with Señor Lion now for not eating what they do.

CONNECTIONS
Christenings. Godparents and godchildren. Hospitality. Interspecies conflict. Lions. Ridicule. Skunks. Status.

---

260. TURTLE AND ONÇA, THE JAGUAR
Livia de Almeida and Ana Portella, *Brazilian Folktales*
Amazonia, Brazil

Monkey laughs that Turtle cannot climb the Inajá tree to eat the fruit like he does. Then, he offers to bring her up, but abandons Turtle high in the palm tree. She has fruit to eat now, but Turtle is afraid of falling down. Onça suggests she jump down, and he will catch her. However, Turtle thinks the jaguar might eat her, which is exactly what Onça has planned. Instead, Turtle tucks inside her shell and hurls herself down on his head. Onça dies. A while later, Turtle returns to the palm tree, takes one of Onça's bones, and carves it into a flute. Another Onça objects that she is singing about having a flute made of jaguar bone. Turtle pretends that the bone is made of something else, but from her hiding place, she cannot resist, singing aloud that it really is Onça's bone. Furious, the second Onça waits to attack her, but she escapes through another hole in the tree.

CONNECTIONS
Anger. Bones. Coexistence. Deceit. Disrespect. Flutes. Interspecies conflict. Jaguars. Monkeys. Power. Trust. Tortoises and turtles.

---

261. ENEMY PLAYMATES: KITTEN AND RAT
Melville J. Herskovits and Frances Herskovits, *Suriname Folk-Lore*
Suriname

Kitten and little Rat like each other and play together every day, but one day little Rat's mother tells him to stop playing with Kitten because he is actually Kitten's favorite food. And Kitten's mother instructs Kitten to hit little Rat when they play because little Rat is his food. The next day, when Kitten asks why Rat isn't coming to play out in the street, little Rat answers that wise people with good advice exist in his village, too.

Connections

Allegories and parables. Cats. Coexistence. Enmity. Friendship. Interspecies conflict. Knowledge. Parents and children. Rats. Trust.

262. The Cat and the Mouse

John O. West in Neil Philip, *Horse Hooves and Chicken Feet* (Introduction)
Mexico

A cat is chasing a mouse, but the mouse escapes into its hole. The cat waits patiently outside and whispers *Meow*. The mouse knows the cat is there and stays hidden. Then the cat barks *Bow, wow!* And mouse thinks it is safe to come out, whereupon the cat pounces on him. The wily cat concludes how useful it is to speak two languages.

Connections

Allegories and parables. Cats. Cleverness. Enmity. Humorous tales. Interspecies conflict. Language. Mice. Tricksters.

263. Why Rabbits Have Long Ears

Robert Hull, *Central and South American Stories*
Maya People

Rabbit falls instantly in love with a beautiful female jaguar who is strolling through the village beside the male jaguar she will marry. Rabbit compliments her and praises his own ingenuity. The male jaguar angrily tells the rabbit to go away, but confident Rabbit does not give up. He tells the female jaguar he is sure she likes him back. She growls that this is nonsense. He gets the male jaguar to agree to ask her which one of them she prefers. Rabbit starts out running alongside Jaguar as they head over to ask, but through clever, polite talking Rabbit ends up putting a harness on Jaguar and riding him there. Other creatures see the rabbit whipping the jaguar to go faster. Rabbit tells the jaguar's sweetheart that he is the smart one. The female jaguar asks if Rabbit would be able to provide game for her. He boasts that riding a jaguar proves that he can do anything. Still, she wants her husband to have teeth that terrify other animals. Rabbit goes to the Creator-Person and requests powerful teeth. The All-Things-Maker tells Rabbit to return with a tooth from a giant and one from a monkey. Playing tricks, Rabbit acquires the teeth. The Creator-Person gives him a pair of large teeth, but when Rabbit asks if the rest of him could be bigger, too, the Creator-Person laughs and pulls his ears long. The female jaguar compliments Rabbit's new look, but says she will stick with Jaguar.

CONNECTIONS

Appearance. Braggarts. Cleverness. Competition. Courtship. Discontent. Ears. Foxes. Giants. Gods and animals. Humorous tales. Interspecies conflict. Interspecies seduction. Jaguars. Monkeys. Origin tales. Rabbits. Ridicule. Teeth. Tricksters.

HOW ELSE THIS STORY IS TOLD

Maya variation:
Why Rabbits Have Long Ears—Douglas Gifford, *Warriors, Gods & Spirits from Central & South American Mythology*

Warao variation from Guyana and Venezuela:
How Rabbit Took Away the Sweetheart of Jaguar—Johannes Wilbert, *Folk Literature of the Warao Indians*. Rabbit and Jaguar both court Fox.

See also The King of the Animals (132) for a straight status competition version of this story and The Rabbit's Ears / Las orejas del conejo (62) and The Affair of the Horns (106) for other explanations of rabbits' long ears.

---

264. DEER AND JAGUAR SHARE A HOUSE
Antonio Rocha in David Holt and Bill Mooney, *More Ready-to-Tell Tales*
Brazil

Deer chooses a spot where he can build himself a house and leaves, planning to start the next day. Later, Jaguar decides the exact same thing at the exact same spot. Neither knows about the other. As they arrive at different times and add floor, walls, and roof to the structure, they each believe that the construction help is coming from the God Tupan. Deer builds one room for himself and one for Tupan. He goes to sleep in his room, and Jaguar, who arrives and thinks it must be Tupan snoring, goes to sleep in the other room. Deer and Jaguar discover each other the next morning and agree to share the house. One day, though, Jaguar returns with a deer he has hunted for their supper, and Deer is upset. The next day, Deer tricks the large anteater, Tamandua Bandeira, into killing a jaguar. The deer brings this jaguar home. Now Jaguar cannot eat, and both stay awake for fear of the other. Deer's antlers hit the wall as his head nods. Hearing the loud bang, Jaguar roars. They both leap up and run out of the house in opposite directions.

CONNECTIONS

Anteaters. Bulls. Coexistence. Deer. Fear. Food. Generosity. Goats. Gods and animals. Houses. Jaguars. Misunderstandings. Interspecies conflict. Trust.

HOW ELSE THIS STORY IS TOLD

Brazilian variations:
The Deer and the Jaguar Share a House—Harold Courlander, *Ride with the Sun* and in Joanna Cole, *Best-Loved Folktales of the World*.
Jaguar and Goat—Livia de Almeida and Ana Portella, *Brazilian Folktales*. Amazonia. A Jaguar and a Goat who have decided to live together run different directions when they each mistake signs of anger in the other.

Kanjobal Maya variation from Guatemala:
The Jaguar and the Deer—Don Pedro Miguel Say. In Fernando Peñalosa, *Tales and Legends of the Q'Anjob'al Maya* and as Deer and Jaguar Live Together—But Not for Long! Also in *Maya Culture—Traditional Storyteller's Tales* (Online). Here, the deer tricks a large bull into killing the jaguar he brings home for food.

---

265. THE REVOLT OF THE UTENSILS

John Bierhorst, *Latin American Folktales*
Tacana People. Bolivia

Once when a man leaves his house, the clay pots go out to the garden for maize and to the stream for water to make maize chicha. They are happily drinking and dancing and chatting with each other until they realize the man will be back soon. So, they clean up. When the man returns, he says things are just as he left them, and the pots laugh. They know better.

CONNECTIONS

Independence. Parties. Pots. Rebellion. Secrets. Status. Supernatural beings.

HOW ELSE THIS STORY IS TOLD

The Clay Pot's Party—Bill Gordh, *Stories in Action*

X

Defenders of the Earth

---

266. EPEREJI: ANIMAL GUARDIAN
Juan Carlos Galeano, *Folktales of the Amazon*
Amazonia, Bolivia

When his wife scolds him for once again coming home empty-handed, a hunter from Conquista returns to the watering hole and kills a tapir. Immediately, a hairy little man climbs down from a tree and slaps the tapir, which comes back to life. The hairy man tells the hunter he is Epereji, caretaker for the animals. He gives the hunter an ox horn to attract animals and warns him to keep the horn secret and to kill sparingly. The hunter's luck changes, until he shares his secret with his wife, who lends the horn to her brother who greedily shoots everything in sight. The next time the hunter shoots a tapir, it gets up and charges at him. When he comes to, Epereji is sitting on the tapir. Epereji says he has been trying to heal the animals his brother-in-law wounded, and the magic horn is gone for good.

CONNECTIONS
Brothers-in-law and sisters-in-law. Cautionary tales. Gifts. Greed. Hunters. Husbands and wives. Magic. Magic horns. Promises. Punishments. Respect for nature. Restoring life. Secrets. Supernatural beings. Tapirs. Warnings.

---

267. THE DOG THAT LOVED TO HUNT ARMADILLOS
Constancio Cnamé in Américo Paredes, *Folktales of Mexico*
Mexico

When a man's dog follows an armadillo down a hole and does not return, the man traces him to the foot of Mactumatzá Mountain. He waits. A guide appears who leads him underground to a large field filled with many-colored deer and other animals. When his own dog runs over, the hunter is ready to go, but the guide tells him that he must first pay for the harm he and his dog have done to many animals. The guide takes him past someone he knew who had died, who is now carrying hay here for wounded animals. He is also taken to see where they roast the buttocks of hunters. The guide brings the hunter to the *patrón*, who refuses to give his dog back because he has hurt too many animals. By refusing to sit down, the man stays free from the *patrón*'s power. The *patrón* angrily orders he be thrown out, and the hunter finds himself above ground. Lost, he meets villagers who have come looking for him, but is afraid of them. The hunter does not become himself again until they rebaptize him.

CONNECTIONS

Armadillos. Cautionary tales. Caves. Changes in attitude. Dogs. Fear. Hunters. Journeys to other realms. Magic. Punishments. Respect for nature. Supernatural beings. Underground worlds. Wounds.

HOW ELSE THIS STORY IS TOLD

The Visit to the Animal Master—Don Enrique. In John Bierhorst, *The Mythology of Mexico and Central America*. Chinantec People. Mexico. Around Valle Nacional, a hunter meets a man on a horse wearing a big charro hat, who transports him to a cave which holds all the animals that the hunter has wounded. The rider warns him to shoot to kill when he goes out hunting and not to leave wounded animals or his dogs will come and eat him. The man never hunts again.

---

268. MAPINGUARI: ONE-EYED OGRE

Juan Carlos Galeano, *Folktales of the Amazon*
Amazonia, Brazil

Despite his wife's advice that he not hunt on Sundays, a hunter goes to shoot game on the banks of the Amazon every day of the week. He insists that people have to eat on Sunday, too. "No domingo também se come," he says, as he pushes his reluctant neighbor to join him. That Sunday all the animals seem to have vanished, though. Then they hear frightful screams, and an ape-like creature with one green eye appears. The hunter's bullets bounce right off, while his friend climbs a tree. The beast tears the hunter apart and eats him piece by piece, saying, "One must also eat on Sundays." When the creature leaves, the friend runs to Tepe, where townspeople tell him the creature must be a Mapinguari. They find the beast and shoot at its bellybutton where its heart is, and the creature runs off. His wife regrets that her husband did not listen to her.

CONNECTIONS

Advice. Calendar. Cautionary tales. Fear. Greed. Hunters. Husbands and wives. Magic. Mapinguari. Monsters. Ogres. Punishments. Respect for nature. Supernatural beings.

---

269. *TRISBA & SULA: A MISKITU FOLKTALE FROM NICARAGUA / UNA LEYENDA DE LOS MISKITOS DE NICARAGUA*

Joan MacCracken
Miskito People. Nicaragua

One day after his father dies, Trisba falls in love with a beautiful woman whom he meets in the forest. They marry. Trisba goes hunting every day to prove to Sula that he is a good provider. Only his mother notices that Sula is sad when he returns with deer meat, which she does not eat. Sula tells him just that she misses her family, which Trisba understands. He hunts even more. A bad dream about Trisba's hunting worries his mother, but Trisba leaves to hunt anyway. Sula transforms into a doe and runs off to warn her father, king of the deer, that Trisba is coming. The king surrounds Trisba with so many deer, that the frightened young man sees no escape. He climbs a tree, but when he shoots an arrow at the king of the deer, the wounded king grows larger and even more frightening. Now the king has two heads and then four, and shakes the tree so hard that Trisba falls out. Sula arrives just then. She changes back into a young woman. Tenderly, she tells Trisba that the animals are her family and that killing more than what they need for food will destroy him, too. Sula's love opens Trisba's heart to return to the wisdom of his father's way of hunting.

Connections

Cautionary tales. Changes in attitude. Deer. Dreams. Fear. Greed. Hunters. Magic. Parents and children. Punishments. Respect for nature. Supernatural husbands and wives. Supernatural beings. Traditions. Transformations.

---

270. The Flute of the Chullachaki

Juan Carlos Galeano, *Folktales of the Amazon*
Amazonia, Peru

A man keeps looking for animals to hunt even after his brothers give up and return home. He comes to a cave, where grandfather Chullachaki, a shape-shifting spirit of the forest, sits. Chullachaki lifts a *nacanaca*, a coral snake. In his hands it becomes a *pifuano*, a flute, which calls animals over with music which only they can hear. Chullachaki gives the man the flute, but warns that he must play it only when his family needs meat to eat. When a Chullachaki woman and some children enter, the man finds it very funny that they have no buttocks. He brings home a wild pig to eat and amuses his family with the story that Chullachakis have no buttocks. The man keeps his promise to use the flute wisely, until one day, after drinking, his brothers and many friends want to kill extra game to sell in Iquitos. A greedy brother puts the flute to his mouth, and it turns into a coral snake and fatally bites him. The man who received the flute from Chullachaki also dies the next morning, while the macaw mockingly laughs about Chullachaki buttocks.

Connections

Brothers and sisters. Cautionary tales. Chullachaki. Gifts. Greed. Hunters. Magic. Magic flutes. Music. Promises. Punishments. Respect for nature. Ridicule. Snakes. Spirits. Storytelling. Supernatural beings. Warnings.

271. THE CURUPIRA
Margaret Read MacDonald, *Earth Care*
Brazil, Paraguay, and Northern Argentina

Carlos leaves tobacco and honey for Curupira, hoping the guardian of the animals will give him better luck with hunting to feed his family. It works, but Carlos begins to resent leaving all these gifts he himself could use. He starts bringing less, and his luck still holds. It even holds when he leaves nothing at all. But then, Carlos kills many animals all at once to sell to a buyer. He has just set the game out to work on when a chick with no feathers walks out of the forest to inspect it. A loud voice asks if his animals are all there. The chick tells Curupira they are, and the voice asks the chick to bring them to him. The chick swiftly pecks each animal back to life, and the animals follow him into the forest. Carlos flees, as the voice of Curupira tells the chick they will come for Carlos next time.

CONNECTIONS
Cautionary tales. Changes in attitude. Chickens. Curupira. Hunters. Magic. Punishments. Respect for nature. Restoring life. Supernatural beings. Supernatural voices.

272. CURUPIRA: GUARDIAN SPIRIT OF THE FOREST
Juan Carlos Galeano, *Folktales of the Amazon*
Amazonia, Brazil

A peasant, out shooting birds in the forest, finds a little blond girl all alone and brings her home, so his wife can care for her. He doesn't know she is really Curupira, guardian of the forest, who can take any shape. That night he dreams that the girl tells him not to shoot the first animal he sees, and he will be able to bring down whatever else he wants. He has the same dream again on another night. The peasant's son comes hunting with him and wants his father to shoot the first deer they see. The man remembers the warning, but gives in as his son keeps pestering. As soon as he pulls the trigger, though, the man is filled with regret. Then the dead deer stands up and walks away. It appears to be laughing. The man thinks the laughing deer must have been the Curupira. In his dream that night, the little girl tells him he broke his promise. He is never again able to shoot another deer that doesn't stand up laughing.

CONNECTIONS
Cautionary tales. Curupira. Dreams. Hunters. Magic. Promises. Punishments. Respect for nature. Restoring life. Spirits. Supernatural beings. Transformations.

273. THE SONGS OF THE BIRDS
Robert Hull, *Central and South American Stories*
Kamaiurá Xingu People. Brazil

Long ago, when birds, animals, and plants all speak like people, some bird-people hear a young man complain about the lack of adventure in his life and tell him their trouble. One man has been killing many macaws, toucans, eagles, and hummingbirds recently. As they speak, the young man realizes he knows that man, Avatsiu, from his village. He calls him a murderer. The bird-people invite him to help them. The eagle chief directs the bird-people to make a skin of eagle feathers for the man, and they teach him to fly. It is not easy; some feathers fall off, and once, during practice, he misses a rock shelf while swooping down to grab a stone and crashes. The bird-people are uncertain whether he will be able to get Avatsiu. When Avatsiu appears, the young man impatiently dives towards him too soon and hits the ground. The bird-people send the ox-blood bird with a message to the man's son, hoping he will want to avenge his father's death. The boy's mother suggests the boy swoop down on Avatsiu from behind. The son flies well and with the help of two eagles, they sink talons into Avatsiu and carry him away. As they drink Avatsiu's blood, however, human language leaves the birds, who ever after thank humans for helping them in many different calls.

CONNECTIONS

Birds. Discontent. Flight. Human helpers. Humans. Language. Murder. Origin tales. Parents and children. Punishments. Respect for nature. Revenge. Supernatural beings.

HOW ELSE THIS STORY IS TOLD

The Language of Birds—Douglas Gifford, *Warriors, Gods & Spirits from Central & South American Mythology*

---

274. STORY OF THE OWL

Ignacio Bizarro Ujpan in James D. Sexton, *Heart of Heaven, Heart of Earth*
Maya People

When a woodcutter shoots the owl who hoots insistently on his rancho roof, the wounded owl goes to the dueno, who checks on people's misdeeds. A few days later, a small young man meets up with the woodcutter and suggests that the woodcutter follow him to better firewood higher up the hill. At the top, however, the woodcutter is brought to the angry-looking dueno of Pulchich Hill. The dueno has 2 teeth pointing up and 2 on the side below. He tells the frightened woodcutter that he must work for four hours to repay wounding one of his policemen. Pus is placed in the woodcutter's mouth, and he is told to heal the owl's wing and infected, broken leg. The woodcutter is shown other wounded animals being worked on by humans, as well as humans being punished when they cannot cure those they have hurt. The man is able to help the owl. Later on, villagers do not believe what he tells them about the hill, and he dies shortly afterward.

CONNECTIONS

Birds. Cautionary tales. Duenos. Healing. Hunters. Journeys to other realms. Magic owls. Owls. Punishments. Respect for nature. Righting a wrong. Storytelling. Supernatural beings. Woodcutters. Wounds.

275. THE CITY OF THE DOLPHINS

Juan Carlos Galeano, *Folktales of the Amazon*
Amazonia, Brazil

Two policemen from Santo Antônio do Içá show up in a speedboat with summons to bring a fisherman who wounded a pink dolphin with his spear to the judge. Just as the fisherman notices that their boat is not heading to Santo Antônio do Içá and that these police hang fish, instead of clubs, from their belts, the boat sinks through netting to the bottom of the river. The fisherman is dry when they reach the city lights down there. Now the police are breathing through holes at the top of their heads, like dolphins. They bring him to a hospital to cure the moaning dolphin he has injured or at least to let them know which metal his spear is made of. He will be shut in jail if the dolphin dies, because dolphins are human. The fisherman is frightened, thinking of his family, and then lights tobacco, knowing it is something dolphins intensely dislike. The dolphins want him taken far away from them, and the police leave him back up on the river's surface. The fisherman's family rejoices at his return, but no one believes him when he says dolphins are like people.

CONNECTIONS

Cautionary tales. Dolphins. Enchanted cities. Fishermen. Healing. Journeys to other realms. Magic. Punishments. Respect for nature. Righting a wrong. Storytelling. Supernatural beings. Water worlds. Wounds.

276. THE HUNTING OF SEA LIONS

Johannes Wilbert, *Folk Literature of the Yamana Indians*
Yaghan People. Islands south of Tierra del Fuego, Argentina

The elder Yoálax from the first family of humans is sad when the special harpoon made by his sister breaks off in a sea lion and is lost. Not only did that harpoon that always hit its mark make hunting sea lions easier, but it returned to his hand and saved him the trouble of crafting new harpoons. The elder's younger brother thinks it is good for people to make weapons with their own hands and become more skillful hunters. Elder brother agrees, which is why hunters now need to learn how to throw their harpoons with just the right force. Elder sister gifts the elder brother with new weapons. Younger brother disapproves and continues to make his own, believing people need to work for their food and care for their own tools.

CONNECTIONS

Allegories and parables. Brothers and sisters. Gifts. Hunters. Knowledge. Magic. Magic harpoons. Perspective. Punishments. Respect for nature. Sea lions and seals. Skills. Supernatural beings. Weapons. Work.

277. Who Cuts the Trees Cuts His Own Life

Victor Montejo, *The Bird Who Cleans the World and Other Mayan Fables*
Jakaltek Maya. Guatemala

A father warns the young narrator that cutting little green trees means that you are cutting short your own life and will die slowly. His son can see the connection between trees and the pollution, deforestation, and erosion around. He knows his father's words are right.

Connections

Allegories and parables. Cautionary tales. Death. Ecology. Life span. Parents and children. Perspective. Punishments. Respect for nature. Trees. Warnings.

---

278. Sachamama: Mother of the Forest

Juan Carlos Galeano, *Folktales of the Amazon*
Amazonia, Peru

Tired from their work collecting latex from rubber trees, a husband and wife decide to camp beside a large fallen tree with balls of shiringa they will deliver the next day. It seems to the woman that the tree trunk is bleeding, but her husband thinks it may just be red sap. They rest in the same spot on their way back. When they build their fire, the shrubs and trees begin shaking until a hard rain puts the fire out. When they wake, a road has replaced the fallen trunk and all of the other trees there. They cannot stop thinking about the tree and the road when they return home. The husband consults a shaman who believes the trunk was Sachamama, who can move from place to place, and does not like to be disturbed. The man returns by another path and finds human and animal bones in a dark place. He finds the trunk which grows larger and leads him to a sunlit meadow with animals and birds frozen in place. He realizes that he has reached the mouth of a beast, an enormous boa who hypnotizes animals and then eats them. He uses his machete to cut the spell of dizziness. The boa raises its head, and he runs.

Connections

Boa constrictors. Ecology. Escapes. Fear. Gods and humans. Husbands and wives. Mysteries. Perspective. Punishments. Respect for nature. Rubber tappers. Shiringa trees. Sachamama. Snakes. Supernatural beings. Trees. Wounds.

---

279. Chullachaki: Owner of Trees and Animals

Juan Carlos Galeano, *Folktales of the Amazon*
Amazonia, Peru

Although he works hard tapping rubber trees along the Nanay River, a shiringuero isn't having enough luck getting latex from them to pay his debts. The Chullachaki, a small fat man with power over the jungle trees and animals, appears and offers the shiringuero a bargain. If the rubber tapper wakes the Chullachaki by kicking him and hitting him hard and then knocks him down three times in a fight, the trees will yield more latex, but if the Chullachaki knocks the rubber tapper down, he will die. Seeing that the Chullachaki has one leg smaller than the other, the shiringuero agrees to fight. He stomps on the Chullachaki's smaller foot which holds his strength and wins. The Chullachaki now says he will show him which trees to tap, but the man must not make the trees cry by taking too much latex. Also, the man must not tell anyone about what happened. The shiringuero's luck changes, until the owner of the trees figures out which trees he is tapping and slashes large holes in them until only what looks like water comes out. The Chullachacki tells them both that this is the end of his help. The owner sickens and dies.

CONNECTIONS

Bargains. Cautionary tales. Chullachaki. Ecology. Greed. Punishments. Respect for nature. Rubber tappers. Secrets. Shiringa trees. Spirits. Supernatural beings. Tears. Trees. Warnings. Wounds.

280. THE MOTHER OF THE JUNGLE / LA MADRESELVA

Rueben Martínez, *Once Upon a Time/Había una vez*
Colombia

The peasant Sebastian thinks it is wrong when he sees that a bearded stranger has cleared many, many trees from the jungle. He does not say anything to him. However, he knows the man has hurt the jungle when he finds the river dry. That night, hearing noise, Sebastian and his dog run to the clearing. Yellow light emerges eerily from the ground. They see a pale woman dressed in leaves and branches grab the frightened, bearded man, who disappears inside her glow and shadow. Then she lifts him, and the man whirls like a twister off the ground, wrapped and shrieking. The light fades, and he falls. The bearded man tells Sebastian that she told him he was harming her. Sebastian knows the Mother of the Jungle had come to its defense.

CONNECTIONS

Amazonia. Cautionary tales. Ecology. Fear. Greed. Madremonte. Parents and children. Perspective. Punishments. Respect for nature. Trees. Supernatural beings. Warnings.

281. CURUPIRA'S SON

Juan Carlos Galeano, *Folktales of the Amazon*
Amazonia

It troubles people that a new settler in the forest begins to clear a great deal of land, more than he needs just to feed himself and his wife. He says he is planting corn and rice to save for the future. Twice, a beautiful girl leads him to a place with many animals, but game he brings home for his wife to cook vanishes from the pot. Then a handsome stranger tells the wife that he will stay for the night since her husband is with a girl in the woods. The man does not return for a day. One day when they are expecting their first child, a stranger shows up and tells the man that the baby is his son, conceived the night the husband spent in the forest. The husband throws his shovel, and the stranger disappears. Back at home, his wife gives birth to a child who has one foot pointed backward. The child runs out and climbs a guama tree right after he is born. When the man climbs a ladder to bring the child down from the tree, the stranger and the girl from the forest shake him off. From the ground, the man sees the boy climb down to them. The three go off together, all with one foot pointed backwards.

CONNECTIONS

Cautionary tales. Curupira. Ecology. Greed. Husbands and wives. Interspecies seduction. Mysteries. Parents and children. Perspective. Respect for nature. Supernatural beings.

282. *THE GREAT KAPOK TREE*
Lynne Cherry
Amazonia

A woodsman falls asleep while chopping down a hard kapok tree. One by one, rain forest animals come down from the tree—snake, bee, monkeys, tree frog, jaguar, tree porcupines, anteaters, and sloth—to whisper all the different ways that this tree shelters them and gives them what they need to survive and how it entwines with their future. Finally, a Yanomamo child asks him to look with new eyes when he awakes, and he does realize the beauty of the canopy and the necessity of the forest, and puts down his ax.

CONNECTIONS

Allegories and parables. Changes in attitude. Ecology. Kapok trees. Messengers. Perspective. Respect for nature. Trees. Warnings. Woocdutters. Yanomami people.

283. LUPUNA: A TREE BECOMES VENGEFUL
Juan Carlos Galeano, *Folktales of the Amazon*
Amazonia, Colombia

When the creeks are too dry to carry their cut logs to the river, one woodcutter whacks a big, round red lupuna tree trunk to bring rain. The next day, his stomach swells painfully. The shaman says that he should not have urinated against the trunk or beaten the belly of a lupuna colorada, whose mother lives there. The shaman goes to speak with the lupuna's mother, who is an old woman, made of leaves and wood. With fiery eyes, she tells him that the logger will have to die for defiling her house. The shaman smokes and drinks to summon courage and strength for the fight ahead. He calls for a jaguar and anaconda to help by scratching and squeezing the trunk. The trunk explodes as the lupuna's mother is forced out. The logger's stomach begins to deflate. Other loggers hit against a white lupuna tree to bring the needed rain. When he is recovered, the logger brings drinks and candy to the lupuna to atone.

CONNECTIONS

Cautionary tales. Changes in attitude. Drought. Ecology. Jaguars. Lupuna trees. Magic trees. Punishments. Respect for nature. Revenge. Shamans. Snakes. Supernatural beings. Trees. Warnings. Woodcutters.

284. THE SILVER MINERS

Geraldine McCaughrean, *The Silver Treasure*
Bolivia

In their lust for silver, the Spanish conquerors overwork native people as slaves to break rocks and carry ore down from Parichata Mountain. The workers apologize to the mountain as they tear it apart against their will. The mule-boy, Maro, is leading his father's mules up the path to make sure they are ready for the morning loads, when a driver hidden under a straw hat roars at him to make way. Forced off the path, Maro watches a train of sleek mules pass by. He hides and sees hundreds of insects crawling up to the silver mines where the indigenous man in the straw hat rolls them onto their backs and transforms them into strong mules with a touch of his rod. Molten silver flows directly from the mountain into panniers the mules are carrying. The mules head down the mountain with solid ingots and disappear. The next morning, there is no silver to mine. With no silver, the Spanish leave. No one can find beetles or any evidence for Maro's story, but he is certain that Parichata himself gave away the silver to save the people from misery.

CONNECTIONS

Cultural conflict. Earth. Ecology. Insects. Magic beetles. Miners. Mysteries. Mountains. Rescues. Respect for nature. Silver. Slavery. Supernatural beings. Transformations. Warnings.

285. SUMÉ

Margaret Campbell, *South American Folklore Tales*
Tamoio People. Brazil

The Tamoyo welcome the man dressed all in white with a long white beard who seems to be walking on the water. He is the messenger, Sumé, sent by Tupán, Lord of Heaven and Earth, to bring prosperity to them and to their barren land. Sumé, teaches that it is better to cultivate the Earth than to fight enemies for what they need. He tells them planting seeds which contain wisdom and love in the Earth will give back to them and keep them from going hungry. Though the land begins to bloom, the warrior men do not like bending their backs to dig and plant seeds. One young man rouses the others against Sumé, saying that he takes away their power. They throw rocks and then a spear at him. Sumé walks back to the sea, pulling out the arrows which hit his back. The women cry out for him to stay, but Sumé disappears into the water, surrounded by light. Each arrow aimed at Sumé now pins a foot of the man who had shot it, and they all die mysteriously. The tribe then turns its back on war and tries to care for the land as Sumé showed them.

Note: This tribe has disappeared, but the Tupi and Guaraní People tell their legends.

CONNECTIONS

Allegories and parables. Cautionary tales. Changes in attitude. Cultural conflict. Ecology. Farming. Gods and humans. Outsiders. Perspective. Punishments. Rebellion. Repentance. Respect for nature. Sumé. Teachers. Warriors.

286. THE WOMAN WHO OUTSHONE THE SUN: THE LEGEND OF LUCIA ZENTENO / LA MUJER QUE BILLABA AÚN MÁS QUE EL SOL: LA LEYENDA DE LUCIA ZENTENO
Alejandro Cruz and Rosalma Zubizarreta
Zapotec People. Oaxaca, Mexico

Lucia Zenteno is a mystery. Colorfully dressed, she appears accompanied by butterflies and an iguana. When she bathes in the river, fish and otters flow from her black hair. The elders say she is a wonder, connected to nature; other people fear her strangeness and treat her meanly. When hostile villagers drive Lucia Zenteno away, the river cannot bear to be parted from her. It clings to her hair and leaves with her. The villagers then suffer from drought. The older people convince them to seek her forgiveness. Lucia Zenteno is sitting with her back turned in the iguana cave. She only responds when the frightened children call. She tells them they must treat even those who are different kindly. She returns to the remorseful village and combs out her hair, so water and its life return to the riverbed. In the excitement, no one sees her go.

CONNECTIONS

Changes in attitude. Coexistence. Cultural conflict. Drought. Forgiveness. Outsiders. Punishments. Resistance. Respect for nature. Righting a wrong. Rivers. Supernatural beings. Unkindness. Zenteno, Lucia.

287. HUAYRAMAMA: SNAKE MOTHER OF THE WIND
Juan Carlos Galeano, *Folktales of the Amazon*
Amazonia, Peru

Through fasting and visionary brews, Don Emilio Shuña, a healer near the Ucayali River, has learned to control forces of the earth, but now he also wants power over the wind and rains. For nine days he fasts and drinks tea from the *huayracaspi* tree believed to be mother of Huayramama, the enormous boa in charge of the sky. The giant boa arrives. With her old woman face, she tells him, he must fast for another forty-five days. She also teaches him songs to calm her evil wind children. When people come to him, Don Emilio uses his new power to help them. He sends rain for crops and keeps the rivers good for fishing. He sends the bad winds to holes under the trees when they blow animals and children through the air. When Don Emilio dies, his tribe buries him in the forest under the *huayracaspi* tree he loves.

CONNECTIONS

Ecology. Gods and humans. Huaira caspi trees. Huairamama. Magic. Magic trees. Power. Respect for nature. Shamans. Snakes. Teachers. Trees.

---

288. *THE JOURNEY OF TUNURI AND THE BLUE DEER: A HUICHOL INDIAN STORY*
James Endredy
Huichol People. Mexico

As the mountain villagers walk to the sacred mountain Wirikuta, Tunuri sometimes picks his own path through the woods to hide from his parents. One morning, though, he loses the group after following a butterfly. A glowing blue deer approaches, saying he has been sent to show the boy the way to Grandfather Fire. Then Blue Deer runs away so swiftly, Tunuri fears he has been abandoned, until he sees he can follow a colorful flower trail of Blue Deer's steps. The deer leads Tunuri to Father Sun, Brother Wind, Sister Water, and Mother Earth, who reassure him respectively of the constancy of their warmth, breath, nourishment and beauty. When they reach Grandfather Fire's cave, Grandfather Fire himself tells Tunuri that with the presence of these relatives in nature, he will never be alone, even when he is lost. Grandfather Fire says it is up to Tunuri to share what he has learned with his human family. Tunuri promises, and Blue Deer directs him back to his family, where Tunuri remembers the magic of his encounters.

CONNECTIONS

Allegories and parables. Deer. Gods and humans. Journeys to other realms. Magic deer. Parents and children. Promises. Respect for nature.

---

289. WHY YOU CAN SEE A RAINBOW WHEN DEER ARE BORN
Rigoberta Menchú, *The Honey Jar*
Maya People. Guatemala

A Man who cuts down trees, pollutes rivers, and kills animals for riches does not know that the bird he hears singing is really Rajaw Juyub', the spirit of everything in the world. A nightmare begins. The mountain path keeps leading the Man right back to where he started in front of a large, growling, black dog. When he heads to a village for safety, a boy who has machete cuts on his legs transforms into a wounded jaguar, and his sister becomes a stalk of sugarcane which bleeds. Now the Man realizes Rajaw Juyub' is telling him that he has selfishly damaged nature and done this to the children. The Man wants to atone. He prays on his knees for days to Ajaw, the Heart of Earth and the Heart of Heaven, who turns him into a creature, sometimes deer and sometimes human. His job is to wander to show animals and people how to live wisely with Mother Nature. When he dies, a rainbow appears in the sky to signal that a new deer has been born.

CONNECTIONS

Allegories and parables. Changes in attitude. Deer. Ecology. Gods and humans. Greed. Magic deer. Messengers. Origin tales. Parents and children. Punishments. Rajaw Juyub.' Rainbows. Repentance. Respect for nature. Righting a wrong. Selfishness. Spirits. Transformations. Trees. Wounds.

XI

Between Husbands and Wives

_____

290. HOW MUCH YOU REMIND ME OF MY HUSBAND
M.A. Jagendorf and R.S. Boggs, *The King of the Mountains*
El Salvador

The old indigenous man's wife misses her husband a lot after he dies. She sits on the bench in front of their hut and wishes aloud that he were here with her in Huizúcar. Just then a buzzard circles down to the tree near her. She tells Tío Buzzard how much he resembles her dear husband, wearing black with a little white cap and sitting hunched up with his head dropped between his shoulders. The buzzard moves, and a tree branch hits her. This, too, she exclaims, is like her husband. The buzzard takes off from the tree, and the woman sighs, for the buzzard is leaving to fly to Heaven just like her husband.

CONNECTIONS
Buzzards. Humorous tales. Husbands and wives. Loneliness. Love. Mourning. Reminiscence. Widows and widowers. Wishes.

WHERE ELSE THIS STORY APPEARS
In Jane Yolen, *Gray Heroes*.

_____

291. BUZZARD MAN
John Bierhorst, *The Monkey's Haircut and Other Stories Told by the Maya*
Tzotzil Maya People. Mexico

A lazy man pretends to his wife that he's working when he leaves each day, but mostly he rests instead of clearing trees. He envies a buzzard's freedom and calls up, asking if the bird would like to change places. The buzzard goes to Our Lord for permission and returns ready to exchange clothes after a few days. The man is now dressed in feathers, and the buzzard teaches him what he needs to know. They plan to meet again in three days. The man compliments the buzzard on all the tree clearing he has

176

accomplished. The buzzard reports that the man's wife has only commented that he smells bad. She accepts the buzzard's explanation that the stench comes from the burning he's doing to clear the land. He invites her to come watch. The man who is now a buzzard mistakenly thinks their rising smoke signals food for him and burns up. His wife thinks this buzzard is not very bright, and her new husband says it was what Our Lord commanded. She brushes off the neighbor who tells her that her husband has turned into a buzzard. He provides so well now that she puts up with the smell.

CONNECTIONS

Buzzards. Clothing. Discontent. Gods and animals. Gods and humans. Humorous tales. Husbands and wives. Laziness. Punishments. Supernatural husbands and wives. Transformations. Work.

WHERE ELSE THIS STORY APPEARS

The Buzzard Husband—John Biershorst, *Latin American Folktales The Mythology of Mexico and Central America.* Tzutuhil Maya People. Guatemala

HOW ELSE THIS STORY IS TOLD

Maya variation from Mexico:
The Buzzard Man—Tonik Nibak. In Robert M. Laughlin, *The People of the Bat: Mayan Tales and Dreams from Zinacantán*

Maya variations from Guatemala:
The Buzzard Husband—John Biershorst, *The Mythology of Mexico and Central America.* Tzutuhil Maya People
The Lazy Man and the Buzzard—Fernando Peñalosa, *Tales and Legends of the Q'Anjob'al Maya.* Kanjobal Maya People. The children run off the husband/father who has become a buzzard.
The Man and the Buzzard—Victor Montejo, *The Bird Who Cleans the World and Other Mayan Fables.* Jakaltek Maya People. Guatemala. When the lazy husband wants to trade back, the buzzard finally agrees if the husband promises to work and take care of his wife as the buzzard did.
The Man and the Buzzard / El hombre y el zopilote—Susan Conklin Thompson, Keith Steven Thompson, and Lidia López de López, *Mayan Folktales.*
The Man Who Became a Buzzard—Rigoberta Menchú, *The Honey Jar.* Buzzard and man both go back to being what they were.
The Story of Mariano the Buzzard—James D. Sexton, *Mayan Folktales: Folklore from Lake Atitlán, Guatemala*

---

292. THE LIVING DEAD MAN / EL HOMBRE MUERTO VIVO
Pedro Cholotío Temó and Alberto Barreno, *The Dog Who Spoke /*
  El perro que habló
Maya People. Santiago Atitlán, Guatemala

Tomás never learned how to cut firewood or do any work, and his wife Lucía despairs about how they will manage. Tomás thinks that dying and going to heaven can solve their problems. Lucía takes a job when she hears that death can be painful, but her husband still thinks dying will bring happiness. Tomás puts on a red shirt and pants so Lucia will recognize him in heaven when she gets there and climbs a high mountain. He's very cold and also frets that his wife might not be able to find him, so he comes back down and lies down in the road near home and waits to die. His lying there frightens some mules whose drivers kick him, and Tomás thinks maybe heaven is a place where you get beaten. Lucía finds him crying. He decides that dying is no fun, and it may be better to go to work.

CONNECTIONS

Changes in attitude. Death. Fools. Humorous tales. Husbands and wives. Laziness. Work.

---

293. THE GIANT AND THE RABBIT

Grant Lyons, *Tales the People Tell in Mexico*
Mexico

A farmer asks his wife to bring him lunch in the sugar fields one day, warning her to follow the sandy fork to get there. She gets lost and is captured by a giant, who plans to eat her. When his wife does not arrive, her concerned husband sets out to find her. The giant just laughs when the man asks if he has his wife and keeps laughing when the husband begs to have his wife back. The man is sadly heading home when a jaguar offers to help. The jaguar fiercely fights the giant, but she has to give up. A bull and then an elephant also offer to help the crying man, but the giant defeats both of them, too. The husband doubts that the small rabbit who volunteers can actually help, but together they return to the giant with supplies the rabbit has requested. The giant laughs when the rabbit asks the giant to return the man's only wife. Then the rabbit makes the giant mad by nimbly whipping and biting him just out of reach. Finally, the rabbit cracks a bowl of cornmeal and blood on his head. The giant falls and thinks he has been fatally wounded. The man rescues his wife. After a while, the giant realizes he will live, but is too embarrassed to have been bested by a little rabbit to go after anyone else.

CONNECTIONS

Animal helpers. Bulls. Captivity. Cleverness. Elephants. Farmers. Giants. Humiliation. Husbands
   and wives. Interspecies conflict. Jaguars. Kindness. Rabbits. Rescues. Size.

---

294. THE CHARCOAL CRUNCHER

John Bierhorst, *The Monkey's Haircut*
Tzotzil Maya People. Mexico

A man is really frightened the night he wakes to find just his wife's body in bed without a head. Her head is chomping hot coals at the fireplace and will not say why. When there is no charcoal to eat, she scares people. His wife is too tired during the day, and he tires of living with her. The man's mother suggests he rub salt on her neck when the head is traveling, which he does. The head returns and cannot reattach to her body. It bounces on the bed and lands on their child and then on him. Now the man has two heads. He leaves her head at the base of a pine tree, saying he will bring nuts down to her. When he does not come down, though, her head bounces up and down, trying to reach him and lands on a deer, which runs off with two heads. This explains why people no longer see Charcoal Crunchers.

Connections

Charcoal Cruncher. Fear. Flying heads. Magic. Identity. Pipil people. Skeletons. Supernatural husbands and wives. Transformations. Warlocks and witches.

How Else This Story Is Told

Brazilian variation:

Akarandek, the flying head, or the ravenous wife—Iaxuí Miton Pedro Mutum Macurap. In Betty Mindlin, *Barbecued Husbands*. A husband is distressed to discover that, no matter how well he provides game, his wife's head goes off each night searching for meat in other huts. Her head attaches to his body when he and his mother bury her headless body. Finally, the head is beaten by villagers.

Variations from El Salvador:

Doublehead—John Bierhorst, *Latin American Folktales*. Pipil People. El Salvador. A priest instructs the man to go looking for the head when it takes off after a running deer. He finds it and buries her head. A calabash tree grows there. When little children emerge from inside the fruit, he brings them home.

The Witch's Head—Robert D. San Souci, *A Terrifying Taste of Short & Shivery: Thirty Creepy Tales*.

Mexican variations:

The Charcoal Cruncher—Manvel K'obyox. In Robert M. Laughlin, *Of Cabbages and Kings* and in *The People of the Bat: Mayan Tales and Dreams from Zinacantán*

The Charcoal Cruncher—Romin Teratol. In Robert M. Laughlin, *Of Cabbages and Kings*

The Witch Wife—Efrain A. Paniagua. In Américo Paredes, *Folktales of Mexico*. Aztec People. Mexico. The flesh drops from a man's wife every night, after which the skeleton grows wings and flies around frightening people. When he sprinkles salt on her chopped-up flesh, the skeleton flies away. Perhaps its appearance now signals that someone has died.

---

295. The Story of the Chonchon

Brenda Hughes, *Folk-tales from Chile*
Mapuche People. Chile

Both wives in a happy Mapuche family share work and help care for each other's children. One night, though, one mother wonders why the other mother is not getting up to comfort her crying child. She sees that the other woman has no head. The other mother must be a chonchon, whose ears become flapping wings as she flies, crying *tue tue tue* mournfully in the night. The husband arrives and sends the wife and children to stay with friends. He turns the body over so the chonchon will not be able to reattach itself and waits. Giant wings beat furiously at dawn, but he does not open the door, torn, because he loves this wife when she is human. The large head with feathers breaks in and cries out when it sees its body turned. The head becomes a dog which paws sorrowfully at him. Because he cares for her, he turns her body right side up. Now reattached, his wife tells him not to be afraid, for she will not harm any of them. He and the other wife promise to keep her identity secret, and they continue to live happily as a family together.

CONNECTIONS

Chonchons. Flying heads. Husbands and wives. Identity. Jealousy. Kalkus. Love. Magic. Secrets. Supernatural husbands and wives. Transformations. Warlocks and witches.

296. THE THREE FOUNTAINS
Margaret Campbell, *South American Folklore Tales*
Mapuche People. Chile

Chief Millacura's youngest wife, Culu-vilu (Golden Serpent) practices sorcery in secret. Jealous of the chief's favoritism for another wife, she tricks Blue Water's three teenage daughters into visiting a witch-doctor, who rips off the jewelry their father has given them and dabs their foreheads with red liquid. When they run outside they become smooth black overlapping stones on Mount Nahuelbuta. The god Pillán pities their mother and changes her into a mountain stream to run over them forever.

CONNECTIONS

Caciques and chieftains. Deceit. Gods and humans. Husbands and wives. Jealousy. Magic. Sorcerers. Supernatural husbands and wives. Transformations.

297. THE WITCH MOTHER-IN-LAW
Petra Guzmán Perrón in Américo Paredes, *Folktales of Mexico*
Mexico

A man in Ojo Caliente is becoming desperate. Not only can no one cure his wife's illness, but the expense is becoming more than he can bear. When a neighbor suggests that his mother has bewitched his wife, the man tells his mother how urgent it is that she make his wife well again. His mother denies having done anything. He warns her that if she is guilty she may get hurt when he tries to break the spell. Still, his mother says nothing. He throws an oiled black hen into a bonfire repeatedly until it dies. The next day, he finds his mother burned. Shortly after that, though, his wife dies.

CONNECTIONS

Deceit. Husbands and wives. Illness. Fathers-in-law and mothers-in-law. Magic. Parents and children. Tests. Warlocks and witches.

298. THE WITCH WIFE
John Bierhorst, *Latin American Folktales*
Colombia

Troubled that his new wife, Celina, hardly eats with him, a man secretly follows her when she sneaks outside one night. There at a cemetery, she and other women eat pieces from a freshly buried corpse. Repulsed, the husband accuses his wife, and she throws a cup of water with red powder into his face. The man becomes a little red dog, which she whips. He escapes to the bake shop, where he helps out by biting coins to alert the baker if they are counterfeit. The princess sends her mother to see this dog with human eyes. The queen brings him to the princess, who also mixes power into water. She sprinkles some on him and tells him to become what he really is. He transforms back into a man. The princess gives him a special solution to use on Celina. The husband overcomes his qualms about hurting his wife and sprinkles her with a few drops. His wife changes into a mare, which he sells to pull a miller's grindstone, where she dies.

CONNECTIONS
Cemeteries. Dogs. Magic. Magic dogs. Magic powders. Princes and princesses. Retaliation. Supernatural husbands and wives. Transformations. Warlocks and witches.

---

299. THE COYOTE TEODORA
John Bierhorst, *Latin American Folktales*
Honduras

A farmer wonders how his wife, Teodora, can fix such fancy meals when they are not rich. One night he secretly sees her transform into a coyote and go out. Frightened, he prays to St. Anthony, but a few nights later he follows her and sees the coyote raiding his neighbor's farms. The farmer speaks with the priest, who tells him to whip her with the rope of St. Francis the instant she becomes fully human again. Nervous, the farmer whips her a little too soon. Partially human, with haunches of a coyote, she runs off into the woods.

CONNECTIONS
Coyotes. Farmers. Fear. Priests and priestesses. Rescues. Supernatural husbands and wives. Transformations. Warlocks and witches.

---

300. AMASANGA WARMI: A FEROCIOUS WIFE
Juan Carlos Galeano, *Folktales of the Amazon*
Amazonia, Ecuador

When it rains hard near the Pataza River animals dive into holes under a kapok tree. Little devil-like juri-juri dogs leap out from the holes, when the villagers throw chili peppers down. Also out from a kapok hole one day comes a young girl with white skin, who does not want anyone to touch her dark hair. She says her name is Amasanga Warmi, "woman of the forest." A family raises her as a Christian until she is ready to marry. One suitor brings ten turkeys and ten monkeys to prove he is capable of supporting a family. He promises Amasanga Warmi he will never touch her head. They are happy together. She routinely picks the lice from his hair, and the husband begins to resent that he cannot touch her head. One day he leaps out from behind and tousles her hair. Under her hair in the back, she has another face, like a juri-juri dog. She sadly asks why. Then her juri-juri face laughs evilly. Her sharp teeth bite through to eat his brains and heart, and she returns to the hole under the kapok tree.

CONNECTIONS

Dogs. Faces. Husbands and wives. Kapok trees. Magic dogs. Murder. Promises. Punishments. Supernatural husbands and wives. Transformations. Trees. Warnings.

---

301. THE HEADLESS MULE
Livia de Almeida and Ana Portella, *Brazilian Folktales*
Brazil

Farmhands are sure a jaguar is the one leaving half-eaten livestock in the field every Friday morning. The farmer waits on Thursday night with a gun. Rounding the shed, however, he is horrified to discover his new wife munching on a lamb. Screaming when she sees him, his wife transforms into a headless mule and flees. The next morning, the farmer cannot speak. Neighbors think this is because his wife has left him. On Thursday nights, however, a headless mule can be seen rampaging through the area. It is possible for her to become a woman again, if someone cuts the mule with a knife. Other headless mules, however, will gallop down the roads, and they must not see the whites of people's eyes or teeth.

CONNECTIONS

Farmers. Fear. Magic mules. Mourning. Mules. Murder. Supernatural husbands and wives. Transformations.

---

302. THE HAWK HUSBAND
Livia de Almeida and Ana Portella, *Brazilian Folktales*
Maue People. Amazonia, Brazil

A mother sends her daughter to meet Anaje, the hawk, whom she thinks will make the best provider of meat as a future husband. Along the way, the girl meets the skunk's and buzzard's mothers, who try to pretend their sons are Anaje. When she reaches the hawk's home, however, his mother tells her to hide because he often returns in a foul temper. However, his hunting has gone well, and Anaje likes the idea of marrying the daughter. After the wedding, however, the buzzard comes looking for the girl. Anaje is able to run him off with his sharp beak and strong claws, but when the buzzard goes home wounded, his mother pours boiling water on his head, which leaves him bald.

CONNECTIONS

Birds. Buzzards. Hawks. Interspecies conflict. Interspecies marriage. Jealousy. Origin tales. Parents and children. Supernatural husbands and wives.

303. THE BEETLE MAN

Livia de Almeida and Ana Portella, *Brazilian Folktales*
Brazil

A young woman who has been declining all her suitors as not special enough, decides on the spot to marry the handsome, well-dressed man she sees outside her window. Her father protests that she does not know the man, but the girl insists. They settle on a farm far from the village. At first, they are content together, but after a while she can never seem to please her husband and grows afraid of his anger. One night, she sees her husband transform into a huge beetle and suck the blood from their last sheep. The following day, she tells her husband that she needs to return home to care for her mother, who has become ill. He commands that she return before the rooster crows three times. At home, she tells her parents everything. They listen to her story unhappily, but tell her she brought this upon herself. Back on the farm, she is terrified when her husband begins to sing that he wants blood to drink. None of their livestock is left, and she is sure he will prey on her next. She flees to her parents and stays inside. Furious, he flies to his father-in-law's garden every night, hoping to capture her, but cannot.

CONNECTIONS

Beetles. Cautionary tales. Escapes. Fear. Interspecies marriage. Magic beetles. Parents and children. Punishments. Stubbornness. Supernatural husbands and wives. Transformations. Vampires.

304. THE POOR WIDOW BULLFIGHTER

Anita Brenner, *The Boy Who Could Do Anything*
Mexico

When her devoted husband Florencio disappears, everyone is sure he must have died. His wife, Widow Mariposa, grinds people's corn to help provide for her children, but still she is quite poor. One day a young man appears and presents her with yarn to weave sashes, like she used to. She guesses he is the magic boy Tepozton. She weaves until she becomes sick in bed. A bull walks in and tells her to take the rope off his neck and suddenly, her Florencio is there. She hides him rolled up in a big mat in the corner. People come looking for the bull when they see hoofprints inside her door, but they do not find him. Florencio changes back into a bull again when the church bells ring. He tells his wife to come to the bullfight the next day and fight against him for the prize of a thousand pesos. Florencio, the bull, acts so fierce, no one will go up against him, except Mariposa. She wins the prize money. It takes a long time for the spell which holds Florencio captive to be broken, but one day, he does return to her.

CONNECTIONS

Bullfighting. Bulls. Enchantment. Love. Magic. Magic bulls. Poverty. Supernatural husbands and wives. Tepozton. Transformations.

---

305. THE ROOSTER'S CLAW / LA PATA DE GALLO
Olga Loya, *Momentos Mágicos / Magic Moments*
Colombia

Raúl and Sofía live lovingly and happily together with their children, until one Saturday when Raúl does not return from the market. No one can find him. Sofía wraps herself in such bitterness even her children do not want to stay near her when they are grown. Lonely, Sofía brings an old chicken to María the curandera, hoping the healer will be able to help her. María gives Sofía a rooster's claw, with which to draw in the dirt and make a wish. The curandera warns her, though, that the claw can be unpredictable. First, Sofía wishes for fifty pesos. Three days later a man delivers her daughter's purse containing the pesos, saying that her daughter was hit by a train and died. Horrified, Sofía does not want to use the claw again. Then, longing for her husband, she draws another circle and wishes for him to appear. The next day his skeleton arrives, and she races inside as it reaches for her. He calls out that some robbers killed him and tries to break down the door. Sofía quickly draws a circle and wishes for Raúl to return to his grave. She never complains again. Things could be worse.

CONNECTIONS

Bargains. Changes in attitude. Discontent. Husbands and wives. Love. Magic claws. Mourning. Perspective. Shamans. Skeletons. Warnings. Wishes.

---

306. THE THREE COUNSELS
Yolanda Nava, *It's All in the Frijoles*
Mexico

Three young men from a small village are heading to the city for work. An old man they meet en route asks if they would prefer a bag of money or wise words to help them get through life. The traveler with a son at home is the only one who decides to take the advice. The old man tells him to stay on well-traveled roads, not to questions things which are not his concern, and not to act hastily. The other two think their compadre made a foolish choice. He shares the first bit of advice with them. However, they do not follow it and take a shortcut, where they are robbed and killed. The third man reaches a large ranch, where he does not question what he sees. Because he has minded his own business the owner gives him a job. After many years, the owner also gives this man all of his wealth. The man returns home to share the good news. He becomes enraged when he sees a priest embracing his wife. Then he remembers the third piece of advice not to jump to conclusions and realizes this priest is his grown son.

CONNECTIONS

Advice. Allegories and parables. Anger. Choices. Husbands and wives. Justice. Misunderstandings. Nosiness. Parents and children. Tests. Thieves. Wise men and wise women.

HOW ELSE THIS STORY IS TOLD

Brazilian variation:
Look Three Times—Elsie Spicer Eells, *The Brazilian Fairy Book*

Mexican variations:
Good Advice—Grant Lyons, *Tales the People Tell in Mexico.* The boy Raymondo has a bad habit of acting hastily. He meets a Viejo who sells him the same three pieces of advice as above for a peso each. He is rewarded with riches when he does not pry into a Bandito's business. When Raymondo reaches the city, he marries a woman, who also follows the same three practices.
The Three Counsels—Riley Aiken. In J. Frank Dobie, *Puro Mexicano*

African American variation from Suriname:
Hide Anger Until Tomorrow—Roger D. Abrahams, *African American Folktales* and in Jane Yolen *Gray Heroes*

307. THE MOTH
John Biershorst, *Latin American Folktales*
Quechua People. Peru

Sad and lonely when her husband leaves on a long journey, a wife spends her nights spinning. She speaks to the moth which flutters nearby. When her young son asks whom she is talking to, she answers that it is a friend who keeps her company and loves her. When her husband returns, their son mentions the friend in the night. Enraged, the man kills his wife. One night later, the boy points to a moth in the room and says that is his mother's friend. The father dies from grief over his mistake.

CONNECTIONS

Allegories and parables. Anger. Choices. Husbands and wives. Insects. Jealousy. Misunderstandings. Moths. Murder. Parents and children. Trust. Words.

308. THE RETURN OF THE GARDENER
Soledad Pérez in Wilson M. Hudson, *The Healer of Los Olmos and Other Mexican Lore*
Mexico

A gardener pushes his wife to invite his friends over to eat dinner with them. She has been refusing because they are quite poor. He keeps insisting, however. Finally she invites them and kills the gardener in order to have meat for the stew. Months later, a light and a bell approach closer each night. Her husband's voice says he has come for his entrails. When he is right by her bedside and says he has caught her, she dies of fright.

CONNECTIONS

Fear. Gardeners. Ghosts. Hospitality. Husbands and wives. Murder. Poverty. Scary tales. Supernatural voices.

---

309. THE DEVIL IN A BOTTLE

Livia de Almeida and Ana Portella, *Brazilian Folktales*
Brazil

The Devil appears at the invitation of a husband who needs to travel for work and does not trust his wife's sociability. He tells his wife that he has hired a servant to help her. This servant is always around. To have some space, the wife gives him a sieve to fetch water with and goes to visit some friends. Upon her return, she flatters the Devil and tricks him into getting inside a bottle for her ring where she traps him. Now the wife is free to go visiting whenever she likes. When her husband returns, she tells him that the servant left. She sends her husband to the church to fill the bottle with holy water. The Devil zooms out and away when the man opens the bottle. The husband never figures it out. There is a saying that a woman will even outwit the Devil to do what she wants to do.

CONNECTIONS

Cleverness. Devil. Humorous tales. Husbands and wives. Servants. Tricksters. Trust.

---

310. FIVE EGGS

Harold Courlander, *Ride with the Sun*
Ecuador

Begging from passersby in town, a poor peasant is able to bring home five eggs to share with his wife. She claims three of the eggs saying that's only fair because she boiled them. The husband thinks he deserves three eggs, and his wife should have two. They argue. His wife pretends to die because she will only receive two eggs, and her husband asks some friends to find a coffin. Back at home, aloud he begs Juanita not to leave him and then whispers that he's going to eat three and she will have two and she whispers back that she will eat three. The public pretense and whispered bantering go on all the way to the cemetery. At the gravesite, Juanita realizes he really is going to lower her down. She sits up in the casket then and says all the eggs are his. They go home. She places five eggs on the table and eats three.

CONNECTIONS

Arguments. Cemeteries. Changes in attitude. Conflict. Eggs. Generosity. Humorous tales. Husbands and wives. Justice. Peasants. Perspective. Poverty. Problem solving.

HOW ELSE THIS STORY IS TOLD

Five Eggs—Pleasant DeSpain, *The Emerald Lizard.* In this version, Jorge earns the eggs by helping an egg merchant.

---

311. THE MAN WHO WAS FULL OF TRUTH

Américo Paredes, *Folktales of Mexico*
Mexico

When a man who has always lied dies, his widow wails that he is leaving with his body "so full of truth." This puzzles her comadre, who gently suggests that the man rarely told a truth. The widow agrees. She says her husband is taking all the truths he never shared with her to the grave.

CONNECTIONS

Death. Deceit. Humorous tales. Husbands and wives. Storytelling. Truth. Widows and widowers. Words.

XII

For Love

---

312. THE WHITE SPIDER'S GIFT

Genevieve Barlow, *Latin American Tales from the Pampas to Mexico City*
Guarani People. Paraguay

    The little white spider, which Piki saved from drowning when he was younger, now greets him each time he fills jars with water at the spring. From there he sees the chieftain's lovely daughter, Tukira, who has returned from a neighboring village. They often meet in the woods gathering berries and flowers and fall in love. The chieftain, however, would like Tukira to marry a warrior and holds a competition for her hand. Piki does well in the physical competitions, but the final test is to return in two moons with the most wonderful and original present for Tukira. Piki and his mother are too poor to purchase something exquisite. Though he prays to the god Tupa, Piki despairs, until the spider tells him she will help. The next day the spider gives him an exquisite lace mantle, which outshines every other gift. Piki and Tukira are wed.

CONNECTIONS
Animal helpers. Class conflict. Clothing. Competition. Death. Friendship. Gifts. Gratitude. Jealousy. Lace. Love. Magic. Ñanduti lace. Origin tales. Outsiders. Parents and children. Rescues. Shroud. Spiders. Weaving.

HOW ELSE THIS STORY IS TOLD
More Beautiful Than the Spider's Web—M.A. Jagendorf and R.S. Boggs, *The King of the Mountains*
The Origin of Ñandutí Lace—Margaret Read MacDonald, *Five Minute Tales*. A chief's son, who goes hunting to give the Guaraní girl he loves a wonderful present, is found years later hanging from a tree beside a jaguar skeleton. His skeleton is wrapped in magnificent cloth specially woven by the spiders. The girl wishes to be the one to weave her love's shroud and watches the spiders weaving for many days, until she is able to create beautiful cloth he can be buried in.
The Origin of Ñandutí Lace / La leyenda del origen del encaje de Ñandutí—Paula Martin, *Pachamama Tales*
The Tale of the Ñanduti—Margaret Campbell, *South American Folklore Tales*

313. WHEN MOUNTAINS BECAME GODS

Carlos Franco Sodja in *Jade and Iron*
Aztec People. Mexico

The Aztec princess Xochiqueztal is filled with joy to see the husband she truly loves among the returning Aztec warriors, for she has been told that he was killed in battle. However, she is now married to the Tlaxcalan who told her this and turns on him for lying to her. Xochiqueztal runs off, filled with shame and sorrow at having been tricked. Her beloved first husband pursues her, and the Tlaxcalan warrior runs after both. The two warriors fight fiercely, and the Aztec kills the Tlaxcalan. Afterwards, however, her beloved finds Xochiqueztal dead. She has taken her own life, overwhelmed with remorse over having remarried. Her husband weeps and covers Xochiqueztal with flowers and incense. The Morning Star of death passes, and there is a tremendous earthquake in the valley of Anáhuac. By dawn two snowy mountains stand there, eternally together. One volcanic mountain looks like a woman resting on white flowers and becomes known as *Ixtachthuatl*, Sleeping Woman. The taller volcano, *Popocateptl*, Smoking Mountain, resembles an Aztec warrior kneeling over her white hair. The deceitful second husband becomes a mountain much further away.

CONNECTIONS

Conflict. Death. Deceit. Gods and goddesses. Husbands and wives. Ixtaccihuatl. Love. Mountains. Mourning. Origin tales. Parents and children. Popocatepetl. Princes and princesses. Punishments. Self-sacrifice. Transformations. Volcanoes. Warriors.

HOW ELSE THIS STORY IS TOLD

Ixtlaccihuatl and Popocatepetl: Mexico's Two Famous Volcanoes—Frances Toor, *A Treasury of Mexican Folkways*

The Love of a Mexican Prince and Princess—M.A. Jagendorf and R.S. Boggs, *The King of the Mountains* and in Marguerite Henry, *Stories from Around the World*

Popcatepetl and Ixtlaccihuatl—Juliet Piggott, *Mexican Folk Tales*

The Sleeping Princess—E. Adams Davis, *Of the Night Wind's Telling*

Sleeping Woman of the Snows—Camilla Campbell, *Star Mountain and Other Legends of Mexico*. Toltec People

The Smoking Mountain—Richard and Judy Dockrey Young, *1492: New World Tales*

The Sweethearts / Los novios—Genevieve Barlow and William N. Stivers, *Stories from Mexico / Historias de México*

The Two Mountains: An Aztec Legend—Eric A. Kimmel. In this telling, the lovers begin as gods and secret lovers and become mortals when Ixcoçauqui disobeys his father by leaving the heavens for earth. When his wife, Coyolxauhqui becomes ill and dies, Ixcoçauqui vows never to leave her, and the gods transform them into two mountains.

---

314. THE YOUNG MAN AND THE STAR MAIDEN

Mercedes Dorson & Jeanne Wilmot, *Tales from the Rain Forest*
Amazonia, Brazil

Caué, the youngest brother, falls in love with the Star Maiden in his father's stories. She is a woman who can come down from the sky to a man who yearns for her. His accomplished elder brother Acauã would also like to marry the Star Maiden, but he is repulsed when it's an old woman who appears to them in a glow. Caué gently brings the old woman home in a gourd. When he goes to show his father the Star Maiden, she jumps out of the gourd as an opossum and lands on a maize plant. His father is sure that corn is dangerous for people, but Caué eats the corn cakes the Star Maiden shows them how to prepare. Caué carries the old woman around all day in the gourd to converse with her when he can. This is a time before farming, and people often go hungry in the rainy season. The old woman asks to be alone to prepare her wedding gift to Caué, which will be seeds from the river and from heaven and training to cultivate the plants. Caué worries when he does not see her for six days. He finds a young woman planting sweet potatoes. She tells him she is the Star Maiden, who appeared as an old woman to test his brother's sincerity. However, when they return to the village, Acauã's friends have burned the family's *maloca* and smashed the gourd from fear. The Star Maiden brings Caué and his father up to her night sky. Back on earth, suspicion and fear keep people from enjoying the wonderful things which exist in the heavens.

CONNECTIONS

Appearance. Brothers and sisters. Farming. Fear. Food. Gifts. Interspecies conflict. Journeys to other realms. Kindness. Longing. Love. Loyalty. Opossums. Outsiders. Punishments. Supernatural husbands and wives. Sky worlds. Stars. Transformations. Unkindness.

HOW ELSE THIS STORY IS TOLD

The Man Who Married a Star—Martin Elbl and J.T. Winik, *Tales from the Amazon.* A young hunter sickens because of his love for one brilliant star. His sister is the only one who sticks by him. When suspicious villagers set fire to the basket in which the star woman hides, she leaps to the sky with her little son in her arms. That night she calls for her husband to journey to her. He brings his hunting dogs and comes.

The Star from the Sky—Lux Vidal. In Johannes Wilbert, *Folk Literature of the Gê Indians, Vol. 2.* Shikrin Gê People. Brazil. When the secret star woman is discovered, the man's mother helps to decorate her, and everyone is kind. She visits her family in the sky and returns with cultivated plants, teaching the tribe how to prepare their fields and grow potatoes, bananas, squash, yams, and manioc.

Star-Girl—Robert Hull, *Central and South American Stories.* A man holds the young woman who has been coming down from the sky and taking his potatoes.

The Star Woman—John Bierhorst, *The Mythology of South America* Apinayé Gê People. Brazil. The star woman comes down to converse with a man after his wife dies, and agrees to live with him in a gourd in his house. She climbs to the sky on cotton thread and brings back yams and potatoes, plus many other crops people now plant and eat. However, when he becomes disloyal to her, she goes back to the sky, taking away the possibility of heaven on earth.

---

315. LORD SUN'S BRIDE

John Bierhorst, *The Monkey's Haircut*
Kekchi Maya

To attract an old man's daughter into thinking he is a great hunter, the Sun carries a deer stuffed with ashes and grass past her house each day. The deer bursts open when he slips on some water she has thrown on the path at her father's suggestion. Embarrassed, Lord Sun borrows a hummingbird's skin. The daughter asks her father to stun the bird with his blowgun so she can keep it as a pet. In the night, the bird becomes a young man who convinces her to run away with him. He obscures her father's seeing stone with soot and puts chili pepper powder in his blowgun, which can suck things back from far distances. When the chili pepper makes him cough and fails to suck his daughter back, her angry father insists that the rain god Chac kill them both with a thunderbolt. When Chac appears above them, Lord Sun becomes a turtle and she becomes a crab, but lightning kills her in the water. The dragonfly helps Lord Sun collect her blood into thirteen jars, which Lord Sun leaves with an old woman. When he returns she wants him to remove the jars, which have been making frightening sounds, and he pours out many buzzing insects and snakes. The daughter is alive in the thirteenth jar, and Lord Sun carries her to the sky to become the moon.

CONNECTIONS

Anger. Blood. Chac. Dragonflies. Emperors, kings & queens. Forbidden love. Gods and humans. Hummingbirds. Hunters. Insect helpers. Journeys to other realms. Lightning. Love. Magic. Moon. Origin tales. Parents and children. Princes and princesses. Restoring life. Shamans. Sun. Supernatural husbands and wives. Transformations. Tortoises and turtles. Volcanoes.

HOW ELSE THIS STORY IS TOLD

The Courtship of Sun and Moon—John Bierhorst, *The Mythology of Mexico and Central America.* The daughter struck by lightning here is a princess. When the Sun comes to collect the bottles, she has become very little, and a shaman tells him a deer must jump over his wife three times. The princess grows so big, she becomes the moon, his wife in the sky.
Note: This story also explains the origins of pink eye (when achiote from the spyglass gets into the king's eye) and of whooping cough (when the king sucks chili pepper in through the blowgun).
The Marriage of the Sun and the Moon—Douglas Gifford, *Warriors, Gods & Spirits from Central & South American Mythology*

316. THE STORY OF THE SUN AND THE MOON

Neil Philip, *Horse Hooves and Chicken Feet*
Mexico

In love, a soldier goes to find the young woman who has mysteriously appeared and then vanished from his room for two nights. He is helped by three magic items, which he takes from brothers who have been arguing over them. Magic boots carry the soldier three leagues with each step to the house of the Sun and then to the Moon, but the beautiful girl has already gone. The soldier travels on to the House of the Wind, where he brings the Wind's mother back to life by hitting her with the magic cudgel. The grateful Wind offers to help him find his love. Each wearing one boot, they reach a witch's house, where the soldier puts on his magic hat of invisibility. He searches the house for his love, who can see him because she is not a witch. They flee, but the old witch comes after them. The witch gets through trees and thick fog the young woman creates by throwing down a comb and then ashes, but she cannot cross the river made by magic salt. The witch curses the daughter, saying that her dreams will dry up at the spring. When they reach the spring, the soldier leaves her to tell his parents the happy news of his love. She ties a handkerchief to his belt to remind him of her and warns him not to let anyone embrace him. The soldier's grandmother, however, hugs him, and he forgets about the maiden at the spring. At his wedding to someone else, the young woman appears and releases two doves. As she asks the male dove about the curse, the spring, and the handkerchief, the young man's memory returns. He tells the bride he is promised to someone else and marries his true love.

Connections

Brothers and sisters. Curses. Enchantment. Gratitude. Journeys to other realms. Longing. Love. Magic. Magic ashes. Magic boots. Magic combs. Magic cudgels. Magic hats. Magic salt. Moon. Parents and children. Quests. Restoring life. Soldiers. Sun. Supernatural beings. Transformations. Warlocks and witches. Warnings. Wind.

---

317. The Llama Herder and the Daughter of the Sun

John Bierhorst, *Black Rainbow: Legends of the Incas and Myths of Ancient Peru*
Inca People. Peru

Acoynapa plays a flute as he tends a herd of white llamas. One day he is awestruck when two dazzling daughters of the Sun ask questions about his flock. Before they leave for the palace, though, one daughter, Chuquillanto, asks Acoynapa his name and where he lives. He removes the silver ornament with a finely etched design of ticks sucking a heart from his forehead. She examines it and hands it back, but she cannot get the design or the herder out of her mind. That night Chuquillanto dreams that she confesses her love to a little bird. She fears she will be killed if she stays in the palace. The bird tells her to sing what is in her heart to the four fountains. If they approve, they will sing back to her, which will give her the power to do what she wishes. Chuquillanto sings to the fountains, and one by one, they sing her song back to her. Outside the palace, Acoynapa's longing for her has made him ill. His mother is fixing him a nettle stew when two of the Sun daughters appear. Acoynapa's mother has told him to hide inside her wooden walking staff. Chuquillanto is disappointed not to see Acoynapa and begs to have the staff, which his mother gives her. She brings it into the palace so openly, the guards who always check to make sure nothing harmful enters the palace, do not stop her. That night Chuquillanto weeps, and the herder is there. At dawn, she sets out for the mountains, but a guard has followed and calls out when he sees Acoynapa emerge from the staff. They flee together, but the angry Sun turns them into stone statues above the town of Calca.

CONNECTIONS

Bird helpers. Interspecies conflict. Disobedience. Dreams. Forbidden love. Gods and humans. Herders. Journeys to other realms. Longing. Love. Magic. Music. Parents and children. Punishments. Stone. Supernatural beings. Transformations.

HOW ELSE THIS STORY IS TOLD

The Daughter of the Sun / La Hija del Sol—Ismael Mascayano. A young daughter of the Sun transforms her flute-playing friend, the llama herder, into a pendant and sneaks him into the palace one night. When she chooses to remain as a mortal and does not return to the palace, the Sun punishes them both with eternal night, but they do not mind, as long as they are together.

---

318. THE QUENA: THE LEGEND OF MANCHAI PUYTU (GLOOMY CAVERN) / LA QUENA: LA LEYENDA DEL MANCHAI PUYTU (CAVERNA TENEBROSA)

Paula Martin, *Pachamama Tales: Folklore from Argentina, Bolivia, Chile, Paraguay, Peru, and Uruguay*
Quechua People. Peru

When their love is frowned upon by the moon and the villagers of Cochabamba, two lovers go to live in a cold cave high in the Andes Mountains. The woman falls ill and dies, and the man is filled with such sorrow he cannot leave her. For days, for months, he stays by her side, watching her and kissing her until all that is left are her bones. He takes one of her tibia bones then and from it makes a flute. The haunting sounds from that quena express the sweet sadness of his love and his loss.

CONNECTIONS

Bones. Death. Devotion. Flutes. Love. Music. Origin tales. Quenas. Sacrifice.

HOW ELSE THIS STORY IS TOLD

The Tale of the Quena—Margaret Campbell, *South American Folklore Tales*. Inca People. Here, the quena's expressive sound comes from the lament a young man sings at having to leave his beloved mountains, just before he gives his left leg bone to a demon to save his sisters' lives.

---

319. THE SORCERER'S DAUGHTER

W.H. Brett, *Guyana Legends* and as William Henry Brett, *Legends and Myths of the Aboriginal Indians of British Guiana*
Guyana

A sorcerer's daughter asks her father to turn her into a dog so she can be near the young hunter she loves in the forest. The sorcerer loves her and is sad to do this, but he gives her a magic skin to wear and hopes she will get over this and come back to him. The young hunter begins his day with four dogs, but one runs off. When he returns to his house after hunting in the woods, cassava bread has been baked and the floor swept. He thinks it may be a spirit helping him. The same dog runs away again, so he ties up the others and peeking through a hole sees a young woman baking bread in his house and the skin hanging on the wall. The young woman captures his heart, and he runs in and throws her skin in the fire, so she will not transform back. He holds her and says they will go to her father and be wed.

CONNECTIONS
Dogs. Hunters. Longing. Love. Magic. Parents and children. Sorcerers. Transformations.

320. THE HUNTER WHO WANTED AIR
Alex Whitney, *Voices in the Wind*
Amerind People. Guyana, Suriname, French Guiana and Brazil

The hunter Mapuri falls in love with Tafeela the minute he sees her weaving a basket, but she tells her father that she only wants to marry someone who shows that he is also wise. Mapuri paddles in his dugout to learn wisdom from Mankato, the wise chieftan of another tribe. Mankato holds Mapuri's head underwater for a long time and then asks Mapuri what he was thinking about while underwater. Mapuri answers that nothing was on his mind but getting air. Mankato tells him he will become wise when he desires wisdom with that same single-mindedness. Mapuri sadly returns to Tafeela and tells her that he only learned that air is more important to him than being wise. Tafeela says she will marry him, believing that his honesty will lead to wisdom.

CONNECTIONS
Honesty. Humility. Hunters. Love. Marriage. Parents and children. Quests. Teachers. Tests. Wisdom.

HOW ELSE THIS STORY IS TOLD
The First Lesson—Pleasant DeSpain, *Thirty-Three Multicultural Tales to Tell*. Brazil. The young woman here praises the hunter's humility as well as his honesty, as steps on the path to wisdom.

321. THE SWEETEST SONG IN THE WOODS
M.A. Jagendorf and R.S. Boggs, *The King of the Mountains*
Maya People. Guatemala

The wise priests tell a Maya king who loves his daughter Nima-cux that choosing a husband will lift the sadness that has suddenly befallen her. The king summons many young noblemen. Her eyes brighten only at the end of the day, when a poor young man arrives singing a beautiful song that lifts her spirits. She tells him that his voice is sweet, but that she will only marry him when he can sing as sweetly as the birds. He requests four moons to try. For months, the young man listens to the birds in the woods and practices every day, but he cannot make his voice match theirs. Time is almost up, when the Spirit of the Woods tells him to cut a small branch from a tree. The Spirit hollows the branch and makes some holes and instructs the young man to practice blowing through the tube. Music as beautiful as a bird song sounds when he returns to the princess, who happily marries him.

CONNECTIONS

Chirimía. Gods and humans. Love. Magic. Music. Parents and children. Perseverance. Princes and princesses. Spirits. Supernatural beings. Tests.

HOW ELSE THIS STORY IS TOLD

Song of the Chirimia: A Guatemalan Folktale / La música de la chirimia: folklore Guatemalteco—Jane Anne Volkmer
The Chirimía—Pleasant DeSpain, *Thirty-Three Multicultural Tales To Tell*

---

322. THE MOUSE AND THE ANT
Angel Vigil, *The Eagle on the Cactus*
Mexico

A lonely ant finds a silver dollar while searching for food in the desert. She drags it to town and buys some new clothes, hoping someone will notice. The dog who runs over seems too rough; the cat's meowing just sounds like noise. No animal seems like the one she might want to settle down with. The ant is leaving town when she hears a lovely voice. It is a mouse, singing to himself. They visit and become friends and get married. The ant never gets tired of hearing the mouse sing to her. One day, the mouse drowns in a pot of soup while the ant is out. She misses him and finds comfort in singing his songs.

CONNECTIONS

Ants. Cockroaches. Friendship. Husbands and wives. Insects. Interspecies marriage. Love. Mice. Mourning. Music. Rescues. Solace.

HOW ELSE THIS STORY IS TOLD

Brazilian variation:
The Cockroach's Wedding—Livia de Almeida and Ana Portella, *Brazilian Folktales*

Mexican variations:
Martina Martínez and Pérez the Mouse—Alma Flor Ada and F. Isabel Campoy, *Tales Our Abuelitas Told.* Martina's friends all express sympathy after Pérez falls into the soup, but it is her aunt Doña Pepa who speeds to the kitchen and saves Raton Pérez, by pulling him out of the pot by the tail.
Pérez the Mouse—María Soledad Orozco. In Américo Paredes, *Folktales of Mexico*
Ratoncito Pérez—Soledad Pérez. In Wilson M. Hudson, *The Healer of Los Olmos and Other Mexican Lore*

323. NACHO AND LOLITA
Pam Muñoz Ryan
Mexico

Nacho, a pitacoche with colorful feathers, sings beautifully at dusk near the Mission at San Juan Capistrano, but he is lonely for the company of other birds. When a small swallow arrives in March, Nacho sings lullabies as she builds her nest, helps to carry grass, brings insects for her to eat, and protects the eggs with his wings. The swallow's name is Lolita, and she tells Nacho he is wonderful. In the fall, Lolita says she must migrate south with the other swallows. She begs him to join her, and he begs her to stay, saying he is too large to fly that far. Lolita brings Nacho a branch so he can rest in the water when he grows tired. He practices, but the water is so choppy that swallows have to lift Nacho to safety. So, Nacho remains in Capistrano and dreams of Lolita. While he waits, he plants all of his colorful feathers, which grow into flowers. The feathers which grow back are all gray, but when Lolita returns, she still finds him wonderful.

CONNECTIONS
Birds. Devotion. Friendship. Kindness. Loneliness. Longing. Love. Magic feathers. Migration. Mourning. Music. Pitacoches. Separation. Swallows.

HOW ELSE THIS STORY IS TOLD
A Tale of Love—Anthony John Campos, *Mexican Folk Tales*. This one has a sad ending. When the pitacochi gets too tired trying to fly away, the swallow leads him back to the cliff top where he waits, but she never returns.

---

324. MOTHER SCORPION COUNTRY / LA TIERRA DE LA MADRE ESCORPIÓN
Harriet Rohmer and Dorminster Wilson
Miskito People. Nicaragua

When his beloved wife Kati dies, Naklili cannot bear to be separated from her and bring eggs and cassava, along with his flute and lance, and lies down beside her in the coffin. He uses the lance to keep any animals from nibbling on her. Suddenly, she wakes and wonders that Naklili is there with her. Kati tells him that she now belongs to the dead, but Naklili insists he wants to stay with her. Kati guides him to the boat which will take them across the lagoon to Mother Scorpion Country, but the frog boatman jumps into the water fearing Naklili who is still alive. Mother Scorpion and the spirits on the other side welcome Kati joyfully, but Mother Scorpion warns Naklili that this land will only be paradise for Kati. Indeed, everything that is beautiful to Kati there appears dismally bleak to Naklili. He realizes he truly does not belong. Kati send him drifting back in a bamboo trunk with instructions that he is not to tell others what he experienced here until the end of his life, when he will also take a string of beads she has left for him in the house. Some of Naklili's relatives welcome him, and some are fearful. When he is ready to leave the land of the living, he reaches for the string of beads and a poisonous snake bites him. He is called by Mother Scorpion, where he knows he will be able to rejoin Kati.

CONNECTIONS

Afterlife. Death. Dogs. Frogs and toads. Gods and humans. Husbands and wives. Journeys to other realms. Love. Mourning. Scorpions. Secrets. Separation. Spirits. Storytelling. Supernatural beings.

HOW ELSE THIS STORY IS TOLD

The Dead Wife—John Bierhorst, *Latin American Folktales and The Mythology of Mexico and Central America.* Here, the man's wife is ferried to the land of the dead by a dog, and the husband swims alongside.

---

325. THE LAND OF THE DEAD

Johannes Wilbert, *Yupa Folktales*
Yupa People. Sierra de Perijá, Venezuela

When a young man is shot in the forest by jealous men from his tribe, the young woman who loves him laments by his grave for a whole week. When her dead lover appears one night, she tells him that death has not changed her love for him. He asks her to drink some *támi* so they can travel together. In the form of cloud and wind he follows her along the forest path to the house of Kopecho, the Lord of Frogs, who commands them each to make something with the reeds he hands them. Kopecho is pleased with the young man's hat, but because the girl's basket is poorly made, he sends her down a different, frightening path with wild beasts and screaming people. One day later, her path converges with her lover's, and they continue on to a great wall, the *taiyáya*, which fences the Land of the Dead. Because he is righteous, her lover can break through the wall with a cudgel, and they travel on to a river. Because he has been kind to dogs in his life, a large dog tows him across. The girl can swim without drowning because she is not dead. They reach a village with round huts and people who look human. She stays for several years, surprised that her husband can do everything live humans do there, except make love, which would kill her. She journeys home alone, and her parents welcome her with a feast. However, intoxicated with a fermented drink, she tells all that she experienced in the Land of the Dead. Then, fearing that her lover will reject her because she has told, she takes her own life.

CONNECTIONS

Afterlife. Death. Frogs and toads. Gods and humans. Jealousy. Journeys to other realms. Love. Mourning. Murder. Righteousness. Secrets. Self-sacrifice. Separation. Storytelling. Supernatural beings.

326. Daughters of the Kalku

Brenda Hughes, *Folk-tales from Chile*
Mapuche People. Chile

Looking for free labor, the village sorcerer, a selfish kalku, challenges his two nephews to cut down his oak trees with a single blow to prove they will make worthy husbands for his daughters. They do, with the help of sharper axes that the powerful spirit Pillan sends crashing down from the heavens. Konkel and Pediu marry the kalku's daughters, but the kalku has ever more tasks for them. When Konkel and Pediu do not return from hunting ostriches and llamas after two days, the kalku is sure they have run away. He orders his reluctant fox servant to kill his daughters. Broken with sadness to find their wives dead, the brothers pull the sun down into a cooking pot with a lid, so darkness will end life on earth. The birds beg them to let the sun out, offering their daughters as wives, but the brothers miss their own wives too much. The kalku dies, as well as many others. Finally, the partridge prods their mule to kick over the pot, so the sun can climb back into the sky. Things begin to live again, but the brothers still grieve. The ostrich asks the brothers to chant while he dances. Two old women appear, and the ostrich cries for them to keep chanting. Now, their wives appear, and Konkel and Pediu are happy to see them. Each wife has only one eye, but the two old women give them each one of their eyes. Konkel and Pediu begin to enjoy life again.

Connections

Bird helpers. Captivity. Death. Eyes. Fathers-in-law and mothers-in-law. Foxes. Gods and humans. Husbands and wives. Love. Magic. Mourning. Murder. Ostriches. Partridges. Restoring life. Revenge. Selfishness. Sorcerers. Sun. Tasks.

---

327. The Tale of Delgadina

Laura Simms in David Holt and Bill Mooney, *More Ready-to-Tell Tales*
Chile

Delgadina gently puts the little red snake she finds into a beautiful box, and by morning it has tripled in size. It keeps growing as she cares for it, until her mother says they do not have enough money to feed it anymore. Delgadina sadly tells the snake that it must go to the ocean. Before he leaves, the snake instructs her to rub her hands on his eyes, and gold coins will fall when she shakes her fingers after washing. Word spreads. A wicked old woman tells the king that she will bring him Delgadina, but she blinds Delgadina on the way there and throws her into the sea. The old woman then presents her own daughter to the king as the magic girl. Wanting gold, he marries her right away. Meanwhile Delgadina is rescued by an old shepherd and sings by the shore every morning. The red snake recognizes Delgadina's voice and cures her eyes. She shakes out coins to thank the shepherd, and the snake carries her back across the sea to her mother. By now the king has realized that his wife is not the true Delgadina. He orders a feast prepared with greasy food and no towels, so guests will need to shake their fingers. The real Delgadina is recognized, and the old woman and her daughter are caught sneaking away. That night Delgadina becomes queen, and the red snake comes whenever they need help solving problems.

CONNECTIONS

Animal helpers. Blindness. Deceit. Emperors, kings & queens. Friendship. Gratitude. Greed. Heroes and heroines. Identity. Kindness. Love. Magic. Punishments. Reversals of fortune. Snakes. Rescues. Supernatural beings. Warlocks and witches.

HOW ELSE THIS STORY IS TOLD

Brazilian variation:
Why the Sea Moans—Elsie Spicer Eells, *Fairy Tales from Brazil* and in Ethna Sheehand, *Folk and Fairy Tales from Around the Wor*ld. When Dionysia marries the prince, she forgets about calling the sea serpent at the hour of her marriage, as she has promised, so the serpent must remain in the sea and calls her name, a sound which you can hear whenever waves break against the shore.

Chilean variation:
Delgadina and the Snake—Yolando Pino-Saavedra, *Folktales of Chile*. The wicked old woman here is a witch, who gets thrown in the oven with her daughter.

---

328. THE CROCODILE MAN
Pleasant DeSpain, *The Emerald Lizard*
Colombia

The vendor Mario runs a successful business in Magangué spinning stories to go with the fruit from his cart, but he yearns to be with Roque Lina, who is always well guarded by her brothers. Roque Lina's father has ordered him not even to speak to her, which makes both Mario and Roque Lina sad. A whirlpool separates the places where men and women bathe in the river. Mario's grandmother has taught him how to transform himself. Each grain of rice Mario eats turns into a crocodile tooth, and one day he becomes a crocodile and swims to the women's side. Everyone flees, but Roque Lina, who does not fear the Crocodile Man. He evades capture and visits with her in the water for two weeks before she climbs onto his back, and they swim down the river together.

Note: A warning chant which Colombian parents sing to children who do not finish their rice is based on this story.

CONNECTIONS

Brothers and sisters. Crocodiles. Forbidden love. Love. Parents and children. Supernatural beings. Transformations. Vendors.

---

329. GREEN BIRD
Mary-Jo Gerson, *Fiesta Femenina*
Mixtec People. Mexico

The Zapotec King, Great Jaguar, has chosen a political match for his daughter Kesne, but she defies him, saying she has pledged her love to the man Tidacuy. Furious, Great Jaguar has court sorcerers change her into a green bird and banish her forever. Green Bird hides in the jungle. She despairs when eagles bring word that Great Jaguar has died, for it means that he will never be able to forgive her and she will always be cursed. However, her mother Serpent Goddess has not forgotten Kesne and goes to the sorcerers who tell her where to find her daughter and what they have to do to soften the Heart of the Sky. Turtledoves and hummingbirds help them fill thirteen jars with tears and nectar from every flower. Other birds help them create a rug of rainbow-colored feathers. The Serpent Goddess brings these things to the temple of the Heart of the Sky and begs him to free her daughter from her father's punishment. He recognizes her unselfish love for Kesne and agrees to undo the magic. Green Bird's feathers slide off in a flash of lightning. She reigns as Queen of the Zapotecs with Tidacuy, her love, as King, and her devoted mother, the Serpent Goddess, nearby.

Connections

Anger. Bird helpers. Birds. Curses. Devotion. Disobedience. Emperors, kings & queens. Enchantment. Forbidden love. Gods and humans. Heroes and heroines. Love. Magic. Parents and children. Perseverance. Punishments. Snakes. Tasks. Transformations. Unselfishness. Zapotec People.

---

330. The Parrot Prince

John Bierhorst, *Latin American Folktales*
Chile

Mariquita presses her father to marry the widow next door, who turns mean once he does. She moves into the little cottage her mother has left for her to escape the cruelty of her stepmother and stepsisters. One evening a parrot offers to help her sweep. Mariquita asks the parrot what she can do for him, and the parrot asks her to leave him a basin of water and some things to groom with. He comes to her windowsill at midnight, bathes, and transforms into a prince. Her loneliness vanishes as they visit each night. The prince leaves money before he goes. The stepmother tells the stepdaughters to find out who is giving Mariquita the money. The youngest stepsister sees the parrot become a prince. Hearing this, the stepmother sets three sharp knives on the windowsill which cut the parrot. He cries that Mariquita has betrayed him. To right the wrong, she must come for him after wearing through the soles of iron shoes. Mariquita never stops searching for the prince in iron shoes. When the soles have worn through, she overhears three duck women speaking, and one says the prince's knife wounds will not heal until a right wing feather from each of the duck women is dipped in their blood and waved over the wounds. Mariquita takes the three wings from the ducks while they sleep and goes to the city, stopping only to change into men's clothing. She tells the king she is a doctor and has come to cure the prince. She waves the wings dipped in blood gently over his wounds, and he is healed. Then Mariquita tells him the whole story, and they are wed.

CONNECTIONS

Bird helpers. Deceit. Dreams. Ducks. Enchantment. Greed. Healing. Iron shoes. Jealousy. Love. Magic. Misunderstandings. Orphans. Parrots. Perseverance. Quests. Reconciliations. Step-mothers and stepdaughters. Transformations. Warlocks and witches.

HOW ELSE THIS STORY IS TOLD

Brazilian variation:

The Parrot of Limo Verde—Elsie Spicer Eells, *The Brazilian Fairy Book*. Senhorita One-eye, Two-eyes, and Three-eyes and their mother are the jealous neighbors who hurt the parrot. The young woman's search for the prince takes her to the Moon and the Great Wind.

Chilean variation:

The Little Orphan Girl—Yolando Pino-Saavedra, *Folktales of Chile*. The young woman does not reveal who she is when she cures the prince in disguise. He only realizes she is not the one who left the knives which cut him, when he comes to seek revenge and sees the ring he gave the doctor in the bowl of water.

Mexican variations:

The Green Bird—Américo Paredes, *Folktales of Mexico*. This young woman works in the kitchen when she arrives in the worn-out iron shoes. The prince recovers after hearing her play the guitar. He says he will marry the one who makes the best cup of chocolate, which is Luisa's, his love.

The Green Bird—Angel Vigil, *The Eagle on the Cactus*. Spanish Colonial People. Maria finds the green bird Quiquiriquí when she becomes lost in the woods. It is in her dream that she sees him wounded by the knives. Wearing the iron shoes, she visits the Sun, the Moon, and the wind. Two doves in a tree say their ashes can end his enchantment.

---

331. *MARIANA AND THE MERCHILD: A FOLK TALE FROM CHILE*

Caroline Pitcher

Chile

Kindly old Mariana lives by the sea, teased by the village children, and lonely. One day after a storm, the shell of the large crab she places into her basket splits to reveal a baby girl with red hair and a silver fish's tail. Mariana immediately loves this girl, and the Wise Woman advises how to care for her. Mariana wants the mother to know her child is safe. She sets the crab shell on a rock and waits. When a Sea Spirit comes in on a wave and sings her child, Mariana emerges from hiding. The Sea Spirit thanks her for saving the baby from sea-wolves and asks her to look after the child while the seas are still wild. The Merchild delights Mariana, and seeing her, the other children no longer run away. Every day, the Sea Spirit teaches her child to swim in a sheltered rock pool and then further out in the water. The time comes when the Sea Spirit sings that she must take the Merchild home. Mariana cries, but she is no longer totally alone. The village children take her hands, and the Merchild and her mother bring fish and pearls.

CONNECTIONS

Babies. Changes in attitude. Gratitude. Kindness. Loneliness. Love. Mermaids and mermen. Old
    age. Parents and children. Rescues. Reversals of fortune. Separation. Spirits. Supernatural
    beings. Wise men and wise women.

---

332. THE GREAT BLESSING OF THE LAND

M.A. Jagendorf and R.S. Boggs, *The King of the Mountains*
Guatemala

Parrot, Coyote, Jaguar, and Eagle bring the creator gods, Bitol and Tzakol, to the
River to see a beautiful boy they have found there. He is the child of Golden Sunbeam
and River. The gods take him home and raise him with their children and call him
Teosinte. Their youngest daughter Ma-ix and Teosinte fall in love and get married.
Teosinte wants to live near River to hear his mother's song. Bitol and Tzakol are sad
that their daughter is moving away and then worried when the newlyweds do not come
to visit. The gods decide to go to River, where all they find are two, tall, graceful plants
in front of the cave with red hair like Teosinte's and fruit with white teeth like Ma-ix's.
They decide the plants are the spirits of their children. They call the one with teeth
Maíz and help it to grow for food all over the land. The corn that is Teosinte grows wild.

CONNECTIONS

Adoption. Corn. Gods and goddesses. Interspecies marriage. Love. Origin tales. Parents and
    children. Spirits. Transformations.

HOW ELSE THIS STORY IS TOLD

The Beginning of Maize—Dorothy Sharp Carter, *The Enchanted Orchard*. Teosinte's lesser status
    as a plant is his punishment for defying the gods.

---

333. THE LITTLE FROG

Yolando Pino-Saavedra, *Folktales of Chile*
Chile

A miserly king gives his three sons leave to see the world if they each return with
a decaliter of silver for him in a year. The elder two sons rudely kick the frog whom
they thought was a young woman singing at cottage, but the youngest son, Juanito, tells
the father he will marry his daughter no matter what she looks like. Juanito does marry
the little frog and lives at their cottage. Though he wishes she weren't a frog, Juanito is
kind to her, and she sings him to sleep. When he needs to return to the castle, but does
not have the required silver, she tells him to add one wood chip to the sack of coal and
bring that. Silver pours out of the sack before his father. Now the queen wants each of
their wives to embroider a tablecloth. Juan is worried, but the frog sends him back with
the most wonderful one of all. Though Juanito's brothers mock him for being the husband of a frog, the puppy she trains can dance on its hind legs. The king wants to meet

all three wives. Juanito and the frog leave in a tub pulled by oxen. They arrive at the castle riding in a coach, and the frog is a beautiful princess. She causes the other wives who copy her to drop horse turds when they dance, while she spins off pearls. When they return home with the king, their cottage has become a beautiful house, and the little frog remains a woman.

CONNECTIONS

Animal helpers. Bargains. Brothers and sisters. Emperors, kings & queens. Enchantment. Frogs and toads. Kindness. Love. Magic. Magic frogs. Magic monkeys. Magic toads. Parents and children. Ridicule. Tasks. Transformations. Unkindness. Warlocks and witches.

HOW ELSE THIS STORY IS TOLD

Brazilian variation:
Princess Toad—Livia de Almeida and Ana Portella, *Brazilian Folktales*

Costa Rican variation:
The Enchanted Monkey—Lupe de Osma, *The Witches' Ride*. The youngest prince frees the monkey being beaten by a witch by saying he will marry her, and she sends him to the king with surprisingly wondrous gifts.

334. THE BIRD BRIDE
John Bierhorst, *The Monkey's Haircut*
Yucatec Maya Speakers. Mexico

A father offers his land to the son who can capture the creature which has been raiding the cornfield. The first two sons angrily dismiss the toad which offers to help them, but the youngest son kindly shares his lunch with the toad and invites him to come along on his search. When the toad shows him a wish-granting pebble, the boy wishes for a bride, a house, and to catch the cornfield thief. They set out together, toad and boy. When they see a bird fly down to the cornfield, the bird begs him not to shoot. She tells him she was changed by a sorceress when she refused to marry her evil son. The boy recognizes this bird as the one meant to be his bride. He invites her to come with them. Back at home, he asks the toad to transform her, and a young woman appears. His father says that this youngest son will inherit the land. The toad lives with them, and the jealous brothers flee in shame.

CONNECTIONS

Animal helpers. Birds. Brothers and sisters. Competition. Enchantment. Frogs and toads. Kindness. Love. Magic. Magic stones. Parents and children. Quests. Rescues. Rewards. Theft. Transformations. Supernatural beings. Wishes.

HOW ELSE THIS STORY IS TOLD

The Three Brothers and the Toad—Alfredo Barrera Vazquez. In Frances Toor, *A Treasury of Mexican Folkways*. Quintana Roo, Mexico

335. THE SHE-CALF / WAKACHA
Teodora Paliza in Johnny Payne, *She-Calf*
Quechua People. Peru

When a woman gives birth to a she-calf, her father sends the child up to the meadow with their servant, who visits the calf each week. One week, the she-calf requests that the servant tell her mother to secretly prepare for her to visit with specific instructions to leave first loaves of bread out of the oven, a first cup of wine, flowers, holy water, and an innocent boy, all in an untouched room with a bed. Her mother does this, borrowing a neighbor's boy. When the she-calf arrives at midnight, she checks to make sure everything is right and then slips out of her calfskin. As she strokes the boy's hair, he wonders who she is and falls back to sleep. The next time the boy comes, he only pretends to fall asleep, but the woman vanishes when he accidentally drips some wax while admiring her beauty. The boy stitches seven pairs of sandals and goes out searching for her, wearing out five pairs before he heads into the jungle. Some frightening condors tell him he does not belong there, but relent when he tells them that he is driven by despair. After they eat the cow he has cut up for them, one condor carries him to the bank of a lake and instructs him to cut open the stomach of each animal he finds inside the goat there. The last will be a white dove, which he is to capture. The boy does all this, but he is heartbroken as the dove flies away and asks an eagle to knock it down. The dove falls to earth and becomes the she-calf girl, who says that she now knows that the young man really loves her and that her enchantment is over.

CONNECTIONS
Bird helpers. Calves. Condors. Doves. Enchantment. Heroes and heroines. Journeys. Love. Magic. Parents and children. Quests. Sandals. Supernatural beings. Transformations.

---

336. HOW NANCO WON A WIFE
Brenda Hughes, *Folk-tales from Chile*
Chile

The cacique's daughter does not want to marry the rich old friend her father has chosen for her, but she knows her father will never agree to let her marry her cousin poor Nanco, though they love each other. When the daughter vanishes one day, the cacique promises that Nanco can marry his daughter if he can find her. Nanco dives into the lake where she was last seen. With thorny branches, he keeps a floating animal skin, a cuero with many eyes, from drowning him and rides it to the entrance of an underwater cave. There Nanco stabs a strange round man with a head on backwards before the creature sees him. His love is one of the girls chained to a wall behind. He hides some of the shiny metallic rocks he finds and returns with the villagers' boat to rescue them. Nanco's uncle, though, reneges on his promise for Nanco to marry his daughter. Nanco demands to fight the cacique's friend and wins. With silver nuggets from the cave, he buys gifts for his bride and her father and a horse with a silver bridle for himself, and eventually, Nanco beomes cacique.

CONNECTIONS

Caciques and chieftains. Captivity. Class conflict. Heroes and heroines. Journeys to other realms. Love. Parents and children. Promises. Rescues. Reversals of fortune. Sorcerers. Supernatural beings. Water worlds.

---

337. THE JEWELS OF SHINING LIGHT

Angel Vigil, *The Eagle on the Cactus*
Spanish Colonial People. Mexico

The royal ministers urge the king to run a contest, saying that his daughter will never get married if she continues to hold out for love. Juanito, a poor shepherd, heads for the palace with his sheep to enter the competition. On the way there, he collects falling stars which transform into glowing jewels, not too hot to pick up. He thanks the saints for these gifts. The king has imagined a wealthy husband for his daughter. He has Juanito imprisoned for showing up with dirty sheep. The princess, however, is intrigued by Juanito and by the bright light which comes from the dungeon. Juanito shows her the jewels, and each night they visit secretly. He gives the jewels to the princess, saying they are meant for her. Later, she hands him a bag to open the next day. When the king is ready to announce the winner of the contest, the princess tells him that the richest prince is there in disguise. Her servants bring Juanito. When the king opens his bag, coins which she placed there, along with his shining jewels, light up the room. Now the king is ready to believe Juanito really is a prince in disguise. The princess has already fallen in love with the wealth of his good heart.

CONNECTIONS

Captivity. Class conflict. Competition. Emperors, kings & queens. Gifts. Gods and humans. Herders. Jewels. Love. Magic. Magic jewels. Parents and children. Princes and princesses. Stars. Transformations.

---

338. JUAN MARÍA AND JUANA MARÍA

John Bierhorst, *Latin American Folktales*
Guatemala

Juan María and Juana María, the son and daughter of two good friends, run away from home when their mothers forbid them to marry. They promise only to marry each other, but are jailed for vagrancy in the first town they reach and placed in separate cells. The governor's daughter falls in love with Juan María, but when Juana María hears that they may marry, she makes a shroud with the help of a female guard. On the night of the wedding, she leaves the prison with a dagger and chain, screaming in the street that she will kill anyone who stops her. Juana María stabs Juan María with the dagger that night at his home and returns to prison. She opens the coffin to stab him again once more in the church. Devils grab her on the church steps, and she calls a farewell to the guard. When the guard calls back that she will remember her, Juana María snags her with the chain to come along.

CONNECTIONS
Captivity. Forbidden love. Guards. Love. Murder. Promises. Punishments. Supernatural beings.

---

339. WHY THE MOON IS FREE
Mary-Jo Gerson, *Fiesta Femenina*
Yaqui People. Mexico

The Sun would love to marry the Moon, but the Moon enjoys being independent. She has stars and planets to talk to and meteors to race. She tells the Sun she will marry him when he brings her a beautiful skirt that fits her perfectly. The Sun has a special skirt woven with golden thread and striped with starlight, but now the Moon is so much thinner. The Sun brings the skirt to a tailor to take in, but the moon has become wider, and the skirt is too tight. For thirty days, the Sun cannot get the size of the skirt right. He does not marry the Moon, but every day he looks at her as she is about to rise and sighs.

CONNECTIONS
Amazon River. Appearance. Bargains. Clothing. Humorous tales. Identity. Independence. Longing. Love. Moon. Origin tales. Rivers. Size. Sun. Tasks. Tears.

HOW ELSE THIS STORY IS TOLD
Brazilian variation:
The Creation of the Amazon River—Livia de Almeida and Ana Portella, *Brazilian Folktales*. The silver Moon meets the golden Sun in the Amazon forest, and they fall in love. They would like to marry, but the Sun, a fierce warrior, realizes that his passion for her would burn all life on earth. And the Moon realizes that the tears she would shed as their love is consummated would flood the Earth. They agree that this marriage cannot happen, but as the Moon cries, yearning for the Sun, her tears create the mighty Amazon River.

Mapuche variation from Argentina and Chile:
The Playground of the Sun and the Moon—Margaret Read MacDonald, *Tuck-Me-in-Tales: Bedtime Stories from Around the World*. The Sun chases the Moon around the paths of day and night, but the Sun is never able to catch the frolicking Moon and be able to travel along in her silver ring.

---

340. RABBIT GETS MARRIED
John Bierhorst, *The Monkey's Haircut*
Kanjobal Maya People

Coyote's daughter tells Rabbit that he is too short to marry her. She gets annoyed when he touches her. He does touch her again and flees. She becomes trapped by a log fence which collapses as she runs after him. Rabbit teases her then, and she tells him he is tall. Her father arrives and asks Rabbit to help get her free, but Rabbit cannot lift the logs and says he is too small. Coyote threatens to eat Rabbit if they cannot free his daughter. Rabbit calls out for a Puma passing by to help. Puma and Coyote both get trapped under a log, but set Coyote's daughter free. She runs off with Rabbit, and they marry.

CONNECTIONS
Captivity. Coyotes. Flirtation. Interspecies conflict. Love. Interspecies marriage. Parents and children. Pumas. Rabbits. Size.

341. THE STORY THAT BECAME A DREAM
José Manuel Reyes in John Bierhorst, *Latin American Folktales*
Chile

Entranced by a beautiful woman, a man new to town finds an excuse to stop by and speak with her. He visits often, and they become lovers. She has told him she is not married, which is wishful thinking as she is disappointed with her husband. The young man also becomes friends with her husband, without knowing the connection. One time when he almost gets caught at her house, the young man even tells the husband about his adventure. The wife keeps hiding the lover in different places. The husband suspects his wife and the friend. He seeks help from his father-in-law. The father-in-law invites both men to dinner. The young man finishes telling the story of his latest escapade by describing the end as a dream he then woke from. The father-in-law is angry that the husband questioned his daughter's honor over a dream. He stabs the husband. The young man continues to visit the father-in-law and marries the woman he loves.

CONNECTIONS
Anger. Deceit. Discontent. Fathers-in-law and mothers-in-law. Husbands and wives. Illicit love. Love. Lovers. Murder. Reputation. Seduction. Storytelling.

342. THE FLEA
Neil Philip, *Horse Hooves and Chicken Feet*
Mexico

A magician tells his daughter that she can marry the boy she loves only if the boy can outsmart him. For three nights, the boy has to pick a place to sleep where the magician cannot find him. The magician does not know that this boy can also do magic. With spells, the magician finds the boy on the tip of the moon and in a shell at the bottom of the sea. For the third night though, the boy becomes a flea and hops onto the magician's sombrero. The magician cannot find him anywhere, and the boy and the daughter get to lead an enchanted life together.

CONNECTIONS

Animal helpers. Bargains. Class conflict. Emperors, kings & queens. Fleas. Foxes. Hats. Humorous
tales. Insects. Lice. Love. Magic. Parents and children. Princes and princesses. Riddles. Sorcerers. Tests. Tricksters. Truth.

HOW ELSE THIS STORY IS TOLD

Brazilian variation:

The Louse-Skin Chair—Livia de Almeida and Ana Portella, *Brazilian Folktales*. Neither the king
nor the princess want this poor man to marry her, even though he is the one who guesses
what the princess's chair is made of. They put him through other tests. He outsmarts them
in the last, where the king would need to embarrass himself to admit the truth.

Chilean variation:

The Wandering Soldier—Yolando Pino-Saavedra, *Folktales of Chile*. A princess says that she will
marry whoever hides so that she cannot find him and will kill those whom she can. She has
found everyone so far, until a drunken soldier is helped by a vixen who puts on iron gloves
and digs a tunnel so the soldier can stand right under the palace doorsill.

---

343. LOVE LIKE SALT

John Bierhorst, *Latin American Folktales*
Mexico

A king asks his three daughters how much they love him. The eldest two answer
more than gold and jewels, but the youngest daughter honestly answers that she loves
him as much as food loves salt. Furious, the king has her little finger cut off and turns
her out. The princess is taken in by a hermit, whom she helps by digging up roots and
hauling water. A prince falls in love with her as she is gathering flowers, and they gallop
away. His parents consent to the marriage. She invites her father to the wedding and
instructs the kitchen not to add any salt to his food. It tastes terrible. When she asks
her father if someone once angered him by saying how valuable salt was to her, her
father asks for her forgiveness.

CONNECTIONS

Anger. Definitions. Forgiveness. Love. Misunderstandings. Parents and children. Princes and
princesses. Punishments. Reconciliations. Salt. Words.

---

344. MARGARITA'S SLIP / LA CAMISA DE MARGARITA

Genevieve Barlow, *Stories from Latin America / Historias de Latinoamérica*
Peru

Luis Alcátar, newly arrived from Madrid in 1765, falls in love with Margarita Pareja,
daughter of Don Raimundo, the Collector General of the Port of Callao, at the procession of Santa Rosa, patron saint of Lima. Margarita has many well-off suitors, but she

also loves Don Luis, who is poor. When Don Raimundo refuses to let them marry because of this, Margarita falls ill. Doctors tell Don Raimundo that only marriage to her love will save her. He appeals to Don Luis's uncle, a miserly rich man who hasn't helped Don Luis so far, but is angry at the way Don Raimundo slighted his nephew. Don Luis's uncle agrees to their marriage only if Margarita receives no money from her father. She is to arrive with just the clothes she is wearing. That's how it happens that the bride's slip Margarita wears to her wedding is decorated with Belgian lace and a diamond collar.

Note: This is the story behind a Liman expression: "It's more expensive than Margarita Pareja's slip."

CONNECTIONS

Class conflict. Cleverness. Clothing. Illness. Jewels. Lace. Love. Marriage. Misers. Parents and children. Uncles and nephews.

---

345. THE LEGEND OF THE POINSETTA / LA FLOR DE LA NOCHE BUENA
Angel Vigil, *The Eagle on the Cactus*
Mexico

María, youngest in the Martínez family, is out of sorts, jealous that she is too young to be an angel and wear wings in the procession reenacting Mary and Joseph's search for lodging in Bethlehem on Christmas Eve. Even though her mother says that singing in the procession is a gift for the baby Jesus, María wants to bring something very special to show her love. She sulks for eight nights. On the last night, María has trouble making cut decorations and gets even more frustrated. She is missing as the children bring up their presents for the baby Jesus. Her brother says she went into a field on the way to Mass. And then María enters with a colorful red and green plant, which usually grows wild with just green leaves. The whole field is filled with these special plants in recognition of her special love.

CONNECTIONS

Festivals. Gifts. Jealousy. Jesus. Las Posadas. Love. Miracles. Origin tales. Parents and children. Plants. Poinsettas.

HOW ELSE THIS STORY IS TOLD

The Legend of the Poinsetta—Tomie dePaola

---

346. THE RAREST THING
Antonio Ramírez in John Bierhorst, *Latin American Folktales*
Guatemala

When all three of the king's sons want to marry his niece, the king tells them that the one who returns with something unique in three months will win her hand. They meet together before heading home. Through magic glasses he has found, the first son sees that the niece is lying in a coffin. The second son flies them swiftly back on his magic carpet. The third son uses the magic apple he found to bring her back to life. They begin to argue which one is most responsible for saving the niece. The king says they all helped equally. He sends them off to find extraordinary wives in the places where they traveled.

CONNECTIONS

Bargains. Brothers and sisters. Competition. Death. Emperors, kings & queens. Heroes and heroines. Journeys. Love. Magic. Magic apples. Magic carpets. Magic glasses. Princes and princesses. Restoring life. Rescues. Teamwork. Uncles and nieces.
See also The Five Brothers (424) for an adventurous rescue spin on this story.

347. THE HACIENDA OWNER'S DAUGHTER / HACIENDAYUQPA USUSIN

Miguel Waman in Johnny Payne, *She-Calf*
Quechua People. Peru

The daughter of a rich hacienda owner has been taught by her father to protect herself by testing potential suitors. Whenever a young man proposes marriage, she warns him that he must go everywhere she does and eat everything she eats. She brings her suitors to a cemetery at night, and, so far, five young men have run away. The caretaker's son, however, really likes her and does not run when they arrive at the cemetery. She opens the funerary niche in the wall with a small key and takes out roast lamb she has prepared, which he eats with gusto. The next morning, they marry. The wealthier suitors just never trusted that the food was lamb.

CONNECTIONS

Cemeteries. Humorous tales. Love. Tests. Trust.

348. THE KING AND THE RIDDLE / EL REY Y LA ADIVINANZA

Rueben Martínez, *Once Upon a Time: Traditional Latin American Tales / Había una vez: Cuneos tradicionales latinoAmericanos*
Chile

The shoemaker's three daughters take turns watering the basil in their garden. The two oldest girls run inside, flustered, when the king stops to ask them how many leaves are on the plant, but on the third day, clever Rosita asks him a riddle back. Now the king is flustered and rides off to think how many stars are in the sky. He returns disguised as a candy vendor, who says he will only sell candy for kisses. Only Rosita makes the trade and gives him a kiss for each piece. The king returns dressed as king and, as they start swapping riddles, he asks how many kisses she would give for candy. Rosita angrily realizes he has tricked her. Time passes, and when she later hears that the king is ill, Rosita disguises herself as a doctor, ready for revenge. She arrives at the palace riding a donkey. She tells the king that he will have to kiss the donkey's tail to be cured. He does. The next morning, the king does feel better. A few days later, he rides past the shoemaker's house and again asks Rosita about the number of leaves on the basil plant. She asks him about the stars; he asks her about the kisses for candy; and she asks him how many times he kissed the donkey's tail. Embarrassed, he huffs off to the palace, but then decides he would like to marry clever Rosita. He challenges that she has to come bathed and not bathed, combed and not combed, on horseback and not on horseback. She does, and they live together happily from then on.

Connections

Brothers and sisters. Cleverness. Disguises. Emperors, kings & queens. Humorous tales. Love. Problem solving. Revenge. Riddles. Tests. Tricksters.

How Else This Story Is Told

Brazilian variation:

The King's Promise—Elsie Spicer Eells, *The Brazilian Fairy Book*. This tale begins where the king commands that a poor fisherman's daughter come to the palace when it is neither day nor night, neither by foot nor upon horseback. When the delighted King tells her she may take whatever pleases her the most from the palace, she bundles him up to bring home.

Chilean variations:

The Basil Plant—Yolando Pino-Saavedra, *Folktales of Chile*
Clever Carmelita—Frances Carpenter, *South American Wonder Tales*

XIII

Supernatural Seducers

---

349. THE LEGEND OF THE YARA

Mercedes Dorson & Jeanne Wilmot, *Tales from the Rain Forest*
Amazonia, Brazil

Jaraguari, the great young hunter is respected by all, even the fish he spears in the Amazon River. Soon after he can wear the warrior's necklace of jaguar teeth, though, Jaraguari seems different, withdrawn. His mother worries that he has encountered the Yara, the Spirit of the Water, who haunts men with her beauty and song and then takes them down into the water. Each dusk, Jaraguari is drawn to travel back alone to Tarumâ Point. Jaraguari's mother and the chieftain want him to leave with them for another village, but Jaraguari tells his sobbing mother that he cannot go. He is last seen the next day standing in a canoe beside the Yara, her pink skin and green hair aglow.

CONNECTIONS

Appearance. Cautionary tales. Enchantment. Hunters. Iaras. Journeys to other realms. Lovers. Parents and children. Music. Secrets. Supernatural seduction. Spirits. Supernatural beings. Water worlds.

HOW ELSE THIS STORY IS TOLD

Brazilian variations:

Iara, the Mother of Water—Daniel Munduruku, *Amazonia*. Tupi People. The fisherman Jaraguari wanders into a lake, lured by the beautiful song Iara, half-fish, half person, sings. He manages to get away, but is never the same, and one day rides off with her by his side.

The Yara—Affonso Arinhos de Melo Franco. In Harriet De Onís, *The Golden Land*

Variation from Guyana:

The Water Woman and Her Lover—Ralph Prince. In Andrew Salkey, *Caribbean Folk Tales and Legends*. Big John is haunted by the naked woman often seen on the Essequibo River, fair-skinned with long, black hair and like a fish below the waist, singing softly to herself. He dreams of her and finds shells or her comb by his bed in the morning. She tells him she will make him rich on earth if he keeps the money she leaves secret, but he cannot keep the secret and disappears. Some say when you see the Water Woman now, a big man stands beside her.

350. A Gift from Yara, an Underwater Seducer
Juan Carlos Galeano, *Folktales of the Amazon*
Amazonia, Peru

A young logger, who has come from Lima to the Manú River, happens to be alone when a beautiful green-eyed girl with white skin walks by his hut and smiles. She disappears, but that night, music awakens him. He thinks perhaps she has returned when he hears something come out of the water and approach his door. Warnings he has heard about people from the water who steal men and women keep him in bed, clutching a dolphin-tooth charm. Towards dawn, he looks out and sees a *dorado* fish flopping in the dirt, but is afraid to touch it. His workers tell the man that it was the dolphin tooth which kept him safe. An indigenous man tells him the fish was a gift, and it will now be hard for him to fall in love with anyone else.

CONNECTIONS
Amulets. Cautionary tales. Fear. Iaras. Magic. Supernatural seduction. Supernatural beings.
Warnings. Water worlds. Woodcutters.

351. Yara: Fish-Woman from the Underwater World
Juan Carlos Galeano, *Folktales of the Amazon*
Amazon and Yavari Rivers near the border of Brazil and Colombia

When a woman returns from the *chakra* one day with fish, in addition to the fruits she usually brings back from the garden plot, she acts strange. She asks if her children are really hers and does not accompany her mother-in-law to the river to wash clothes. The woman says she already spends much time in the water. The mother-in-law alerts her son, who follows his wife when she leaves the house that night. He realizes his wife is not meeting another man, when he sees her fish tail as she slides into the water. This woman is a Yara, half-woman and half-snake, who killed his wife in the *chakra* to be his lover. Villagers hunt the Yara down.

CONNECTIONS
Deceit. Desire. Fathers-in-law and mothers-in-law. Husbands and wives. Iaras. Identity. Murder.
Supernatural beings. Transformations. Water worlds.

352. Mawaris: Aquatic Abductors
Juan Carlos Galeano, *Folktales of the Amazon*
Amazonia, Venezuela

A young man is paddling home from his girlfriend's house, when he sees her motioning him over to pick her up from the banks of the Negro River. He is surprised, of course, for he has just left her. They paddle, and then she jumps into the river. He follows her down to a city of Mawaris, enchanted people who can live in or out of the water. She is a tonina and wants him now to stay with her, so the young man becomes a dolphin. After a while, though, he misses his family and knows that they are looking for him. The Mawaris tell him he may only leave if any children he fathers resemble them. Back up on land, he marries his real girlfriend. Their children do look like Mawaris, blond with pink skin and soft bones. He loves these children, who only seem animated and talk when they are by the river, but their otherness bothers his wife. She leaves when he tells her about his journey into the river. The husband continues to care for the children on land before he moves with them to the Mawari's underwater city.

CONNECTIONS

Babies. Bargains. Deceit. Dolphins. Enchanted cities. Husbands and wives. Iaras. Identity. Journeys to other realms. Lovers. Mawaris. Outsiders. Parents and children. Rejection. Rivers. Supernatural seduction. Supernatural beings. Transformations. Water worlds.

HOW ELSE THIS STORY IS TOLD

Brazilian variation:
Mario and the Yara—Frances Carpenter, *South American Wonder Tales*

---

353. LEGENDS OF THE WARAUS. THE STORY OF KOROBONA
W.H. Brett, *Guyana Legends*
Warao People. Guyana

Though they have been forbidden by the Great Spirit Kanonatu to swim in the lake, one sister convinces another to go in. The elder sister, Korobona, grabs hold of a piece of wood in the water, without knowing it has been charmed. As she holds the wood, Wahma, a spirit at the bottom of the lake, rises. The wood transforms into a man, who takes her underwater. Korobona conceives and comes home to give birth. She convinces her brothers not to kill the baby then. However, her brothers pierce him with an arrow when they see Korobona hide him at the edge of the lake to go underwater with Wahma, who comes, sometimes as a serpent, sometimes as a man, sometimes as both. The child does not die, however, and Korobona cares for him in secret. When her brothers find the boy again, this time they shoot many arrows and cut him into pieces. Korobona curses the Warau people and covers her son with leaves and red flowers. She stays with him, and one day he appears as a warrior with red marks on his cheeks. He is the first of the Carib tribe, fierce enemy of the Waraus.

CONNECTIONS

Babies. Brothers and sisters. Carib people. Conflict. Curses. Disobedience. Heroes and heroines. Journeys to other realms. Lakes. Lovers. Mourning. Murder. Origin tales. Outsiders. Parents and children. Restoring life. Supernatural seduction. Spirits. Supernatural beings. Transformations. Tribes. Warnings. Water worlds.

How Else This Story Is Told

The Legend of Korobona—John Bierhorst, *The Red Swan*

Legend of Korobona—William Henry Brett, *Legends and Myths of the Aboriginal Indians of British Guiana*. In verse.

The Sky People—Douglas Gifford, *Warriors, Gods & Spirits from Central & South American Mythology*. This telling begins with the Warao people's descent to earth before moving into the murder of Korobona's child and the beginnings of the warrior Carib people.

354. Yakuruna: Male Lover from the Underwater World

Juan Carlos Galeano, *Folktales of the Amazon*
Amazonia, Ecuador

When a family's oldest daughter disappears while fetching water from the Napo River, the shaman transforms himself into a dolphin to find her. He reports that the girl is set to marry a Yakaruna, a handome underwater city man who faces backwards. The shaman smokes and chants for days to bring her back, and, at last, the daughter emerges from the water. Her parents are so happy to have her home, but their daughter has nothing but praise for the underwater world. She runs back to the river, where a wave sent by the Yakaruna carries her away from her father into the water. Her family yearns for her to return, but the shaman tells them she is already married and lives in a shell and coral house with servants who are half-women, half-fish with anacondas, turtles, and crabs as furnishings. Though her parents keep the other two daughters from the river, the girls secretly wish this will happen to them, too.

Connections

Cautionary tales. Enchanted cities. Journeys to other realms. Lovers. Mermaids and mermen. Mourning. Parents and children. Supernatural seduction. Shamans. Supernatural beings. Transformations. Water worlds. Yakurunas.

355. The Dolphin's Children

Juan Carlos Galeano, *Folktales of the Amazon*
Amazonia, Colombia

A man and woman own a little store on the banks of the Amazon, where they sell supplies to fishermen. Sometimes a certain pink dolphin frolics nearby the woman when her husband has gone to town for supplies. The wife dreams about dolphins and their underwater city. Once, when her husband goes to Atacuri for a few days, the dolphin comes very close to her by the river, and she hears squelching sounds in the hut at night. She begins to feel pains, and the healer tells her that she is carrying a dolphin's child. The woman is upset, for she loves her husband. Her husband is very angry and moves away. Her sister-in-law comes to help, and when she gives birth to two dolphins, the healer advises her to return them to the river so they will be well. She does, and that night she dreams that the dolphin thanks her for bringing his children.

CONNECTIONS

Anger. Babies. Dolphins. Dreams. Healers. Husbands and wives. Lovers. Parents and children. Rejection. Supernatural seduction. Supernatural beings. Water worlds.

356. MARÍA AND THE DOLPHINS
Juan Carlos Galeano, *Folktales of the Amazon*
Amazonia, Colombia

María watches the pink dolphins frolic as she washes clothes in the Amazon River every morning. They remind her of the light-skinned young man who sings love songs to her in her dreams. One morning she playfully asks one dolphin to bring her a *gamitana* fish. He returns with many, and she hears the music from her dreams. After that he waits her for each morning. Her father does not approve of the handsome young man who starts walking by their house at night. He notices that his footprints vanish near the water. Despite her parents' concerns and the shaman's warning about how dolphins lure young women to underwater palaces, María is no longer interested in any other young man.

CONNECTIONS

Cautionary tales. Dolphins. Parents and children. Supernatural seduction. Supernatural beings. Transformations. Water worlds.

357. THE GIRL AND THE ANACONDA
Juan Carlos Galeano, *Folktales of the Amazon*
Amazonia, Colombia and Peru

A lonely girl likes to spend time at the pond near her home. She falls in love with an anaconda there, who wraps himself around her waist in the water and gives her many fish to bring home. She tells her family, she has caught them herself, but her brother follows her one day and sees how she calls the anaconda with a gourd. He secretly does the same, and then he and his friends shoot the snake. Heartbroken when she finds the anaconda floating, dead, the girl tells her mother everything and also that she is pregnant. Her parents do not turn her out, like the neighbors think they ought to. They build wooden box cradles for the little anacondas she gives birth to. When the anaconda children are old enough, they go to live in the pond and leave fresh fish for their mother.

CONNECTIONS

Anacondas. Fish. Love. Lovers. Murder. Outsiders. Parents and children. Snakes. Supernatural beings. Supernatural seduction.

How Else This Story Is Told

African American variation from Venezuela:

The Swordfish—Harold Courlander, *A Treasury of Afro-American Folklore*. A girl sings to a fish who grows with his pond. Her brothers and father discover their friendship and kill the fish. The pond is dry when the girl gets there, and all her parents find is her hair sticking out of the ground.

---

358. The Snake's Lover

Jane Yolen, *Favorite Folktales from Around the World*
Quechua People. Peru

A daughter, who has been taking the cattle along up to graze on the mountain, is seduced by a young man into becoming his lover. A snake, he runs on many tiny little feet, but to her always appears as a tall, thin young man. When she becomes pregnant, he says they should go live with her parents. He will enter through a hole near the mortar in the storeroom and she will sleep nearby, telling her parents she is keeping watch for thieves. The daughter would have preferred not to keep him secret from her parents, who want to know who the father is. When she begins to suffer from birth pains but cannot give birth, her parents go to the Guesser, who tells them that the man is a snake and that there is a remedy in a neighboring town. Once she is away, the Guesser says they should chop off the snake's head and bury it. However, the daughter returns while the men are still trying to club the head which is jumping around. Little snakes come out of her, and the men go after those, too. Then they bury all the serpents. She tells her parents about how the snake man came to the pasture. They care for her, and when her spirit has healed, she marries a kind man.

Connections

Babies. Cautionary tales. Love. Lovers. Mourning. Murder. Parents and children. Supernatural seduction. Snakes. Supernatural beings. Transformations.

---

359. The Snake Sister

Douglas Gifford, *Warriors, Gods & Spirits from Central & South American Mythology*
Inca People. Peru

Soon after a strange snake stares fixedly at her, an unmarried woman becomes pregnant and gives birth to twins, one human daughter and one snake. The woman is relieved when she dreams that the snake child asks to live in the garden. Her human daughter never knows she has a snake sister. She marries a man from a distant village. When the man leaves to visit his family, a snake appears and warns the wife that her husband will bring a horse which she must not ride. Instead, she should travel on the donkey, which will be there. The snake also instructs her to bring certain items and to travel at the back. She does all this. The wife feels uneasy as they approach a farmhouse on their journey. Just as she realizes that the door leads to hell and turns her donkey back, her husband turns into the devil and rides after her. As he gets closer, she throws out the thread, and then the soap, comb, and wool, which the snake told her to bring. They create mist, rain, thorns, and forest which slow him down, but the devil still gets through. Just as the devil reaches for her donkey's tail, she throws the scissors at him, which open into a cross, and he stops. The donkey transforms into a snake, her sister, who warns her to marry someone she knows the next time before she slithers away.

CONNECTIONS

Animal helpers. Babies. Brothers and sisters. Cautionary tales. Devil. Dreams. Escapes. Heroes and heroines. Magic. Magic thread. Magic soap. Magic yarn. Parents and children. Seduction. Snakes. Supernatural beings. Supernatural husbands and wives. Twins. Warnings.

360. THE CONDOR SEEKS A WIFE
John Bierhorst, *Latin American Folktales*
Quechua People. Bolivia

A condor who has fallen in love with a shepherdess transforms into a young man, but she does not want to marry him. He suggests she come to see his mountaintop, and when she refuses that, too, he goes away. He pesters her the next day again, but she repeats that she is attached to her sheep and her mother. This time, however, the condor tricks her into climbing onto his back to scratch an itch and flies off with her to his mountain cave with the other condors. He is kind, but she is hungry and homesick. She grows feathers and lays eggs. Chicks hatch. A parrot tells her mother that he will rescue her daughter in exchange for corn and space to nest. When the young woman is alone, he carries her back. Her mother washes her and soothes her. The angry condor eats the parrot whole. The parrot passes right through his body intact, so he swallows him in pieces. Each piece emerges as a little parrot.

CONNECTIONS

Babies. Bargains. Bird helpers. Birds. Captivity. Cautionary tales. Condors. Deceit. Foxes. Herders. Origin tales. Parents and children. Parrots. Rescues. Revenge. Supernatural seduction. Supernatural beings. Transformations. Warlocks and witches.

HOW ELSE THIS STORY IS TOLD

The Witch-Fox and the Condor—Margaret Campbell, *South American Folklore Tales*. Aymará People. Bolivia. Lulu is first tricked and carried away by a witch-fox and then by a condor, who drops the fox, who has comes looking for his wife, on the rocks. She is rescued by her family when a leke-leke bird tells them where she is. Lulu vows never to listen to strangers again.

361. THE CREATURE OF THE NIGHT
Margaret Read MacDonald, *Five Minute Tales*
Brazil

Maria lives alone and longs for company. When she hears a man's low voice call her name in the distance, she waits expectantly. The calls come closer. Once his shadow arrives at her house, however, her dog sings out that she is not here. Annoyed, Maria kicks her dog and scolds him. The next day she ties the dog in the yard, but it cries through its muzzle for the dark stranger to go away. Maria is even angrier at the dog, but the dog sings out even after she kills it and burns its body. After Maria throws the dog's ashes into the sea, she waits for the man as the voice comes closer and closer, and this time when she opens the door....

CONNECTIONS

Anger. Dogs. Loneliness. Murder. Mysteries. Scary tales. Supernatural beings. Supernatural seduction. Supernatural voices.

HOW ELSE THIS STORY IS TOLD

Creature of the Night—Livia de Almeida and Ana Portella, *Brazilian Folktales*

---

362. BLANCA AND THE WILD MAN
Verónica Uribe and Carmer Diana Dearden in *Jade and Iron*
Venezuela

Blanca lags behind the other children, listening to sounds of the forest, when their grandmother takes them to the swimming hole. She is certain someone is following her and thinks about how girls warn about the Wild Man who enchants beautiful young women and carries them off into the jungle. Now she is afraid to go swimming again, but even from her porch she hears spooky sounds from the forest. She feels that someone is lifting her up to look down on the village. Her grandmother teases that perhaps Blanca has been bewitched by the Wild Man and laughs that he is just a story. But on the day after she turns fifteen, Blanca, with her yellow-green eyes and curly hair, disappears.

CONNECTIONS

Fear. Forests. Mysteries. Scary tales. Supernatural seduction. Supernatural beings. Warnings.

---

363. CELINA AND EL SOMBRERÓN, THE MAN WITH THE BIG HAT / CELINA Y EL SOMBRERÓN
Olga Loya, *Momentos Mágicos / Magic Moments*
Guatemala and Mexico

One rock and then another come through the window. Then Celina hears guitar music, and someone is singing to her, but her mother cannot see anyone outside. Celina would like to know who sings so hauntingly, but she can hear that the horses are nervous and stays inside. The next day they find the horses' manes tightly knotted. The mysterious singing goes on at night. Celina is thrilled and frightened by the love songs only she can hear. She stops eating and becomes ill. The priest tells her mother it is El Sombrerón and advises them to put a table and a new guitar under an orange tree. When a rock comes in her window, Celina walks outside and sees the little man with a big mustache and giant hat who has been singing to her. He tells her he would like to take her away. She says she will go with him if he will sing her the song they sing in heaven. He pulls his hat down and walks away.

CONNECTIONS

Bargains. Love. Sombrerón. Music. Parents and children. Supernatural seduction. Supernatural beings.

HOW ELSE THIS STORY IS TOLD

The Tears of Sombrero Grande—Luis Alfredo Arango. In *Jade and Iron*. When Celina stops sleeping, haunted by Sombrero Grande's love songs, her mother locks her in a church on the other side of town. There, Celina dies of sadness. That night Sombrero Grande sings of love once more and leads his mules away, weeping and leaving crystal tears behind.

364. THE BEAUTIFUL DEER

Daniel Munduruku, *Amazonia*
Manao People. Brazil

The young women flock to a handsome young man fishing in the Rio Negro, though he stays quiet. One touches him, and he says his name is Piripiri and runs into the river with three women. The woman who touched him and the other three women he leaves further downstream now exude a sweet fragrance. Piripiri has told them his mother does not want him to marry while he still drinks her milk, but all of the other women want to smell good, too. They search for months, and when one young woman sees Piripiri turn into a deer and nurse from the doe, they all run to that grotto. The doe becomes a hawk and carries Piripiri across the river. Still, the young women will not give up. They go to a wise man and then to his son Supi. Piripiri easily breaks their ropes, but at last they secure him with single hairs. Piripiri sings to the stars and ignores them. Supi warns them not to touch him while his mind is wandering. The young women fall into a deep sleep. When they wake Piripiri is gone, but a small plant with an enchanting scent has grown from him.

CONNECTIONS

Deer. Flirtation. Origin tales. Parents and children. Piripiroca. Plants. Scent. Seduction. Supernatural beings. Transformations.

XIV

Tricksters and Fools

Pedro de Urdemalas

365. PEDRO AND THE MONEY TREE / PEDRO Y EL ARBOL DE VINERO

Angel Vigil, *The Eagle on the Cactus*
Spanish Colonial People. Mexico

Unable to find work and desperate, Pedro de Ordimales washes his last few coins in the river and hangs them on the branches of a mesquite tree. He then pretends to be watering the tree. Two travelers see the shiny coins and want to buy the tree. Pedro refuses, even when they say he can name his own price. The tree is too special to sell. He keeps refusing their offers, until they say they will give him the coins off of this tree, if he sells them the tree itself. At last, Pedro agrees. He advises them to be patient as they wait for new coins to grow.

CONNECTIONS

Cleverness. Gullibility. Humorous tales. Illusions. Money. Pedro de Urdemalas. Reversals of fortune. Storytelling. Trees. Tricksters.

HOW ELSE THIS STORY IS TOLD

Kanjobal Maya variation from Guatemala:
Pedro Rimares and His Money Tree—Fernando Peñalosa, *Tales and Legends of the Q'Anjob'al Maya*

Mexican variations:
Pedro de Urdemalas—Riley Aiken. In J. Frank Dobie, *Puro Mexicano*. This medley includes six tricks Pedro plays.
Stories of the Bandit Pedro de Urdemales—Frances Toor, *A Treasury of Mexican Folkways*. Mexico. Pedro pulls three clever tricks in this group.

Variations from Chile, Guatemala, and Mexico:
The Money Tree—Maria Cristina Brusca and Tona Wilson, *Pedro Fools the Gringo*

366. THE MAGIC POT
Maria Cristina Brusca and Tona Wilson, *Pedro Fools the Gringo*
Chile, Argentina, Mexico, and Guatemala

Pedro buys a little clay cooking pot and some beans with his last coins and builds a fire by the road. He places the pot of beans with water over some coals in a hole, so it looks like the cooking pot is sitting on the ground and steaming away. Pedro is singing to his magic pot when two travelers ride up. They want to know how the beans can cook without fire, and Pedro tells them all he has to do is sing to this magic pot and it cooks all by itself. They offer money for the pot, and Pedro finally accepts a thousand gold coins and leaves. They never discover how the "magic" pot works, until they've finished eating the beans.

CONNECTIONS
Cleverness. Cooking. Gullibility. Horsemen. Humorous tales. Illusions. Mischief. Pedro de Urdemalas. Pots. Storytelling. Tricksters.

HOW ELSE THIS STORY IS TOLD
Chilean variation:
Pedro Urdemales Cheats Two Horsemen—Yolando Pino-Saavedra, *Folktales of Chile* and in Richard M. Dorson, *Folktales Told Around the World*. Three episodes of Pedro's clever tricks are included in this medley.

Mexican variations:
Pedro and the Magic Pot / Pedro y la olla mágica—Angel Vigil, *The Eagle on the Cactus*. Spanish Colonial People. Pedro tricks some threatening mule drivers into buying his pot and offers to show them how to trick the pot into accepting a new master.
Pedro de Urdemalas—Riley Aiken in J. Frank Dobie, *Puro Mexicano*. This medley includes six tricks Pedro plays.

367. THE GOLDEN PARTRIDGE
Maria Cristina Brusca and Tona Wilson, *Pedro Fools the Gringo*
Chile

Pedro needs to go to the bathroom, but there are none in sight. He squats right by the road. As two men ride up, Pedro covers the dung with his hat. They want to know why he is holding his hat to the ground. Pedro tells them he has caught a golden partridge. He asks if they will watch the hat and if he may borrow one of their horses to fetch his brother who will help him sell the golden bird. The men readily agree, thinking they will make off with the treasure themselves, until one reaches underneath to grab the partridge.

Connections

Birds. Brer Rabbit. Cleverness. Excrement. Gullibility. Horsemen. Humorous tales. Orphans. Pedro de Urdemalas. Rabbits. Storytelling. Thieves. Tricksters.

How Else This Story Is Told

Chilean variations:

Antonio and the Thief—Saul Schkolnick. In *Jade and Iron*. Three times a boy outwits the thief who keeps coming after him on his way to the other side of the mountain to fetch butter and flour for his mother. There is nothing at all under the hat here.

Pedro Urdemales Cheats Two Horsemen—Yolando Pino-Saavedra, *Folktales of Chile* and in Richard M. Dorson, *Folktales Told Around the World*. Three episodes of Pedro's clever tricks are included in this medley.

Mexican variations:

The Adventures of Peter—Romin Teratol. In Robert M. Laughlin, *Of Cabbages and Kings* and at Smithsonian Institution Library (Online). Tzotzil Maya. Zinacantán, Mexico. Six tricks played by the orphan Peter, with ethnographic texts in English and Tzotzil.

Stories of the Bandit Pedro de Urdemales—Frances Toor, *A Treasury of Mexican Folkways*. Mexico. Pedro pulls three clever tricks in this group.

Warao variations from Guyana and Venezuela:

Brer Rabbit—Johannes Wilbert, *Folk Literature of the Warao Indians*. The trickster here is a rabbit, who hides his dung under his hat.

---

368. Pedro Malasartes Herds Pigs

Livia de Almeida and Ana Portella, *Brazilian Folktales*
Brazil

Pedro goes to work for the pig farmer, after his brother complains that the farmer refuses to pay him. The farmer sends Pedro to watch the pigs, but he sells six pigs to a traveler, keeping their tails which he sticks in the swamp. Then Pedro tells the farmer that the pigs are stuck in the swamp mud. Their tails come right off when the farmer tries to pull them out, so he sends Pedro back to his house for two shovels to help dig the pigs out. Pedro tells the farmer's wife that the farmer sent him for two bags full of gold coins. She hollers out asking if the farmer wants her to give him both, and he yells back yes. And Pedro takes off with the gold.

Connections

Cleverness. Farmers. Gullibility. Humorous tales. Illusions. Justice. Mischief. Owners. Pedro de Urdemalas. Pigs. Rabbits. Storytelling. Tricksters.

How Else This Story Is Told

Maya variation:

Rabbit as Swineherd Tricks the Boss (The Rabbit As Swineherd)—Don Pedro Miguel Say. In Fernando Peñalosa, *Maya Culture—Traditional Storyteller's Tales* (Online). Rabbit is the trickster here.

Mexican variations:

The Adventures of Peter—Romin Teratol. In Robert M. Laughlin, *Of Cabbages and Kings* and at Smithsonian Institution Library (Online). Tzotzil Maya. Zinacantán, Mexico. Six tricks played by the orphan Peter, with ethnographic texts in English and Tzotzil.

Pedro and the Pig Tails—Angel Vigil, *The Eagle on the Cactus.* Spanish Colonial People

Pedro de Urdemalas—Riley Aiken. In J. Frank Dobie, *Puro Mexicano.* This medley includes six tricks Pedro plays.

Variation from Argentina, Chile, Mexico, and Guatemala:

Pig Tails in the Swamp—Maria Cristina Brusca and Tona Wilson, *Pedro Fools the Gringo.*

---

369. PEDRO URDIMALE, THE LITTLE FOX, AND THE MARE'S EGG

Yolando Pino-Saavedra, *Folktales of Chile*
Chile

When Pedro Urdimale sees a squash which looks just like an egg, he takes it from the farmer's field. A newly arrived horseman asks what he is carrying, and Pedro tells the man it is a mare's egg, just about to hatch into a racing horse. The naïve gringo presses Pedro to sell it to him. Finally Pedro sells the squash for thousands of pesos and advises the man not to let it fall. The squash does slip away from the horseman while he is riding, however. It smashes, startling a fox who streaks away. The horseman is sure that fox is his wonderful racing colt.

CONNECTIONS

Cleverness. Eggs. Foxes. Gringos. Gullibility. Horsemen. Humorous tales. Illusions. Pedro de Urdemalas. Squash. Storytelling. Tricksters.

HOW ELSE THIS STORY IS TOLD

The Mare's Egg—Josepha Sherman, *Trickster Tales*
Pedro Fools the Gringo—Maria Cristina Brusca and Tona Wilson, *Pedro Fools the Gringo*

---

370. PAINTED HORSES

Maria Cristina Brusca and Tona Wilson, *Pedro Fools the Gringo*
Mexico

A priest hires Pedro Urdemalas when he is young to clean out his horse stalls for only a little pay. Pedro buys paint and paints some brown, black and gray spots on the priest's white horses. He sells all the spotted horses and moves to another town. Two years later, he sees that the rain has washed all the spots off the horses. He steals the white horses, paints them again, and this time sells them to the priest. The priest buys his own horses back from Pedro, without recognizing him ... or them, until the spots don't stay.

CONNECTIONS

Cleverness. Gullibility. Horses. Humorous tales. Illusions. Mischief. Paint. Pedro de Urdemalas. Priests and priestesses. Storytelling. Tricksters.

HOW ELSE THIS STORY IS TOLD

Stories of the Bandit Pedro de Urdemales—Frances Toor, *A Treasury of Mexican Folkways*. This is one of three clever tricks Pedro pulls in this group.

---

371. THE MAGIC BURRO

Josepha Sherman, *Trickster Tales*
Mexico

Pedro de Urdermalas doesn't have anything to ride and is carving a burro out of a piece of wood, when a gringo rides up on a good horse. Pedro pretends he is going to mount his wooden burro and ride away, and the gringo laughs. Pedro tells the man not to insult this magic burro. The gringo wants to know how it is magic. Pedro tells him she turns real when you get on, and then she runs faster than the wind. Now the gringo wants to buy her. Pedro says the burro is too special to sell. The gringo proposes a trade for his horse. Pedro says that they had better trade clothes, too, and that the man should wait until he is out of sight, so his burro will not be upset by a stranger.

CONNECTIONS

Burros. Cleverness. Disguises. Gringos. Gullibility. Humorous tales. Pedro de Urdemalas. Reversals of fortune. Storytelling. Tricksters.

HOW ELSE THIS STORY IS TOLD

Pedro de Urdemalas and the Gringo (53b)—Ireneo Serrano Soto. In Américo Paredes, *Folktales of Mexico*

---

372. THE HELPER RABBIT

Maria Cristina Brusca and Tona Wilson, *Pedro Fools the Gringo*
Argentina

The wealthy Don José has threatened to kill Pedro Urdemalas for playing tricks on him, so Pedro and his wife Teresa prepare a new trick to stop him. When Don José jumps out at Pedro who is returning from town, Pedro pulls a little gray rabbit out from his jacket and instructs it to run home and tell Teresa to fix asado with sausages for company. The rabbit hops off. Don José is curious and heads home with Pedro to eat the food. Teresa has already cooked it, as she and Pedro planned. She pretends, though, that the gray rabbit tied to a stake outside is the one which told her to prepare. Amazed, Don José asks to have that messenger rabbit in exchange for Pedro's life. Pedro Urdemalas considers the offer and finally accepts Don José's gold for the rabbit. But the next day, Don José has an unpleasant surprise when he invites some important townspeople to his house and brags how he will send this magic gray rabbit with the message and food will be ready for them.

CONNECTIONS

Cleverness. Gullibility. Humorous tales. Husbands and wives. Illusions. Pedro de Urdemalas. Rabbits. Storytelling. Tricksters.

HOW ELSE THIS STORY IS TOLD

Brazilian variation:

Pedro Malasartes Sells Rabbits—Livia de Almeida and Ana Portella, *Brazilian Folktales.* Pedro sells two rabbits to a gentleman who didn't know that Pedro doesn't own them and that the rabbits run right back to their owner's garden. With the gentleman now out to get him, Pedro Malasartes secretly cuts the belly of a sheep and tucks its tripe inside his shirt. He tells the sheep's owner that someone is after him and pretends to cut open his own belly, letting the tripe fall on the floor. He tells her he will now be able to run away from him much faster without his entrails. When the gentleman reaches the woman, she tells him what Pedro did, and he really cuts his own belly open to catch up with Pedro.

---

373. BURRO GOLD

Maria Cristina Brusca and Tona Wilson, *Pedro Fools the Gringo*
Mexico and Guatemala

Once again, Pedro finds himself in Mexico needing money. He feeds his last gold coins to his burro. Something clinks as they walk. Pedro stops. Coins drop with the burro's manure. When a wealthy horseman comes up, Pedro is separating the coins out. He tells the gringo that his burro's stomach turns grass to gold several times a day. The horseman's offers to buy this burro, and Pedro refuses. The horseman keeps offering more, until, in the end, Pedro gets to ride off on the gringo's horse with many pesos, plus the man's mules.

CONNECTIONS

Burros. Cleverness. Excrement. Gringos. Humorous tales. Illusions. Pedro de Urdemalas. Reversals of fortune. Storytelling. Tricksters. Horsemen. Gullibility.

HOW ELSE THIS STORY IS TOLD

Pedro de Urdemalas and the Gringo (53a)—Guillermo Serrano Martínez. In Américo Paredes, *Folktales of Mexico*

---

374. "GOOD-BYE TO YOUR MACHETES..."

Maria Cristina Brusca and Tona Wilson, *Pedro Fools the Gringo*
Chile, Guatemala, and Mexico

The many people Pedro has tricked in Guatemala tie him up in a big sack and prepare to throw him off a ravine into the river. While they sleep, he frees himself and gathers up all of their weapons and tools and secures those inside the bag and hides. The men throw the heavy bag far off the cliff, calling good-bye to Pedro de Urdemalas. As it splashes down, however, they hear an echo from Pedro, bidding farewell to all their things.

CONNECTIONS

Captivity. Cleverness. Escapes. Humorous tales. Mischief. Mule drivers. Pedro de Urdemalas. Retaliation. Sheep. Storytelling. Tricksters.

HOW ELSE THIS STORY IS TOLD

Brazilian variation:

Pedro Malasartes in the Bag—Livia de Almeida and Ana Portella, *Brazilian Folktales.* When the king's soldiers nab Pedro and leave the bag he's in unattended, Pedro convinces a shepherd to take his place inside in order to marry the king's daughter. Villagers are amazed when Pedro appears with the shepherd's flock, which he says he found at the bottom of the ocean when he was thrown in.

Chilean variation:

Pedro Urdemales Cheats Two Horsemen—Yolando Pino-Saavedra, *Folktales of Chile* and in Richard M. Dorson, *Folktales Told Around the World.* Three episodes of Pedro's clever tricks are included in this medley.

Guatemalan variation:

Pedro Rimares and the Muleteers—Fernando Peñalosa, *Tales and Legends of the Q'Anjob'al Maya.* Maya People. Guatemala. The muleteers put Pedro in a sack because he cut off their mules' lips. After he escapes, they do not realize it's their food they've thrown in the river.

Mexican variations:

The Adventures of Peter—Romin Teratol. In Robert M. Laughlin, *Of Cabbages and Kings* and at Smithsonian Institution Library (Online). Tzotzil Maya. Zinacantán, Mexico. Six tricks played by the orphan Peter, with ethnographic texts in English and Tzotzil.
Pedro and the Mule Drivers—Angel Vigil, *The Eagle on the Cactus.* Spanish Colonial People
Pedro de Urdemalas—Riley Aiken. In J. Frank Dobie, *Puro Mexicano.* This medley includes six tricks Pedro plays. At the end he shows up with sheep he claims to have obtained from people in the river.

---

375. PEDRO URDEMALES AND THE GIANT / PEDRO URDEMALES Y EL GIGANTE

Rueben Martínez, *Once Upon a Time / Había una vez*
Chile

Pedro Urdemalas answers with total aplomb when he wakes to find a giant challenging him in a mountain cave. He agrees to stay and compete for a 1000 peso prize. For the rock-throwing contest, Pedro tosses a small bird into the air, which flies out of sight. When it comes to punching the deepest hole in a rock, Pedro pre-chisels his so his arm goes in to his shoulder. To carry the most firewood, Pedro wraps a rope around the trees and pretends that he's going to carry the forest. He never actually has to do that or the spear throwing, for the giant stops him when Pedro says he is aiming his spear across the ocean to Spain where it will pierce the giant's mother. Pedro wins and continues to make mischief in the world.

Connections

Cleverness. Competition. Giants. Humorous tales. Pedro de Urdemalas. Storytelling. Supernatural beings. Tricksters.

How Else This Story Is Told

Mexican variations:

The Adventures of Peter—Romin Teratol. In Robert M. Laughlin, *Of Cabbages and Kings* and at Smithsonian Institution Library (Online). Tzotzil Maya. Zinacantán, Mexico. Six tricks played by the orphan Peter, with ethnographic texts in English and Tzotzil.

Pedro and the Giant—Angel Vigil, *The Eagle on the Cactus*. Spanish Colonial People. Pedro first unnerves the giant by telling him he is yelling for someone he threw up in the sky three days ago to stop bothering him. When the giant wants to do hand-to-hand combat, Pedro tricks him by pre-setting a scene of total destruction and saying he just vanquished that man who returned from the air.

Pedro de Urdemalas—Riley Aiken in J. Frank Dobie, *Puro Mexicano*. This medley includes five other tricks, too, which Pedro plays.

---

376. Pedro and the Hanging Tree

Angel Vigil, *The Eagle on the Cactus*
Spanish Colonial People. Mexico

Down on his luck, again, Pedro de Ordimalas goes to the king, who gives him a job in the royal kitchen. But Pedro makes a mistake of playing a trick on the king at a royal banquet. Angry and humiliated, the king commands that Pedro hang in the morning. However, beginning to regret his sentence, the king allows Pedro to choose his own hanging tree. Pedro picks a large sunflower, which bends over and sets his feet right back on the ground.

Connections

Cleverness. Emperors, kings & queens. Humorous tales. Pedro de Urdemalas. Punishments. Retaliation. Reversals of fortune. Tricksters.

---

377. Clever Little Pedro

Maria Cristina Brusca and Tona Wilson, *Pedro Fools the Gringo*
Mexico

When a priest asks where the road goes, Pedro Urdemales tells him that it always stays in the same place. The priest offers young Pedro work as his servant plus an education. Pedro gives many word play answers, which amuse and exasperate the priest. One day Pedro eats the priest's hidden cheese and tells the priest he used his library to do it. What he actually did was pile up books to reach the cheese. When he sneaks a drumstick on the way to serving dinner, and the priest complains that the chicken only has one leg, Pedro shows him how all the chickens in the henhouse sleep standing on one leg. He tells the priest he should have called to that chicken, and it would have put its other foot on the ground.

CONNECTIONS
Cleverness. Humorous tales. Illusions. Mischief. Pedro de Urdemalas. Priests and priestesses. Storytelling. Tricksters. Words.

HOW ELSE THIS STORY IS TOLD
Pedro de Urdemalas and the Priest— Manuel Guevara. In Américo Paredes, *Folktales of Mexico.*

378. PEDRO RIMALES, THE HEALER
Rafael Rivero Oramas in *Jade and Iron*
Venezuela

Pedro Rimales arrives in another country with no money and pretends to be a healer. When no one comes to him for help, he thinks he might be able to make some money if he can cure someone better than the king can, for the king considers himself an expert healer. Pedro finds a man who is holding his breath and pretending to be dead to get out of work. He knows the man is just pretending because he can see his shirt rise and fall. Pedro suggests they call in the king to bring this man back from the dead. None of the king's medicines rouse the man. Now Pedro says he will try. He mixes up leaves with water in a gourd and blows in smoke and feeds this to the man, while secretly pushing his lit cigar against the man's backside. The man jumps up, yelping. Pedro Rimales is named king for his wonderful healing. He rules until he gets bored and is ready to move on.

CONNECTIONS
Competition. Emperors, kings & queens. Healers. Humorous tales. Pedro de Urdemalas. Reversals of fortune. Storytelling. Tricksters.

379. PEDRO THE TRICKSTER
Neil Philip, *Horse Hooves and Chicken Feet*
Mexico

One tale in this medley about Pedro Ordimalas describes what happens to Pedro at the end of his mischievous life. Always short of money, Pedro borrows fifty centavos from his friends. They don't want to lend it to him if he is going to hand it to beggars. He says he will not, but does. The beggars turn out to be the Lord and Saint Peter, who offer Pedro a reward. He asks for fifty centavos, so he can show his friends he has their money, and then he asks for a deck of cards that always wins, a drum that will not stop beating, and the promises that he will not have to leave someplace if he does not want to and that his family will be accepted into heaven. He also requests that Lord take his body and soul. Pedro always wins at cards now. When the Death who rides a horse says she was sent to bring him, Pedro tricks her into beating the drum that never stops, until she gives him extra years and goes. He also wrangles extra years from the Death with a scythe. It takes the Death who drives a cart to carry him off. The Lord sends Pedro to limbo and then Purgatory, and Hell, and he misbehaves in all three. Pedro drives the devils' sheep to a beautiful mansion, which Saint Peter is guarding. He asks for a look inside, but then won't leave the doorway. Pedro says the Lord promised he would not have to leave any place he does not want to. The Lord will not let him enter heaven, but agrees that Pedro can stay as a stone at the entrance to watch everything going on.

CONNECTIONS

Charity. Cleverness. Death. God. Gods and humans. Humorous tales. Life span. Mischief. Pedro de Urdemalas. Peter, Saint. Promises. Punishments. Rewards. Storytelling. Tricksters. Transformations. Wishes.

HOW ELSE THIS STORY IS TOLD

Chilean variation:
Pedro Urdimale Gets into Heaven—Yolando Pino-Saavedra, *Folktales of Chile*. Pedro asks to peek inside of heaven, and when Saint Peter opens the gates a crack, Pedro convinces the saint to open them a bit more. That is just wide enough for Pedro to squeeze in enough to push the door open, at which point Saint Peter slams the gates and cuts Pedro in half. Pedro tells Saint Peter and then God it's the sinful part of him that got left outside. God pulls the bottom half of Pedro in then and Pedro gets to stay in heaven all put together.

Mexican variation:
Pedro Goes to Heaven—Maria Cristina Brusca and Tona Wilson, *Pedro Fools the Gringo*

More People Tricksters

380. THE LITTLE, LITTLE FELLOW WITH THE BIG, BIG HAT
M.A. Jagendorf and R.S. Boggs, *The King of the Mountains*
Maya People. Guatemala

Exasperated with the trouble one of his twins is always getting into, a hatmaker goes to the *brujo* for advice. The brujo prays and tells the father that God has instructed him to make a giant sombrero, which the brujo will weave magic into. When this is done, the father brings home the giant, heavy sombrero and puts it in the middle of the floor of his house. That night he discovers the hat moving. His son has gone there to hide after some mischief and is stuck underneath. The hat really won't come off the boy, even when his father tugs. People call the boy El Sombrerón, The Big Hat. He stays short because of the weight of the hat, but that does not stop him from making trouble. El Sombrerón learns to make himself invisible and frighten people and ride horses to exhaustion at night. He brings presents to a girl he likes, but her mother is not happy with El Sombrerón and decides that the only way to get rid of him is to secretly move away. However, her daughter lets El Sombrerón know where they are going. So, when he shows up, laughing, with the mother's missing cooking pot, she lets El Sombrerón marry her daughter.

CONNECTIONS

Courtship. Disobedience. Hatmakers. Hats. Humorous tales. Magic hats. Mischief. Parents and children. Punishments. Sombrerón. Tricksters. Warlocks and witches.

---

381. THE PRICE OF HEAVEN AND THE RAIN OF CARAMELS

John Bierhorst, *Latin American Folktales*
Mexico

A man from the city who goes to wakes, instead of working, overhears a country husband ask how much it will cost for his wife to be able to get to heaven. Relatives suggest different amounts, and the husband places one thousand pesos in the coffin. After the burial, the man from the city digs up the coffin and stands it up against their door. The dead woman's body falls on the son. The family decides that they must not have put enough pesos into the coffin. They add more and rebury her. The man from the city takes some of the money and brings the body back to the house again. The husband gives the man from the city money to add to the coffin and see to the burial. The man keeps the coffin money and buries the body for good. Later in life, the man from the city gets married. He tells his wife that he overheard some mule drivers say they would bury money in the woods. His wife pretends not to believe him, but goes and digs up the money herself and hides it in the house. She tells the man his mind is slipping and sends him to school, after instructing him to tie the dog up with sausage links. She spreads candies all over the patio and later lets him think that it has rained candy. When the mule drivers come to the village to find out who took their money, they ask the old man questions and he tells them the truth. It all sounds so absurd with the dog tie of sausages and a candy rain, that the mule drivers think the man and his wife are both nuts and go away.

CONNECTIONS

Burials. Deceit. Gullibility. Humorous tales. Husbands and wives. Storytelling. Theft. Treasure. Tricksters. Truth.

---

382. THE MISER'S JAR

John Bierhorst, *The Monkey's Haircut and Other Stories Told by the Maya*
Kekchi Maya People

An old miser has set a high price on a beautiful jar which many want to buy. His daughter tells him three people—a gentleman, a man, and a priest—have come by separately to see the jar. Her father instructs her to pretend to each one that she will secretly sell him the jar without letting her father know and to give each one a different time to arrive. As each man arrives, she sends the one already there up to the loft to hide from her father. The father arrives and sets fire to his sack of dried chilis. Smoke inhalation kills all three men. The girl summons the fool who is in love with her and tells him that a priest choked to death while dining with them. The love-sick fool says he will dispose of the body, if she promises to marry him. She agrees and sneakily dresses the gentleman as a priest. The fool buries that body and then another and another, when she accuses him each time of not having done the job. As the girl and her father flee, the miser falls into a pool. The daughter jumps in to save him, but the weight of his special jar full of money and her grindstone pulls them both under. The fool follows their tracks to the pool. Crying over losing his love, he becomes a bird.

Connections

Accusations. Deceit. Fools. Humorous tales. Misers. Murder. Parents and children. Pedro de Urdemalas. Priests and priestesses. Tricksters.

Where Else This Story Appears

In *Latin American Folktales*.

How Else This Story Is Told

Chilean variation:

Pedro Urdimale and the Dead Priests—Yolando Pino-Saavedra, *Folktales of Chile*. A girl tells Pedro Urdimale she will marry him if he disposes of the priest she has killed, but it is actually three dead priests. She accuses him three times for not doing the job. Finally, Pedro gets frightened by an encounter with a living priest and decides to forget about this girl.

---

383. The Art of Lying
Angel Vigil, *The Eagle on the Cactus*
Mexico

One smart *compadre* is trying to teach his not-so-smart friend how to lie. Working as a team, the slower *compadre* will corroborate what the smarter *compadre* is saying. If a story is getting too unbelievable, he will pull the storyteller's shirttail. In the first town, the smart *compadre* is telling a group that they have come from a place where rattlesnakes are a mile long. His *compadre* pulls his shirttail. The storyteller keeps amending the snake's size down to smaller and smaller lengths, until it doesn't seem much of a story. Afterwards, the smart *compadre* tells his partner that listeners get mad when the story loses its wonder, even if it isn't the truth. In the next town, when the smart *compadre* says he has seen a baby with seven heads, the slower *compadre* backs him up by saying he saw the little shirt with seven collars. People enjoy that story so much, they want to hear more. From then on, the two *compadres* earn their living telling tall tales together.

CONNECTIONS

Comadres and compadres. Deceit. Emperors, kings & queens. Friendship. Humorous tales. Storytelling. Tall tales. Teachers. Teamwork. Tricksters. Truth.

HOW ELSE THIS STORY IS TOLD

Chilean variation:

The Chilean Swindlers—Yolando Pino-Saavedra, *Folktales of Chile*. From walls of cheese to babies with nine arms to a large cabbage plant in the middle of Africa that can fit armies inside, two educated friends work as a team and are well-rewarded, telling and verifying outlandish stories of things they have seen to Latin American and European kings.

Mexican variation:

Keeping the Shirt-Tail In—Riley Aiken. In J. Frank Dobie, *Puro Mexicano*

---

384. THE MAGIC CAP

Angel Vigil, *The Eagle on the Cactus*
Mexico

Instead of helping out his poor *compadre*, a rich *compadre* tells the man that he should have worked harder and suggests the man sell his old cap for money. The poor *compadre's* fortune improves a little, and he decides to play a trick on the rich *compadre*. He buys a fancy new hat and a suit to wear and then prepays for a cheap watch, imitation pearls, and a restaurant meal which he will pick up later. The poor *compadre* arranges with those merchants that he will say, "Charge it to the cap" when he returns with the rich *compadre*. The rich *compadre* is amazed that the poor *compadre* can purchase these things without money. He offers to buy the special cap. The poor *compadre* tells him it has no magic, but finally accepts $10,000. The rich *compadre* gets his comeuppance when he blithely says "Charge it to the cap," and the merchants expect him to pay.

CONNECTIONS

Comadres and compadres. Deceit. Hats. Humorous tales. Retaliation. Storytelling. Tricksters. Unkindness.

HOW ELSE THIS STORY IS TOLD

Charge This to the Cap—Riley Aiken in J. Frank Dobie, *Puro Mexicano*

Animal Tricksters

385. THE WAX DOLL, THE COYOTE, AND RABBIT

Dan Storm, *Pictures Tales from Mexico*
Mexico

Little Conejo the rabbit raids a certain garden every day, and the owner has had it. That night when Rabbit arrives, a little man is standing in the middle of a row. Rabbit does not know that the little man is a doll the farmer has made of wax and pitch to catch him. He keeps asking to pass by. When the little man continues to ignore Rabbit, Conejo slaps him. First his hands and then his feet get totally stuck. In the morning, the farmer ties Rabbit in a tree and sets a kettle of water to boil. Rabbit gets Señor Coyote to take his place by saying the farmer is going to force him to stay with chickens. Señor Coyote manages to escape before getting stewed, but he is certainly looking for a way to get even with Rabbit after that.

CONNECTIONS

Anansi. Captivity. Cleverness. Conflict. Coyotes. Dolls. Emperors, kings & queens. Escapes. Farmers. Foxes. Guinea pigs. Humans. Humorous tales. Mice. Monkeys. Prophecies. Punishments. Rabbits. Spiders. Storytelling. Theft. Traps. Tricksters.

HOW ELSE THIS STORY IS TOLD

Brazilian variations:

The Monkey and the Wax Doll—Enid D'Oyley, *Animal Fables and Other Tales Retold: African Tales in the New World*. African American People

The Old Lady and the Monkey—Livia de Almeida and Ana Portella, *Brazilian Folktales*. As the old lady is stewing the monkey she caught stuck to the wax doll, a singing voice warns her at each step of the way to cook him gently, to eat him gently, to digest him gently, or to let him go. She ignores the warnings, but after eating her stomach keeps swelling. Finally, she tells the monkey to go, and dozens of monkeys explode out.

Chilean variation:

The Tarbaby—Yolando Pino-Saavedra, *Folktales of Chile*. It's two men stealing figs who get stuck to the sticky figurine here.

Mam-Kekchi Maya variation from Guatemala:

Rabbit and Coyote—John Bierhorst, *The Monkey's Haircut and Other Stories Told by the Maya*. After coyote gets free and goes looking for rabbit, rabbit tricks coyote again by throwing a green sasparilla ball into his mouth which breaks coyote's teeth. Then he gets coyote to try to get cheese from the well.

Mexican variations:

The Fox and the Coyote / El zorro y el coyote—Angel Vigil, *The Eagle on the Cactus*. Coyote thinks Fox is dancing with the little man, and Fox tells Coyote if he takes his place, he'll go get chickens for both of them.

The Rabbit and the Coyote—Américo Paredes, *Folktales of Mexico*. This is the first episode in a medley of six stories where Rabbit tricks Coyote, and Coyote is never able to get even.

Sister Fox and Brother Coyote—Riley Aiken in J. Frank Dobie, *Puro Mexicano*. 'Mana Zorro tricks coyote five different times.

The Tale of Rabbit and Coyote—Tony Johnston. Juchitán, Mexico. Rabbit tricks Coyote here in six different ways, including this one.

Peruvian variations:

Guinea Pig and Fox—Josepha Sherman, *TricksterTales.* The first of three tricks Guinea Pig plays on gullible Fox is to tell him that he is stuck to the farmer's tar statue because he is waiting for the magic tar to make him taller so he can marry the farmer's daughter.

Love and Roast Chicken—Barbara Knutson. Andes Mountains, Peru and Bolivia. The last of three tricks which Cuy the Guinea Pig plays on Tío Antonio the Fox is this one, where the Cuy gets stuck to the farmer's clay figurine covered in eucalyptus tree sap and complains to Tío Antonio that he, a vegetarian, is being held captive to be made to eat chicken.

The Mouse and the Fox—Richard M. Dorson, *Folktales Told Around the World.* Quechua People. In the first of four tricks, a captured mouse tricks a fox into taking his place, saying that the owner is holding him to marry his daughter and he's afraid of getting stepped on.

Zorro and Quwi—Rebecca Hickox. In the first of four tricks, Quwi the guinea pig pretends that he is being held captive to marry the garden owner's daughter. He tells Fox he is afraid the daughter is too big and will step on him and kill him. Naïve Zorro is thrilled to take his place. (Quwi was not caught by a sticky sticky figurine, but the structure of the story is the same.)

African American variations from Suriname:

Tar Baby: Monkey as Thief—Melville J. Herskovits and Frances Herskovits, *Suriname Folk-Lore.* Anansi is beaten to death when he is found stuck to the corncob doll.

Tar Baby: God Above 1—Melville J. Herskovits and Frances Herskovits, *Suriname Folk-Lore.* Anansi the spider gets stuck to a large tar doll the King has put in his yard to catch the culprit who has been stealing palace food. The King plans to kill him, and Anansi asks his children what they will do to help him. The youngest says he will hide in a tall tree at the execution site and sing about how the whole country will flood and everyone will die, if they kill Anansi. The King hears this song and believes (with a nudge from Anansi) that the voice is a prophecy from God. Anansi goes free.

---

386. Rabbit and Puma

John Bierhorst, *The Monkey's Haircut*
Yucatec-Tzutuhil Maya People. Mexico

Puma spies Rabbit under an overhanging rock and is absolutely sure he has him this time. Rabbit immediately puts his front paws up to push against the rock. He says Puma can't eat him because he is holding up the roof that will keep the sky from falling. Rabbit asks Puma to hold it, so he can go find some sticks to help them. He tells Puma to ring the bell if he gets tired. Puma holds, and Rabbit hops off. Puma pushes and pushes until he can press no more. He pulls the bell, which turns out to be a stinging wasps' nest. Puma goes after—and gets outsmarted by—Rabbit two more times in this medley.

Connections

Cleverness. Conflict. Coyotes. Foxes. Guinea pigs. Humorous tales. Juan Tul (Trickster). Mice. Monkeys. Opossums. Pumas. Rabbits. Sheep. Squirrels. Tricksters.

HOW ELSE THIS STORY IS TOLD

Bolivian variation:

The Fox and the Monkey—Moisés Alvarez. In John Bierhorst, *Latin American Folktales*. Aymara People. The monkey tricks the fox four times.

Chilean variation:

Antonio and the Thief—Saul Schkolnick. In *Jade and Iron*. Three times a boy outwits the thief who keeps coming after him on his way to the other side of the mountain to fetch butter and flour for his mother.

Maya variation:

Juan Tul—John Bierhorst, *The Red Swan*. Maya People. Juan Tul's first trick on Squirrel Woman begins when he pretends to hold up the cave roof. He then sets fire to her grassy bundle, causes a vine to shrink and swing her up into a tree, disguises himself with leaves, and gets her drunk so she can no longer pursue him.

Mexican variations:

Borreguita and the Coyote—Verna Aardema. Ayutla, Mexico. A lamb tricks a coyote three different ways.

The Coyote and the Fox—Frances Toor, *A Treasury of Mexican Folkways*. Yaqui People. The fox is the trickster in this medley of four fox and coyote tales.

The Coyote and the Tlacuache—Frances Toor, *A Treasury of Mexican Folkways*. Coyote, usually the victim in most of the tales, tricks opossum twice here. The second time the coyote throws a hard cherimoya with prickles that gets stuck in the tlacuache's throat.

The Fox and the Coyote / El zorro y el coyote—Angel Vigil, *The Eagle on the Cactus*. Here is the second of five tricks Fox plays on Coyote.

It's About to Fall!—Martha Hamilton and Mitch Weiss, *Through the Grapevine*. The fox tricks the coyote here.

The Rabbit and the Coyote—Américo Paredes, *Folktales of Mexico*. The rabbit tricks the coyote six times.

Señor Coyote and Señor Fox—Lila Green, *Folktales of Spain and Latin America*. The fox tricks the coyote here.

Señor Coyote and Señor Fox—Dan Storm, *Picture Tales from Mexico*. The fox tricks the coyote here.

Sister Fox and Brother Coyote—Riley Aiken. In J. Frank Dobie, *Puro Mexicano*. 'Mana Zorro tricks coyote five different times.

The Tale of Rabbit and Coyote—Tony Johnston. Juchitán, Mexico. Rabbit tricks Coyote here in six different ways, including this one.

The Tlacuache and the Coyote / El tlacuache y el coyote—Rueben Martínez, *Once Upon a Time / Había una vez*. The opossum tricks the coyote in two different episodes.

Peruvian variations:

The Fox and the Cuy / El zorro y el cuy—Paula Martin, *Pachamama Tales*. The guinea pig tricks the fox.

Guinea Pig and Fox—Josepha Sherman, *TricksterTales*. Guinea Pig tricks gullible Fox three times.

Love and Roast Chicken—Barbara Knutson. Andes Mountains, Peru and Bolivia. The three tricks which Cuy the Guinea Pig plays on Tío Antonio the Fox begin with this one.

The Mouse and the Fox—Richard M. Dorson, *Folktales Told Around the World*. Quechua People. A little mouse tricks a fox four times.

Zorro and Quwi—Hickox, Rebecca. Though the fox tries to catch the guinea pig every night, the guinea pig outfoxes him four times.

---

387. *Borreguita and the Coyote*
Verna Aardema
Ayutla, Mexico

A little lamb outfoxes a gullible coyote three times. In the middle vignette, Borreguita convinces the coyote that cheese will taste much better than she does. She tells the coyote to meet her at the pond at night. There is a glowing cheese in the water, which she urges him to swim out and take. But, as hard as the coyote swims, the cheese, which is the moon's reflection, stays just out of reach.

Connections
Cheese. Cleverness. Conflict. Coyotes. Devil. Foxes. Humorous tales. Illusions. Monkeys. Opossums. Origin tales. Rabbits. Raccoons. Sheep. Tricksters.

How Else This Story Is Told
Bolivian variation:
The Fox and the Monkey—Moisés Alvarez. In John Bierhorst, *Latin American Folktales*. Aymara People. In the last of four tricks, the monkey gives the fox a taste of some stolen cheese and makes the fox promise that he won't ever hurt him if the monkey shows him where he can get more. More is down at the river, where the impulsive fox leaps in after the reflection of a half-moon and drowns.

Kanjobal Maya variation from Guatemala:
The Rabbit and the Coyote—Fernando Peñalosa, *Tales and Legends of the Q'Anjob'al Maya* and as Rabbit Tricks Coyote Twice (The Rabbit and the Coyote)—Don Pedro Miguel Say. Also in Fernando Peñalosa, *Maya Culture—Traditional Storyteller's Tales* (Online). Rabbit tricks the coyote here.

Mexican variations:
Brother Rabbit, Señor Coyote, and the Cheese—Dan Storm, *Pictures Tales from Mexico*. Rabbit tricks the coyote here.

The Fox and the Coyote / El zorro y el coyote—Angel Vigil, *The Eagle on the Cactus*. In one from a medley of five tricks, Fox tells Coyote to stay and get the cheese in the pond, when it floats closer to him, while Fox goes to get chicken for Coyote (so he says).

The Coyote and the Fox—Frances Toor, *A Treasury of Mexican Folkways*. Yaqui People. The fox is the trickster in this medley of four fox and coyote tales.

'Mano Coyote—Camilla Campbell, *Star Mountain and Other Legends of Mexico*. A dog of the Devil gets tricked by a raccoon at the end of a series of stories where the Devil's dogs refuse to get along with humans.

Mother Fox and Mr. Coyote / Mamá Zorra y Don Coyote—Victor Villaseñor. When her babies get trapped between the coyote and the water, a mother red fox convinces the hungry coyote that the freshly made cheese in the pond would taste much better.

The Rabbit and the Coyote—Américo Paredes, *Folktales of Mexico.* This is the first episode in a medley of six stories where Rabbit tricks Coyote, and Coyote tries unsuccessfully to get even.

Sister Fox and Brother Coyote—Riley Aiken. In J. Frank Dobie, *Puro Mexicano.* 'Mana Zorro tricks coyote five different times.

The Tale of Rabbit and Coyote—Tony Johnston. Juchitán, Mexico. Rabbit tricks Coyote here in six different ways, including this one. After Coyote is so bloated with water, Rabbit convinces him to climb to the moon and pulls the ladder away, which is why Coyote howls.

The Tlacuache and the Coyote / El tlacuache y el coyote—Rueben Martínez, *Once Upon a Time/ Había una vez.* Some say after being tricked by the tlacuache, the coyote jumped to the moon, where he still howls.

---

388. *LOVE AND ROAST CHICKEN*
Barbara Knutson
Peru and Bolivia

   In his second trick, Cuy the Guinea Pig sees Tío Antonio the Fox coming after him and starts energetically digging a hole into the side of the hill. He tells Tío Antonio he will need this den to be safe from the rain of fire which is on its way and will destroy the world. Tío Antonio does not want to be tricked by the guinea pig again, but he isn't sure about this rain of fire. Not taking a chance, Tío Antonio wriggles into the den and pushes Cuy out. Cuy blocks the entrance with rocks to keep sparks from getting in and asks the fox to remember his good deed. All through the night, Tío Antonio worries about all that will be gone when the world ends. He decides to peek out, sees flames, and tucks back in again. In the morning, there are no flames, and the whole world looks the same, except for the little circle right in front where Cuy built a campfire.

CONNECTIONS
Coyotes. Conflict. Fire. Foxes. Guinea pigs. Humorous tales. Mice. Rabbits. Storytelling. Tricksters.

HOW ELSE THIS STORY IS TOLD
Mexican variations:
The Coyote and the Fox—Frances Toor, *A Treasury of Mexican Folkways.* Yaqui People. The fox is the trickster in this medley of four fox and coyote tales.

The Fox and the Coyote / El zorro y el coyote—Angel Vigil, *The Eagle on the Cactus.* In one from a fox-coyote medley, the fox tells the coyote that they can jump out and surprise the king's servants who are going to come by carrying food. He tells Coyote to wait in the tall grass on the other side and sets it on fire.

Rabbit and Puma—John Bierhorst, *The Monkey's Haircut.* Yucatec-Tzutuhil Maya People. In the last of four tricks Rabbit play on Puma, Rabbit gets Puma to help him carry hay to the village so they can sell it and split the profit. Instead, however, Rabbit sets fire to the hay and runs and gets rid of Puma for good.

The Rabbit and the Coyote—Américo Paredes, *Folktales of Mexico.* As one of the episodes in a medley where Rabbit tricks Coyote over and over, Rabbit sets fire to the cane all around a clearing, after telling Coyote to shut his eyes and shout and dance at a wedding party where there will be food and fireworks.

Sister Fox and Brother Coyote—Riley Aiken. In J. Frank Dobie, *Puro Mexicano*. 'Mana Zorro tricks coyote five different times.

Peruvian variations:
Guinea Pig and Fox—Josepha Sherman, *TricksterTales*. Guinea Pig tricks gullible Fox three times.
The Mouse and the Fox—Richard M. Dorson, *Folktales Told Around the World*. Quechua People. In the third of four tricks which mouse plays on fox, he tells fox he's digging a hole for him to be safe from a rain of fire.
Zorro and Quwi—Rebecca Hickox. Though the fox tries to catch the guinea pig every night, the guinea pig outfoxes him four times.

---

389. THE KING OF THE LEAVES
M.A. Jagendorf and R.S. Boggs, *The King of the Mountains*
Nicaragua

The king has had enough of the rabbit Tío Conejo's tricks and wants him gone from the land. When Tío Conejo overhears that there is a plan to catch him at the water hole, knowing he will get thirsty sooner or later, he comes up with a mischievous plan of his own. When the shoemaker goes inside to get him a drink of water, he steals a pair of shoes from outside. Tío Conejo leaves one shoe in the road in one place and a second further on. Then he steals the gourd of honey a man has set down in order to go back and retrieve the first shoe. Tío Conejo pours honey over himself and rolls on the ground until dead leaves stick all over him. He frightens people when he comes hopping into the village. The king's men are waiting at the water hole to catch him, but no one recognizes this strange creature. Tío Conejo, King of the Leafy Beasts, gets to drink all the water he wants.

CONNECTIONS
Agoutis. Disguises. Escapes. Foxes. Humans. Jaguars. Juan Tul (Trickster). Leaf monster. Mischief. Monkeys. Rabbits. Retaliation. Squirrels. Tigers. Tricksters.

WHERE ELSE THIS STORY APPEARS
The King of the Leaves—M.A. Jagendorf and R.S. Boggs in Lila Green, *Folktales of Spain and Latin America*

HOW ELSE THIS STORY IS TOLD
Brazilian variations:
How Agouti (Cotia) Fooled Onça—Livia de Almeida and Ana Portella, *Brazilian Folktales*. Amazonia. After the cotia fools the jaguar by disguising herself in honey and termites, she begs not to be thrown into the thorny bushes, which is exactly what the cotia wants and needs for escape. This telling also includes the storm trick.
Jaguar and Fox—John Bierhorst, *The Red Swan*. Mundurucú People. Amazonia. As one in a series of pranks, the fox escapes when he tricks the jaguar into thinking he is chief of the Leafy Beasts his grandfather told him about. With advice from other animals, the jaguar tries to lure fox by playing dead, but the fox says aloud that his grandfather farted just before he died. Jaguar thinks that's what he must do and farts, giving himself away, again.

The Monkey Buys Corn—Enid D'Oyley, *Animal Fables and Other Tales Retold: African Tales in the New World*. African American People. The monkey disguises himself from tiger who wants revenge. Once monkey escapes, he throws rocks at the tiger's teeth which he can see after tiger has hidden and asked others to cover him up with leaves.

See The Monkey Buys Corn (124) under Making Bargains for the first part of this story on why the tiger wants to get even with the monkey.

Maya variations:

Juan Tul—John Bierhorst, *The Red Swan*. Squirrel Woman does not recognize the rabbit Juan Tul who has rubbed balche leaves on his face.

---

390. THE RABBIT AS COWHERD

Fernando Peñalosa, *Tales and Legends of the Q'Anjob'al Maya*
Kanjobal Maya People. Guatemala

The rabbit sells the owner's cows he has been hired to tend. He then places some empty gourds in the tops of tall trees, which make a mooing sound when the wind blows. The rabbit tells the owner that he was threatened by thieves, who stole all the cows. He brings the livestock owner to the place where cows had been grazing before. The owner hears mooing. When he agrees that they should separate to follow the mooing sounds, to look for the cows, the rabbit makes his escape.

CONNECTIONS

Cows. Herders. Humorous tales. Mischief. Owners. Rabbits.

WHERE ELSE THIS STORY APPEARS

As Rabbit as Cowherd Tricks the Boss—Don Pedro Miguel Say. In Fernando Peñalosa, *Maya Culture—Traditional Storyteller's Tales* (Online)

---

391. HOW AGOUTI (COTIA) FOOLED ONÇA

Livia de Almeida and Ana Portella, *Brazilian Folktales*
Amazonia

Running through the forest, the small rodent Cotia scares Onça the jaguar by saying a storm with strong winds is coming. Onça asks Cotia to tie her to a tree so she will not blow away and gets stuck there for days, until a termite helps to eat away the ropes that hold her. Grateful, Onça invites the King of the Termites to a banquet, but it is Cotia who shows up in disguise, covered in honey with termites sticking on to look like a king. Cotia stuffs itself, but in the night rain washes away the honey and lets the little termites crawl away. Alerted by her son that their sleeping guest is Cotia, Onça ties Cotia to a tree. When she tells Cotia she will drown Cotia in the pond, Cotia pretends that a bath to wash off the honey would be great. So Onça says she will throw Cotia in the thorny bushes, which, though the rodent protests will kill her, is exactly what Cotia needs to get away.

Connections

Agoutis. Cleverness. Coyotes. Disguises. Foxes. Humorous tales. Jaguars. Leaves. Rabbits. Raccoons. Rescues. Squirrels. Storms. Storytelling. Termites. Tricksters.

How Else This Story Is Told

Brazilian variation:

Jaguar and Fox—John Bierhorst, *The Red Swan*. Mundurucú People. Amazonia. The fox tricks the jaguar into thinking he'll be safe from a storm, if the jaguar ties him to a leafy vine which shrinks, holding him captive up in a tree. The fox then has plenty of other creative tricks in store.

Chilean variation:

Antonio and the Thief—Saul Schkolnick. In *Jade and Iron*. Three times a boy outwits the thief who keeps coming after him on his way to the other side of the mountain to fetch butter and flour for his mother. In this one, Antonio pretends that he plans to tie himself to the locus tree because the earth is about to turn upside down. The man does not want to fall off the earth and asks to be tied up instead. Antonio does and leaves him there.

Mexican variation:

Señor Coyote and Little Señor Coon—Dan Storm, *Pictures Tales from Mexico*. Señor Tejon the coon talks Señor Coyote out of eating him, by scaring him into getting into a hollow log to be safe from a dangerous hail-storm Señor Tejon says is coming. The coon throws handfuls of large stones at the log to simulate hail.

---

392. Uncle Coyote's Last Mischief

Harold Courlander, *Ride with the Sun*
Nicaragua

Uncle Rabbit tempts Uncle Coyote to sneak into the Padre's garden with him, where they share a ripe watermelon, which Uncle Coyote rips open. Then they overhear the Padre's housekeeper say the Padre will be eating ripe watermelon for dinner. Uncle Coyote is sure he will be blamed for raiding the garden. Uncle Rabbit suggests that they fill the watermelon rind with mud and push the two halves back together so no one will know. When Uncle Rabbit goes back later to check, the housekeeper is ranting about Uncle Coyote and the mud. Uncle Rabbit tells her he will bring the coyote there for justice. He is wondering how he is going to do that, when he finds Uncle Coyote in pain with broken teeth. Uncle Rabbit suggests he go to the Padre's housekeeper for something to stop the pain. When Uncle Coyote shows up, however, she lights his tail on fire. He runs to the river and then far away.

Connections

Accusations. Coyotes. Housekeepers. Mischief. Punishments. Rabbits. Tricksters. Watermelons.

393. ZORRO AND QUWI
Rebecca Hickox
Peru

Zorro the fox would like to eat Quwi the guinea pig, but Quwi always gets the best of him in the Andes Mountains. The last of four episodes begins after Quwi convinces Zorro to get into a hole to be safe from a rain of fire and then pokes Zorro with stinging thornbushes. When Zorro emerges from his hole and sees that the earth has not been burned, he wants revenge. To make peace, Quwi brings a small dish of sweetened corn-meal to Zorro's home. Zorro enjoys the mazamorra and wants more. He follows Quwi to a human house to find more. But Zorro's head gets stuck inside the clay pot of mazamorra there. He calls out to Quwi for a rock to break the pot, and Quwi leads him over to the bald head of a sleeping man to knock against. The man startles, throwing Zorro against the wall. Zorro escapes when the pot breaks. In the end, he decides Quwi would be too tough to eat.

CONNECTIONS
Captivity. Cleverness. Foxes. Guinea pigs. Humorous tales. Mice. Monkeys. Tricksters.

HOW ELSE THIS STORY IS TOLD
Bolivian variation:
The Fox and the Monkey—Moisés Alvarez. In John Bierhorst, *Latin American Folktales*. Aymara People. The monkey tricks the fox four times. When the fox's head gets stuck in a pot of quinoa, the monkey tells him to hit it against a rock, which turns out to be the native servant's head. The pongo brings the monkey to his patrón who ties him up. The monkey tricks the fox into taking his place, telling him he is being forced to marry the patrón's daughter.

Quechua variation from Peru:
The Mouse and the Fox—Richard M. Dorson, *Folktales Told Around the World*. In the fourth trick which a little mouse plays on the fox, the mouse shows the fox the pot of *mazamorra* inside a house, where the fox gets stuck. The fox cracks the pot off on the old man's head, and the old man is sure his wife has another husband when she says the fox did it.

394. SEÑOR COYOTE PLAYS SCHOOLMASTER FOR THE RABBIT
Dan Storm, *Pictures Tales from Mexico*
Mexico

Rabbit deflects Señor Coyote's desire to eat him one day by bringing him to a school where he says he has been hired to make sure the children keep studying their numbers and letters. Rabbit tells Señor Coyote he was offered three chickens for the work, but he cannot leave the students unattended to get them. He offers Señor Coyote two of the three promised chickens if he takes over and pokes a stick inside the school to nudge the children back to studying when he doesn't hear the hum of their lessons anymore. Señor Coyote agrees. Rabbit goes. Things get too quiet, and Señor Coyote pokes the stick inside. Only then, when hundreds of angry hornets come out buzzing and stinging, does Señor Coyote learn what kind of school rabbit brought him to.

CONNECTIONS
Bees. Coyotes. Foxes. Hornets. Humorous tales. Insects. Mischief. Rabbits. Schools. Tricksters. Wasps.

HOW ELSE THIS STORY IS TOLD
Coyote Rings the Wrong Bell—M.A. Jagendorf and R.S. Boggs, *The King of the Mountains*. Hare says he'll go get something more tender for Coyote to eat if he rings the bell when it is time for the tender little hares at school to come out. Hare goes off, and Coyote shakes the tree with all his might, and hornets sting him everywhere.
The Fox and the Coyote / El zorro y el coyote—Angel Vigil, *The Eagle on the Cactus*. In a medley of many tricks, the fox tells the coyote to poke a stick inside a bag where he says children are trapped.
The Rabbit and the Coyote—Américo Paredes, *Folktales of Mexico*. This is the middle episode in a medley of six stories where Rabbit tricks Coyote and Coyote tries unsuccessfully to get even.
Rabbit and Puma—John Bierhorst, *The Monkey's Haircut* Yucatec-Tzutuhil Maya People. This is the second of four tricks Rabbit pulls on Puma.
The Tale of Rabbit and Coyote—Tony Johnston. Juchitán, Mexico. Rabbit tricks Coyote here in six different ways, including this one.
Sister Fox and Brother Coyote—Riley Aiken. In J. Frank Dobie, *Puro Mexicano*. 'Mana Zorro tricks coyote five different times.

---

395. A LIE HURTS MORE THAN A WOUND
Melville J. Herskovits and Frances Herskovits, *Suriname Folk-Lore*
African American People. Suriname

Anansi and the King disagree, and Anansi wants to prove to him that a lie can hurt more than a physical wound. He has his child eliminate in front of the door. Then Anansi invites the King to hear how the earth can speak. The King invites all the other kings to come listen to the earth speak, too. Anansi has his child hide under the excrement. When everyone is there, Anansi calls out to the earth, asking whose excrement is there. The voice from the excrement says it is the King's. The King is so humiliated, he rewards Anansi with half of his kingdom.

CONNECTIONS
Anansi. Deceit. Emperors, kings & queens. Excrement. Humiliation. Humorous tales. Mischief. Parents and children. Rewards. Spiders. Storytelling. Tests. Tricksters. Words. Wounds.

396. *Just a Minute: A Trickster Tale and Counting Book*
Yuyi Morales
Mexico

Señor Calavera, Death, comes to Grandma Beetle's door and says it is time for her to come with him, but Grandma Beetle tells him to wait—she has one house to sweep, then two pots of tea to boil, then three pounds of corn to make into tortillas, four fruits to slice, five cheeses to melt, six pots of food to cook, seven piñatas to fill with candy, eight platters of food to arrange. Once polite, Señor Calavera is now getting impatient. Nine grandchildren troop in to celebrate Grandma Beetle's birthday. Afterwards, Grandma Beetle is ready to go, but Señor Calavera has gone, leaving a note that he wouldn't think of missing her party next year.

Connections
Beetles. Counting tales. Death (Character). Humorous tales. Insects. Parties. Procrastination. Tricksters.

397. What's in the Pot, Stays in the Pot!
Dorothy St. Aubyn, *Caribbean Fables: Animal Stories from Guyana and the Antilles*
Guyana

A hungry Tiger lures some little Saciwinkie monkeys down from their tree to hear an urgent story he says he needs to tell them. The Tiger reports that he has just come back from Monkey Land where the monkeys are dying. The Sackiwinkies are worried now that this will happen to them, too, but the Tiger tells them he knows the cure. They need to start a fire and jump into the pot of water on top, pulling the lid over. The Tiger shows them how, when the water is first getting started and not hot. He jumps out of the pot, and the Sackiwinkies jump in. Tiger holds the lid down, and only one Sackiwinkie escapes without getting cooked. A while later, that Sackiwinkie is present when Tiger shows the cure to another group of monkeys. The monkeys ask many questions, and the pot is hot by the time Tiger gets in. When he does, they all jump on top of the lid.

Connections
Deceit. Monkeys. Revenge. Storytelling. Teamwork. Tigers. Tricksters.

398. *Conejito*
Margaret Read MacDonald
Panama

On his way to visit Tía Monica, a little rabbit bumps into Señor Zorro, Señor Tigre, and then Señor Lion, who each want to eat him. Conejito tells each one that he's "Flaquito! Flaquito! Flaquito!"—too skinny—and suggests they wait for his return from his Auntie who is going to feed him all sorts of sweet things until he gets fat. The fierce animals let Conejito go on to his Auntie, but now the little rabbit is afraid to go home. His Tía Monica puts him in a barrel which rolls down the mountain past the animals. She also starts a fire in her yard with smoke they can see. From inside the barrel, Conejito calls out that the mountain is on fire, and the fox, tiger, and lion all run away.

Connections
Aunts and nephews. Billy Goats Gruff tales. Escapes. Foxes. Humorous tales. Lions. Rabbits. Teamwork. Tigers. Tricksters.

Where Else This Story Appears
El Conejito—Margaret Read MacDonald, *Shake-It-Up Tales*
Tío Rabbit and the Barrel—Dorothy Sharp Carter, *The Enchanted Orchard*

399. Fat Sheep, Lean Sheep, and Señor Coyote
Dan Storm, *Pictures Tales from Mexico*
Mexico

Señor Coyote surprises one fat and one lean sheep. Gordo, the fat one, tells the coyote that he is too fat to eat, and Flaco, the lean one, says he does not have enough meat. Each proposes that the coyote eat the other one first. Señor Coyote suggests a contest. He makes a line going lengthwise in the road and tells one sheep to come from one side and the other from the other side. The first one to cross the line will be eaten last. Señor Coyote stands in the middle and signals for the race to start. Both sheep run toward the middle very hard. He is sure they will butt heads, but instead they veer, knock into him hard and escape.

Connections
Competition. Coyotes. Escapes. Humorous tales. Sheep. Tricksters.

400. Señor Coyote Hides in the Rabbit's House
Dan Storm, *Pictures Tales from Mexico*
Mexico

Señor Coyote has hidden himself in the grass outside Rabbit's little cave to keep watch. Rabbit has gone out and just before he returns, Señor Coyote squeezes himself into Rabbit's home. Something makes Rabbit suspicious and he calls out, the way Spanish Americans used to do when approaching the home of another Christian. He calls out, "Hail Mary, my little cave—Ave maria, cuevita mia," as if expecting his house to answer him. Señor Coyote does not answer, so Rabbit calls out to his little cave again.

Now, Señor Coyote thinks he had better answer for the cave. He calls back, and Rabbit runs off amused.

Connections

  Conflict. Coyotes. Greetings. Humorous tales. Jaguars. Rabbits. Tricksters. Words.

How Else This Story Is Told

Brazilian variation:

Jaguar and Fox—John Bierhorst, *The Red Swan.* Mundurucú People. Amazonia. After the squirrel frees the jaguar by chewing the vine where fox has tricked him into thinking he'll be safe from a storm, jaguar hides in fox's hollow tree to get even with fox. He gives himself away, though, by answering when the suspicious fox calls out to his tree to see if jaguar is hiding there. Jaguar also gives himself away when playing dead by farting when the fox says that's what his grandfather did before he died.

Mexican variation:

The Rabbit and the Coyote—Américo Paredes, *Folktales of Mexico.* After being tricked by the rabbit several times, the coyote actually runs away from his own cave when he calls out several times and realizes rabbit is hiding inside.

---

401. The Coyote and the Rooster

Dan Storm, *Pictures Tales from Mexico*

Mexico

When the coyote asks to hear Senor Gallo sing, he knows the rooster will close his eyes to crow. Senor Gallo knows not to trust the coyote, but when the coyote keeps complimenting him, he does. The coyote pounces and runs off with him. As he is being carried in coyote's teeth, the rooster bets that he can hold a single note longer than the coyote can. He also disparages the coyote's singing and boasts that he can sing more loudly and more manly. The coyote puts the rooster down and starts to sing very loudly, but that is all Senor Gallo needs to get away.

Connections

Cleverness. Coyotes. Flattery. Music. Roosters. Tricksters. Trust.

Fools

402. The Mule Drivers Who Lost Their Feet

Neil Philip, *Horse Hooves and Chicken Feet*

Mexico

The simplest things can confuse people from Lagos de Moreno in Jalisco, Mexico. They are famous for being fools. One day some Lagos mule drivers stretch out their legs for a siesta under a tree. Their legs get tangled up. When they awaken, they cannot figure out whose legs are whose. And so, they can't stand up. For the longest while, they sit there uncomfortably. A stranger offers to help them for a price. His solution? He pokes the bottom of each man's foot with a sharp stick, and now the owner of that foot yelps and knows.

CONNECTIONS
Feet. Fools. Humorous tales. Identity. Knowledge. Lagos. Mule drivers. Problem solving.

HOW ELSE THIS STORY IS TOLD
The Drovers Who Lost Their Feet—María de Jesús Navarro ide Aceves. In Américo Paredes, *Folktales of Mexico*
The Drovers Who Lost Their Feet—Jane Yolen, *Favorite Folktales from Around the World*

403. THE HOLES OF LAGOS
M.A. Jagendorf and R.S. Boggs, *The King of the Mountains*
Mexico

The bobos of Lagos find foolish ways to solve their problems. There is a deep hole in the central plaza, and the mayor Señor Alcalde worries that people may get hurt. He wants to see the hole filled in. The town policeman agrees and rounds up some men to fill in the hole. When the job is done, Señor Alcalde finds another hole nearby. It is the one they took the earth out of to fill the plaza hole. He calls the policeman to fill it in. This goes on all day, filling in one hole and creating another until they reach the next town over.

CONNECTIONS
Fools. Holes. Humorous tales. Lagos. Mayors. Problem solving. Tasks. Work.

WHERE ELSE THIS STORY APPEARS
In Lila Green, *Folktales of Spain and Latin America*

404. THE SOMBREROS OF THE MEN OF LAGOS
M.A. Jagendorf, *Noodlehead Stories from Around the World*
Mexico

Six men sit on a long bench in Lagos just fine, but with their large sombreros next to them there is no room for another six. They think the bench has shrunk. They put on their sombreros and pull on the bench to stretch it so the next six can sit, too, but each time they sit down, they put their large sombreros down, again, and there's no room for the others anymore. But the one time all twelve sit down with their sombreros on, they fit. The men of Lagos are sure they must have finally stretched the bench.

CONNECTIONS
Fools. Hats. Humorous tales. Lagos. Problem solving. Size.

405. A SAD TALE OF A SILLY FELLOW
M.A. Jagendorf and R.S. Boggs, *The King of the Mountains*
Uruguay

A foolish man snaps at a stranger who says he should not be sitting on the tree limb he is sawing. But when the limb falls with him on it, he runs after the stranger, certain the man is a fortuneteller. The stranger humors the fool and tells him that he will die when his horse stops to drink three times while he is traveling. One hot day, the foolish man leaves on a long journey, and his horse drinks from two creeks as they go along. The man suddenly remembers the prediction and faints when his horse drinks a third time. The fool insists to his rescuers that he is dead, until they are afraid he really is a ghost and end his life, as the fortune teller said.

CONNECTIONS
Death. Fools. Gullibility. Horses. Humorous tales. Misunderstandings. Perspective. Prophecies. Rescues. Storytelling.

HOW ELSE THIS STORY IS TOLD
Argentinian variation:
When Ingele Believed He Was Dead / Cuando Ingele se creyó muerto—Paula Martin, *Pachamama Tales*

---

406. LET SOMEBODY BUY YOU WHO DOESN'T KNOW YOU
John Bierhorst, *Latin American Folktales*
Guatemala

Don Jesús Nutmeg, called Don Chús, is a faithful Catholic. He buys a mule at the farmer's market in Chinatla, without knowing that two thieves have been sizing him up. He ties the mule where he will be lodging and keeps checking during the night. Between his checks, one thief takes the mule and ties the other man to the stake in its place. Don Chús crosses himself when he sees a man on his hands and knees where his mule should be. The man tells him he was bewitched for bad behavior and was told he would endure hardships as a mule until a sincere religious man owned him. Don Chús lets the man go and returns to the market to buy a new mule. However, he stops to scold the mule which looks identical to the one he bought the day before, sure the man must have misbehaved and been changed back into a mule again.

CONNECTIONS
Deceit. Faith. Fools. Gullibility. Humorous tales. Identity. Kindness. Misunderstandings. Mules. Storytelling. Thieves. Tricksters.

407. SOME IMPATIENT MULE-DRIVERS

Anita Brenner, *The Boy Who Could Do Anything*
Mexico

Some mule-drivers on their way to a fair notice that the mules carrying sponges go faster than those carrying hot chili peppers. One chili mule-driver rubs some hot pepper on the legs of his slow mules, and they take off running. The other mule-drivers copy him. The mules with pepper burning their legs outrun all the others. So, the sponge mule-drivers try it, too. On the way back, though, when they try the same chili trick, all of the salt they are carrying dissolves when the horses plunge into the river to cool their burning legs.

CONNECTIONS

Chili peppers. Fools. Humorous tales. Imitation. Mules. Mule drivers. Speed.

408. WHEN A MAN IS FOOLISH

M.A. Jagendorf and R.S. Boggs, *The King of the Mountains*
Guyana

Some men traveling to a neighboring village, leave the *corial* to hunt. One man rests in his hammock instead. Then he sees an anteater curled up with its eyes closed. He thinks how lucky it is that this anteater is already dead, and he won't have to use an arrow to shoot it. He asks the anteater if it is dead, and when it doesn't answer, he pokes it, but the anteater doesn't move. He can see that it is fresh, warm and still breathing. He asks the anteater other questions, but the anteater still doesn't move. He tells the anteater he is going to find some bark with which to carry him onto the *corial*. When he returns, the anteater is gone, and the others in his group laugh when he tells them it was stolen.

CONNECTIONS

Anteaters. Fools. Humorous tales. Hunters. Misunderstandings.

409. SIMPLE SIMÓN

Ignacio Bizarro Ujpan in James D. Sexton, *Heart of Heaven, Heart of Earth*
Maya People

Simón is sure he just has bad luck all the time. He thinks his godfather has given him two pairs of *caites* that do not fit. Then his wife notices that he has taken two sandals for the same foot. He tells her the ones at home do not fit either. Another time, he has no luck catching fish when he tries to make a seashore at home by putting well water in a vat and spreading some sand around. It worries Simón's wife that he makes these mistakes, but he shrugs it all off and goes swimming in the vat.

CONNECTIONS

Fools. Fortune. Humorous tales. Husbands and wives. Misunderstandings.

Lucky Fools

410. THE ADVENTURES OF JUAN BOBO / LAS AVENTURAS DE JUAN BOBO

Genevieve Barlow, *Stories from Latin America / Historias de Latinoamérica*
Mexico

Juan's mother sends him to the market with instructions to be polite to all he meets. Juan tries to do the right thing. However, when he gives his deepest sympathy to a wedding party, they get angry and tell him he is supposed to cheer. So, Juan cheers when he next meets a butcher with pigs, and the startled pigs run away. This goes on, with Juan always politely saying the wrong thing the people before have told him to say—to a farmer burning weeds and to two men fighting. He buys the hen and bag of rice his mother requested and climbs a tree to nap on the way home. It starts to rain and thieves take refuge under that tree. They start to quarrel. When Juan calls down for them not to fight and the bag of rice breaks open, they think the storm god is angry with them and flee, leaving their gold coins behind. Juan brings the coins home, showing his mother the treasures which good manners can bring.

CONNECTIONS

Fools. Humorous tales. Juan Bobo. Magic brooms. Manners. Misunderstandings. Parents and
    children. Reversals of fortune. Thieves. Warlocks and Witches. Words.

HOW ELSE THIS STORY IS TOLD

Argentinian variation:
Five Kilos of Corn / Cinco kilos de maíz—Paula Martin, *Pachamama Tales*. A boy repeats what
    he has been told and applies the phrases inappropriately.

Costa Rican variation:
The Witches' Ride—Lupe de Osma, *The Witches' Ride*. The bobo misremembers the witches'
    chant which sent him riding high on a spare broom and crashes down into some robbers,
    who think the Devil has come for his share of the loot.

Mexican variation:
John, the Silly Boy / Juan Bobo, el rico—Maite Suarez-Rivas, *An Illustrated Treasury of Latino
    Read-Aloud Stories*.

411. ASHES FOR SALE

Pleasant DeSpain, *The Emerald Lizard*
Mexico

Naldo's sack contains flour, but gullible Pedro believes Naldo when he says it is full of ashes to sell in León, where people use them for fertilizer. Pedro only gets laughed at when he tries to sell ashes in León. A boy there, though, offers to trade Pedro his demon mask for the two sacks. That night, Pedro shares a campfire with some thieves. When he gets scared by an owl's hooting, he puts on the mask to keep death away. One of the thieves sees him and is sure the Demon of Death is here. He wakes the others. As they steal away, Pedro shouts to reassure them that it is just a mask, but now they are even more certain that the demon has come to punish them for their evil ways. Pedro collects all the loot the thieves have left behind and earnestly tells Naldo he obtained the treasure from selling ashes in León.

CONNECTIONS

Ashes. Fear. Fools. Gullibility. Humorous tales. Masks. Misunderstandings. Reversals of fortune. Superstitions. Thieves.

HOW ELSE THIS STORY IS TOLD

Ashes for Sale—Grant Lyons, *Tales the People Tell in Mexico*
Ashes for Sale / Se venden cenizas—Angel Vigil, *The Eagle on the Cactus*

---

412. THE TWO BROTHERS AND THE FORTUNE

Ignacio Bizarro Ujpan in James D. Sexton, *Heart of Heaven, Heart of Earth*
Maya People

Two lazy orphaned brothers are sent off the land by the owner. The older brother takes the wooden door of the *ranchito* and the younger takes the wooden window. They part ways, wishing each other fortune with God's help. The older brother is having no luck selling the door and sleeps in the forest, up in a tree with the door, to be safe from wolves and coyotes. Four thieves with machetes settle under the tree and begin to shoot dice. They just think it is raining when the brother urinates down on them, but when he throws down the wooden door to scare them, they think part of the sky has fallen. The thieves run off, leaving their money and machetes behind. With this money, the brother is able to buy land and settle down. His younger brother tries to copy him, but throws down the window without urinating on the thieves first. It misses, and the thieves chop him to pieces.

CONNECTIONS

Brothers and sisters. Changes in attitude. Doors. Fear. Fools. Humorous tales. Misunderstandings. Names. Orphans. Reversals of fortune. Ridicule. Windows.

HOW ELSE THIS STORY IS TOLD

Costa Rican variations:

The Lucky Table—Lupe de Osma, *The Witches' Ride* and in Joanna Cole, *Best-Loved Folktales of the World*. Here, the bobo's table falls from the tree onto the thieves below.
The Lucky Table—Leslie Goldman, *Dora's Favorite Fairy Tales*. Pedro's brother cannot believe he traded the family cow for a table.

Mexican variation:
Dumb Juan and the Bandits—Anita Brenner, *The Boy Who Could Do Anything.* Juan's brother can no longer call him names after he inadvertently drops a door down on some bandits.

---

413. PINE CONE THE ASTROLOGER
John Bierhorst, *Latin American Folktales*
Panama

Pine Cone, newly arrived from the countryside, decides to try for the reward the king has offered to an astrologer who can find his lost ring. To test if this man can read the stars, the king shows him a pineapple, unknown in those parts, and asks him what it is called. Pine Cone calls himself by name, for he has no idea. The king mistakes "pinecone" for "pineapple" and gives him the job. He sends Pine Cone to the tower to read the stars for his missing ring. Pine Cone notices two servants whispering. When his wife comes to visit, he asks her to hide under the bed and call out "Thief" when each servant comes in. They think he has figured out that they stole the ring and bring it to him. Pine Cone promises to keep their theft a secret if they hide the ring in the peacock's food. They do. Pine Cone is rewarded when he tells the king to kill the peacock, and there the ring is.

CONNECTIONS

Astrologers. Emperors, kings & queens. Fools. Humorous tales. Names. Problem solving. Rewards. Rings. Tests. Thieves. Tricksters. Words.

---

414. PRINCE SIMPLEHEART
John Bierhorst, *Latin American Folktales*
Costa Rica

Prince Simpleheart follows when his two older brothers go adventuring, even though they do not want their naïve younger brother along. Near their camp, he overhears three birds talking about how they drop magic objects whenever they sing. In the early morning, he collects those three objects and brings them to his brothers. One takes the knapsack that fills itself with money, one takes the violin that makes people keep dancing, and Prince Simpleheart takes the cloak of invisibility. The two brothers sneak away from him. Simpleheart eats some fruit that smells sweet and suddenly he grows antlers. Then they vanish when he falls into a pool. Now that he knows how to reverse the magic, Simpleheart sells a basket of that sweet fruit to the king. The whole royal family now has antlers, and he borrows the violin from his brother to make them dance out onto the palace balconies where everyone can see. Embarrassed, the king offers a reward for the music to stop. Simpleheart stops the music, but when he enters the palace for the reward, the king recognizes him as the fruit vendor and has him locked up. Simpleheart is to hang at dawn, but he slips out in his magic cloak, purchases doctor's clothes with money from the knapsack. He removes the antlers by lashing them a little (except the princess) and then holding members of the royal family underwater. All of the antlers disappear. So, Prince Simpleheart not only marries the princess a few days later, but is crowned king. Kind-hearted, he even finds a place for his brothers as ministers in the kingdom.

CONNECTIONS

Antlers. Brothers and sisters. Disguises. Emperors, kings & queens. Fools. Humorous tales. Invisibility. Magic. Magic cloaks. Magic violins. Magic bags. Magic fruit. Music. Princes and princesses. Rewards.

415. THE PRINCESS AND THE RIDDLE
Brenda Hughes, *Folk-tales from Chile*
Chile

The King has chopped off the heads of many young men who have failed to compose a riddle which the clever Princess cannot solve in one day. Tiburce is not especially clever, but he wants to leave the farm and try. His mother is sure he will also be killed and bakes some tortillas with poison, so he will die painlessly before he reaches the palace. That night, Tiburce is too tired to eat, but his donkey finds the tortillas and dies peacefully. Tiburce notices that the birds of prey who feed on the donkey also die. He strings those birds together. Some hungry robbers snatch them from him and eat the birds, and they die, too. With their rifle, he shoots at a dove and misses, but is able to eat her eggs. Tiburce arrives at the palace, ragged and dusty. Everyone laughs at him, but the Princess is angry that she cannot unravel the riddle he tells. Tiburce's riddle is the story of his adventures, obliquely told with numbers, so that the dead donkey killed four; four killed seven, and so on. Still, the King says he must keep his word, and Tiburce gets to marry the Princess, much to his mother's happy surprise.

CONNECTIONS

Competition. Emperors, kings & queens. Fools. Humorous tales. Parents and children. Poison. Princes and princesses. Riddles. Storytelling.

HOW ELSE THIS STORY IS TOLD
Costa Rican variation:
Bobo and the Riddles—Lupe de Osma, *The Witches' Ride*

Mexican variation:
The Princess and Jose—Anita Brenner, *The Boy Who Could Do Anything*. The riddle Jose asks the king is: "What is it that goes first on four legs, then two, then three?"

XV

Heroic Rescues and Magical Escapes

416. *Land of the Icy Death /*
Tierra de la muerte glacial
Harriet Rohmer and Jesús Guerrero Rea
Yahgan People. Chile

Wild hairy creatures are terrorizing the Yahgan people, dragging them under to die in icy water. One day, the monsters encircle Na Ha's canoe. The strong young man fights back bravely, but he is outnumbered and taken to the bottom of the sea. Na Ha escapes, though, and travels along the bottom of the ocean to a wise woman, whose white coral hair grows to the cavern walls. She listens with empathy to the story of his people's troubles and gives Na Ha a giant shell to call forth the icy death that lives beneath the seas. Blowing the shell, she tells Na Ha, will free his people but bring his own death. The land people who saw Na Ha fighting with the hairy creatures rejoice now to see him return. He convinces them to travel north for a while. They set out in their canoes all together, and once he is sure that everyone has left, Na Ha blows the magic shell. The blast brings sudden thick ice that traps the monsters on land. They suffer and shrink to become wide-eyed creatures afraid of Na Ha. When his people return Na Ha is an ice statue welcoming them and the creatures are now harmless seals.

CONNECTIONS
Fear. Heroes and heroines. Ice. Interspecies conflict. Magic. Monsters. Origin tales. Sea lions and seals. Self-sacrifice. Magic seashells. Supernatural beings. Water worlds. Wise men and wise women.

---

417. THE SEARCH FOR THE MAGIC LAKE
Genevieve Barlow, *Latin American Tales from the Pampas to Mexico City*
Inca People. Ecuador

A voice from the Great Ones tells an old emperor that his son must drink water from the magic lake at the end of the world to become well again. The emperor offers a great reward to the person who can make this journey, but no one knows how to find the lake. The sons of a poor farmer try, but they are imprisoned when each pretends that water from different lakes is the real thing. Their little sister Súmac thinks that the emperor may forgive her brothers if she finds the water. She sends her llama home so it will not be devoured by a puma. Some sparrows she once shared corn with each give her a wing feather to hold like a fan, which will take her wherever she wishes to go and protect her when she holds it to her face. They warn her that three fierce creatures guard the lake. Súmac uses the fan to reach the lake, where she puts a threatening black crab, a giant alligator, and a flying blood-red serpent to sleep. The magic water she brings back in the golden flask saves the prince's life. When the grateful emperor and empress ask what reward she would like, Súmac asks for her brothers to be freed, for the feathers to return to the sparrows, and for her parents to receive a new farm with llamas, vicuñas, and alpacas so they will no longer be poor. And then, she returns home.

CONNECTIONS

Alligators. Bird helpers. Brothers and sisters. Courage. Crabs. Emperors, kings & queens. Feathers. Healing. Heroes and heroines. Illness. Journeys to other realms. Kindness. Lakes. Magic. Magic fans. Magic feathers. Magic flasks. Magic jars. Magic waters. Monsters. Parents and children. Quests. Rewards. Snakes. Sparrows. Supernatural beings. Unselfishness.

WHERE ELSE THIS STORY APPEARS

The Search for the Magic Lake—Genevieve Barlow. In Joanna Cole, *Best-Loved Folktales of the World* and in Ethel Johnston Phelps, *Tatterhood and Other Tales*

HOW ELSE THIS STORY IS TOLD

Inca variations from Ecuador:
The Magic Lake—Pleasant DeSpain, *The Emerald Lizard.* Inez does not have anything to carry the water in when she reaches the lake where the land ends and the sea begins, but a llama appears with a crystal jar, which she fills with water. The only creature she encounters at the lake here is a fierce alligator.

The Search for the Magic Lake—Heather Forest, *Wonder Tales from Around the World* (Audio CD and e-book)

Inca variation from Peru:
Miro in the Kingdom of the Sun—Jane Kurtz. Miro, who dreams of becoming a royal chasqui runner like her brothers, is given feathers for a magic fan by the macaw who says Miro does not hunt the birds like the other Inca do.

---

418. THE FLOWER OF LIROLAY / LA FLOR DE LIROLAY

Rueben Martínez, *Once Upon a Time / Había una vez*
Argentina

A king who has gone blind promises his crown to the son who can bring him the magical flower of Lirolay, which the wise men say will cure him. The flower grows at a special spot on a mountaintop and may only be seen by someone with a generous heart.

The three sons follow different paths at the fork to find it. The elder two, however, speak rudely and no one gives them any information. The younger son goes straight to Salta and asks for help and is shown where to go. Still, the route is dangerous and difficult with raging rivers and frightening gnomes. He reaches the mountaintop and collects the flower when it blooms at midnight. Back at the fork, his jealous brothers bind his hands and feet. They bury him in a deep hole and bring the flower to their father. A tree grows where the prince is buried, and a shepherd makes a flute from its wood. When the flute plays a song that tells what the princes did to their brother, he brings the flute for the king to hear. The king recognizes his son's voice and sends his brothers to dig him up. He lays the lirolay flower on the prince, who revives and gets to rule the kingdom.

CONNECTIONS

Blindness. Brothers and sisters. Competition. Deceit. Emperors, kings & queens. Flowers. Flutes. Gnomes. Healing. Herders. Jealousy. Magic flowers. Magic flutes. Murder. Music. Parents and children. Princes and princesses. Quests. Rescues. Restoring life.

HOW ELSE THIS STORY IS TOLD

Costa Rican variation:
The Flower of Sweet Content—Lupe de Osma, *The Witches' Ride*

Mexican variation:
The Flower of Lily-Lo—Jorge Carlos González Avila. In John Bierhorst, *Latin American Folktales* and in Américo Paredes, *Folktales of* Mexico. It is the mother who falls sick in this story, and when a boy blows on the flower which grows where the brothers buried their youngest brother, it sings the song of what they did.

Venezuelan variation:
The Singing Flute—Harold Courlander, *Ride with the Sun*. The healing flower here is an olive blossom, which an old woman tells the youngest son how to find when he shares his food with her. The flute which sings his story is made from reeds which grow over his body.

419. THE MACHI AND THE NGURUVILU
Brenda Hughes, *Folk-tales from Chile*
Mapuche People. Chile

The only safe way across a deep river separating the villagers is by dugout canoe, since waders frequently drown at the ford. Two native Mapuche bring horses decorated with silver bridles and stirrups to the machi, a good shaman sure that there is a monster in the river and sure of his powers to get rid of it for a price. The machi disappears into a whirlpool and comes up holding a nguruvilu. Four times, he threatens the fox-snake with death if it kills any more people. The machi is moving the knife and threatens to cut off the nguruvilu's appendages. Between the hypnotic knife and the drumming on the banks, the nguruvilu gives up, and the machi brings him back down. The whirlpool gradually disappears, and even children can safely cross the ford.

Heroes and heroines. Monsters. Nguruvilus. Rescues. Rivers. Shamans. Supernatural beings.

420. THE KIBUNGO AND THE BOY WITH THE SACK FULL OF FEATHERS
Livia de Almeida and Ana Portella, *Brazilian Folktales*
Brazil

No one knows why the boy collects feathers. He says they will be useful sometime and hauls that bag along when the whole family goes on a fishing trip. Hearing a snort, the men run back from the riverbank, fearing a vicious Kibungo. There is not time enough to get home, and the boy lines everyone up and gives each person one wing feather to put between his teeth and one tail feather for under his arm. When the fearsome Kibungo appears and reaches for the first person, the boy sings out from the back that it is his father, "fall, don't fall." The Kibungo snatches his hand back, and the boy identifies his mother, and so on down the line through all the relatives. The Kibungo has not been able to eat anyone. They all start flapping their feathers like wings and escape. Back at home, the boy tells his family to prepare a deep hole with a sharp stick hidden under banana leaves and mud with a doll sitting right beside the pit. The Kibungo attacks the doll and falls into the pit, where the stick pierces him. The boy's parents now praise their son's cleverness. This boy whom everyone thought strange has outsmarted the Kibungo and kept them safe.

CONNECTIONS
Changes in attitude. Cleverness. Feathers. Heroes and heroines. Interspecies conflict. Kibungo.
    Parents and children. Rescues. Supernatural beings. Tricksters.

421. NEIMA'S RESCUE
Nina Jaffe, *Patakin*
Goajiro People. Venezuela

Orphans Kaliwaa and Neima escape from an aunt who beats them and become self-sufficient in the forest, with four puppies they find who are also alone. Yolujaa, the spirit of the dead, has fallen in love with Neima, but since Neima has promised her brother she will stay inside while he is hunting, Yolujaa asks the witch Chaama to try to lure her away for him. Chaama has her own plans, though, and after she tricks Neima into stepping outside by pretending to be an old woman, she whisks the girl to her house and cuts her into pieces to eat her. A chuuta bird helps Kaliwaa find Chaama, and Kaliwaa and his dogs force the witch to bring Neima back to life. On their way home, the dogs attack an evil wanuluu spirit riding on the back of a fox, who demands Neima in payment. When Kaliwaa refuses, the wanuluu turns the dogs into dust and rides off with Neima anyway. Kaliwaa is bereft. Molokoona, the turtle drummer, offers to go find Neima. He locates the wanuluu at a party of spirits. The spirit demands that Molokoona perform, but tries to get him drunk first. Molokoona pours the rum down his neck (which explains turtles' wrinkled necks) and works up to a drumming crescendo which excites the spirits. He discovers Neima in the kitchen and hides her inside his drum, but the wanuluu catches up with them, for the drum is heavy. Molokoona fights the wanuluu, drumsticks against whip, and finally the spirit runs off. There is great rejoicing when Molokoona and Neima return to Kaliwaa.

CONNECTIONS

Animal helpers. Bird helpers. Brothers and sisters. Captivity. Cleverness. Despair. Dog helpers. Drums. Heroes and heroines. Journeys. Music. Monsters. Origin tales. Orphans. Rescues. Restoring life. Spirits. Supernatural beings. Tortoises and turtles. Wanuluu. Warlocks and witches. Yoluja.

---

422. ROSHA AND THE SUN

Mary-Jo Gerson, *Fiesta Femenina*
Maya People. Mexico

Now that Rosha is older, she often goes off on her own, which angers her older brother Tup. When their parents leave to sell corn in the village, Tup thinks of a way to force Rosha to play with him. He cuts off her long black hair while she is sleeping and makes a nest with it to catch the sun. Rosha yells at her brother when she sees the sun trapped at the edge of the woods. The corn will not be able to grow without it. She tries desperately to release the sun, but its flames scorch her fingers. Neither the deer nor the wild turkey will help her, but a shivering mole volunteers. Warm in Rosha's rebozo, the mole dreams of being powerful. When he wakes, he jumps inside the nest and quickly bites the tangled strands of hair so the sun can float back up into the sky. The grateful sun promises the mole safe shelter underground. To Rosha who freed him, and to all Maya women, the sun grants eyes that shine with his golden light.

CONNECTIONS

Animal helpers. Brothers and sisters. Captivity. Dreams. Gratitude. Heroes and heroines. Moles. Origin tales. Rescues. Rewards. Sun.

---

423. THE ENCHANTED COW

Magdalena Muñoz in John Bierhorst, *Latin American Folktales*
Chile

Pancho would never abandon his family, so people think he must have drowned when the cow he was selling shows up back at the house, wet and alone. His wife Dolores takes the two children and the cow, which she loves, to a house near the sea. One day her son Joaquín is bathing his baby sister when a wave separates them, and she disappears. Then the cow speaks to the boy. She tells Joaquín that his sister was taken by the same witch woman's spirits who took his father away. The cow tells Joaquín to spread her skin on the water and ride, pulling one of her tail hairs when there is danger. Her eyeballs will let him see into water and earth. Joaquín reluctantly kills the cow to rescue his sister and pockets the eyes. Single hairs from the tail enable him to fight against snapping fish, large birds which try to sink the hide, and icebergs. The cow's eyeball shows him a castle on an island ahead. Through its walls he can see his father chained to a column and his sister in the hand of someone holding a knife. Joaquín uses the next to last tail hair to make a ladder to enter the castle and rescue his father and his sister. They fill their pockets with treasure and ride home on the hide. Their mother welcomes them joyfully, and Pancho tells how the Lost Soul witch held him captive when he refused to marry her. Joaquín gathers all the parts of their beloved cow and burns her last tail hair. The cow becomes herself again when the match accidentally falls onto her skin. All goes well for the family from then on.

CONNECTIONS

Animal helpers. Brothers and sisters. Captivity. Cows. Heroes and heroines. Journeys to other realms. Magic. Magic eyes. Parents and children. Restoring life. Self-sacrifice. Supernatural beings. Unselfishness. Warlocks and witches. Water worlds.

---

424. THE FIVE BROTHERS
Yolando Pino-Saavedra, *Folktales of Chile*
Chile

Five brothers, traveling together with their father's blessing, decide to follow different forks in the road and meet in one year with a gift for their sister. They become apprentices in different fields. Pedro learns how to become a thief. Diego learns to hunt birds. José learns bone-setting. Juan learns to resuscitate cadavers. Manuel learns how to tell fortunes. When they meet again, they test their gifts on a partridge—finding it, shooting it, stealing and setting its wing, and then bringing it back to life. A nearby king hears about the sons' talents and promises his daughter's hand in marriage to the one who can retrieve her from captivity. Manuel knows that Old Long Arms, who lives on the Island of Ivories, is holding the princess. The brothers sail there, and working as a team, bring her on board the ship. They are sailing away when Old Long Arms comes after them and smashes the ship, which José rebuilds. However, the frightened girl has died. Juan resuscitates her, and when Old Long Arms reappears, Diego shoots him for good. Back at the palace, the princess tells her father how the brothers all rescued her. The King says the one who shoots an arrow the furthest will marry her, and his four other daughters marry the other boys.

CONNECTIONS

Brothers and sisters. Competition. Emperors, kings & queens. Giants. Heroes and heroines. Hunters. Monsters. Parents and children. Princes and princesses. Promises. Rescues. Restoring life. Supernatural beings. Talents. Teamwork. Thieves.

WHERE ELSE THIS STORY APPEARS

The Five Brothers—Yolando Pino-Saavedra. In Joanna Cole, *Best-Loved Folktales of the World*
See also The Rarest Thing (346) for a love spin on this story.

425. THE WATERFALL OF WISDOM

Angel Vigil, *The Eagle on the Cactus*
Spanish Colonial People. Mexico

Two magic red waterfalls come down from the mountain. One flows with red wine, which brings wisdom; the other flows with red blood, which turns bathers to stone. The king is going to immerse in the wine to become a better ruler. His beloved daughter, the princess, heads over there, too, without telling him. She impulsively leaps into the first red falls and is turned to stone before she can escape. Her stone statue becomes worn down and covered in a ruby red shell as the water flows over her for years. A prince who has heard about the two waterfalls sees the ruby and carefully brings it home to put in an amulet. The royal jewelers, though, sense a presence in this ruby and take it to the royal wizard, who tells the prince that a princess is trapped inside. He tells the prince to bathe the ruby in the waterfall with wine. He does, and the princess returns to herself. They use the waters of wisdom to break the enchantment of the other stone statues. The king rejoices to see his daughter again. The prince and princess marry and reign with wisdom.

CONNECTIONS

Emperors, kings & queens. Enchantment. Heroes and heroines. Impulsivity. Love. Magic. Magic waters. Magic wine. Parents and children. Princes and princesses. Rescues. Stone. Transformations. Waterfalls. Wizards.

426. THE TURQUOISE RING

Pleasant DeSpain, *The Emerald Lizard*
Chile

When all Jacinto, the dreamer, can bring home to their poor mother is a seashell, his brothers send him away. However, just as two unsavory men ride up, Jacinto discovers the silver ring inside which can make him invisible when he turns its turquoise stone toward his palm. He toys with the men, and they flee, terrified, thinking that the Seven-Headed Beast they stole from is now coming after them. Jacinto brings their treasure and horses home. When his brothers squander the riches, he moves his mother to a new village. With his ring of invisibility, Jacinto is able to cut off all seven heads of the Seven-Headed Beast who has been taking one child each day from that village. He then goes after the notorious One-Legged Pirate at the request of a young woman whose brother was captured. Jacinto allows himself to be taken and, once on board the ship frees the captives and pushes the pirate captain overboard. The grateful woman marries Jacinto, and the grateful town tells him he has earned the pirate's treasure to keep.

Connections

Brothers and sisters. Captivity. Gratitude. Heroes and heroines. Invisibility. Magic. Magic rings. Monsters. Pirates. Rescues. Reversals of fortune. Rings. Seashells. Supernatural beings.

How Else This Story Is Told

The Magic Ring—Brenda Hughes, *Folk-tales from Chile*. In this more detailed version, an indigenous man and woman who have been eaten spring out from the huge seven-headed animal when the hero cuts off all of its heads and tails. They bring the young man to their village by the sea, where a girl tells him that her father, the cacique has been kidnapped by men in an enchanted boat who all share one leg. Turning invisible, he is able to kill the crew and free the prisoners before setting the magic boat on fire, so it will never endanger anyone else again.

The Ring in the Seashell—Frances Carpenter, *South American Wonder Tales*

---

427. The Dragon Slayer
John Bierhorst, *Latin American Folktales*
Mexico

Two jealous sisters frame the youngest one, so their father believes this daughter has been stealing. He leaves her in the forest with a few tortillas. The daughter shares food with an old woman, the Virgin Mary, who tells her to go to Quiquiriquí and request work in the king's palace. The Blessed Virgin also gives her a magic wand which will give information with Heaven's power. Working in the palace kitchen, the girl notices that the king is sad. The wand tells her that it is because he must send his son to the dragon with seven heads or the dragon will eat everyone else in the kingdom. The wand also tells her how to kill that dragon. She goes to the dragon's lair and then cuts the seven tongues from its seven heads. However, a man reaches the palace first with the dragon's seven heads themselves and claims to have slain it. The daughter produces the seven tongues to show he is lying and says she would like to marry the prince. The king wants better than kitchen help as his son's bride, but does not renege on his promise to grant any wish to the dragon slayer. The daughter asks the Virgin Mary for help with a dress. She looks so beautiful in the gold gown that both the prince and the king fall in love with her. The wand tells her that the king is planning to kill his son and to stop this with a giant's tooth ring. She takes the ring from the sleeping giant and wishes that the king become a wild pig ... which the prince then shoots.

Connections

Brothers and sisters. Courage. Deceit. Disguises. Dragons. Giants. Heroes and heroines. Jealousy. Magic. Magic rings. Magic wands. Monsters. Parents and children. Princes and princesses. Promises. Reversals of fortune. Supernatural beings. Transformations. Virgin Mary.

---

428. The Feast for Tepozteco
Nina Jaffe, *Patakin*
Aztec People. Mexico

A young woman, who swallows a small seed while sweeping in the temple to the god Ometochtli, gives birth to a baby boy. Ashamed, she leaves the child near a stream, where an old couple finds him and raises him as their own. They call him Tepozteco, and when he is ten years old, the boy says he will go in his father's place to be the one delivered to the monster Xochicalcatl, who demands one old person to eat each day. He tells his fearful parents to watch for a white cloud, which will mean he has killed the monster. Tepozteco picks up sharp pieces of obsidian on his walk east to Xochical-catl. The monster objects to Tepozteco's small size, but swallows him whole anyway. Once inside, Tepozteco cuts his way out, which kills the monster. Later, Tepozteco becomes king, and stories of his heroism spread. Four neighboring kings invite him to join their council. When the royal drum announces Tepozteco's arrival, the others are insulted by his sandals and simple clothing. He returns dressed magnificently and proceeds to pour the food all over himself, saying they hadn't really invited him, just his clothes. They give chase and he flees to the top of La Montana del Aire. Tepozteco's drums shake down a cliff barricade to stop them. From there, Tepozteco continues to protect his people of Tepoztlán.

Connections

Appearance. Clothing. Courage. Emperors, kings & queens. Giants. Gods and humans. Heroes and heroines. Leadership. Magic. Monsters. Sacrifice. Supernatural beings. Tepozteco. Unselfishness.

How Else This Story Is Told

How Tepozton Killed the Giant—Anita Brenner, *The Boy Who Could Do Anything.* After Tepozton cuts his way out of the giant and is crowned king, he rides the clouds, which turn into all kinds of animals, and often disguises himself as an ordinary person to help others.

Legends of the Tepoztecatl—Frances Toor, *A Treasury of Mexican Folkways.* In this telling, Tepoztecatl is the child of a princess who gives birth after she picks up a clay doll which vanishes from her hands.

The Sacred Drum of Tepozteco—M.A. Jagendorf and R.S. Boggs, *The King of the Mountains.* Tepozteco's drums taunt the pursuing kings with sounds of battle. He remains in the mountain of clouds to protect his people, but does not return to earth.

Tepoztecatl—Juliet Piggott, *Mexican Folk Tales*

Tepozton—Anita Brenner, *The Boy Who Could Do Anything* and in *Frances Frost, Legends of the United Nations.* This telling centers on Tepozton's childhood. He is the son of a god who comes to earth and falls in love with a human girl, who first hides the baby in a maguey plant which drips sweet juice into his mouth. She moves the baby to a box by the river, where he is discovered by the old fisherman who brings him home. When Tepozton discovers his magical powers, he rides clouds and can shoot an arrow into the air and still catch game. Some legends say that in the end, Tepozton goes to join his father, a god; others say that he continues to live on earth and help people.

429. The Boy and the Bull

Fernando Peñalosa, *Tales and Legends of the Q'Anjob'al Maya*
Kanjobal Maya. Guatemala

The king is not sure he wants this poor boy working for him, but when the boy does well feeding orphan calves, the king gives him a skinny bull. The boy and bull become friends. When the king orders the boy to kill him, the bull tells the boy how they will escape to the mountains. They do, and anything the boy needs comes out of the bull's horns when he asks. When, three times, the boy refuses to turn the bull over to giant serpents with multiple heads that want to eat him, the bull fights them and wins. However, he is getting tired. The bull tells the boy to give him to the serpent with four heads, but to keep his horns and skin for himself. The boy makes a rope from the bull's skin. He works for a different king, who also thinks he is too dirty and too young. His daughters send the boy to watch the sheep, warning him about a killer animal up there. The boy lassoes the giant sheep-eating serpent who killed his bull and forces him go to his plantation, where the boy chooses a horse of seven colors to ride and slays the serpent. Back at the palace, there is to be a contest for the eldest princess's hand. In disguise, on the horse of seven colors, the boy is able to grab the contest ring. The king and queen disapprove of the boy as a potential husband, until he sends mules loaded with money down from the serpent's bank. The boy goes to live on the serpent's plantation after the wedding and tells the servants who work there that he is now their master and will treat them better and pay them more.

Connections

Animal helpers. Bulls. Changes in attitude. Class conflict. Friendship. Herders. Heroes and heroines. Interspecies conflict. Leadership. Magic. Magic bulls. Magic horns. Monsters. Reversals of fortune. Snakes. Supernatural beings. Tests.

---

430. The Horse of Seven Colors
Carmen Dolores Maestri in John Bierhorst, *Latin American Folktales*
Venezuela

A father's two oldest sons doze off when they are sent to see what is eating the wheat field, but the youngest boy keeps himself awake by sticking pins in his hammock and playing his guitar. He catches a little multi-colored horse in the field just before dawn. The horse begs that it will help the boy forever and not eat the wheat if the boy spares his life. He agrees and the grateful horse gives him a secret magic wand to call him with. At harvest time, when the two older sons are rude to an old woman who asks what they are carrying, they end up with horse manure and stones to sell in town. The youngest boy stops to get the old woman a drink of water and brings good money back to his father. The older two leave home, disgusted, and blind the younger boy when he rushes to follow them. He makes his way to a tree where he overhears three witches tell how he can cure his blindness with three leaves from the tree. This works, and he reaches the town where his brothers now live. He does not tell them how he got his eyesight back, and he works as their cook and housekeeper. The boy summons the horse when he hears about a contest to win the hand of the princess. Riding on the horse of seven colors, he tosses an apple onto her bosom where she sits on the balcony and wins. The princess falls in love with him, and they marry. He pardons his brothers and then summons the little seven-colored horse to bring his father, after which the little horse says his debt is paid and disappears.

Connections

Animal helpers. Bargains. Blindness. Brothers and sisters. Competition. Escapes. Horses. Jealousy. Kindness. Magic. Magic horses. Magic leaves. Magic wands. Princes and princesses. Resentment. Supernatural beings. Unkindness. Warlocks and witches. Wounds.

How Else This Story Is Told

Brazilian variation:

The Three Horses—Elsie Spicer Eells, *The Brazilian Fairy Book* and in Frances Frost, *Legends of the United Nations*. In a less-complex telling, a young man finds work in a royal garden which is being trampled by wild horses every night. Black, white, and sorrel—three horses come as Joaquim plays softly on his guitar and help him ride swiftly up the steep stone steps to the Princess's balcony and win her hand by taking the carnation from her hair.

Guatemalan variation:

The Horse of Seven Colors—Hector Felipe Cruz Corzo. In *Jade and Iron: Latin American Tales from Two Cultures*. The jealous older brothers throw the hero in a well, here, rather than blinding him. The competition for the princess's hand involves passing a silver needle through the princess's gold ring as the horse races by.

Note: A lively version of this story, the Little Horse of Seven Colors, which is set in New Mexico, appears in *Tales Our Abuelitas Told* by Ada and Compoy. The section with blindness comes to the New World from Jewish Sephardic tellings of The Wonderful Healing Leaves.

---

431. The Three Stolen Princesses
Yolando Pino-Saavedra, *Folktales of Chile*
Chile

A king who wants only sons has a hag turn his three daughters into oranges. The giant Hairy Dog strikes down the watchman and takes two oranges for his brothers, Shameless and Terrible. A bird fights Manuel, who is guarding the last orange, and flies off with it. Manuel follows the bird's blood to a rock too heavy for him to turn over alone, but two companions help him. Underneath is a hole. Only Manuel is not frightened to go all the way down in the basket. He tells the men to check for him every day. Manuel finds two of the princesses and slays Terrible and Shameless. Hairy Dog is watching the third princess and asks Manuel whether he wants to fight face to face or back to back. Choosing back to back, Manuel jumps on top of the giant and is about to slice off his arm, when Hairy Dog bargains to help if Manuel doesn't kill him. Manuel sends the princesses up in a basket, and the youngest princess gives him her magic ring, in case his companions leave before lifting him up, which they do. They also pretend to the king that they are the ones who saved the princesses. Meanwhile, the magic ring brings Manuel to a place under the earth where he sadly works as a shepherd for the King of the Pigmies for a long time. An eagle offers to fly him out of there for the price of bread and lamb. When the food runs out, Manuel feeds the eagle both of his own calves, which the bird spits out after he sets Manuel down, so he can walk again. Manuel calls for Hairy Dog, who carries him to the palace orchard and tells the youngest princess that Manuel is there. The delighted princess tells the king and queen that she will marry Manuel, who saved her.

CONNECTIONS

Bird helpers. Captivity. Deceit. Eagles. Emperors, kings & queens. Giants. Heroes and heroines. Humorous tales. Journeys to other realms. Magic. Magic rings. Oranges. Parents and children. Princes and princesses. Rescues. Supernatural beings. Transformations. Underground worlds. Warlocks and witches.

HOW ELSE THIS STORY IS TOLD

Grim, Grunt and Grizzle-Tail—Fran Parnell. In this light-hearted version for younger children, the king has transformed his three daughters into oranges because they are naughty.

---

432. JUAN OSO
Angel Vigil, *The Eagle on the Cactus*
Spanish Colonial People. Mexico

A boy always gets into trouble because of his bear-like strength. His mother suggests that people are afraid of Juan, and it is time for him to leave to seek his fortune. People hire him to work, but one day Juan hears a person singing that he can move a river. Juan sings back that he is stronger than that. They wrestle about equally and decide to travel on together. This man, *Mudarrios* the River Mover, tells Juan about *Mudacerros* the Mountain Mover, who joins them. For three nights, a troublemaking forest elf, a *duende*, makes off with their food by disparaging their strength, but Juan sees him disappear into a hole in the ground. The other two lower Juan down, and he finds the *duende's* treasure, along with three captive princesses whom he rescues from a giant, tiger, and a serpent. *Mudarrios* and *Mudacerros* bring up the princesses, but abandon Juan down there, thinking to collect more of the reward for themselves. When the *duende* returns, Juan dangles him by his feet until the elf points the way out of the cavern. When Juan shows up, the two princesses say Juan is really the one who rescued them. *Mudarrios* and *Mudacerros* say it was too dark to know for sure, but then Juan shows the two jewels which the third princess gave him from her crown.

CONNECTIONS

Captivity. Deceit. Devils. Elves. Emperors, kings & queens. Heroes and heroines. Magic. Princes and princesses. Rescues. Reversals of fortune. Strength. Tests. Tricksters. Underground worlds.

HOW ELSE THIS STORY IS TOLD

Juan Oso—Américo Paredes, *Folktales of Mexico*. The troublemaking elf is a devil here.

433. THE GRAPEFRUIT GIRL

Douglas Gifford, *Warriors, Gods & Spirits from Central &*
    South American Mythology
Maya People

The Creator God gives a prince who wants to marry a wife from the world of plants a stone, a cup of water, and a thorn to do it with and warns him that others may interfere. The grapefruit he picks turns into a woman when he whispers, "Give me water." They run from robbers. The thorn he throws down becomes a thicket and the water, an ocean, which swallows them. A witch at the well falls in love with the prince. She presses a thorn into the grapefruit girl's arm, which turns her into a dove, and then passes herself off as the girl. When they arrive at the castle, the dove hovers, calling for the prince. The gardeners catch it and put it in a cage for the prince. When he rides off to war, the witch wants to roast the dove, which cries out to be buried in the garden, rather than being cut up. The witch buries her, and a grapefruit tree grows in that spot. The prince picks a grapefruit for the king's birthday and remembers the young woman. He whispers for this grapefruit to give him water as he did before, and she becomes human again. The witch vanishes, and they live happily together.

CONNECTIONS

Birds. Doves. Gods and humans. Grapefruit. Magic. Magic pins. Magic thorns. Magic waters.
    Plants. Princes and princesses. Rescues. Supernatural beings. Transformations. Warlocks
    and witches.

HOW ELSE THIS STORY IS TOLD

Costa Rican variation:

Three Magic Oranges—Lupe de Osma, *The Witches' Ride* and in Joanna Cole, *Best-Love Folktales
    of the World.* The prince is enchanted that the young woman who appears when he cuts
    open the third orange does not vanish like the other two, but the witch's pin now turns her
    into a dove.

Mexican variation:

La Reina Mora / The Gypsy Queen—Angela Ruiz. At *Magic Tales of Mexico* (Online). The young
    woman who emerges from an orange is replaced by a gypsy witch, who pushes a pin into her
    head.

434. BLANCA ROSA AND THE FORTY THIEVES

Yolando Pino-Saavedra, *Folktales of Chile*
Chile

Before her mother dies, she gives Blanca Rosa a magic mirror, where her daughter can see her and which will give her what she desires. The new stepmother takes the mirror away, when she sees the girl speaking to it. She asks the mirror to tell her who is prettiest. When the mirror answers that it is Blanca Rosa, the stepmother hires men to kill her. They abandon her, and Blanca Rosa hides near the hideout of forty thieves. She helps herself to their food. The guards think the Virgin of Heaven has come to punish them for stealing, until their Chief catches Blanca Rosa, who tells them she is only a poor girl thrown out by her stepmother. The thieves continue to worship beautiful Blanca Rosa, but the stepmother tracks her down and hires a witch to kill her. The witch, disguised as a poor fruit vendor, sticks a magic needle into Blanca Rosa's head, which puts her in a deep sleep. The thieves think she is dead and seal her into a casket with jewels, which they throw into the sea. A prince pulls the casket from the water and finds Blanca Rosa. She looks alive, but he cannot revive her until one day he dislodges the needle while combing her hair. Blanca Rosa sits up. She is so upset about where the thieves have gone, the prince puts the needle back in her head to think. Then he removes the needle again and offers to protect her as his wife, while he searches for the thieves. His two sisters have been spying, and when he leaves the room, they strip Blanca Rosa and toss her into the street. An old cobbler takes Blanca Rosa in until the prince finds her. He punishes his sisters, and the forty thieves attend Blanca Rosa's joyful wedding.

CONNECTIONS

Appearance. Beauty. Brothers and sisters. Deceit. Disguises. Heroes and heroines. Kindness. Love. Magic. Magic mirrors. Magic needles. Princes and princesses. Punishments. Rescues. Snow White tales. Stepmothers and stepdaughters. Thieves. Warlocks and witches.

---

435. THE TALKING BIRD, THE SINGING TREE AND THE FOUNTAIN OF GOLD

Carmen Heny in Carmen Diana Dearden, *Little Book of Latin American Folktales*

Venezuela

A king falls in love with and marries the sister he has overheard saying she would like to marry the king. He brings her older sisters to the palace, too, to marry the royal baker and cook they dreamed of. However, the jealous sisters steal each of the queen's babies as they are born and secretly send them down the river in baskets. Distressed, the king reluctantly believes what they tell him—that the queen is an ogre who eats her babies. He puts her in a cage. A farmer and his wife lovingly raise the two boys and the sister they have pulled from the river. When they die, the oldest boy wants to go find the talking bird, singing tree and fountain of gold that they have heard of. The girl worries for his safety, but he tells her that he will only be in trouble if the knife blade he leaves behind turns cloudy. An old man he meets on the way warns him that people do not return from that mountain. He advises the boy not to look back after the magic marble he gives him stops rolling. When the blade turns cloudy, the second brother goes to find his brother. He does not return either, and the sister sets off to find them both. Wonderful music from the mountain peak stops her just as she is going to turn around. Up there she finds the singing tree and the talking bird in the cage. The bird tells her to pour water from the fountain over the stone people to bring them back to life. Her brothers are free. The bird instructs her to bring him, a tree branch, and a jug of fountain water back home with her. The fountain begins to flow with gold. One afternoon the brothers save the king from a wild boar. After lunching at the palace, they invite him to their place. The bird tells her to make pearl cakes from pearls she finds under the singing tree. The king is amazed by the fountain and the pearls, but the bird tells him that most amazing of all is that he is sitting at a table with his children. The king hears their story and rushes back to free his wife.

CONNECTIONS

Bird helpers. Brothers and sisters. Deceit. Emperors, kings & queens. Enchantment. Heroes and heroines. Jealousy. Journeys. Magic. Magic feathers. Magic fountains. Magic marbles. Magic trees. Music. Parents and children. Quests. Rescues. Stone. Transformations. Warlocks and witches.

HOW ELSE THIS STORY IS TOLD

Brazilian variation:

The Three Sisters and the Children with Golden Stars on Their Brows—Livia de Almeida and Ana Portella, *Brazilian Folktales*

Colombian variation:

The Three Sisters—John Bierhorst, *Latin American Folktales*. The queen's children are taken in by a gardener and his wife when one by one the sisters switch the babies for a dog, a cat, and a stick. After the rescues, the bird reproves the king for not having been surprised before when his wife gave birth to a dog, a cat, and a stick of wood as he is by the pearls he finds inside the little squashes.

Mexican variation:

The Enchanted Forest—Angel Vigil, *The Eagle on the Cactus*. Spanish Colonial People. The deceitful sisters here substitute animals for the babies they steal. Then they plot to kill the girl by sending a witch to entice her into going to find an enchanted forest with a talking bird, magic fruit tree, and river of one thousand colors, so she will get turned to stone.

---

436. THE MAGIC EAGLE

Genevieve Barlow, *Latin American Tales from the Pampas to Mexico City*
Timote People. Venezuela

The gold eagle is a gift from the god Ches, which has been treasured by generations of chieftains, to bring victory to the Timotean people in battle and good fortune during peace. The first chieftain promised to guard it until Ches asked for its return. A young princess is the leader now, strong in wisdom and kindness, but also very ill. One morning, the princess tells her friend Mistafá that she has dreamed that the god Ches requested that the eagle be returned to his temple on the mountain top. She insists that Mistafá take it up there, but Mistafá quakes. Only chieftains go to the temple, and she does not know the way. The princess reassures her that god Ches will guide her. Mistafá is to bury the eagle and call to god Ches three times, and the god will answer. Mistafá makes it to the temple and digs the hole with a sharp rock. She buries the eagle and calls out to god Ches and falls asleep, exhausted. When she wakes a second time, a bush with green leaves and purple flowers is growing where she buried the eagle. A voice tells her to gather its leaves for the priests to use to make tea for the princess. With joy and hope for her friend, Mistafá brings the leaves down. And the tea makes the princess well.

CONNECTIONS

Ches. Courage. Dreams. Eagles. Gods and humans. Healing. Heroes and heroines. Illness. Journeys. Leadership. Magic leaves. Magic statues. Plants. Princes and princesses. Rescues. Talismans.

WHERE ELSE THIS STORY APPEARS

In Kathleen Ragan, *Fearless Girls, Wise Women, and Beloved Sisters*

437. IN THE CITY OF BENJAMIN
Rosa Salas in John Bierhorst, *Latin American Folktales*
Ecuador

None of the many wives King Benjamin marries last more than three nights because he locks them up when their stories run out. A poor girl thinks she will try to marry the king, even though people say he beheads his wives. She leaves off at the exciting part of the story every night and is still queen seven days later. The queen becomes pregnant and says she cannot tell King Benjamin the end of the story because it would horrify him. Now he really wants to know. She has found where the women are being held captive and offers to trade him the end of the story for their release. The king is uncertain. The queen takes matters into her own hands and secretly lets some women go each night. She tells the king the end of the story before giving birth. She is well, the baby is well, and the kingdom is well. King Benjamin is ready for their marriage to thrive.

CONNECTIONS

Captivity. Changes in attitude. Cleverness. Emperors, kings & queens. Heroes and heroines. Husbands and wives. Rescues. Reversals of fortune. Storytelling.

438. THE FAIRY'S GIFTS
Elsie Spicer Eells, *The Brazilian Fairy Book*
Brazil

Searching for his brothers who have left home, José meets a little old woman, a fairy, who tells him there will be trouble, but to follow the path to the sea. She gives him a sponge and a wand, saying only that he is clever and will figure out how to use them. José finds his brothers in the King's court, though they pretend not to recognize him and lie to the King, saying José has offered to find the missing princess. The King tells José his daughter was enchanted by a wicked fairy and has been shut up in a chest in a rock in the sea. Now, José knows what the magic objects are for. He rides the sponge to the rock in the sea and strikes it with the fairy's wand. The wand also opens the chest inside, and inside that is a tiny white egg. With the egg on his head, he rides the sponge back to shore, where the King awaits. Though his brothers mock him, José taps the egg gently with the wand, and the Princess he is to marry emerges.

CONNECTIONS

Brothers and sisters. Deceit. Eggs. Emperors, kings & queens. Fairies. Heroes and heroines. Journeys. Magic. Magic eggs. Magic sponges. Magic wands. Princes and princesses. Rescues. Ridicule. Supernatural beings. Water worlds.

---

439. THE WISE WOMAN OF CÓRDOBA

Hinojosa, Francisco, *The Old Lady Who Ate People*
Mexico

Despite the fact that she helps the poor who come to her for help with money or love troubles, some say this beautiful woman has connections with the devil. Some say no, she is wise and can make wishes come true. Some say she can appear different to different people at the same time. Some say she can fly. Then she is arrested and brought to Mexico City to be burned as a witch. News arrives that she has escaped in a ship drawn in charcoal on the wall. She has asked a judge what the drawing needed, and when he said someone to sail it, she leaped aboard and steered the ship across the wall and away.

CONNECTIONS

Accusations. Captivity. Escapes. Kindness. Magic. Rumors. Supernatural beings. Warlocks and witches. Heroes and heroines.

HOW ELSE THIS STORY IS TOLD

The Enchantress of Córdoba—Francisco Serrano. In *Jade and Iron*. The enchantress who helps people is a beautiful black woman called Mulata, who never seems to grow old and has never married.

---

440. HOW A WITCH ESCAPED

John Bierhorst, *The Monkey's Haircut*
Kekchi Maya People

People blame the old witch for annoying the snake who lives underground and causing him to shift and make the earth shake. They want to punish her. When they go to her cave, she says she needs to say goodbye to her boatmen first and steps into the picture of a boat drawn on the floor and disappears. So, she is gone and it has been quiet for a while, but the earth is shaking again so badly that the great horned serpent is spewing fire and ash into the air. The witch holds maguey thread when the messengers bring her to the market. She says the horned serpent has a worm in his tooth which she can drive out, but she has to go to the clouds to get his medicine. She ties the thread to a stick in the ground and tosses the ball of thread in the air, climbs up it and is gone.

CONNECTIONS

Accusations. Escapes. Healers. Heroes and heroines. Illness. Snakes. Supernatural beings. Teeth. Volcanoes. Warlocks and witches.

HOW ELSE THIS STORY IS TOLD

The Snake's Toothache—Melinda Lilly. The Snake is bad-tempered, and the witch uses her healing magic to try to keep him calm so his volcanic fire will not destroy her village. First the chief has a worm in his tooth, and she calls upon the snake's power to help him. Then the Snake himself is in pain and tells her, as the ground rumbles, that he needs to eat her to get well, but she cures his toothache and saves herself and the village.

---

441. THE GIRL AND THE PUMA
M.A. Jagendorf and R.S. Boggs, *The King of the Mountains*
Argentina

Around 1535, indigenous people who are battling to keep from being enslaved have surrounded the Spanish settlement at Buenos Aires. The Spanish captain has ordered that anyone who leaves without his permission will be hung. Young Señorita Moldonado is too hungry and slips out one afternoon, crawling to find bits of fruit. When dusk comes, she creeps into a cave and is terrified by a puma's growl. Then the young woman notices that the puma has just given birth and is in pain. She sets her fear aside and helps another cub be born. After this, she stays with the puma family until a band of Querandí people capture her when she goes out for water. She lives in their village and is treated well. Spaniards on a raiding party find her there and bring her back to the settlement. The captain is going to hang Señorita Moldonado for disobeying orders, but the people in the colony plead for her. Instead, he orders her tied to a tree for the wild animals to consume. When people go to check a week later, however, she is unharmed. The puma has helped her stay alive. They bring her back, and the captain relents. Señorita Moldonado's story spreads, and much later, across the Plata River in Uruguay, a city is named in memory of her kindness and courage.

CONNECTIONS

Animal helpers. Courage. Cultural conflict. Disobedience. Gratitude. Heroes and heroines. Kindness. Moldonato, Senorita. Pumas. Punishments. Rescues. Sieges. Soldiers.

HOW ELSE THIS STORY IS TOLD

The Girl and the Puma—Jane Yolen, *Mightier Than the Sword*
The Señorita and the Puma—Pleasant DeSpain, *The Emerald Lizard*

XVI

Strange and Mysterious Encounters

---

442. THE HUNTER AND THE CURUPIRA
Juan Carlos Galeano, *Folktales of the Amazon*
Amazonia, Brazil

A skilled hunter along the Iça River lies down to rest after catching a large bird and some monkeys before heading home. At dusk pounding on the tree wakes him, and a creature with a hairy face and one foot pointed backward sits down next to him. The hunter realizes that it is a Curupira, forest guardian, who now asks for a piece of his arm to eat. The hunter gives him a monkey arm. When the Curupira asks for his heart, he hands over a monkey's heart, which the Curupira eats with pleasure. Then Curupira demands the hunter's knife, saying he meant the hunter's own heart. The hunter stabs the Curupira with his knife. The Curupira becomes a tree trunk. When the hunter and his wife come back to see what kind of wood it is, the wood is too hard for his machete, so he whacks the trunk with an axe. The Curupira comes out of the tree grateful to have been woken up.

CONNECTIONS
Conflict. Curupira. Hunters. Magic. Magic arrows. Supernatural beings. Transformations.

HOW ELSE THIS STORY IS TOLD
Curupira and the Hunter—Livia de Almeida and Ana Portella, *Brazilian Folktales*. After he kills the Curupira, João returns to take back his knife. When he pulls it out, however, the Curupira wakes up and thanks João for coming back. He gives João an enchanted arrow, which will bring him whatever game he wants on the condition he never show it to anyone. After João shows the arrow to his wife, the tapir he aims at turns into a flying serpent and disappears.

The Hairy Man from the Forest—Frances Carpenter, *South American Wonder Tales*. The curupira here takes the hunter's clothes when he falls asleep and goes to his house, pretending to be the hunter. He's very shaggy, though, and in the night, the hunter's wife runs away with her son. When the curupira cannot find them, he returns to the hunter and demands his heart in payment for having slept under his tree. The hunter tricks him with monkey's heart, but then the curupira, who is not so smart, thinks he will cut out his own heart to eat. He seems to die, only rising again when the hunter hits his hard head with an axe to collect his green teeth. The curupira thanks the man for waking him and gives him a magic arrow.

443. SMART DAI-ADALLA
M.A. Jagendorf and R.S. Boggs, *The King of the Mountains*
Guyana

Dai-adalla much prefers to stay home than go to the fiesta in a neighboring village with her parents, and so they leave her to do chores and observe the forest animals. A noise draws her outside, and a dear friend she hasn't seen for a long time says she has come to spend the night. Dai-adalla does not know her friend is really an evil wood spirit in disguise. Because she knows her friend likes to eat frogs, she suggests they separate to catch some. When the spirit calls that it is eating many frogs, Dai-adalla becomes frightened—people do not eat frogs alive. She calls back for the spirit to be quiet so the frogs will not be frightened and runs home. Once there, Dai-adalla turns over all the clay pots and climbs up onto the roof. The evil spirit knows Dai-adalla has tricked him when she no longer answers at all. He turns up all the pots to find her and screeches that he should have eaten her with the frogs. She waits quietly, while the spirit races around all night. It leaves at daybreak. After that, Dai-adalla always accompanies her parents on their outings.

CONNECTIONS
Cautionary tales. Cleverness. Conflict. Disguises. Escapes. Fear. Parents and children. Spirits. Supernatural beings.

---

444. THE COURIER
Lulu Delacre, *Golden Tales*
Quechua People. Bolivia

The Quechua Josucho, a courier, is sent by the mayor to bring two urgent letters over the mountains to the capital. When he reaches the raised stone for the spirit of the mountain at Apachita, he picks up a stone to leave on the altar and says a prayer. But before he can place the stone, he sees an *allqö*, a strange hairy dog, sitting there. Frightened, he puts the stone in his slingshot and hits the dog. The dog screams and limps away. He continues walking. A young girl appears, winding black yarn into a ball. He is attracted to and also a little frightened of this beautiful girl who knows his name and accompanies him. When it starts to grow dark, she shares his food, but when he kisses her and his hand brushes her hip, she howls that it hurts from where he hit her with the rock before. She transforms into a snarling dog, and Josucho runs. When he returns, the villagers of Ayllukullama hunt down and burn this hairy dog which had possessed a young girl.

CONNECTIONS
Accusations. Dogs. Fear. Identity. Messengers. Possession. Punishments. Supernatural beings. Transformations. Unkindness.

445. The Dog Who Spoke / El perro que habló

James D. Sexton and Fredy Rodrígues-Mejía, *The Dog Who Spoke*
Maya People. Sololá, Guatemala

Eerie things begin to happen to people who have built *ranchos* on some land which used to belong to an old man and woman. Pots and beds move by themselves; they hear sweeping sounds; and a hairy arm once reaches across the room and then vanishes. A *secreto* ritual does not chase any evil spirits away. One family buys a dog to guard the house, but the man beats it when it will not stop barking. The next day the dog rebukes the man, saying he was barking at an old man and woman. The man is shocked to hear the dog speak. The dog says the master will now take his place and see for himself. He rubs the man's eyes and dies. The dog-man now behaves like a dog, running out to the porch, but he cannot bark. When he sees an old couple sweeping, moving from one rancho to another, he wants to tell his family, but he cannot. This is because he unfairly hit a dog who was doing his job.

Connections

Abuse. Accusations. Cautionary tales. Dogs. Ghosts. Punishments. Supernatural beings. Transformations. Unkindness.

446. Yanapuma: Black Jaguar Vampire

Juan Carlos Galeano, *Folktales of the Amazon*
Amazonia, Peru

Everyone scoffs when the hunter hired to find game for the logging camp cook says that they should move from the Pachitea River for he has seen a Yanapuma, the devil's jaguar, in the woods. The hunter warns them that the white jaguar will only attack at night, but no weapon works against it except for a spear. The loggers say that they cannot leave the cedar and mahogany trees. The hunter finds them all dead the next day at dusk. Marks on their necks show where the Yanapuma sucked their blood. Their rifles were useless. Sad and angry, the hunter climbs a tree to wait for the Yanapuma. The beast roars and tries to climb his tree, but the hunter spears it and the female, too. It is still night when the hunter starts out to notify their relatives, and he hears the loggers' voices apologizing.

Connections

Fear. Hunters. Magic jaguars. Monsters. Revenge. Supernatural beings. Vampires. Warnings. Woodcutters. Yanapuma.

447. Renacal: A Grove of Magical Trees

Juan Carlos Galeano, *Folktales of the Amazon*
Amazonia, Peru

A father-in-law warns the men who are leaving to catch fish in the lake near the Samira River that a giant anaconda owns the fish there, but they go anyway. It storms in the night and the island of renaco trees which was across the lake the day before vanishes and then reappears, only closer to shore. One man says that he dreamed that a tall woman came out of the renaco trees with anaconda fingers which caught fish for her. She told him everything there—fish, trees, and animals—come from her body, and they should go somewhere else. The men do stay and fish from a raft that day, but when another storm rises and the whole the island of renacos starts moving very quickly in the lightning and thunder. They pole back out of there as quickly as they can.

CONNECTIONS

Anacondas. Dreams. Fear. Islands. Renaco trees. Magic snakes. Magic trees. Supernatural beings. Trees. Warnings.

448. BOA PLANTS: PLANTS TURN INTO ANIMALS

Juan Carlos Galeano, *Folktales of the Amazon*
Amazonia, Peru

A young couple on the banks of the Huallaga River enjoys the two boa plants they were given by their uncle. They do not mind that the plants turn into two boa constrictors at night, unwinding from their spots and slithering to the pond. The woman cares for the plants, which keeps rats away, and when the man's job takes them away to Iquitos, she thinks the plants will thrive better if they stay. She pays the new owner to take care of them. The new owner tells the wife that her husband finds the plants evil. One day, when the wife comes back to visit, the plants are gone. The new owner says her husband attacked the plants one night. Blood sprayed everywhere, which turned into dried leaves in the morning.

CONNECTIONS

Boa constrictors. Boa plants. Conflict. Fear. Husbands and wives. Magic plants. Magic snakes. Plants. Snakes. Supernatural beings. Transformations.

449. SERINGA: MOTHER OF THE RUBBER TREES

Juan Carlos Galeano, *Folktales of the Amazon*
Amazonia, Brazil

A lonely man taps rubber trees by himself on the bank of the Yavari River. When he comes home one day to find smoked tapir with farinha already cooked for him, he is delighted, but puzzled. The same thing happens the next day, but this time "Humans don't know what trees know" is carved beside the food. A little worried now, he returns early the next day and hides behind a nut tree. A young woman walks out of the seringa tree, wearing bark clothes. She holds a bird to fan the kitchen fire and then lets it go. She keeps glancing back as if she knows the tapper is hiding, but when he actually steps out, she disappears, right through the walls of his little house. She only returns once in a dream to ask why he could not be happy just with what she was giving. After that, the trees yield less and less latex and he leaves.

Connections

Accusations. Dreams. Gifts. Loneliness. Punishments. Magic trees. Shiringa trees. Supernatural beings. Trees.

450. Taina

Johannes Wilbert, *Folk Literature of the Warao Indians*
Warao People. Venezuela and Guyana

A Warao man and woman who are trapping fish meet a friendly stranger who invites them to stay with him. He tells them he has been raising peccary in the forest of this island to replenish the supply killed off in an epidemic. He is kind and it is peaceful there, and so they stay. The people from their village who have been sent to bring them back also end up staying. One man, Taina resists being herded into line by the peccary raiser. He reports that over time the people begin to walk bent over and change more and more into peccary. He keeps spying. The women's breasts lengthen and multiply. The people make a huffing whistle sound and their bodies become covered with bristles. Horrified, Taina yells that he is going to kill them, but the peccaries flee into the forest when he goes home for weapons. He curses the peccary people saying that villagers will hunt them from now on.

Connections

Captivity. Conflict. Curses. Escapes. Identity. Magic peccaries. Origin tales. Peccaries. Scary tales. Supernatural beings. Transformations.

451. Evil Rocks and the Evil Spirit of Peru

M.A. Jagendorf and R.S. Boggs, *The King of the Mountains*
Inca People. Peru

When a goat goes missing in the Andes Mountains, an Inca woman leaves her daughter to play by two tall rocks while she searches further on. The Devil, *la vieja Capusa*, comes down in a dark cloud looking just like the girl's mother. She lures the girl inside the two magic rocks, which resemble the girl's home when they open and then close to become rocks again. No one can find the child. Her parents grieve, and one day her father climbs up to those rocks, and there is his daughter, tossing little colored stones by the entrance. He is afraid to approach any closer. She disappears back inside, and the rocks close behind her. He returns with villagers in the hope of rescuing his daughter. When the rocks open and his daughter comes out to play, her father throws a big stone into the opening. The rocks close, and her father rushes to her, but the girl will not stop crying for the Capusa mother. She does not ever recognize her real mother and dies soon after, despite work by the witch doctor. Ever since then, children are taught to cross themselves when they see a lone dark cloud and to render Capusa harmless by asking her to show them her vulture feet.

CONNECTIONS
Captivity. Cautionary tales. Devil. Disguises. Evil. Fear. Identity. Magic. Magic rocks. Parents and children. Rescues. Shamans. Supernatural beings. Transformations.

---

452. LAMPARILLA: GLOWING GHOST
Juan Carlos Galeano, *Folktales of the Amazon*
Amazonia, Peru

Sometimes a schoolteacher from the city who now works on the Tapiche River drinks a little too much. The villagers warn him to beware the Lamparilla who kills drunkards, but he dismisses this as an ignorant story. One night during Carnaval, though, he turns when he senses that someone is following him along the banks of the Tapiche River. There is a person with a light at the height of his chest. The teacher walks faster, but now the light is trapping him from all sides. He stops and prays to God. Just then, people from the party appear, and the Lamparilla disappears, for it cannot take souls when people are there. That is the last time he gets drunk. One night he dreams that the lamprilla tells him that they would now be traveling together had the teacher been evil.

CONNECTIONS
Cautionary tales. Changes in attitude. Dreams. Drink. Escapes. Fear. Ghosts. Lamparilla. Monsters. Punishments. Scary tales. Teachers. Warnings.

---

453. HORSE'S HOOVES AND CHICKEN FEET
Aureliano Guzmán in Américo Paredes, *Folktales of Mexico*
Mexico

Silvestre Guzmán goes to a dance one night with some of his friends and does not leave until late. He and his friends hear music and head over that way, not ready to stop partying. They follow the music to a patio where they have never been before, far from San Pedro. They are dancing with partners when one man notices that all of the women there have chicken feet and all the men have hooves. They leave rapidly and walk home past dawn. Talking it over, they decide they must have entered a witch's ball.

CONNECTIONS
Cautionary tales. Dances. Fear. Identity. Supernatural beings. Warlocks and witches.

HOW ELSE THIS STORY IS TOLD
Horse Hooves and Chicken Feet—Neil Philip, *Horse Hooves and Chicken Feet*

454. THE FLYING SKELETON / EL ESQUELETO VOLADOR

Olga Loya, *Momentos Mágicos / Magic Moments*
Chol People. Mexico

Three boys who live with their uncle think it's odd that he sleeps until afternoon and stays up all night. He tucks them in at night, after leaving a big white hat and small broom by the door, and tells them not to get up. However, the oldest boy, Pedro, hears the door open and wonder where his uncle goes. One night, Pedro hears voices in the kitchen and peeks. The room is full of skeletons in many different kinds of hats having a party. One skeleton has a white hat just like his uncle's. The next night, Pedro and his brothers follow their uncle. Hiding, they hear him tell his flesh to go away. He becomes a skeleton with transparent wings and flies away. At dawn, their uncle returns and his flesh winds back onto his bones. The boys now fear their uncle. Several days later, they pour salt, lemon juice, and chili powder on the flesh he leaves behind. Their uncle shrieks when he cannot put himself back together and flies away with the sound of bones breaking.

CONNECTIONS

Brothers and sisters. Curiosity. Fear. Identity. Scary tales. Skeletons. Supernatural beings. Transformations. Uncles and nephews.

455. THE TEETH

Alvin Schwartz, *In a Dark, Dark Room*
Suriname

Coming home late at night, one man is stopped by another man who asks him what time it is. He tells him, and the stranger lights a match, studies the watch, and then smiles, and his teeth are three inches long! The first man takes off running. A second stranger asks why he's running, and he tells him. And then this man grins and his teeth are even longer. The man takes off running again. He meets another stranger whose teeth are the longest of all and runs home.

CONNECTIONS

Cautionary tales. Fear. Scary tales. Supernatural beings. Teeth.

HOW ELSE THIS STORY IS TOLD

Yorka Teeth 1—Melville J. Herskovits and Frances Herskovits, *Suriname Folk-Lore.* This telling ends with the proverb: "Experience will teach you."

456. THE SKELETON'S REVENGE

Robert D. San Souci, *Even More Short & Shivery:*
　　Forty-Five Spine-Tingling Tales
Mexico

Kind and respected Padre Juan feels responsible to learn more about the wealthy nobleman, Don Duarte, who has been aggressively courting his niece Margarita, an orphan. In Mexico City he hears about Don Duarte's reckless and womanizing past and forbids Margarita to see him again. Don Duarte persists, however. One night he waits for the priest on the stone bridge which leads to his house outside of Santiago. The nobleman promises to reform. When he sees that Padre Juan does not believe him, Don Duarte plunges his knife into the priest's head. He cannot remove the knife and pushes the padre off the bridge and goes. No one knows what has happened to the priest. Don Duarte cannot forget Margarita. He knows she returned his love. However, as he crosses the bridge to persuade her to come away with him, Don Duarte is strangled by a skeleton with a dagger in his skull.

CONNECTIONS

Forbidden love. Gamblers. Love. Murder. Orphans. Priests and priestesses. Punishments. Revenge. Scary tales. Skeletons. Supernatural beings. Uncles and nieces.

HOW ELSE THIS STORY IS TOLD

The Avenging Skeleton—E. Adams Davis, *Of the Night Wind's Telling*

The Hand of Death—Arielle North Olson and Howard Schwartz, *Ask the Bones: Scary Stories from around the World*

Skeleton's Revenge: A Tale from Tlacopán—Richard and Judy Dockery Young, *1492: New World Tales*. Aztec People. An Aztec warrior who has gambled his life into slavery playing patolli stabs the winner in the skull. One year later, the skeleton pulls the knife from his skull and stabs him.

---

457. THE OLD LADY WHO ATE PEOPLE

Francisco Hinojosa, *The Old Lady Who Ate People: Frightening Stories*
Mexico

A frighteningly evil and smelly old woman from Guatemala now lives in a cave near Tuxtla Chico. Not only is she squat and unwashed, but she lures travelers in and then transforms into a fearsome beast to eat them. A witch-man arrives from Guatemala to avenge some harm she once did him. This man, who looks like a farmer, but is really made of stone, promises to get rid of her. Unknowing, the woman takes him in to spend the night and prepares to eat him as she did the others, but when she bites, her teeth and paws break against his stone. Only rags are left in the morning, and the air in Tuxtla Chico clears.

CONNECTIONS

Conflict. Disguises. Monsters. Revenge. Stone. Supernatural beings. Transformations. Warlocks and witches.

458. THE DEAD MAN WHO WAS ALIVE
Anita Brenner, *The Boy Who Could Do Anything*
Mexico

An epidemic of Yellow Cholera is causing quick burials, as people fear getting sick. Pedro is a gravedigger and sometimes leaves water and bread in the graves, in case the dead get hungry. But then Pedro dies. He is buried straight into the ground with water and bread, since there is no time for a coffin. Once the disease has abated, people come to visit the cemetery. A little boy who is stomping on top of Pedro's grave is startled when a voice asks him to stop because dirt is getting in his eyes. When people ask, Pedro answers that he is both dead and alive. He tells the priest he would love to get some fresh air. They dig Pedro up. He isn't sure he wants to go home with the priest and work, until the priest tells him he can ring the church bells. That sounds fine to Pedro, and people wonder if he really died or is just being Pedro.

CONNECTIONS
Cemeteries. Death. Humorous tales. Illness. Mysteries.

459. ELVES (B)
Francisco Quintero in Américo Paredes, *Folktales of Mexico*
Mexico

Elves abound in the old days and play mean tricks, like drowning a man in the flour at his own mill. When a family tries to sneak away from their house and their elf, the elf pipes up that it has brought the broom.

CONNECTIONS
Conflict. Elves. Humorous tales. Supernatural beings.

HOW ELSE THIS STORY IS TOLD
The Big Hatted Duede / El duende sombrerudo—Paula Martin, *Pachamama Tales*

460. *FUNNY, FUNNY*
Anita Brenner, *The Boy Who Could Do Anything*
Mexico

Pancho shoots when he hears a nahual scream in his cornfield at night. The next morning a stranger arrives with a hurt leg. Pancho finds something suspiciously unsettling about the man and refuses to help him. The next day when Pancho bends over to take juice from the magueys, something butts him again and again, though he sees nothing. When he arrives home bruised, a bird with a human head scolds him to be kinder to others. Time goes by and Pancho marries and has a daughter who falls in love with a lazy man, Felipe. For six months Felipe pretends to be a nahual, calling from the tree that Pancho has to let him marry his daughter. Pancho isn't sure that Felipe isn't a nahual. His wife thinks they should go ahead and let them marry, but now Felipe is stand-offish, and so they promise Felipe he will not have to work. Felipe turns out to be a good son-in-law, though Pancho hesitates to ask if he is a nahual.

CONNECTIONS

Bargains. Courtship. Fathers-in-law and mothers-in law. Identity. Marriage. Mysteries. Nahuals. Parents and children. Supernatural beings.

461. LITTLEBIT
Manuel Oporto in John Bierhorst, *Latin American Folktales*
Chile

The day after a poor wife says that having a child, "even a little bit of a thing," could help them in the hard times, a tiny baby boy wriggles out of her sleeve into the washtub. The parents love their finger-sized child, whose voice and strength grow far beyond his height. When Littlebit goes to the butcher for some scraps of meat and says he can manage more, the butcher tests him with a whole steer, which Littlebit carries just fine. The same with bread, sugar, and tea. Going for onions, Littlebit is swallowed by a cow and cuts his way out with a penknife. Stories about him spread, and now the king wants to meet him. Littlebit trains a mouse to be his horse and rides with his penknife as a sword. Intrigued, the king asks him to stay, but when Littlebit says his parents need him, the king brings them to the palace, too. Littlebit serves in the army and enjoys his success in the spotlight.

CONNECTIONS

Appearance. Babies. Emperors, kings & queens. Humorous tales. Loyalty. Magic. Parents and children. Size. Strength. Supernatural beings. Tests.

462. THE WILD CHERRY TREE
Bill Gordh, *Stories in Action*
Mexico

When a little old man and woman need water, the tomato rolls off their table to fetch some. On the way to the river, however, the tomato stops to eat cherries from the cherry tree. When the tomato does not return, they send the onion and then the chili pepper, which also stop to eat cherries. The man and woman go to get the water themselves and also stop at the cherry tree. The river floods and floats the tree with them all in it into the Gulf of Mexico. They swim to shore, walk home, and sit back down at the table, still thirsty.

CONNECTIONS

Cherry trees. Floods. Journeys. Magic chili peppers. Magic onions. Magic tomatoes. Magic trees. Plant helpers. Supernatural beings. Thirst. Tomatoes. Water.

463. THE INSIDE-OUT ROBE

Alex Whitney, *Voices in the Wind*
Quiché Maya People. Guatemala

Cabrakan's work is to make sure none of the fires go out in the vessels at Temple of the Seven Flames, which have been burning with oil for hundreds of years. When Raxah, High Priestess of the temple, wishes that she could hear the tiny ku-bird chirp every day, Cabrakan secretly decides to capture one for her. He heads into the rain forest, but he does not know it well and becomes lost and frightened by sounds. Crashing through the undergrowth, Cabrakan at last stumbles upon his own footprints and follows them back. He oversleeps the next morning and leaps up, suddenly remembering that he needs to fill the vessels. He first hurriedly pulls his robe on inside out, takes time to reverse it, and then runs. Trying to avoid a collision with Raxah, though, Cabrakan overturns the vessels, and all of the fires go out. He blames his robe; she tells him he has been careless. Cabrakan worries about being punished, but when he finds Raxah, she happily tells him that a ku-bird built a nest in the garden while he was gone. Still, he makes sure never to reverse his robe again.

CONNECTIONS

Accidents. Birds. Clothing. Cu (bird). Fear. Fire. Lost. Priests and priestesses. Quests. Supernatural beings. Superstitions. Tasks.

464. MATINTA-PERERA: DEVIOUS PEOPLE TURN INTO BIRDS

Juan Carlos Galeano, *Folktales of the Amazon*
Amazonia, Brazil

The children of a couple who run a small store are enchanted by the owlet one logger walks in with. He gives the owl to the store owner on the condition that he can visit and frequently arrives with bread and milk for the owl. The storekeeper's servant suspects that the owl is a Matinta-perera, a bird with a person inside who bothers others until it is promised something which it cannot refuse. The storekeeper's wife thinks that is just a story, but a bird starts whistling after midnight now. It disappears before the villagers can invite the creature for coffee in the morning and find out who it might be. When the servant hears the whistling at night and shines a flashlight on the aviary, she sees the owl missing. Yet it is back eating breakfast in the morning. She tells the storekeeper who hides behind a tree the next night. When he hears whistles coming from the wood carver's shop, he shouts, "Friend, come by for coffee." The next day the wood carver appears, embarrassed to have been found out.

CONNECTIONS
Birds. Identity. Magic owls. Matinta perera. Mysteries. Owls. Supernatural beings. Tests. Transformations. Vendors. Wood carvers.

---

465. THE MYSTERY OF ELM GROVE STREET / EL MISTERIO DE LA CALLE DE OLMEDO

Genevieve Barlow and William N. Stivers, *Stories from Mexico / Historias de México*
Mexico

A man stops a priest one cold night in Mexico City and asks him to come to hear the confession of his sister who is very ill. The priest accompanies him to an elegant house on Elm Grove Street, where a weak young woman thanks the priest for coming to give her last rites. The man sits and reads while the woman and priest pray. An hour later, the priest is surprised when the man rushes him out. They exit, and the man heads off. The priest hears a terrifying scream from the house, but cannot get back in. Unsettled, the priest heads to the monastery, but remembers he left his rosary on her bed. The next day, a policeman helps the priest enter the house, where neighbors say no one has lived for many years. A skeleton lies with hands together and the rosary by its side.

CONNECTIONS
Ghosts. Kindness. Mysteries. Prayer. Priests and priestesses. Skeletons. Supernatural beings.

---

466. GIRL IN WHITE

S.E. Schlosser, *American Folklore.net* (Online)
Mexico

A man is not happy to come to a dance without his girlfriend, who stayed home to take care of her mother. When his friend suggests he dance with someone else, he sees a pale girl with dark eyes behind a fern. When they dance, he wants to get angry at the man who keeps bumping into her. And then, his friend teases that he is dancing alone. The man is annoyed at his friend, until he brings the girl a drink outside and realizes he can see through her. She fades, he runs, and his friend tells him the next day the spirit was Consuela, who died long ago before her first ball.

CONNECTIONS
Dances. Fear. Ghosts. Supernatural beings.

---

467. THE PHANTOM CHILDREN

Américo Paredes, *Folktales of Mexico*
Mexico

An older woman tells this story of when her mother was younger and would play with her brother near the lake with some children they meet where the woods are thick. At first their parents dismiss the story as make-believe because no one else lives near. However, when the children repeat this story every day, complete with details about what the little blonde girl and boy look like, their mother follows them one day. She becomes frightened when she sees what looks like a part of white skirt whisk behind a bush. The mother goes to an old sheepherder who lives nearby. The sheepherder also sees something hide behind the bush and runs at it with his stick. No children are there, but a black dog with fiery eyes growls at him. He crosses himself, but when the dog does not run, the sheepherder backs away. Men with guns and machetes come, and a priest prays at the spot, but no one ever sees anything unusual there again. Some say that a brother and sister, traveling from Texas long ago, had been killed at that spot by their uncle, who wanted their money.

CONNECTIONS

Fear. Ghosts. Magic dogs. Murder. Mysteries. Parents and children. Storytelling. Supernatural beings.

---

468. THE VOICE OF THE DEAD

Artemio de Valle-Arizpe in Francisco Hinojosa, *The Old Lady Who Ate People*

Mexico

One midnight when the nuns go to chapel to sing, a high sweet voice joins in. Sometimes the voice sounds sad and desperate. They do not know who it can be. A young nun tells Mother Superior that she has counted one more nun walking in the line to chapel than are in the choir. The voice returns and begins to sound more anxious. Mother Superior follows the line of nuns one night, and the last nun separates and heads to the cemetery and vanishes. The next night, the Mother Superior commands the last nun to state if she belongs to this world and what she wants. It is the ghost of Sister Luisa who recently died. She says she repents the vanity of her youth, the way she never helped the other sisters, and skipped prayers, and seeks forgiveness from Mother Superior in order to rest. Mother Superior forgives her, but tells the ghost she must now leave. The voice joins the choir one more night and goes in a flash of light.

CONNECTIONS

Changes in attitude. Forgiveness. Ghosts. Music. Mysteries. Repentance. Righting a wrong. Selfishness. Supernatural beings. Vanity. Supernatural voices.

---

469. THE MAN WHO WANTED TO LEARN TO BE A BRUJO AND A CHARACOTEL

Enrique Miguel Menéndez in James D. Sexton, *Heart of Heaven, Heart of Earth*

Maya People

Young Quique Miguel is heading for trouble and does not want a regular job. A brujo agrees to teach him to be a warlock if Quique Miguel can pass eight cemetery tests. By the third test, however, Quique Miguel is frozen with fear. He does not want to be picked up in a whirlwind by a fierce man and poked with a lance. His father, the shaman, has to perform rituals in the cemetery to cure him. Quique Miguel apprentices to a characotel with a cat spirit, who helps Death to bring spirits to the other world. For three nights the characotel tries to confuse an old man into dying with the sound of breaking bowls and pots. Relatives run in and find no broken pots. When the man does not die, the characotel tells Quique Miguel it is his turn to try. Because Quique Miguel does not yet have an animal spirit, the clay pots really do break. When the relatives run in, he falls and breaks his bones. Quique Miguel spends the rest of the night in pain. Again, his shaman father has to perform a costumbre for his soul. After that, Quique Miguel gives up sorcery as a career.

CONNECTIONS

Bargains. Demons. Fear. Humorous tales. Magic. Parents and children. Shamans. Sorcerers. Supernatural beings. Tests. Warlocks and witches. Work.

---

470. THE EARTH ATE THEM

John Bierhorst, *Latin American Folktales*
Argentina

A stingy old man makes his three daughters promise they will bury him with the sack containing all of his gold and silver coins. They do this, but are living in such poverty, they decide to take the bag back from his grave. The eldest daughter brings home the coins. That night, their father returns from the dead and knocks. Frightened, they do not open the door and replace the bag in the morning. Still, they really need the money, and the second daughter retrieves the coins. Again that night, their father comes knocking, and again they return the bag in the morning. Now the youngest daughter takes the bag and hides it. When their father knocks that night, she opens the door and leads him to his chair. When she asks where his legs are, he hollowly answers that the earth has eaten them. He answers the same about the other parts of his body. When she then asks where the bag of coins is, he believes that if they do not know then they are not the ones who took it, and he runs angrily away.

CONNECTIONS

Fear. Humorous tales. Justice. Misers. Misunderstandings. Money. Parents and children. Promises. Supernatural beings. Thieves. Tricksters.

HOW ELSE THIS STORY IS TOLD

Variation from Paraguay:

Endnote to The Earth Ate Them—John Bierhorst, *Latin American Folktales*. A thief sneaks into the cemetery to steal a rich widow's jewels from her coffin, but the corpse opens its eyes when he is pulling a fancy comb from her hair. In a comedy of errors, his poncho then catches. The terrified thief thinks the corpse is reaching for him and eventually manages to run off, now totally white-haired and out of his mind.

Appendix A
Indigenous Peoples by Country, with Alternate Names

Common languages are provided for tribes with smaller populations, which are often grouped by those languages.

Tales identified as coming from Amazonia may include indigenous populations from any of the following countries: Bolivia, Colombia, Ecuador, French Guiana, Guyana, Peru, Suriname and Venezuela.

Tales identified as coming from the Andes Mountains may include indigenous populations from any of the following countries: Argentina, Bolivia, Chile, Colombia, Ecuador, Peru, and Venezuela.

ARGENTINA

Guaraní
Inca "Children of the Sun": Quechua, *also* Quichua, Kichwa
Mapuche. Araucanian speakers
Mocoví
Ona, *also* Onawo, Selk'nam
Pilaga
Tehuelche
Toba, *also* Qom
Yahgan, *also* Yamana, Yagán, Tequenica. Islands south of Tierra del Fuego

BELIZE

Maya: Kekchi, *also* Q'eqchi'; Mopan, *also* Mopan Maya; and Yucatec Maya Speakers

BOLIVIA

Aymara, *also* Aimara, Aymará
Bororo. Gê speakers
Chimane, *also* Tsimané
Guaraní
Inca "Children of the Sun": Quechua, *also* Quichua, Kichwa, Runakuna, Ingas

Tacana
Toba, *also* Qom

BRAZIL

Anambé
Apinagé, *also* Apinayé, Apinajé. Gê language speakers
Bororo. Gê language speakers
Caraja, *also* Carajá, Karaja, Karajá, Iny. Gê language speakers
Carib, *also* Karina, Kalina
Cayapo, *also* Kayapó, Mebengokre. Gê language speakers
Crenye. Gê language speakers
Guaraní
Kamaiurá, *also* Kamaiurá Xingu, Kamayura
Kulina
Manao. Arawakan language speakers
Maue, *also* Sateré-Mawé, Sateré-Maue
Mundurucú, *also* Munduruku, Wuy Jugu
Opaye, *also* Ofayé
Pemón, *also* Jaricuna; Kamarakoto; Macuxi or Makuxi; Taurepang: Arecuna, *also* Arekuna; Taurepang: Tualipang

287

Shikrin. Gê language speakers
Tamoio, *also* Tupi
Tapuyu, *also* Tapui
Tupi
Yanomami, *also* Yạnomamö, Yanoma, Ye'k-
  wana, Ye'Kuana, Yekuana, Yequana,
  Yecuana, Dekuana, Maquiritare, Makir-
  itare

Chile

Aymara *also* Aimara, Aymará
Inca "Children of the Sun": Quechua, *also*
  Quichua, Kichwa
Mapuche. Araucanian language speakers
Ona, *also* Onawo, Selk'nam
Tehuelche

Colombia

Chibcha, *also* Muisca
Cuna, *also* Guna, Kuna
Goajiro, *also* Guajiro, Wahiro, Wayu,
  Wayuu, Wayúu
Inca "Children of the Sun": Quechua, *also*
  Kichwa, Quichua
Yupa, *also* Yukpa, Yuco, Yucpa, Yuko

Ecuador

Amazonia "Children of the Sun": Quechua,
  also Quichua, Kichwa, Runakuna, Ingas

El Salvador

Pipil, *also* Cuzcatlecs

French Guiana

Carib *also* Karina, Kalina

Guatemala

Maya
  Cakchiquel, *also* Kaqchikel Kakchiquel,
    Cachiquel, Caqchikel
  Chorti
  Jakaltek, *also* Jacalteco
  Kanjobal, *also* Q'Anjob'al and Kanhobal
  Kekchi, *also* Q'eqchi Indians
  Lacandon Maya
  Mam
  Mopan, *also* Mopan Maya
  Pokomchi, *also* Poqomchi'
  Quiche, *also* K'iche'
  Tzutihil, *also* Sutujil, Tzutujil, Tz'utujil,

Yucatec Maya language speakers. Most
  Kekchi Maya

Guyana

Carib, *also* Karina, Kalina
Pemón, *also* Arecuna, Arekuna, Aricuna
  Jaricuna, Kamarakoto, Taurepang
Warao, *also* Guarao, Guarauno, Warau,
  Warrau

Honduras

Maya
Miskito, *also* Miskitu

Mexico

Aztec (who refer to themselves as Mexica):
  Otomi, Nahautl
Chinantec
Chol
Cora (who refer to themselves as Náayerite)
Huichol (who refer to themselves as
  Wixáritari, "The People")
Maya: Lacandon Maya; Mam Maya; Tzeltal
  Maya, *also* Tsetal; Tzotzil Maya. Most
  are Yucatec Maya Speakers
Mixtec
Mazahua
Mazatec
Seri (who refer to themselves as Comcáac)
Tarahumara, *also* Rarámuri
Toltec
Totonac
Trique, *also* Triqui
Yaqui, *also* Yoeme
Zapotec

Nicaragua

Miskito, *also* Miskitu
Nicarao

Panama

Cuna, *also* Guna, Kuna

Paraguay

Guaraní
Toba, *also* Qom

Peru

Aymara, *also* Aimara, Aymará
Inca "Children of the Sun." Quechua speakers

Quechua, *also* Quichua, Kichwa,
  Runakuna, Ingas
Kulina

SURINAME

Carib, *also* Karina, Kalina
Warao, *also* Guarao, Guarauno, Warau,
  Warrau

URUGUAY

Guaraní

VENEZUELA

Carib, *also* Karina or Kalina: Acawai, *also*
  Akawaio; Kalinago
Goajiro (not Wayuu), *also* Wayu, Wayúu,
  Guajiro, Wahiro
Pemón, *also* Arecuna, Aricuna Jaricuna,
  Kamarakoto, Taurepang
Timote
Warao (Boat People), *also* Guarao, Gua-
  rauno, Warau, Warrau
Yanomami, *also* Yąnomamö, Yanomama

Appendix B

Glossary

achiote—a seed which is ground for use in culinary spice and as an orange dye. Achiote is also called annatto and urucul, and, according to folklore, may be the source of the first pinkeye.

agouti—small, smart rodent that lives in the Amazon rain forest; the fruits it buries to save for later, help to grow more trees.

aguamiel—sweet juice from the maguey plant, used as a medicine and also fermented for drink.

ahuehuetes—big cypress trees.

amambā—tomorrow.

Amazonia—Amazon rainforest, largest and most diverse tropical rainforest and jungle area in the world, mostly located in Brazil, with the ecoregion extending into Peru, Colombia, Venezuela, Ecuador, Bolivia, Guyana, Suriname, and French Guiana.

Anansi—the beloved mischief-making spider man, a folk hero god, whose stories of outwitting kings and larger foes traveled with the slaves from Africa.

Andes Mountains—the world's longest continuous mountain range (4,500 miles long) with the highest peaks outside of Asia; runs along the western coast of South America through seven countries, from Venezuela, Colombia, Ecuador, Peru, Bolivia, Chile, down to Argentina.

asado—meat roasted by fire.

batata—sweet potato or potato.

bobo—a fool.

bola—a rope with attached weights thrown by gauchos to catch cattle and game animals by entangling their legs.

brujo—Maya wise man who gives advice and cures illnesses and can perform magic; a warlock or witch.

cacique—local chieftain.

caites—open-toed sandals.

Capusa, la Vieja—the shape-shifting female Devil of Peruvian lore, who can assume any appearance, but cannot hide her clawed black vulture's feet.

Chac—Maya rain god, composed of four entities with powers essential for cultivating crops, a presence in the **Popul Vuh**.

chakra—small plot garden, often cleared in the forest.

characotel—a Maya demon, who serves death by carrying spirits into the next world.

chasqui—specially trained royal runners who delivered messages throughout the Inca Empire.

Ches—Supreme god for many Andean tribes; the Timote People of Venezuela made sacrifices to Ches to insure a good harvest and the well-being of their culture.

chicha—homemade fermented or non-fermented drink, most often made from maize, but sometimes manioc root or fruit are used.

chirimía—a reed wind instrument, akin to an oboe.

chirrionera—a supernatural snake that stands on its head and whips its tail in the air to strike at things; it moves by biting its own tail and rolling.

Chonchon—a feared Mapuche flying human head, whose ears flap like wings as she mournfully cries in the night; a magically transformed **kalku**, who may also drink human blood.

chontal—foreigner; also refers to indigenous people from Tabasco, Mexico.

Chullachaki—a shape-shifting owner of the rain forest; a spirit with one leg smaller than the other who can read people's minds.

comadre—godmother, neighbor, gossip.

compadre—a friend, godfather.

conejo—rabbit; sometimes short for *conejo de Indias*, another term for a guinea pig.

corial—dugout canoe.

Cosijogui—Zapotec god of lightning.

costumbres—traditional customs and rituals of a region.

cotia—*see* **agouti**

Cucuy—a supernatural creature with a large, red left ear, who hears when children are misbehaving and may sometimes be summoned to carry them away.

cuero—an animal skin; in Latin American folklore, the skins floating on water often have magical properties.

curandera—an indigenous medicine woman; the male healer is *curandeiro*.

Curupira—a supernatural guardian of the forest with his feet on backwards, which makes him tricky to avoid or track; some say this frightening creature rides on a wild boar to chase woodcutters out of the forest.

Cuscatlán—Nahuatl name for El Salvador.

cuy—Spanish for guinea pig in Ecuador, Peru, and Bolivia.

La Diosa Hambrienta- Hungry Mother, the Aztec Mother Earth.

dueña and **dueño**—female and male for owner or landlord, which may refer to a human in charge of a ranch, for instance, or a spirit in charge of a lake or hill.

duende—a forest elf who causes mischief in the human world.

El Dorado—symbolizes the Spanish conquistadors' quest for the mythical kingdom or man of gold; from the Colombian legend of caciques who covered their bodies in gold dust and entered Lake Guatavita as reported in the chronicles of Sebastián de Benalcázar.

Enemigo Malo—the Devil.

farinha—manioc flour.

Feathered Snake—refers to different deities for different indigenous people; *see* **Quetzalcoatl** and **Gucumatz**.

Gabicha—Zapotec god of the sun, strongest Zapotec deity.

gaucho—cowboy who herds grazing cattle on the plains of Argentina.

grillo—cricket.

gringo—a newly arrived European or North American, who doesn't know too much about farming or ranching; a person who is not Hispanic or Latino.

guaro—Maya sugarcane rum.

Gucumatz—the Feathered Serpent god in the Quiché Maya mythology of the **Popul Vuh**, who participated in the creation of humans; also spelled as Q'uq'umatz and Kucumatz.

habanero—very hot chili pepper.

hambrienta—hungry.

Hant Caai—Seri god of creation.

hermano—brother, often shortened to 'mano in addressing someone.

Huairamama—the enormous Amazonian boa in charge of the sky.

huipil—dress.

Huitzilopochtili—the Aztec god of war and the sun; also patron of the city of Tenochtitlan to whom many human sacrifices were made to insure victory for the Mexica people in battle.

Hunab Ku—Yucatec Maya creator deity; "One God" encompassing opposites in the universe.

Huracan—Quichí Maya sky deity, with power over wind, storm, and fire; the Heart of the Sky, who participated in the creation of humans.

Iara (Yara)—alluring half-fish, half female being who enchants fishermen in the waters of Amazonia; also known to different cultures as Water Mother, *mami wata*, *Yemanya, or Yemaya*, Mohana, *Madre de agua*, Mamadilo, Watramama, Water-mama; sometimes described as half-woman and half-snake.

Juan Tul (John Rabbit)—rabbit trickster of modern Maya tales from the Yucatan, sometimes portrayed as a tall man with a long moustache.

kalku—an evil Mapuche sorcerer or witch who works with malevolent spirits such as the **Nguruvilu**; can transform another kalku so that its head can be removed to create a **Chonchon** which will carry out acts of black magic.

Kaputano—most supreme of all Carib Ancestors inhabiting Heaven; after living on earth as a culture hero, he ascended to the sky, where he was transformed into Orion.

Kenos—creator god of the Ona, an Ancestor responsible for organizing the shape of the earth and life upon it from elders reborn.

Kibungo—fearsome supernatural creature who swallows his victims (mostly women and children) whole into a stomach opening in his back.

Kopecho—Lord of the Frogs, Yupa god of the dead.

Kuben-niêpre—supernatural bat with a man's body.

machi—a benevolent Mapuche shaman or sorcerer.

machincuepa—somersault.

Madremonte (Mother of the forest)—a protector of forest life, who can become punitive when animals or trees are being mistreated. Also known as Mother Nature, Mistress of the Animals, and Marimonda.

mãe d'agua—a Portuguese water mother, who works magic in lakes and rivers; like the mermaid **Iara**, sometimes malevolent in nature, sometimes benign.

Makunaima (Macunaima)—the great Creator god of the Acawai and neighboring Carib tribes. Makunaima is often said never to have been seen by mortal man. His name means "He Works by Night."

maloca—communal house in the Amazon regions of Brazil and Colombia, built with designs unique to different indigenous communities.

mam—the four Maya thunder lords; also refers to the second most widely spoken Maya language in Guatemala and parts of Mexico.

Mama Cocha (Mamaqucha)—Inca sea and fish goddess.

manioc—a starchy, edible root, a staple food in South America; also known as cassava and yuca.

Mapinguari—a ferocious monster who helps to protect the Amazon rain forest, with ape-like arms and red or black fur.

matinta perera—a supernatural bird with a shrill whistle who permits a person to use its body to haunt Brazilian forest villages at night; it will only stop when promised something, like tobacco, coffee, or rum, and then must show up the next day to claim the gift.

mawari—from Venezuelan lore, an enchanted person, able to transform into an animal and live in or out of the water.

mazamorra—a Miskito dessert of sweetened cornmeal.

Montezuma II (Moctezuma)—ninth Aztec emperor of Mexico, who reigned from 1502 to 1520 and welcomed the white-bearded Spanish conquistador, Hernán Cortés, whom he mistakenly and disastrously believed to be the prophesied returning god **Quetzalcoatl**.

muchacho—boy.

nahual (nagual)—a sorcerer from Mexican and Central American lore who can magically transform into an animal, physically or spiritually.

Nahuaques—aspects of the Aztec supreme deity, **Tezcatlipoca**, with supernatural powers.

Nakawé—the revered Huichol great-grandmother Mother Earth.

Nanahuatzin—the humble Aztec god who threw himself into the fire to create sun for the earth; his name means "full of sores."

naturales—natives.

Nguruvilu—a malevolent water-dweller from Mapuche folklore, who causes dangerous whirlpools to drown those who want to cross a river; like a fox with a snake's body and clawing fingernails on the end of his tail.

Noçoquém—the mythological Eden where ancient Maue People could find every plant and animal they needed.

nopál—a tall, thorny cactus with heart-shaped branches, akin to a prickly pear with sweet fruit which was used for food by indigenous tribes; legendary as the plant on an island in Lake Texcoco where the Aztecs found an eagle perched holding a snake in its mouth which signified their new homeland.

onça—jaguar.

paca—nocturnal Central and South American rodent with a reddish-brown coat and white spots, which is hunted for food.

Pacha Kamaq (Pachacamac)—the ancient Peruvian "Earth Maker," creator god with a palace in the sun.

Pachamama—Inca earth mother goddess who oversees all the planting and harvesting necessary to sustain life.

paisano—fellow countryman in Mexico.

paloma—dove.

pampas—low-lying grasslands of Argentina, Uruguay, and Brazil from the Quechua word for plains.

patolli—a gambling game of the Aztecs, played on a game board with dice made of human knuckle bones and markers of painted squash seeds.

patrón—boss, owner.

peccary—a wild pig-like animal with dark coarse hair, sharp teeth, a snout, and hooves; also known as a javelin.

Pedro de Urdemalas—beloved Latin American mischief-maker; also called Pedro de Ordimales, Pedro de Ordinalas, Pedro Malasartes, Pedro Rimales, Pedro Tecomate, Pedro Urdimalo, depending on country where the trickster tale is told.

Pillan—lord of the axe, Mapuche spirit from Chile in control of lightning, thunder, volcanic eruptions, and earthquakes.

piripirioca—aromatic and medicinal plant in the Sedge family, native to the Amazon, with a specific light, spicy scent with floral notes.

pongo—disparaging term for an indigenous servant.

Popocatépetl—an active volcano in Central Mexico, also known as Smoking Hill and linked in romantic legend to the nearby dormant volcanic mountain, Iztaccihuatl, Lady of the Snows.

Popul Vuh—creation story of the Quiché Maya told by an anonymous Guatemalan Indian in the mid-1500s; narrates origins, traditions and history, including the word spark which led to formation of the earth itself, frustrations of the gods to create humans on earth who would appreciate them, and the end of the Quiché tribes.

pulque—alcoholic drink made from the fermented sap of the maguey (agave) plant.

quena—a musical pipe which makes a melancholy sweet sound; now made of reeds, but once made from hollowed human or animal bone.

Quetzalcoatl—"Feathered Snake," one of the four important Aztec creator gods; a restless deity who commands the winds, the dawn, the arts, and knowledge.

quwi—Quechua word for guinea pig.

Rajaw Juyub'—Maya spirit, who judges the way people keep nature's laws.

rancho—cane or pole hut with a palm-leaf roof, which houses ranch workers.

raton—mouse.

rebozo—shawl.

Sachamama (Sach'amama)—Amazon mother of the forests, portrayed as a two-headed serpent; she rarely moves and may be mistaken for a fallen tree and hypnotize and swallow hunters or animals.

secreto—ritual or magic act or sacred object performed to protect someone or to reverse a bad situation.

shaman—intermediary between people and the ancestors and gods of the spirit world; keeper of a tribe's traditions and values; may also be a healer and predict the future.

shiringa (seringa)—Amazonian rubber tree.

shiringuero—Amazonian rubber tapper who makes four to ten incisions in the trunks of trees to extricate the milky latex used to make rubber.

Sukunkyum—Maya deity of the underworld who judges souls and who feeds the sun when it becomes weak each night and carries it on his back through the underworld to the east, so it can rise with strength to again begin its journey across the sky.

Sumé—legendary hero who taught the Tamoio people civilization in the form of agriculture and social organization.

tacacá—Brazilian soup with prawns and paracress in soured manioc broth.

tamalitos—little tamales of seasoned meat or beans rolled in cornmeal from the first harvest of corn.

Tamusi—Carib grandfather god who created humans and animals on earth and guards the sun with a sword from sending serpents to attack the earth.

tenca—Chilean mockingbird, a song bird from Chile and Argentina.

Tenochtitlan—capital city and religious center of the Aztec empire, located on an island in Lake Texcoco in what is now Mexico City.

Tepozteco (Tepozton)—legendary mischievous son of an Aztec god and a mortal who confronted the bloodthirsty giant Xochicalcatl and went on to become ruler and then perhaps continued protector of his people.

Tezcatlipoca—"Lord of the *Smoking Mirror*," one of the supreme Aztec creator gods, who also controls the night, divination and sorcery, time, of the north, and war. His name comes from the Nahuatl description of obsidian.

tilma—woven blanket or cloak.

tlacuache—opossum (in Mexico); small gray mammal who pretends he's dead when in trouble. Name also refers to a weasel; chucha, cuicla, zarigüeya in other Latin American countries.

tonina (boto, bufeo)—pink Amazon river dolphin.

Tonotiuh—Aztec sun god.

usmiq—buzzard.

viejito—old man.

Viracocha—Inca creator god.

viscachas (vizcachas)—rodents closely related to chinchillas, which look like rabbits with longer tails and live in the brush of the pampas.

Voladores—Four flyers, who climb a thirty-foot wooden pole in a ritual Totonac ceremony to invoke prosperity from the gods of the sun and the four winds, then fling themselves off, dancing and twirling and spinning down to earth on their ropes, as a fifth man plays songs on his flute and drum from the platform at the very top.

wanuluu—long dead Goajiro spirits dressed in white or black which ride on mules and shoot arrows which bring illness and death.

witranalwe—ghoul seen only in outline, at night and on horseback, giving off a whitish hue and leading travelers astray (Chile). *Witranalwe* are also big humans, mounted on huge horses, who gallop and attack the living (Chile).

xkokolché—kind-hearted bird in a Mexican fable whose beautiful song calls others to help the poor hummingbird prepare for her wedding.

Xochicalcatl—the Aztec monster-king of Xochicalco, who subjugated the people of Morelos by demanding victims to eat. **Tepozteco** took the place of his adopted father who was to be sacrificed and cut his way out of the giant with a piece of obsidian.

Yakuruna—a mythical being who takes care of fish and animals at the bottom of the Amazon River; he sleeps with one eye open during the day and takes the form of a handsome man, with his face turned backwards, who paddles on the river at night on a black crocodile canoe with a giant boa necklace to seduce young women with magical powers and bring them down to become yakaruna spirits in his underwater city.

yerba mate—tea-like beverage made from an infusion of naturally caffeinated leaves from a species of rainforest holly tree.

yolujaa—a Goajiro spirit of the dead which has crossed the Milky Way to the peninsula of dead society before becoming lost, being reburied, and returning to earth as a positive force of rain or evil **wanuluu**.

zorro—fox.

Bibliography

Aardema, Verna, reteller. *Borreguita and the Coyote.* Illus. Petra Mathers. New York: Knopf, 1991.

Abrahams, Roger D., ed. and comp. *African American Folktales: Stories from Black Traditions in the New World.* Originally published as *Afro-American Folktales.* New York: Pantheon Books, 1985.

Ada, Alma Flor. *The Lizard and the Sun / La Lagartija y el Sol.* Bilingual English/Spanish. Illus. Felipe Dávalos, trans. Rosalma Zubizarreta. New York: Doubleday Books for Young Readers, 1997.

_____. *Mediopollito / Half-Chicken.* Bilingual English/Spanish. Illus. Kim Howard, trans. Rosalma Zubizarreta. Garden City, NY: A Doubleday Book for Young Readers, 1995.

Ada, Alma Flor, and F. Isabel Campoy. *Tales Our Abuelitas Told: A Hispanic Folktale Collection.* Illus. Felipe Dávalos, Viví Escrivá, Susan Guevara, and Leyla Torres. New York: Atheneum Books for Young Readers, 2006.

Alexander, Ellen. *Llama and the Great Flood: A Folktale from Peru.* New York: Thomas Y. Crowell, 1989.

Almeida, Livia de, and Ana Portella. *Brazilian Folktales.* Ed. Margaret Read MacDonald. Westport, CT: Libraries Unlimited, 2006.

Anaya, Rudolfo. *La Llorona: The Crying Woman.* Bilingual: English and Spanish, Rev. ed. of *Maya's Children.* Trans. Enrique Lamadrid, Illus. Amy Córdova. Albuquerque: University of New Mexico Press, 2011.

_____. *Maya's Children: The Story of La Llorona.* Illus. Maria Baca. New York: Hyperion Books for Children, 1997. Open Library.

Ardagh, Philip. *South American Myths & Legends.* Illus. Syrah Arnold. Chicago: World Book, 2002.

Baden, Robert, reteller. *And Sunday Makes Seven.* Illus. Michelle Edwards. Niles, IL: Albert Whitman & Company, 1990.

Baker, Betty. *No Help at All.* Illus. Emily Arnold McCully. New York: Greenwillow Books, 1978.

Baltuck, Naomi. *Apples from Heaven: Multicultural Folk Tales About Stories and Storytellers.* North Haven, CT: Linnet Books, 1995.

Barlow, Genevieve. *Latin American Tales from the Pampas to Mexico City.* Illus. William M. Hutchinson. Chicago: Rand McNally, 1966.

_____. *Stories from Latin America / Historias de Latinoamérica.* Bilingual English/Spanish. Illus. Robert Borja and Julia Scharf. Chicago: McGraw-Hill, 2010.

Barlow, Genevieve, and William N. Stivers. *Stories from Mexico / Historias de México.* Bilingual English/Spanish. Chicago: McGraw-Hill, 2009.

Belting, Natalia M. *Moon Was Tired of Walking on Air.* Illus. Will Hillenbrand. Boston: Houghton Mifflin, 1992.

Bernhard, Emery. *The Tree That Rains: The Flood Myth of the Huichol Indians of Mexico.* Illus. Durga Bernhard. New York: Holiday House, 1994.

Bierhorst, John, ed. *Black Rainbow.* New York: Farrar Straus & Giroux, 1976.

_____. *The Hungry Woman: Myths and Legends of the Aztecs.* Illus. Aztec artists of the Sixteenth Century. New York: William Morrow, 1984.

_____, ed. *Latin American Folktales: Stories from Hispanic and Indian Traditions.* New York: Pantheon Books, 2002. Open Library.

_____. *The Monkey's Haircut and Other Stories Told by the Maya.* Illus. Robert Andrew Parker. New York: William Morrow, 1986. Open Library/Internet Archive.

_____. *The Mythology of Mexico and Central America.* New York: William Morrow, 1990.

_____. *The Mythology of South America.* New York: William Morrow, 1988. Open Library.

_____. *The Red Swan: Myths and Tales of the American Indians.* New York: Farrar Straus & Giroux, 1976.

Blackmore, Vivien. *Why Corn Is Golden: Stories About Plants.* Illus. Susana Martínez-Ostos. Boston: Little, Brown, 1984.

Brenner, Anita, reteller. *The Boy Who Could Do Anything & Other Mexican Folk Tales.* Illus. Jean Charlot. Hamden, CT: Linnet Books, 1992.

Brett, W.H. *Guyana Legends.* Georgetown, Guyana: Release Publishers, 1931.

_____. *Legends and Myths of the Aboriginal Indians*

of British Guiana. London: William Wells Gardner, 1880. Open Library.

Brusca, María Cristina, and Tona Wilson. *Pedro Fools the Gringo and Other Tales of a Latin American Trickster*. Illus. María Cristina Brusca. New York: Holt, 1995.

____, retellers. *The Blacksmith and the Devils*. Illus. María Cristina Brusca. New York: Holt, 1992.

Campbell, Camilla. *Star Mountain and Other Legends of Mexico*. Illus. Frederic Marvin. New York: McGraw, 1946.

Campbell, Margaret, ed. & reteller. *South American Folklore Tales*. Illus. Arturo Fine. El Monte, CA: Latin American Village Press, 1942.

Campos, Anthony John, ed. and trans. *Mexican Folk Tales*. Illus. Mark Sanders. Tucson: The University of Arizona Press, 1977.

Carpenter, Frances. *South American Wonder Tales*. Illus. Ralph Creasman. Chicago: Follett Publishing Company, 1969.

Carter, Dorothy Sharp. *The Enchanted Orchard, and Other Folktales of Central America*. Illus. W.T. Mars. New York: Harcourt Brace Jovanovich, 1973.

Cherry, Lynne. *The Great Kapok Tree: A Tale of the Amazon Rain Forest*. San Diego: Harcourt Brace Jovanovich, 1990. Open Library.

Climo, Shirley, reteller. *The Little Red Ant and the Great Big Crumb*. Illus. Francisco X. Mora. New York: Clarion Books, 1995. Open Library.

____. *Monkey Business: Stories from Around the World*. Illus. Erik Brooks. New York: Henry Holt, 2005.

Cole, Joanna. *Best-Loved Folktales of the World*. Illus. Jill Karla Schwarz. New York: Doubleday, 1982. Open Library.

Cordova, Gabriel, comp. "Magic Tales of Mexico, 1951." http://www.g-world.org/magictales. Accessed Feb. 10, 2014.

Courlander, Harold, ed. *Ride with the Sun: An Anthology of Folk Tales and Stories from the United Nations*. Illus. Roger Duvoisin. New York: Whittlesey House/McGraw-Hill Book Company, 1955. Open Library.

____. *A Treasury of Afro-American Folklore*. Illus. Enrico Arno. New York: Crown, 1976.

Crespo, George, reteller. *How Iwariwa the Cayman Learned to Share: A Yanomami Myth*. New York: Clarion Books, 1995.

Crossley-Holland, Kevin, ed. *The Young Oxford Book of Folk Tales*. Oxford: Oxford University Press, 1998.

Cruz, Alejandro. *The Woman Who Outshone the Sun: The Legend of Lucia Zenteno / La Mujer Que Brillaba Aún Más Que el Sol: La Leyenda de Lucía Zenteno / from a Poem by/ Basado en el Poema de Alejandro Cruz Martinez*. Bilingual English/Spanish. Retellers Rosalma Zubizarreta, Harriet Rohmer, and David Schecter, Illus. Fernando Olivera. San Francisco: Children's Book Press, 1987. Open Library.

Davis, E. Adams. *Of the Night Wind's Telling: Legends from the Valley of Mexico*. Illus. Dorothy Kirk. Norman: University of Oklahoma Press, 1946.

Dearden, Carmen Diana, ed. *Little Book of Latin American Folktales*. Simultaneously published in Spanish in Caracas. Trans. Susana Susana Wald, et al. Berkeley, CA: Groundswood Books/ Douglas & McIntyre, 2003.

Delacre, Lulu, reteller. *Golden Tales:Myths, Legends, and Folktales from Latin America*. New York: Scholastic, 1996.

De Onís, Harriet, compiler, ed. & trans. *The Golden Land: An Anthology of Latin American Folklore in Literature*. New York: Knopf, 1948.

De Osma, Lupe. *The Witches' Ride: and Other Tales from Costa Rica*. New York: William Morrow, 1957.

DePaola, Tomie. *Adelita: A Mexican Cinderella Story*. New York: G. P. Putnam's Sons, 2002. Open Library.

____. *The Lady of Guadalupe*. New York: Holiday House, 1980. Open Library.

____, reteller. *The Legend of the Poinsetta*. New York: Putnam Books for Young Readers, 1994.

DeSpain, Pleasant, reteller. *Eleven Turtle Tales*. Illus. Joe Shlichta. Little Rock, AR: August House, 1994.

____, reteller. *The Emerald Lizard: Fifteen Latin American Tales to Tell*. Trans. Mario Lamo-Jiminez, Illus. Don Bell. Little Rock, AR: August House, 1999. Open Library.

____, reteller. *Thirty-Three Multicultural Tales to Tell*. Illus. Joe Shlichta. Little Rock, AR: August House, 1993.

Dewey, Ariane, reteller & illustrator. *The Thunder God's Son: A Peruvian Folktale*. New York: Greenwillow Books, 1981.

Dobie, J. Frank, ed. *Puro Mexicano*. Texas Folklore Society Publication Number XII. Dallas: Southern Methodist University Press, 1935.

Dorson, Mercedes, and Jeanne Wilmot, retellers. *Tales from the Rain Forest: Myths and Legends from the Amazonian Indians of Brazil*. Foreword by Barry Lopez. Hopewell, NJ: The Ecco Press, 1997.

Dorson, Richard M., ed. *Folktales Told Around the World*. Chicago: University of Chicago Press, 1975.

D'Oyley, Enid. *Animal Fables and Other Tales Retold: African Tales in the New World*. Illus. Larissa Kauperman. Trenton, NJ: Africa World Press, 1988.

Edwards, Carolyn McVickar. *The Return of the Light: Twelve Tales from Around the World for the Winter Solstice*. Illus. Kathleen Edwards. New York: Marlowe & Company, 2000, 2005.

Eells, Elsie Spicer. *The Brazilian Fairy Book*. Illus. George Hood. New York: Frederick A. Stokes Co., 1926. http://www.worldoftales.com/Brazilian_folktales.html. Accessed Oct. 30, 2013.

____. *Fairy Tales from Brazil: How and Why Tales from Brazilian Folk-Lore*. Chicago: Dodd, Mead and Company, 1917.

Ehlert, Lois. *Cuckoo: A Mexican Folktale / Cucú: In Cuento Folklórico Mexicano*. Bilingual English/Spanish. Trans into Spanish Gloria de Aragón Andújar. New York: Harcourt, 1997.

_____. *Moon Rope: A Peruvian Folktale/Un Lazo a la Luna: Una Leyenda Peruana*. Bilingual. Trans into Spanish Amy Prince. New York: Voyager Books/Harcourt, 1992. Open Library.

Elbl, Martin, and J.T. Winikand, retellers. *Tales from the Amazon*. Illus. Gerda Neubacher. Burlington, Ontario: Hayes Publishing, 1986.

Endredy, James. *The Journey of Tunuri and the Blue Deer: A Huichol Indian Story*. Illus. María Hernández de la Cruz and Casimiro de la Cruz López. Rochester, VT: Bear Cub Books, 2003.

Fagundes, Mani. *"Vitoria Regia." Stories from the World's Greatest Rivers*. Auckland, New Zealand: Auckland Museum, 2011. YouTube. https://www.youtube.com/watch?v=GwzIhWg-q6M. Accessed Nov. 29, 2014.

Finger, Charles J. *Tales from Silver Lands*. Illus. Paul Honoré. Garden City, NY: Doubleday Page & Company, 1926. Open Library.

"The First People." *Legends of Guyana's Amerindians: Legends of the Caribs*. OoCities.org. http://www.oocities.org/thetropics/shores/9253/legends3.html. Accessed Oct. 30, 2014.

Forest, Heather. *Wisdom Tales from Around the World*. Little Rock, AR: August House, 1996.

_____. *Wonder Tales from Around the World*. Illus. David Boston. Little Rock, AR: August House, 1995.

_____. *Wonder Tales from Around the World*. Audiobook. Prince Frederick, MD: Recorded Books, 2013.

_____. *World Tales of Wisdom and Wonder*. CD or Downloadable audio file. Little Rock, AR: August House Audio, 2002.

Frost, Frances. *Legends of the United Nations*. Whittlesey House/McGraw-Hill Book Company, 1943.

Galeano, Juan Carlos. *Folktales of the Amazon*. Trans. Rebecca Morgan and Kenneth Watson, Foreword by Michael Uzendoski. Westport, CT: Libraries Unlimited, 2009.

Gerson, Mary-Joan. *Fiesta Femenina: Celebrated Women in Mexican Folklore*. Illus. Maya Christina Gonzalez. Cambridge, MA: Barefoot Books, 2001. Open Library.

_____, reteller. *How Night Came from the Sea*. Illus. Carla Golembe. Boston: Little, Brown, 1994. Open Library.

_____, reteller. *People of Corn: A Mayan Story*. Illus. Carla Golembe. Boston: Little, Brown, 1995.

Gifford, Douglas. *Warriors, Gods & Spirits from Central & South American Mythology*. Illus. John Sibbick. New York: Schocken, 1983. Open Library.

Goldman, Judy. *Whiskers, Tails and Wings: Animal Folktales from Mexico*. Illus. Fabricio Vanden-Broeck. Watertown, MA: Charlesbridge, 2013.

Goldman, Leslie, reteller. *Dora's Favorite Fairy Tales*. Illus. A & J Studios. New York: Simon Spotlight/Nick Jr., 2004.

González, Lucía M., reteller. *Señor Cat's Romance and Other Favorite Stories from Latin America*. Illus. Lulu Delacre. New York: Scholastic Press, 1997.

Gordh, Bill. *Stories in Action: Interactive Tales and Learning Activities to Promote Early Literacy*. Westport, CT: Libraries Unlimited, 2006.

Green, Lila. *Tales from Hispanic Lands; Originally Published as Folktales of Spain and Latin America*. Illus. Donald Silverstein. Morristown, NJ: Silver Burdett Company, 1979.

Hamilton, Martha, and Mitch Weiss. *How & Why Stories: World Tales Kids Can Read and Tell*. Illus. Carol Lyon. Little Rock, AR: August House Publishers, 1999. Open Library.

_____. *Tales Kids Can Tell*. Illus. Annie Campbell. Golden, CO: Fulcrum Publishing, 1996.

_____. *Through the Grapevine: World Tales Kids Can Read and Tell*. Illus. Carol Lyon. Little Rock, Arkansas: August House, 2001. Open Library.

Hayes, Joe. *¡El Cucuy! A Bogeyman Cuento in English and Spanish*. Bilingual. Illus. Honorio Robledo. El Paso, TX: Cinco Puntos Press, 2001.

_____. "Joe Hayes Narrates El Cuycuy!" 2011. YouTube. https://www.youtube.com/watch?v=xsQ-h8L4Xfg. Accessed Nov. 22, 2104.

_____. "La Llorona—A Hispanic Legend." *Teaching from a Hispanic Perspective & A Handbook for Non-Hispanic Adult Educators*, 2011. Literacynet.org. http://www.literacynet.org/lp/hperspectives/llorona.html. Accessed Nov. 30, 2014.

_____. *La Llorona / The Weeping Woman: An Hispanic Legend Told in Spanish and English*. Bilingual Spanish/English. Illus. Vicki Trego Hill and Mona Pennypacker. El Paso, Texas: Cinco Puntos Press, 2004. Open Library.

_____. "La Llorona Told by Joe Hayes, 2011." YouTube. http://www.youtube.com/watch?v=xsQ-h8L4Xfg. Accessed July 19, 2014.

Herrmann, Marjorie E. *Las Manchas del Sapo / How the Toad Got His Spots*. Bilingual English/Spanish. Lincolnwood, IL: National Textbook Company, 1987.

Herskovits, Melville J., and Frances Herskovits. *Suriname Folk-Lore*. New York: Columbia University Press, 1936.

Hickox, Rebecca. *Zorro and Quwi*. Illus. Kim Howard. New York: Delacorte Press, 1997.

Hinojosa, Francisco, adapter. *The Old Lady Who Ate People: Frightening Stories*. Illus. Leonel Maciel. Boston: Little, Brown, 1984, English translation.

Hoffman, Mary. *A Twist in the Tail: Animal Stories from Around the World*. Illus. Jan Ormerod. New York: Holt, 1998. Open Library.

Holt, David, and Bill Mooney, eds. *More Ready-to-Tell Tales from Around the World*. Little Rock, AR: August House, 2000.

Hudson, Wilson M., ed. *The Healer of Los Olmos and Other Mexican Lore*. Texas Folklore Society: Number XXIV. Introd. by J. Frank Dobie. Dallas, TX: Austin Southern Methodist University Press, 1951, ebook, 2000.

Hughes, Brenda. *Folk-Tales from Chile*. London: George G. Harrap & Co., 1962; republished 1998 by Hippocrene Books, New York.

Hull, Robert. *Central and South American Stories*. Simultaneously published by Thompson Learning, New York as *Pre-Columbian Stories*. Illus. Vanessa Cleall and Claire Robinson. Sussex, England: Wayland Publishers, 1994.

Jade and Iron: Latin American Tales from Two Cultures. Ed. Patricia Aldana. Trans. Hugh Hazelton, Illus. Luis Garay. Toronto: A Groundwood Book/Douglas & McIntyre, 1996.

Jaffe, Nina. *Patakin: World Tales of Drums and Drummers*. Illus. Ellen Eagle. New York: Holt, 1994. Open Library.

Jagendorf, M.A. *Noodlehead Stories from Around the World*. Illus. Shane Miller. New York: The Vanguard Press, 1957. Open Library.

Jagendorf, M.A., and R.S. Boggs. *The King of the Mountains: A Treasury of Latin American Folk Stories*. Illus. Carybé. New York: The Vanguard Press, 1960. Open Library.

Janvier, Thomas Allibone. *Legends of the City of Mexico*. New York: Harper & Brothers, 1910. Google eBook.

Jardim, Luis. *The Armadillo and the Monkey: A Folktale of Brazil*. Trans. Maria Cimino. New York: Coward-McCann, 1942.

Johnston, Tony. *The Tale of Rabbit and Coyote*. Illus. Tomie DePaola. New York: G.P. Putnam's Sons, 1994.

Keding, Dan. *Elder Tales: Stories of Wisdom and Courage from Around the World*. Westport, CT: Libraries Unlimited, 2008. Northwestern Polytechnic University and at http://npu.edu.ua/!ebook/book/djvu/A/iif_kgpm_Keding_Elder_Tales.pdf.pdf.

Ketteman, Helen. *Señorita Gordita*. Illus. Will Terry. Chicago: Albert Whitman & Company, 2012.

Kimmel, Eric A., reteller. *The Two Mountains: An Aztec Legend*. Illus. Leonard Everett Fisher. New York: Holiday House, 2000.

_____, reteller. *The Witch's Face: A Mexican Tale*. Illus. Fabricio Vanden Broeck. New York: Holiday House, 1993.

Knutson, Barbara. *Love and Roast Chicken: A Trickster Tale from the Andes Mountains*. Minneapolis: Carolrhoda Books, 2004.

Kurtycz, Marcos, and Ana García Kobeh. *Tigers and Opossums: Animal Legends*. Trans. Felicia M. Hall. Boston: Little, Brown, 1984.

Kurtz, Jane. *Miro in the Kingdom of the Sun*. Illus. David Frampton. Boston: Houghton Mifflin, 1996. Open Library.

Larson, Bonnie, reteller. *When Animals Were People/Cuando los Animals Eran Personas*. Bilingual English/Spanish. Illus. Modesto Rivera Lemus. Santa Fe, NM: Clear Light Publishers, 2002. Open Library.

Lattimore, Deborah Nourse. *Why There Is No Arguing in Heaven: A Mayan Myth*. New York: Harper, 1989.

Laughlin, Robert M., compiler & trans. *Of Cabbages and Kings: Tales from Zincantán*. Bilingual English/Tzotzil. Washington, D.C.: Smithsonian, 1977. And at Smithsonian Institution Libraries. http://www.sil.si.edu/smithsoniancontributions/

Anthropology/pdf_hi/SCtA-0023.pdf. Accessed Jan. 5, 2015.

_____, compiler & trans. *The People of the Bat: Mayan Tales and Dreams from Zinacantán*. Bilingual, English and Tzotzil. Ed. Carol Karasik. Washington, D.C.: Smithsonian, 1988. Open Library.

"The Legend of the Vitória Régia." *Reminiscence Site of Untold Stories*. Momentum Arts, 2008. http://www.untoldstories.org.uk/storytelling/brazilian/br_story01.html, Accessed Nov, 29, 2014.

Lewis, Richard. *All of You Was Singing*. Illus. Ed Young. New York: Atheneum, 1991.

Lilly, Melinda. *Aletín and the Falling Sky*. Illus. Charles Reasoner. Vero Beach, FL: The Rourke Press, 1999.

_____. *Mira and the Stone Tortoise*. Illus. Charles Reasoner. Vero Beach, FL: The Rourke Press, 1999.

_____. *The Moon People*. Illus. Charles Reasoner. Vero Beach, FL: The Rourke Press, 1999.

_____. *The Snake's Toothache*. Illus. Charles Reasoner. Vero Beach, FL: The Rourke Press, 1999.

Lippert, Margaret H., reteller. *The Sea Serpent's Daughter: A Brazilian Legend*. Felipe Davalos. Mahwah, NJ: Troll Associates, 1993. Open Library.

López de Mariscal, Blanca. *The Harvest Birds/Los Pájaros de la Cosecha*. Bilingual English/Spanish. Illus. Enrique Flores. Emeryville, CA: Children's Book Press, 1995.

Lowery, Linda, and Richard Keep, adapter. *The Tale of La Llorona*. Illus. Janice Lee Porter. Minneapolis: Millbrook Press, 2008.

Loya, Olga. *Momentos Mágicos / Magic Moments*. Bilingual: English/Spanish. Spanish trans. Carmen Lizardi-Rivera. Little Rock, AR: August House, 1997. Open Library.

_____, told by. *Tío Conejo / Uncle Rabbit. Four tales from Tío Conejo (Uncle Rabbit) and Other Latin American Trickster Tales*. Little Rock, AR: August House Audio, 2006. CD.

Lupton, Hugh. *Tales of Mystery and Magic*. With CD. Illus. Agnese Baruzzi. Cambridge, MA: Barefoot Books, 2007.

Lyons, Grant. *Tales the People Tell in Mexico*. Exec. eds. Andrew Antal and Doris K. Coburn. New York: Julian Messner, 1972.

MacCracken, Joan, reteller. *Trisba & Sula: A Miskitu Folktale From Nicaragua/Trisba & Sula: Una Leyenda de los Miskitos de Nicaragua*. Bilingual: English and Spanish. Illus. Augusto Silva, trans. Isabel Macdonald, Adán Silva Mercado, and María Fuentes. Orono, Maine: Tiffin Press, 2005.

MacDonald, Margaret Read. *Conejito: A Folktale from Panama*. Illus. Geraldo Valério. Little Rock, AR: August House, 2006.

_____. *Earth Care: World Folktales to Talk About*. North Haven, CT: Linnet Books, 1999. Open Library.

_____. *The Farmyard Jamboree*. Illus. Sophie Fatus. Cambridge, MA: Barefoot Books, 2005.

_____. *Five Minute Tales: More Stories to Read and*

Tell When Time Is Short. Illus. Yvonne Davis. Atlanta, GA: August House, 2007.

_____. *Shake-It-Up Tales: Stories to Sing, Dance, Drum, and Act Out.* Illus. Yvonne Davis. Little Rock, AR: August House, 2000.

_____. *Tuck-Me-in-Tales: Bedtime Stories from Around the World.* Illus. Yvonne Davis. Atlanta, GA: August House, 2005.

MacDonald, Margaret Read, Jennifer MacDonald Whitman, and Nathaniel Forrest Whitman. *Teaching with Story: Classroom Connections to Storytelling.* Illus. Yvonne Davis. Atlanta, GA: August House, 2013.

Maggi, Maria Elena. *The Great Canoe: A Karina Legend.* Illus. Gloria Calderón, trans. Elisa Amado. Toronto, Ontario: Groundswood Books/ Douglas & McIntyre, 1998. Open Library.

Mahabir, Kumar, comp. *Caribbean Indian Folktales.* Bilingual: Dialect and English. Foreword by Vobert C. Cambridge, Illus. Angali Dabideen and Preddie Partap. San Juan, Trinidad and Tobago, West Indies: Chakra Publishing House, 2005.

Martin, Paula, reteller and trans. *Pachamama Tales: Folklore from Argentina, Bolivia, Chile, Paraguay, Peru, and Uruguay.* Bilingual: Spanish/English. Ed. Margaret Read MacDonald. Westport, CT: Libraries Unlimited, 2014.

Martínez, Reuben. *Once Upon a Time: Traditional Latin American Tales/Había una Vez: Cuneos Tradicionales Latinoamericanos.* Bilingual: English/Spanish. Illus. Raúl Colón, trans. David Unger. New York: HarperCollins, 2010.

Martinez del Rio, Amelia. *The Sun, the Moon and a Rabbit.* Illus. Jean Charlot. New York: Sheed & Ward, 1935.

Mascayano, Ismael. *The Daughter of the Sun / La Hija del Sol.* Bilingual: English/Spanish. Toronto: Kids Can Press, 1978.

Mayo, Margaret. *Mythical Birds and Beasts from Many Lands.* Illus. Jane Ray. New York: Dutton Children's Books, 1977.

_____. *When the World Was Young: Creation and Pourquoi Tales.* Illus. Louise Brierley. New York: Simon & Schuster Books for Young Readers, 1995.

McCaughrean, Geraldine. *The Golden Hoard: Myths and Legends of the World.* Illus. Bee Willey. New York: Margaret K. McElderry Books, 1995. Open Library.

_____. *The Silver Treasure.* Illus. Bee Willey. New York: Margaret K. McElderry Books, 1996.

McDermott, Gerald. *Jabuti the Tortoise: A Trickster Tale from the Amazon.* New York: Harcourt, 2001.

_____. *Musicians of the Sun.* New York: Simon & Schuster Books for Young Readers, 1997.

Menchú, Rigoberta. *The Honey Jar.* With Dante Liano, Trans. David Unger, Illus. Domi. Toronto: Groundwood Nooks/House of Anansi Press, 2002.

"Mexican Folklore." American Folklore.net, 2014. http://americanfolklore.net/folklore/mexicanfolklore/. Accessed Feb. 13, 2015.

Mike, Jan M., reteller. *Opossum and the Great Firemaker: A Mexican Legend.* Illus. Charles Reasoner. Mahwah, NJ: Troll Associates, 1993. Open Library.

Milord, Susan, reteller. *Tales Alive! Ten Multicultural Folktales with Activities.* Illus. Michael A. Donato. Charlotte, VT: Williamson Publishing, 1955. Open Library.

Mindlin, Betty. *Barbecued Husbands.* Trans. Donald Slatoff. London: Verso, 2002.

Montejo, Victor. *The Bird Who Cleans the World and Other Mayan Fables.* Trans. Wallace Kaufman, Introd. by Allan Burns. Willimantic, CT: Curbstone Press, 1991.

Moore, Elizabeth, and Alice Couvillon. *How the Gods Created the Finger People: A Mayan Fable.* Bilingual. Illus. Luz-Maria Lopez. Gretna, LA: Pelican Publishing, 2011.

Mora, Pat, reteller. *The Night the Moon Fell.* Illus. Domi. Toronto: Douglas & McIntyre, 2000.

_____. *The Race of Toad and Deer.* Illus. Maya Itzna Brooks. New York: Orchard Books, 1995. Open Library.

Morales, Yuyi. *Just a Minute: A Trickster Tale and Counting Book.* San Francisco: Chronicle Books, 2003.

Munduruku, Daniel, reteller. *Amazonia: Indigenous Tales from Brazil.* Illus. Nikolai Popov, trans. Jane Springer. Toronto: Groundwood Books/House of Anansi Press, 2013.

Nagarajan, Nadia Grosser. *Pomegranate Seeds: Latin American Jewish Tales.* Introd. by Ilan Stavans. Albuquerque: University of New Mexico Press, 2005.

Nava, Yolanda, ed. *It's All in the Frijoles: 100 Famous Latinos Share Real-Life Stories, Time-Tested Dichos, Favorite Folktales, and Inspiring Words of Wisdom.* New York: Fireside/ Simon & Schuster, Inc., 2000. Open Library.

Ober, Hal, reteller. *How Music Came to the World.* Illus. Carol Ober. Boston: Houghton Mifflin, 1994.

Olson, Arielle North, and Howartd Schwartz. *Ask the Bones: Scary Stories from Around the World.* Illus. David Linn. New York: Viking Press, 1999. Open Library.

Palacios, Argentina. *The Hummingbird King: A Guatemalan Legend.* Illus. Felipe Davalos. New York: Troll Associates, 1993.

_____. *The Llama's Secret: A Peruvian Legend.* Illus. Charles Reasoner. New York: Troll Associates, 1993.

Paredes, Américo, ed. and trans. *Folktales of Mexico.* Foreword by Richard M. Dorson. Chicago: The University of Chicago Press, 1970.

Parker, Vic. *Traditional Tales from South America; Based on Myths and Legends Retold by Phlip Ardagh.* Illus. Syrah Arnold. North Mankato, MN: Thameside Press, 2001.

Parnell, Fran. *Grim, Grunt and Grizzle-Tail.* Illus. Sophie Fatus. Cambridge, MA: Barefoot Books, 2013.

Patent, Dorothy Hinshaw. *Quetzal: Sacred Bird of the Cloud Forest.* Illus. Neil Waldman. New York: Morrow Junior Books, 1996. Open Library.

Payne, Johnny, compiler, trans. & ed. *She-Calf and Other Quechua Folk Tales*. Bilingual: English/Quechua. Albuquerque: University of New Mexico Press, 2000.

Peñalosa, Fernando, trans. and ed. "Maya Culture—Traditional Storyteller's Tales." Page prepared by Paula Giese, *Stories told by don Pedro Miguel Say*. Native American Indian Resources, 1995. http://www.kstrom.net/isk/maya/mayastor.html. Accessed Nov. 3, 2014.

_____, trans. and ed. "Mayan Folktales. Told by don Pedro Miguel Say." FolkArt.com, 2007. http://www.folkart.com/folktale/. Accessed Nov. 3, 2014.

_____. *Tales and Legends of the Q'Anjob'al Maya*. Illus. Adrián Say and Virves García. Rancho Palos Verdes, CA: Yax Te' Press, 1995.

Petersen, Patricia. *Voladores*. Illus. Sheli Petersen. Legends of the Americas. Beverly Hills, CA: Peter Bedrick Books/McGraw-Hill Children's Publishing, 2002.

Phelps, Ethel Johnston, ed. *Tatterhood and Other Tales*. Illus. Pamela Baldwin-Ford. New York: The Feminist Press, 1978. Open Library.

Philip, Neil, reteller. *Horse Hooves and Chicken Feet: Mexican Folktales*. Illus. Jacqueline Mair. New York: Clarion Books, 2003. Open Library.

Piggott, Juliet. *Mexican Folk Tales*. Illus. John Spencer. New York: Crane Russak, 1973.

Pino-Saavedra, Yolando, ed. *Folktales of Chile*. Trans. Rockwell Gray, Foreword by Richard M. Dorson. Chicago: The University of Chicago Press, 1967.

Pitcher, Caroline. *Mariana and the Merchild: A Folk Tale from Chile*. Illus. Jackie Morris. Grand Rapids, MI: Eerdmans Books for Young Readers, 2000.

Purnell, Idella. *The Merry Frogs*. Illus. Nadine Wenden. London: Suttonhouse, 1936.

The Puyhuy Birds. Story cards. Trilingual: English/French/Spanish. Miami, Florida, and Spain: Miniland Educational Corporation.

Ragan, Kathleen, ed. *Fearless Girls, Wise Women and Beloved Sisters: Heroines in Folktales from Around the World*. Foreword by Jane Yolen. New York: W.W. Norton, 1998.

Richards, Michael, reteller. *The Rainmaker: A Tzutijil Maya Story from Guatemala*. Illus. Angelika Bauer. Guatemala: Litoprint, 1997.

Rockwell, Anne. *The Good Llama: A Picture Story from Peru*. Cleveland, OH: The World Publishing Company, 1968. Open Library.

_____. *The Monkey's Whiskers*. New York: Parents' Magazine Press, 1971. Open Library.

Rohmer, Harriet, reteller. *Cuna Song/Cancion de los Cunas*. Bilingual English/Spanish. Illus. Irene Perez. San Francisco: Children's Book Press, 1976.

_____, reteller. *The Legend of Food Mountain / La Montaña del Alimento*. Bilingual English/Spanish. Illus. Graciela Carrillo, trans. Alma Flor Ada and Zubizarreta. San Francisco: Children's Book Press, 1982. Open Library; Internet Archive.

_____, reteller. *Uncle Nacho's Hat: A Folktale from Nicaragua / El Sombrero del Tío Nacho: Un Cuento de Nicaragua*. Bilingual English/Spanish. Illus. Veg Reisberg, trans. Rosalma Zubizareta. San Francisco: Children's Book Press, 1989. Open Library.

Rohmer, Harriet, and Mary Anchondo, retellers. *How We Came to the Fifth World / Cómo Vinimos al Quinto Mundo*. Bilingual English/Spanish. Ed. Harriet Rohmer and Rosalma Zubizarreta. Illus. Graciela Carrillo. San Francisco: Children's Book Press, 1988 (1976).

Rohmer, Harriet, Octavio Chow, and Morris Vidaure, retellers. *The Invisible Hunters / Los Cazadores Invisibles*. Bilingual English/Spanish. Illus. Joe Sam, trans. Rosalma Zubizarreta and Alma Flor Ada. San Francisco: Children's Book Press, 1987. Open Library.

Rohmer, Harriet, and Jesús Guerrero Rea, retellers. *Land of the Icy Death / Tierra de la Muerte Glacial*. Bilingual English/Spanish. Illus. Xavier Viramontes. San Francisco: Children's Book Press, 1976. Open Library.

_____, retellers. *The Treasure of Guatavita / El Tesoro de Guatavita*. Bilingual English/Spanish. Illus. Carlos Loarca. San Francisco: Children's Book Press, 1978.

Rohmer, Harriet, and Dorminster Newton Wilson. *Mother Scorpion Country / La Tierra de la Madre Escorpión*. Bilingual English/Spanish. Illus. Virginia Stearns, trans. Rosalma Zubizarreta and Alma Flor Ada. San Francisco: Children's Book Press, 1987.

Rothenberg, Jerome. *The Flight of Quetzalcoatl*. Brighton: Unicorn, 1967.

_____. "The Flight of Quetzalcoatl," 1969. Spoken Web: Concordia University—Jerome Rothenberg at SGWU, 1969. http://spokenweb.concordia.ca/sgw-poetry-readings/jerome-rothenberg-at-sgwu-1969/. Accessed Jan. 5, 2014.

_____. *Shaking the Pumpkin: Traditional Poetry of the Indian North Americas*. Garden City, NY: Doubleday & Company, 1972. Open Library.

Ryan, Pam Muñoz. *Nacho and Lolita*. Illus. Claudia Rueda. New York: Scholastic Press, 2005.

St. Aubyn, Dorothy. *Caribbean Fables: Animal Stories from Guyana and the Antilles*. Trinidad and Tobago: Paria, 2007.

StJohn, Amanda, reteller. *Medio Pollito (Half-Chick): A Mexican Folktale*. Illus. Sue Todd. Mankato, MN: The Child's World, 1980.

Salkey, Andrew, comp. *Caribbean Folk Tales and Legends*. Illus. Gordon DeLaMothe. London: Bogle-L'Ouverture, 1980.

San Souci, Robert D. *Even More Short & Shivery: Forty-Five Spine-Tingling Tales*. Illus. Jacqueline Rogers. New York: Delacorte Press for Young Readers, 1997.

_____. *A Terrifying Taste of Short & Shivery: Thirty Creepy Tales*. Illus. Lenny Wooden. New York: Delacorte Press for Young Readers, 1998.

Schuman, Michael A. *Mayan and Aztec Mythology*.

Berkeley Heights, NJ: Enslow Publishers, 2001. Open Library.

Schwartz, Alvin, reteller. *In a Dark, Dark Room and Other Scary Stories.* Illus. Dirk Zimmer. New York: Harper, 1984.

Sexton, James D., trans. and ed. *Mayan Folktales: Folklore from Lake Atitlán, Guatelmala.* New York: Anchor Books/Doubleday, 1992.

Sexton, James D., ed. and trans., Ignacio Bizarro Ujpán, reteller. *Heart of Heaven, Heart of Earth and Other Mayan Folktales.* Washington, D.C.: Smithsonian, 1999.

Sheehan, Ethna, comp. *Folk and Fairy Tales from Around the World.* Illus. Mircea Vasiliu. New York: Dodd, Mead & Company, 1970.

Sherman, Josepha, reteller. *Merlin's Kin: World Tales of the Hero Magician.* Little Rock, AR: August House, 1998. Open Library.

_____, reteller. *Trickster Tales: Forty Folk Stories from Around the World.* Illus. David Boston. Atlanta, GA: August House, 1996. Open Library.

Shetterly, Susan Hand. *The Dwarf-Wizard of Uxmal.* Illus. Robert Shetterly. New York: Atheneum, 1990.

Sierra, Judy. *Nursery Tales Around the World.* Illus. Stefano Vitale. New York: Clarion Books, 1996.

Stern, Anita. *World Folktales: An Anthology of Multicultural Folk Literature.* Chicago: National Textbook Company, 1994.

Stiles, Martha Bennett, reteller. *James the Vine Puller.* Illus. Larry Thomas. Minneapolis: Carolrhoda Books, 1974. Open Library.

Storm, Dan. *Picture Tales from Mexico.* Illus. Mark Storm. New York: J.B. Lippincott, 1941. Open Library.

Suarez-Rivas, Maite, ed. *An Illustrated Treasury of Latino Read-Aloud Stories.* Trans. Alma Mora, illus. Ana López and Luis Fernando Gerrero Escrivá, et al. New York: Black Dog and Leventhal Publishers, 2004. Open Library.

Temó, Pedro Cholotío, and Alberto Barreno, retellers in Spanish, James D. Sexton, ed. and trans., Fredy-Mejía Rodrígues, eds & trans. *The Dog Who Spoke and More Mayan Folktales / El Perro Que Habló y Más Cuentos Mayas.* Bilingual English/Spanish. Norman: University of Oklahoma Press, 2010.

Thompson, Susan Conklin, Keith Steven Thompson, and Lidia López de López. *Mayan Folktales / Cuentos Folklóricos Mayas.* Bilingual: Spanish/English. Westport, CT: Libraries Unlimited, 2007.

Toor, Frances. *A Treasury of Mexican Folkways.* Illus. Carlos Merida. New York: Crown Publishers, 1947.

Troughton, Joanna, reteller & illustrator. *How Night Came: A Folk Tale from the Amazon.* New York: Peter Bedrick Books, 1986.

Van Laan, Nancy, reteller. *The Legend of El Dorado.* Illus. Beatriz Vidal. New York: Alfred A. Knopf, 1991. Open Library.

_____, reteller. *The Magic Bean Tree: A Legend from Argentina.* Illus. Beatriz Vidal. Boston: Houghton Mifflin Company, 1998. Open Library.

_____. *So Say the Little Monkeys.* Illus. Yumi Heo. New York: Atheneum Books for Young Readers, 1998.

Vigil, Angel. *The Eagle on the Cactus: Traditional Stories from Mexico.* Partially bilingual: English/Spanish. Trans. Francisco Miraval, Illus. Carol Kimball. World Folklore Series. Englewood, CO: Libraries Unlimited, 2000.

Villaseñor, Victor. *The Frog and His Friends Save Humanity / La Rana y Sus Amigos Salvan a la Humanidad.* Bilingual English/Spanish. Trans. Edna Ochoa, Illus. José Ramírez. Houston, TX: Piñata Books/Arte Publico Press, 2005.

_____. *Mother Fox and Mr. Coyote / Mamá Zorra y Don Coyote.* Bilingual English/Spanish. Trans. Guadalupe Vanessa Turcios, Illus. Felipe Ugaide Alcántara. Houston, TX: Piñata Books/Arle Publishing Press, 2004.

Volkmer, Jane Anne, reteller. *Song of the Chirimia: A Guatemalan Folktale / La Música de la Chirimia: Folklore Guatemalteco.* Bilingual: English and Spanish. Trans. Lori Ann Schatschneider. Minneapolis: Carolrhoda Books, 1990.

West, David. *Mesoamerican Myths.* Graphic nonfiction. Illus. Mike Taylor. New York: The Rosen Publishing Group, 2006.

Whitney, Alex. *Voices in the Wind: Central and South American Legends.* New York: David McKay Company, 1976.

Wilbert, Johannes, ed. *Folk Literature of the Selknam Indians: Martin Gusinde's Collection of Selknam Narratives.* Los Angeles, CA: UCLA Latin American Center Publications, 1975.

_____, ed. *Folk Literature of the Yamana Indians: Martin Gusinde's Collection of Yamana Narratives.* Berkeley: University of California Press, 1977.

_____. *Folk Literature of the Gê Indians.* Vol. 1 & 2. With Karin Simoneau. Los Angeles, CA: UCLA Latin American Center Publications, 1978.

_____. *Folk Literature of the Warao Indians.* Los Angeles: University of California Press, 1970.

_____. *Yupa Folktales.* Berkeley: University of California Press, 1974.

Wolkstein, Diane, reteller. *Lazy Stories.* Illus. James Marshall. New York: Clarion Book/The Seabury Press, 1976. Open Library.

Yolen, Jane, ed. *Favorite Folktales from Around the World.* New York: Pantheon Books, 1986.

_____, ed. *Gray Heroes: Elder Tales from Around the World.* New York: Penguin Putnam, 1999.

_____, ed. *Not One Damsel in Distress: World Folktales for Strong Girls.* Illus. Susan Guevara. New York: Harcourt, 2000.

Young, Richard, and Judy Dockrey Young. *1492: New World Tales.* Atlanta, GA: August House, 2013.

Story Title Index

References are to story numbers.

Subject Index

References are to story numbers.

310